SHOCKED
BY THE BIBLE
2

CONNECTING THE DOTS IN SCRIPTURE TO REVEAL
THE TRUTH THEY DON'T WANT YOU TO KNOW

JOE KOVACS

bancroft
press

I wish to thank God's Holy Spirit for opening my eyes to even more truth as we prepare for everlasting life.

Table of Contents

Introduction:
Cracking the window into the spirit dimension

Welcome back, Bible fans!

I'm thrilled to see you still have an interest in learning Bible truth, because it's quite a rarity these days. So many people are very busy spending their days distracted by other activities, whether it's making money, watching TV, listening to music, traveling, looking for romance, checking social media or posting funny photos and videos about their pets on the Internet, that they have no time left to consider and pursue the very reason they exist. And that reason has everything to do with their Creator, the God of the Bible. And the Bible is the one book you can confidently read, knowing that what you're seeing on its pages is the truth.

When the original "Shocked by the Bible" was published, there was strong reaction, both favorable and unfavorable. The positive reaction came from people who understood what I was doing, and that was to stun and enlighten people with verses from their own Bibles to reveal how different the truth of Scripture is from what so many erroneously believe. So to all those who have helped to champion Bible truth, I thank you with all of my heart.

The negative reaction came from people who thought I was somehow trashing the Bible, or attacking Christianity, when nothing could be farther from the truth. So as I start this book, I again need to stress that the Bible is completely true. I want people to read the words on the pages of their own Bibles, and believe them. It is when people don't believe the Word of God that confusion and errors are created.

The first book was a primer that covered a wide variety of topics. Some were very serious, like the fact that people don't go to heaven immediately upon death. Others were rather light-hearted, such as the numerous appearances of hemorrhoids in the Holy Writ. While some may have viewed the book as a collection of random facts, I was merely showing people how to read the Bible, and that is to accept the words that are on the page. The reason it was needed is because too many people, including many self-professing Christians, do not even know what's in the Bible or claim that it doesn't mean what it says. It most certainly does.

Incidentally, some folks have wondered about my own religious affiliation. The answer is that I am a Bible-believing Christian, a worshiper of God our Father and the Lord Jesus Christ, as is revealed in the Holy Bible. I don't belong to any particular denomination, because the people in Scripture did not belong to any. They merely worshiped God in spirit and in truth, which is the type of person whom Jesus said His Father is seeking. So for those trying to lump me in with some organized church or man-made religion, you won't be able to because I'm not part of any of them.

A few readers of the first book told me they were not too shocked by the material, because, as they explained, they read the Bible regularly and have a good understanding of the basics. I don't doubt them on that, because there is nothing in the first book that people who have read all of Scripture should be shocked by if they accept what the Bible states.

But being shocked is in the eye of the beholder because many others indicated they were completely stunned by the content of the highlighted Scriptures. Reading the first book caused them to dig deeper into the Bible for themselves, which is what I had hoped for. It's not an easy task to ascertain the exact level of Biblical insight a reader has at any given moment, so I try to provide both some basics and more advanced material.

This new book that you're reading should seem a little different than the first, because it is not a bunch of random facts. It needs to be read in order, as concepts often build upon each other through the chapters. It is definitely more advanced, because it's time to grow and mature into the person you're meant to be, making the transition from spiritual milk to spiritual meat. There is an extraordinary purpose to the Bible, and this book will help you understand that purpose.

Now that you know how to read the Bible, accepting it for what it says, this book will connect the dots on a variety of issues that will give you a much greater understanding of what God intends for us. We all need to keep growing spiritually, and if we avoid studying Scripture just because we think we know it already, then we are in danger of stopping our growth. We need to put what is on the page into practice, letting God's Holy Spirit guide us as we continue to have our personal character perfected.

Many don't realize that the Bible is more than an ordinary book. It is actually a code. It is the code for living now in this physical world, and it is the code that will get us into the spirit world. It is like a treasure map that has tremendous riches awaiting us at the final destination in the kingdom of God. If we don't follow the map's directions, we'll never reach the destination with the treasure, which is everlasting life. And there are forces, both seen and unseen in this world, which keep you from understanding the Bible and the real reason for your existence, thus preventing you from reaching your intended destiny.

One specific feature of this book is that it will crack open a window into the unseen dimension of heaven, the spirit dimension that remains invisible right now to our physical eyes. Please allow me to explain. As you read, you'll note that on occasion I will focus on a certain passage to highlight more than one meaning, because many verses of the Bible have more than just a single essence. There is an ostensible, physical meaning that is often obvious, but there is often a secondary connotation, a spiritual meaning, that should be considered as well. After all, the Bible is a book ultimately designed and produced by a Spirit being, and He is broadcasting ideas that apply both in our physical, flesh-and-blood world, as well as in the spirit dimension that we don't see at this moment. Here's a simple example of a Scripture that has both a physical and spiritual meaning:

> The wicked worketh a deceitful work: but to him
> that soweth righteousness shall be a sure reward.
> (Proverbs 11:18 KJV)

On the physical level here on Planet Earth, this passage talks about two opposite types of people. There is a wicked person who deals deceptively with others, and there is a righteous person who follows God's instructions and will have a sure reward for obedience. This is quite obvious.

But there is a higher, spiritual meaning as well, and it does not negate the physical meaning. So let's now crack open the window to peer into the spirit dimension for a moment. To grasp the spiritual meaning, just keep in mind that God and all his angels – both good angels and bad angels – are all spirit beings, and God's Word applies to them as well. Thus, it should be easy to now see that "the wicked" mentioned in the above proverb can refer to the most wicked one in the spirit dimension, who is none other than Satan the devil.

And there is no doubt in anyone's mind that Satan performs deceitful work, as the Bible calls him a liar and the father of lies in John 8:44. In fact, as a mental exercise, you can substitute the name of Satan every time you see "the wicked" mentioned in Scripture. In many instances, it will immediately crack open the window into the spirit world a little more, allowing you to understand the Scripture on the spirit level.

Meanwhile, the same proverb also talks about the opposite character of the devil, and that is the ultimate Person who sows righteousness and has received a sure reward. That is obviously the righteous Spirit being, who is Jesus Christ. So, we can see that the proverb applies to both the wicked and righteous here in our physical world, as well as "the wicked" and "the Righteous" in the unseen spirit dimension. I realize this concept may be new to some of you, so I'll make sure to highlight the secondary meaning whenever I think it's appropriate.

In addition to connecting the dots and looking at Scriptures on the spirit level, another theme you'll find in this book is something that I like to call Opposite World. This is a concept that is very easy to understand, because I think we all have experienced it to one degree or another. Opposite World is the world in which we live, the society whose ways stand in direct opposition to the way things are supposed to be – the ways that are approved by God. It is a world where seemingly everything that is right is portrayed as wrong, and everything that is wrong is portrayed as right. Throughout the chapters, I'll mention a handful of examples of today's beliefs or practices that are the reverse of what has been intended by our Creator, and the conclusion of the book will put into focus how upside-down and opposite our world has become.

There is also a fun chapter near the end of this book that shows how God's messages are being broadcast through major motion pictures and TV shows these days. Important Bible themes are secretly embedded inside Hollywood productions that you might never think have anything to do with the Bible. These include some of the most famous titles ever, such as "The Matrix," "Star Wars," "Willy Wonka & the Chocolate Factory," "The Big Short," "Blade Runner," "The Shawshank Redemption," "Groundhog Day," "The Truman Show," and "The Walking Dead." And there are many more. But you'll need to read the rest of the chapters first to understand many of the Biblical points I will highlight in the films.

As I did in the first "Shocked," I will be quoting from a variety of the most popular Bibles, sometimes with emphasis on certain words so you don't miss any important information. The Bibles include the King James Version, New King James Version, New Living Translation, New International Version, Holman Christian Standard Bible and New American Standard Bible, among others. Some people may wonder why I quote from more than one version, and the answer is simple. I want you to understand what God is telling you, and so I am choosing the version that is the clearest, most comprehensible on any given passage. But I encourage everyone to look up the verses in their own Bible, and in other Bibles.

There is no "official Bible" of God in the English language. Holy Scripture was written in ancient Hebrew, Greek and Aramaic, so every translation that we have in English today is really an interpretation by the people who happened to translate the words from the original language. So reading more than one translation is a very helpful and edifying practice. If there's something you might not understand in the archaic English of King James, for example, you may be able to understand it better in a more modern version. Today, there are many Bible study tools online, such as blueletterbible.org, that allow you to view numerous translations at the same time, and they're absolutely free. So have at it and dig deep!

I also wish to note that I am printing all personal remarks from God in red letters, whether they're from the Old Testament or the New Testament. As was proven in the first "Shocked," the God of the Old Testament is Jesus Christ, so there's no reason why His words should be in red in the New Testament only. Once you see His Old Testament instructions in color, your eyes will open further into the spirit dimension and your understanding will rocket to new life.

Finally, I would like to acknowledge the tremendous help I have received from God's Holy Spirit in the production of this book. There are certain topics I have never written about or even thought about before, yet God brought them to the forefront of my mind, inspiring and surprising me with new revelations from Scripture. Yes, I myself continue to be shocked by the Bible, and many of the fresh concepts God has shown me have found their way into prominent portions of this writing. I personally believe the new observations are the most noteworthy sections of the book. But my opinion about what is best may differ greatly from what you think is the most outstanding. So I'll leave it to you and your own interaction with God's Spirit to make that determination for yourself.

I know you're eager to get started, so without any further ado, let's jump into the Holy Word of God and get shocked by the Bible once again.

Chapter One:
The Coal Kids Club and every green tree

Have you ever had one of those "aha!" moments when you suddenly see or hear something, and then everything you ever wondered about instantly clicks into place, becoming absolutely clear, with your nagging questions and concerns finally receiving solid answers that make complete sense?

I recently had one of those startling epiphanies during a shopping trip, and I wish to share it with you because it may go a long way toward answering some of the questions that have been bothering you over the years. I saw a message containing just four words, and those four words brought to my mind the entire expanse of the Bible and human history. They put into focus God's Master Plan, the ongoing battle between the forces of good and evil, the truth concerning the real God of heaven versus the deception from the fraudulent god of this world, and the final destinies for those in rebellion against their Maker. Those four words are: "the Coal Kids Club."

Now, I realize you might be thinking something along the lines of, "What in the world is this guy talking about? How can those four words encompass all that?" If you'll be so kind as to grant me a few minutes, I'm happy to explain. I'm confident it'll be well worth your time, because I'm going to connect the dots from the Bible and human history, painting a portrait of what's really taking place, and why it's all happening. You'll learn why many people do what they do, even if they themselves are clueless about the precise reasons. I'm also going to open up a window into the invisible spirit dimension, allowing you to finally get a clear, panoramic view of the unseen world where God and the angels dwell, and how they interact with you and me.

Hiding in plain sight

The morning of December 24, 2015, was just like any other typical morning for me, but the appearance of an item in a local shopping center caught my attention in a very unusual way, and it inspired me to write this chapter.

I wasn't doing any Christmas shopping at the time, for I had stopped celebrating the traditional holiday years ago in my teens. But that morning, I happened to be in an Old Navy clothing store, thinking about buying a pair of jeans. Now if you wish to make fun of me for looking at clothes at Old Navy, go right ahead because it doesn't bother me one bit.

I noticed one store item on sale for Christmas was a white T-shirt featuring a bold printed message in large black letters on its front side, stating: "the Coal Kids Club." I had never seen that message before, but I purchased the shirt and snapped a photo of it, because that's when the moment of clarity struck, and I've been thinking about it ever since.

I went online to look for comments about the shirt, and one woman from Toronto, Canada, noted: "Great for a silly day! Bought this for a holiday work function, got lots of laughs." I, too, got the joke immediately, as the Coal Kids Club is obviously a humorous reference to the legend of Santa Claus, the fictional bearer of Christmas gifts who is famously said to leave a lump of coal for children who have been more naughty than nice.

But my revelation suggested there might be something more to this Coal Kids Club. I sense a hidden meaning to which the makers and marketers of the shirt are undoubtedly oblivious, so I'm not implying a shred of ill intent on their part. It's a secret message hiding in plain sight that becomes unlocked in our consciousness only when we start digging into our Bibles to learn true history.

The Original Coal Kids Club

Many portions of the Bible are rarely discussed. Sometimes it's because people just aren't reading their Bibles as they should, or they don't understand what they're reading. Perhaps the words on the page stand in opposition to what their pastors teach, or the subject matter, for whatever reason, simply makes them uncomfortable. This is one of those avoid-at-all costs areas that we're not going to avoid any longer.

We will now discuss a topic that may be difficult for some of you to handle because of its horrific nature. But it's in the Holy Word of God—many times. It's there for an important reason, and it sheds divine light on what people have done in the past, as well as what they're doing at this very second in both the United States and countries across the globe. But no matter how bad it seems to get as you read, I urge you to stick with this entire chapter, because the end reveals a bright and glorious future. Truly and thankfully, there is a happy ending.

Millions of God-professing Christians remain unaware that Scripture actually talks about a practice that I shall call the Original Coal Kids Club. This ancient club is not a pleasant or jolly place in any respect. In fact, it's the polar opposite of all that is happy, uplifting, joyful and sacred. It is among the vilest practices that have ever taken place on Planet Earth. It is so evil, in fact, that the Creator of the universe admits it never even entered His mind that people should do this despicable thing. And yet, despite its unsavory nature, a twisted version of the practice continues today.

While it bothers me to write some of these words, I'm compelled to tell you how wickedly sick men and women can be. The atrocious practice to which I'm referring is the human sacrifice of infant children. As unbelievable as it sounds, Scripture talks countless times about mothers and fathers taking their newborn infants and other young children, dropping their offspring into searing coal fires, and burning them alive in the scorching flames. This wretched activity was done willingly, ostensibly to appease the unseen god – not the Maker of all things or the Son of God, but rather the pretender who wants to be like the Most High, and that is "the sun god," Satan the devil.

To understand this, let's introduce you to a few characters in Scripture with which many of you may be unfamiliar. One character is named Molech. It is spelled different ways in different Bibles, sometimes appearing as Molek, Moloch or even Milcolm and Malcham. It's a corrupted form of the Hebrew word "melech" (sometimes spelled "melek") which simply means "king" and is translated more than 2,500 times as "king."

The other character closely associated with Molech is Chemosh. Both are the titles of some of the pagan sun gods (most often referred to in Scripture as "Baal," which, interestingly, means "the Lord") that the Israelites and the surrounding nations wrongfully worshiped.

The Jewish Encyclopedia notes that "Chemosh ... was in general a deity of the same nature as Baal. On critical occasions a human sacrifice was considered necessary to secure his favor (compare 2 Kings 3:27), and when deliverance came, a sanctuary might be built to him." The encyclopedia adds that "both Chemosh and Moloch were developed, in different environments, from the same primitive divinity, and possessed many of the same epithets."
(Jastrow, Morris, and Barton, George, A. "Chemosh," In "Jewish Encyclopedia."
[http://www.jewishencyclopedia.com/articles/4296-chemosh]. 1906.)

Molech and Chemosh are merely two alternate names for the sun god Baal, the "king" of all demons, and the devil himself, as we shall now see.

The first place Molech is mentioned is in Leviticus, as the Creator sternly warns the Israelites not to sacrifice their children to this demonic king by passing them through flames. Here are two Bible versions of the same verse so it's clear what He meant:

> 'And you shall not let any of your descendants pass through the fire to Molech, nor shall you profane the name of your God: I am the LORD. (Leviticus 18:21 KJV)

> "Do not permit any of your children to be offered as a sacrifice to Molech, for you must not bring shame on the name of your God. I am the LORD. (Leviticus 18:21 NLT)

Yes, it's simply mind-boggling to realize that human beings were engaged in this debased activity. Not only is it shocking to us, it's even more astonishing to our Maker, who eviscerated His own people for adopting what He calls a "horrible deed" and "incredible evil":

> They have built pagan shrines to Baal, and there they burn their sons as sacrifices to Baal. I have never commanded such a horrible deed; it never even crossed my mind to command such a thing! (Jeremiah 19:5 NLT)

> They have built pagan shrines to Baal in the valley of Ben-Hinnom, and there they sacrifice their sons and daughters to Molech. I have never commanded such a horrible deed; it never even crossed my mind to command such a thing. What an incredible evil, causing Judah to sin so greatly! (Jeremiah 32:35 NLT)

As the Bible explains, it's clear the sacrifices were to fallen angels called devils and demons:

> Yea, they sacrificed their sons and their daughters unto devils (Psalm 106:37 KJV)

> They sacrificed unto devils, not to God; to gods whom they knew not, to new gods that came newly up, whom your fathers feared not. (Deuteronomy 32:17 KJV)

> "They shall no more offer their sacrifices to demons, after whom they have played the harlot. (Leviticus 17:7 NKJV)

Even the famed King Solomon, who asked for and received a tremendous amount of wisdom from God, was apparently far from wise on this matter. He, too, got involved in the worship of these satanic sun gods:

> On the Mount of Olives, east of Jerusalem, he even built a pagan shrine for Chemosh, the detestable god of Moab, and another for Molech, the detestable god of the Ammonites. (1 Kings 11:7 NLT)

> For Solomon has abandoned me and worshiped Ashtoreth, the goddess of the Sidonians; Chemosh, the god of Moab; and Molech, the god of the Ammonites. He has not followed my ways and done what is pleasing in my sight.
> (1 Kings 11:33 NLT)

> The king also desecrated the high places that were east of Jerusalem on the south of the Hill of Corruption – the ones Solomon king of Israel had built for Ashtoreth the vile goddess of the Sidonians, for Chemosh the vile god of Moab, and for Molek the detestable god of the people of Ammon. (2 Kings 23:13 NIV)

On some occasions, the burning of children would take place on the seventh day of the week, which is God's holy Sabbath day of rest. And after the youngsters were broiled to death, people would go back to the temple of the true God for their regular worship practice. This incited God's temper even more:

> They have committed both adultery and murder – adultery by worshiping idols and murder by burning as sacrifices the children they bore to me. Furthermore, they have defiled my Temple and violated my Sabbath day! On the very day that they sacrificed their children to their idols, they boldly came into my Temple to worship! They came in and defiled my house.
> (Ezekiel 23:37-39 NLT)

As you can imagine, this regular massacre of children prompted God to command a harsh penalty. And that, unsurprisingly, was the death penalty:

"Say to the Israelites: 'Any Israelite or any foreigner residing in Israel who sacrifices any of his children to Molek is to be put to death. The members of the community are to stone him. I myself will set my face against him and will cut him off from his people; for by sacrificing his children to Molek, he has defiled my sanctuary and profaned my holy name.
(Leviticus 20:2-3 NIV)

And if the people of the community ignore those who offer their children to Molech and refuse to execute them, I myself will turn against them and their families and will cut them off from the community. This will happen to all who commit spiritual prostitution by worshiping Molech.
(Leviticus 20:4-5 NLT)

The little drummer boys

It's time now to give you some specific information on how the children were immolated. People would bring their offspring to a large, metallic idol, often made of iron or brass, with a giant figure seated on a throne, since the object of their adoration was their supposed "king." Remember, the term Molech comes from the same Hebrew word meaning king. These humongous idols had the body of a man, except for its head, which was that of a beast. Yes, a beast. Sometimes it featured the head of a calf, for the Israelites were notorious for calf worship (including the famous golden calf of Exodus 32:4), or it could possess the head of a different beast, such as that of a goat.

In fact, some Bibles actually translate the word "devils" from the King James as "goat idols" in connection with these child sacrifices:

They must no longer offer any of their sacrifices to the goat idols (Leviticus 17:7 NIV)

Now take a close look at this illustration.

The image you're examining is among the best I've seen to shed light on the infernal activity of the sinful parents. It's from the 1897 book, "Bible Pictures and What They Teach Us" by Charles Foster. Here is the original caption for the drawing:

> This is an idol named Molech. A great many people used to pray to this idol. It had the head of a calf, and was made of brass, and it was hollow inside. There was a place in the side to make a fire in it. When it got very hot the wicked people used to put their little children in its arms. The little children were burned to death there. This man in the picture is just going to put a little child in the idol's arms. Other men are blowing on trumpets and beating on drums, and making a great noise, so that no one can hear the poor little child cry.

I realize that many of you have never seen nor heard anything like this before, but I assure you it's real, and it's well-documented in both Holy Scripture and non-sacred histories. God even has a name for this sordid action. He calls it "Tophet" (also spelled "Topheth" or "Topeth" depending on which Bible translation you have). And we'll look at some of these Scriptural passages in a moment.

This word "Tophet" is among the most fascinating words in Scripture, because it has two different connotations, both of which apply to this nasty business of burning children. The first meaning is "the drumming place." The root word for Tophet in Hebrew is "toph" (in English, it rhymes with loaf), and it simply means "drum." It's one of those onomatopoeic terms, so merely saying the word sounds like the action it performs. Bees buzzing is an example of onomatopoeia, and, in similar fashion, a drum makes a sound like a *boom-boom*, *tom-tom* or *toph-toph*.

The word "toph" is also applied to other percussion instruments, and it's sometimes rendered as timbrel, tambourine or tabret. The very first use of the word in Scripture shows Miriam, the sister of Moses and Aaron, celebrating with a hand-held version of one of these toph instruments, translated here as "timbrel":

> And Miriam the prophetess, the sister of Aaron,
> took a timbrel [toph] in her hand; and all the
> women went out after her with timbrels [toph]
> and with dances. (Exodus 15:20 KJV)

Thus, Tophet is the place where people would play drums (along with other musical instruments) at the very moment the youngsters were placed in the scorching lap of the false deity seated on his throne. The noisemaking, which also featured the jingling of bells, was intentionally as loud as possible, to completely drown out the horrific screams of the children offered as sacrifice.

The second connotation to Tophet is simply "fireplace." It was the precise location where all this dreadful burning was taking place. Now, with these two meanings in mind – the drumming place and fireplace – you can easily understand now what the Bible is talking about in verses mentioning "Tophet":

> And they have built the high places of Tophet,
> which is in the valley of the son of Hinnom, **to
> burn their sons and their daughters in the fire**;
> which I commanded them not, neither came it
> into my heart. (Jeremiah 7:31 KJV)

Throughout Scripture, God has been shown to send his prophets directly into the places where evil was most rampant, and Jeremiah was no exception. The Creator sent him to confront the top government officials of the time (yes, even the king of Judah himself was sacrificing his own kids on the lap of the sun god), and God excoriated them for their horrendous spilling of "the blood of innocents:"

> And go forth unto the valley of the son of
> Hinnom, which is by the entry of the east gate,
> and proclaim there the words that I shall tell
> thee, And say, Hear ye the word of the LORD,
> O kings of Judah, and inhabitants of Jerusalem;
> Thus saith the LORD of hosts, the God of Israel;
> Behold, I will bring evil upon this place, the
> which whosoever heareth, his ears shall tingle.

> Because they have forsaken me, and have
> estranged this place, and have burned incense in
> it unto other gods, whom neither they nor their
> fathers have known, nor the kings of Judah, and
> have filled this place with <u>the blood of innocents</u>;
> They have built also the high places of Baal, to
> **<u>burn their sons with fire for burnt offerings</u>**
> **<u>unto Baal</u>**, which I commanded not, nor spake it,
> neither came it into my mind: Therefore, behold,
> the days come, saith the LORD, that this place
> shall no more be called <u>Tophet</u>, nor The valley of
> the son of Hinnom, but The valley of slaughter.
>
> (Jeremiah 19:2-6 KJV)

In the same warning, God told Jeremiah that He would shatter sinful Jerusalem like a clay jar, causing the metropolis to be invaded and its large populace slaughtered. Therefore, the city would become the same type of mass graveyard as the outdoor fireplace of Molech, where all those drummer boys played as kids shrieked in agony:

> And shalt say unto them, Thus saith the LORD
> of hosts; Even so will I break this people and this
> city, as one breaketh a potter's vessel, that cannot
> be made whole again: and they shall bury them
> in <u>Tophet</u>, till there be no place to bury. Thus will
> I do unto this place, saith the LORD, and to the
> inhabitants thereof, and even make this city as
> <u>Tophet</u>: And the houses of Jerusalem, and the
> houses of the kings of Judah, shall be defiled as
> the place of <u>Tophet</u>, because of all the houses
> upon whose roofs they have burned incense unto
> all the host of heaven, and have poured out drink
> offerings unto other gods.
>
> (Jeremiah 19:11-13 KJV)

Not only are these shocking accounts found in the Bible, they're also described in graphic, blood-soaked detail in other famous literature.

Gustave Flaubert, one of the most well-known writers in history, was a 19th century French novelist who was an expert in historical realism, known for his scrupulous devotion to his literary style. He painstakingly researched what history was like at any given time to make his writing reflect reality as closely as possible. After publishing "Madame Bovary" in 1857, Flaubert traveled to Carthage in 1858 to conduct extensive historical research for a work titled "Salammbô," which was published in 1862 and became a best-seller. Chapter 13 of "Salammbô"* focuses on "Moloch the Devourer," and although it is *not* the Bible, the story does provide an exceptionally vivid description of what was said to have taken place at these fiery human sacrifices, at least in Carthage in the 3rd century B.C.

(Flaubert, Gustave. "Salammbô." [http://www.gutenberg.org/files/1290/1290-h/1290-h.htm#link2HCH0013]. 1862.)

Flaubert explains that the children were sacrificed as **presents** to the unseen gods, to coax the powers of the unseen world to help them with a variety of causes, from bringing forth rain to winning military battles. People would sing worship songs while loudly playing their musical instruments to hide the shrieks of their burning kids. Here's an excerpt:

Then the men in the red cloaks chanted the sacred hymn:

"Homage to thee, Sun! king of the two zones, self-generating Creator, Father and Mother, Father and Son, God and Goddess, Goddess and God!" And their voices were lost in the outburst of instruments sounding simultaneously to drown the cries of the victims.

While the scorching idol was itself stationary, having to be rolled out on large cylinders, Flaubert says its arms were movable by a pulley-type system, making it appear that this giant beast was actually drawing the young victims toward its mouth or belly, as if it were eating the children. Remember, this devil was known as Moloch the Devourer. And the author explains that adults would not only offer their children to the sun god Baal, they would bring other valuable presents as well:

By degrees people came into the end of the passages; they flung into the flames pearls, gold vases, cups, torches, all their wealth; the offerings became constantly more numerous and more splendid. At last a man who tottered, a man pale and hideous with terror, thrust forward a child; then a little black mass was seen between the hands of the colossus, and sank into the dark opening. The priests bent over the edge of the great flagstone,—and a new song burst forth celebrating the joys of death and of new birth into eternity. ...

The victims, when scarcely at the edge of the opening, disappeared like a drop of water on a red-hot plate, and white smoke rose amid the great scarlet color.

Nevertheless, the appetite of the god was not appeased. He ever wished for more. In order to furnish him with a larger supply, the victims were piled up on his hands with a big chain above them which kept them in their place. Some devout persons had at the beginning wished to count them, to see whether their number corresponded with the days of the solar year; but others were brought, and it was impossible to distinguish them in the giddy motion of the horrible arms. This lasted for a long, indefinite time until the evening. Then the partitions inside assumed a darker glow, and burning flesh could be seen. Some even believed that they could descry hair, limbs, and whole bodies.

Night fell; clouds accumulated above the Baal. The funeral-pile, which was flameless now, formed a pyramid of coals up to his knees; completely red like a giant covered with blood, he looked, with his head thrown back, as though he were staggering beneath the weight of his intoxication.

In proportion as the priests made haste, the frenzy of the people increased; as the number of the victims was diminishing, some cried out to spare them, others that still more were needful. The walls, with their burden of people, seemed to be giving way beneath the howlings of terror and mystic voluptuousness. Then the faithful came into the passages, dragging their children, who clung to them; and they beat them in order to make them let go, and handed them over to the men in red. The instrument-players sometimes stopped through exhaustion; then the cries of the mothers might be heard, and the frizzling of the fat as it fell upon the coals.

This, dear friends, though not in the Bible, agrees with the spine-chilling events that God did have his holy prophets decry and write down for you to read today. It is this cult of human immolation, this "pyramid of coals" designed to melt children down in the belly of a demonic beast, that I am now calling the Original Coal Kids Club. And there's more. Much more.

Every green tree (and groves)

Another illuminating yet overlooked fact from the Bible is that these child sacrifices took place in the proximity of trees – green trees, as a matter of fact. Sometimes these trees were in groves, and sometimes these trees would be cut down from the groves and carried to a location where they would be tied up so they wouldn't fall down. Is any of this starting to sound familiar yet?

Here is just a small sampling of the many Bible verses mentioning the groves and the grisly activity taking place among them:

But ye shall destroy their altars, break their images, and **cut down their groves**: For thou shalt worship no other god: for the LORD, whose name is Jealous, is a jealous God: Lest thou make a covenant with the inhabitants of the land, and they go a whoring after their gods, and do sacrifice unto their gods, and one call thee, and thou eat of his sacrifice; And thou take of their daughters unto thy sons, and their daughters go a whoring after their gods, and make thy sons go a whoring after their gods. (Exodus 34:13-16 KJV)

For he built again the high places which Hezekiah his father had broken down, and he reared up altars **for Baalim**, and **made groves**, and worshipped all the host of heaven, and served them. (2 Chronicles 33:3 KJV)

But thus shall ye deal with them; ye shall destroy their altars, and break down their images, and **cut down their groves**, and burn their graven images with fire. (Deuteronomy 7:5 KJV)

And the children of Israel did evil in the sight of the LORD, and forgat the LORD their God, and **served Baalim and the groves**. (Judges 3:7 KJV) For the LORD shall smite Israel, as a reed is shaken in the water, and he shall root up Israel out of this good land, which he gave to their fathers, and shall scatter them beyond the river, because **they have made their groves**, provoking the LORD to anger. (1 Kings 14:15 KJV)

Now therefore send, and gather to me all Israel unto mount Carmel, and the prophets of Baal four hundred and fifty, and **the prophets of the groves** four hundred, which eat at Jezebel's table. (1 Kings 18:19 KJV)

There are many more similar Scriptures mentioning the groves, but I think you get the idea. Now take a look at how often the Bible speaks of green trees associated with this murderous activity that God can't stomach:

> are ye not children of transgression, a seed of falsehood, Enflaming yourselves with idols **under every green tree**, **slaying the children** in the valleys under the clifts of the rocks?
> (Isaiah 57:4-5 KJV)

> Ye shall utterly destroy all the places, wherein the nations which ye shall possess served their gods, upon the high mountains, and upon the hills, and **under every green tree**: And ye shall overthrow **their altars**, and break their pillars, and **burn their groves** with fire; and ye shall hew down the graven images of their gods, and destroy the names of them out of that place.
> (Deuteronomy 12:2-3 KJV)

> For they also built them high places, and **images, and groves**, on every high hill, and **under every green tree**. (1 Kings 14:23 KJV)

> And he **sacrificed** and burnt incense in the high places, and on the hills, and **under every green tree**. (2 Kings 16:4 KJV)

> And they set them up **images and groves** in every high hill, **and under every green tree**:
> (2 Kings 17:10 KJV)

> He **sacrificed** also and burnt incense in the high places, and on the hills, and **under every green tree**. (2 Chronicles 28:4 KJV)

> For of old time I have broken thy yoke, and burst thy bands; and thou saidst, I will not transgress; when upon every high hill and **under every green tree** thou wanderest, playing the harlot.
> (Jeremiah 2:20 KJV)

The LORD said also unto me in the days of Josiah the king, Hast thou seen that which backsliding Israel hath done? she is gone up upon every high mountain and **under every green tree**, and there hath played the harlot. (Jeremiah 3:6 KJV)

Only acknowledge thine iniquity, that thou hast transgressed against the LORD thy God, and hast scattered thy ways to the strangers **under every green tree**, and ye have not obeyed my voice, saith the LORD. (Jeremiah 3:13 KJV)

Whilst their children remember their altars and their **groves by the green trees** upon the high hills. (Jeremiah 17:2 KJV)

Then shall ye know that I am the LORD, when their slain men shall be among their idols round about their altars, upon every high hill, in all the tops of the mountains, and **under every green tree**, and under every thick oak, the place where they did offer sweet savour to all their idols. (Ezekiel 6:13 KJV)

You're doing it wrong

The Biblical passages above are quite eye-opening. Over and over, the Creator mentions "green trees" with which people have been hypnotically obsessed for countless centuries. As we see in the first Scripture in this list, God even mentions the green trees in the same sentence as the sinful slaughter of the children. Here it is again, being spoken by God Himself:

are ye not children of transgression, a seed of falsehood, Enflaming yourselves with idols under **every green tree, slaying the children** in the valleys under the clifts of the rocks?
(Isaiah 57:4-5 KJV)

What is really being said here? He is addressing "children of transgression," meaning a people who transgress or break the eternal laws of God. He calls them "a seed of falsehood." In other words, their parents have filled their minds with so much deception, that they, too, have become liars and committers of fraud, perhaps not even knowingly. In this same verse, the NKJV calls them the "offspring of falsehood," the NIV labels them "offspring of liars." The Holman Christian Standard Bible gets right to the point, with God declaring: "you rebellious children, you race of liars" (Isaiah 57:4 HCSB).

The Creator is dealing with people who are in rebellion because they've been lied to generation after generation. Therefore they, themselves, have become liars and deceivers, and it's not totally their own fault.

Now what about this green-tree business mentioned in the same divine thought from God? While the King James Version says, "Enflaming yourselves with idols under every green tree," the New King James renders it as: "Inflaming yourselves with gods under every green tree." Yes, it uses the words "gods," instead of "idols." When we look at the Hebrew word from whence it comes, it's even more stunning. It is "El," the shortened form of Elohim. El is a word that also applies to the true Maker of all things, and is translated 213 times in the KJV as "God," not with a little g, but with a capital G.

What I'm getting at is that while these people were worshiping fraudulent gods, which in actuality were demons and the devil himself, they likely thought in the imagination of their own minds, and with the purest of intent in their own hearts, that they were worshiping the **true** God, El, the Creator of all things! They believed this then, and millions believe it today. They engaged in this hoax of worship because their minds had been influenced by the devil, corrupted over many centuries with deception flourishing in their own personal homes, having been taught from their own parents! They had been **tricked** by the dark side of the unseen world into thinking they were worshiping the light of the real God!

And what was associated with this phony style of worship? The Creator says these people were passionate worshipers, "inflaming themselves" with a lust for god – either the real God or the false god, or both – **under every green tree**! Yes, my friends, the Bible says over and over again that deceived people have been tricked into using green trees, thinking that they're somehow honoring God, when the polar opposite is true: they are breaking God's very explicit instructions on how He wants to be worshiped. He refuses to have people worship Him with the nonsense of tree idols:

> "I am the LORD; that is my name! I will not yield my glory to another or my praise to idols.
> (Isaiah 42:8 NIV)

And what else were these people doing? The very same verse of Isaiah 57:5 says they were murdering their own children! Let's read these two verses again in their entirety. Remember, it is the true God speaking here, addressing people who are passionately, but erroneously, worshiping:

> Whom do you ridicule? Against whom do you make a wide mouth And stick out the tongue? Are you not children of transgression, Offspring of falsehood, Inflaming yourselves with gods under every green tree, Slaying the children in the valleys, Under the clefts of the rocks?
> (Isaiah 57:4-5 NKJV)

God is saying that these folks who are hot in their desire to worship (not just figuratively, but literally, as evinced by the burning of their kids) are worshiping incorrectly, transgressing (going against) His instructions. In other words, God is shouting at people: "You're doing it wrong!"

These adult children have been lied to so often by their parents and their parents before them, that despite their claims to love their Maker with all their heart, they have come to the point where they're using green trees to somehow "honor" God. And beyond the tree factor, many were even killing their kids as readily as they would throw a Yule log into the fireplace, and playing worship music at the same time.

Yule be horrified

Speaking of which, you'll probably be alarmed when you learn what the word "Yule" means in its most ancient language. Please sit down for this, if you're not sitting already. The word Yule, in the ancient Chaldean language of Babylon dating back to the time shortly after the Flood of Noah, is "baby" or "child." That's correct. Child! What an unnerving connection! It matches perfectly into this gruesome scenario of people tossing their own children (their own personal yules) into a burning fireplace fueled by lumps of coal, all the while singing Yule-tide carols and shaking jingle bells as little drummer boys were pa-rum-pum-pumming!

This is no joke, people. This is the mind-numbing forerunner of what many people still do today, as I'm certain you've recognized by now. God has said worship using these customs is worthless, and it actually ridicules Him. As we just read, He explained it's like sticking out your tongue to His face, even if it's done unknowingly.

God broadcast this same rebuke through the prophet Jeremiah, exposing and blasting this ancient worship service that, in reality, is a devious, satanic hoax:

> For mine eyes are upon all their ways: they are not hid from my face, neither is their iniquity hid from mine eyes. And first I will recompense their iniquity and their sin double; because they have defiled my land, they have filled mine inheritance with the carcases of their detestable and abominable things. ...
>
> the Gentiles shall come unto thee from the ends of the earth, and shall say, Surely **our fathers have inherited lies, vanity,** and things wherein there is **no profit**.
>
> Shall a man make gods unto himself, and **they are no gods**?
>
> Therefore, behold, I will this once cause them to know, I will cause them to know mine hand and my might; and they shall know that my name is The LORD.
>
> The sin of Judah is written with a pen of iron, and with the point of a diamond: it is graven upon the table of their heart, and upon the horns of your altars; Whilst their children remember **their altars** and **their groves by the green trees** upon the high hills. (Jeremiah 16:17-17:2 KJV)

In just these few verses, God has summed up what took place not only back then among his own people and among pagans, but what still takes place today worldwide every single year at the winter solstice in December, when the sun starts providing more light in the Northern Hemisphere. He said that at some point, people will recognize their traditions are merely **lies** that were inherited (handed down) from their fathers, their very own parents. God uses the term "vanity," which means "nothingness," "worthlessness," and "futility," denoting a veritable fraud. And that is what these traditions are, a brilliantly conceived hoax designed by the master of deception, the trickster-in-chief, "that serpent of old, called the Devil and Satan, who deceives the whole world." (Revelation 12:9 NKJV)

And there's still more. The Creator got specific about some of these tree-related customs that people engaged in then, and continue to take part in today:

> Thus says the LORD:
> "Do not learn the way of the Gentiles ...
> For the customs of the peoples are futile;
> For one cuts a tree from the forest,
> The work of the hands of the workman, with the ax.
> They decorate it with silver and gold;
> They fasten it with nails and hammers
> So that it will not topple.
> They are upright, like a palm tree,
> And they cannot speak;
> They must be carried,
> Because they cannot go by themselves.

(Jeremiah 10:2-5 NKJV)

After all you have read thus far in this chapter, if you can't perceive what God is talking about here, then you are blinding yourself to the truth, perhaps even on purpose. I'll still spell it out for you.

God Himself is telling everyone throughout all time periods, including us in the here and now, not to learn and adopt the practices and traditions that come from the Gentiles, people who worshiped pagan gods such as

Baal, Molech, Chemosh or any other false god of the heathens. And why? Because their customs are futile. They're worthless. A bunch of nothingness. A steaming pile of heathen B.S. that doesn't profit us in any way toward reaching the goal of eternal life in the coming kingdom of God.

The Creator then provided a specific example of one such custom where people would cut down a tree in the forest. That fallen tree then needed to be "trimmed" by those who cut it down. And because it could not go anywhere on its own, it had to be carried by someone to its destination.

Then, it needed to be properly positioned, and that is always "upright," just like a palm tree stands erect. In order to do this, people in ancient times would use nails and hammers or whatever other tools necessary to get the tree to appear to stand up on its own. Today, most people merely purchase devices called Christmas tree "stands" to make sure their personal tree is standing "upright."

Deck THIS!

Then, the decorating began. And what did God say these heathen worshipers of Satan would use to adorn their tree? "They decorate it with silver and gold" (Jeremiah 10:4 NKJV).

Scripture does provide a bit more information about the decking process. And astonishingly, God called these silver and gold decorations for the trees by the same name that is used today: ORNAMENTS!

> Ye shall defile also the covering of thy graven images of silver, and the **ornament** of thy molten images of gold (Isaiah 30:22 KJV)

Notice how He mentioned that these ornaments of gold were molten, which means melted down, so they could be shaped properly. That's how it was done in the old days. But melting is the precise method of how glass ornaments are made for decorating trees today, where bulk quantities of glass are melted and flowed in a ribbon over a series of molds. Once dry, they're coated with different colors to make them appear like gold and silver. Today, hundreds of millions of people deck their trees with all sorts of shiny ornaments, from tinsel to garland and those popular ornament balls, and we're all well aware the colors adorning the trees are often silver and gold. It's utterly amazing how timeless and accurate the Word of God is.

The book of 2 Kings tells us more about some other dangling ornaments from the trees, as it mentions "women wove hangings for the grove" (2 Kings 23:7 KJV). So people would actually spend time manufacturing ornaments by hand to hang from the tree.

This was mentioned during an inspiring time of repentance and obedience under Josiah, a king of Judah who was faithful to the instructions of God, and who put an end, at least temporarily, to this idolatrous lunacy:

> And he did that which was right in the sight of the LORD, and walked in all the way of David his father, and turned not aside to the right hand or to the left. (2 Kings 22:2 KJV)

When Josiah was twenty-six years old, he ordered the Temple of God to be repaired, and during the construction work, a book of God's eternal law had been rediscovered:

> And Hilkiah the high priest said unto Shaphan the scribe, I have found the book of the law in the house of the LORD. (2 Kings 22:8 KJV)

King Josiah then read it aloud to his people to get them to return to the ways of the true Maker, and abandon their pagan nonsense. Now, as you read this much-avoided passage of Scripture, please pay attention to all the facts that connect the practice of decorating trees in the groves to sun worship and the worship of demons, including the burning of children as an offering to Molech. It's all neatly wrapped up with a bow for you in this single section:

> And the king stood by a pillar, and made a covenant before the LORD, to walk after the LORD, and to keep his commandments and his testimonies and his statutes with all their heart and all their soul, to perform the words of this covenant that were written in this book. And all the people stood to the covenant.

And the king commanded Hilkiah the high priest, and the priests of the second order, and the keepers of the door, to bring forth out of the temple of the LORD all the vessels that were made **for Baal**, and **for the grove**, and **for all the host of heaven**: and he burned them without Jerusalem in the fields of Kidron, and carried the ashes of them unto Bethel.

And he put down the **idolatrous priests**, whom the kings of Judah had ordained to burn incense in the high places in the cities of Judah, and in the places round about Jerusalem; them also that burned incense unto **Baal**, to the **sun**, and to the **moon**, and to the **planets**, and to **all the host of heaven**.

And he **brought out the grove** from the house of the LORD, without Jerusalem, unto the brook Kidron, and burned it at the brook Kidron, and stamped it small to powder, and cast the powder **thereof upon the graves of the children** of the people.

And he brake down the houses of the sodomites, that were by the house of the LORD, where the **women wove hangings for the grove**. ...

And he defiled **Topheth**, which is in the valley of the children of Hinnom, that no man might **make his son or daughter to pass through the fire to Molech.** (2 Kings 23:3-10 KJV)

Not only would people hang ornaments on the green trees, they actually would bring all sorts of **gifts** to the scene as part of their worship of Molech!

You worship them with liquid offerings and grain
offerings. ...
Do you think all this makes me happy?
You have committed adultery on every high mountain.
There you have worshiped idols and have been
unfaithful to me.
You have put pagan symbols on your doorposts
and behind your doors.
You have left me and climbed into bed with these
detestable gods.
You have committed yourselves to them. ...
You have given olive oil to Molech with many gifts
of perfume. (Isaiah 57:6-9 NLT)

Is it making sense to you yet? The worshipers of the true Maker of all things have for centuries engaged in this colossal deception. Encouraged by deceptive priests and pastors, whether in ancient Israel or the churches of today, people who claim to love and worship the true God have glommed on to practices that God says are disgusting to Him, from the seemingly harmless decoration of green trees that people make stand upright, to the placing of presents under those trees, to the worship of the sun, moon, planets and stars (including worship at the winter solstice, the spring equinox, as well as astrology), to the intentional slaughter of their own children to the "king" demon Molech, who is none other than Satan, "the god of this world" (2 Corinthians 4:4). And just like Moloch the Devourer had an unquenchable appetite for human flesh, the New Testament says: "Your enemy the devil prowls around like a roaring lion looking for someone to devour." (1 Peter 5:8 NIV)

You may recall the famous statement from Jesus in the gospel of John concerning people who don't obey His instructions, and instead follow the devil:

You belong to your father, the devil, and you
want to carry out your father's desires. He was a
murderer from the beginning, not holding to the
truth, for there is no truth in him. When he lies,
he speaks his native language, for he is a liar and
the father of lies. (John 8:44 NIV)

In this one sentence, you can see how Yeshua identified Satan as the ultimate father from whom people have inherited their lies. He alluded to the brutal slaughter of children from people worshiping the devil, noting Satan was "a murderer from the beginning." And Jesus said people who don't adhere to His instructions today actually **want** to carry out the desires of their father, the devil.

What God thinks

I've heard countless times from people that even though they're fully aware their annual traditions were birthed from pagan practices, they don't feel they're engaging in any sort of wrongful worship, especially that of the devil. But let's see what God Himself had to say about worshiping Him, the true God, using customs based on heathen traditions:

> do not fall into the trap of following their customs and worshiping their gods. Do not inquire about their gods, saying, 'How do these nations worship their gods? I want to follow their example.' You must not worship the LORD your God the way the other nations worship their gods, for they perform for their gods every detestable act that the LORD hates. They even burn their sons and daughters as sacrifices to their gods.
> (Deuteronomy 12:30-31 NLT)

This could not be clearer. God plainly says that He *hates* it when people who claim to follow Him get sucked into the trap of using customs practiced by those pagan devil worshipers. He says we must not worship Him, Jesus the Christ, with the same traditions as the pagans, since they have engaged in all sorts of activities He cannot stand, the worst of which being the scorching of their sons and daughters in the fire "as sacrifices to their gods." So just because people today may not burn their kids in fires to kill them (they instead use abortion clinics to get the job done), God says we still must not worship Him using their customs. These so-called "cute" and "fun" practices actually remind Him of the bloody days of the Original Coal Kids Club.

As for the "all kinds of detestable things the LORD hates," Jesus got quite specific in a brief list later in Deuteronomy, as He instructed:

> When you enter the land the LORD your God is giving you, do not learn to imitate the detestable ways of the nations there. Let no one be found among you who sacrifices their son or daughter in the fire, who practices divination or sorcery, interprets omens, engages in witchcraft, or casts spells, or who is a medium or spiritist or who consults the dead. Anyone who does these things is detestable to the LORD; because of these same detestable practices the LORD your God will drive out those nations before you.

(Deuteronomy 18:9-12 NIV)

It's ironic how millions of self-proclaimed Bible believers today have little problem objecting to witchcraft, sorcery and other occult-related practices. But they don't even realize that cutting down trees, standing them up in their homes and churches, and decorating them with silver and gold is engaging in something just as detestable to their Maker. And they're being taught by their dishonest pastors that such rebellious activity, even if it's done through the deception of the devil, is perfectly fine. They might wish to revisit this warning from Scripture:

> For rebellion is as the sin of witchcraft, and stubbornness is as iniquity and idolatry.

(1 Samuel 15:23 KJV)

In the name of God

Will the worthless practices including annual tree decoration ever cease? The Bible does provide a solid answer, and there are many surprises that will come to light as we examine additional Scriptures on the matter.

The entire twentieth chapter of the book of Ezekiel is one of those portions of Scripture that spans thousands of years, revealing specifics about what God has done in the distant past, and what He'll do in the soon-to-come future. It's rarely talked about in Christian circles, so I urge you to read the whole chapter in your own Bible, while I provide some key portions here. Knowing what you know now about the history of God's people and their worthless worship of Him using ancient pagan practices, your eyes should be opened to some new astonishment.

The Creator told Ezekiel to relate the following scathing indictment to the people who claim to worship the true God:

> "Son of man, bring charges against them and condemn them. Make them realize how detestable the sins of their ancestors really were. Give them this message from the Sovereign LORD: When I chose Israel—when I revealed myself to the descendants of Jacob in Egypt—I took a solemn oath that I, the LORD, would be their God. I took a solemn oath that day that I would bring them out of Egypt to a land I had discovered and explored for them—a good land, a land flowing with milk and honey, the best of all lands anywhere.

> Then I said to them, 'Each of you, **get rid of the vile images you are so obsessed with**. Do not defile yourselves with the idols of Egypt, for I am the LORD your God.'

> "But they rebelled against me and would not listen. They did not get rid of the vile images they were obsessed with, or forsake the idols of Egypt. Then I threatened to pour out my fury on them to satisfy my anger while they were still in Egypt. (Ezekiel 20:4-8 NLT)

God recounted how He withheld His hand from destroying His own people, as He brought them into the wilderness for forty years where He'd have their full attention, teaching them that obedience to His laws would lead them to everlasting life:

> There I gave them my decrees and regulations so they could find life by keeping them.
> (Ezekiel 20:11 NLT)

You probably already know that the Israelites continuously rejected the divine instructions, and that prompted God to take a solemn oath against His people in the wilderness:

> I swore I would scatter them among all the nations because they did not obey my regulations. They scorned my decrees by violating my Sabbath days and **longing for the idols of their ancestors.**

> I gave them over to worthless decrees and regulations that would not lead to life. I let them pollute themselves with the very gifts I had given them, and I allowed them to **give their firstborn children as offerings to their gods**—so I might devastate them and remind them that I alone am the LORD.

> "Therefore, son of man, give the people of Israel this message from the Sovereign LORD: Your ancestors continued to blaspheme and betray me, for when I brought them into the land I had promised them, they **offered sacrifices** on every high hill and **under every green tree they saw!** They roused my fury as they offered up **sacrifices to their gods**. ...

> "Therefore, give the people of Israel this message from the Sovereign LORD: Do you plan to **pollute yourselves** just as your ancestors did? Do you intend to keep prostituting yourselves by worshiping **vile images?**

> For when you **offer gifts** to them and **give your little children to be burned as sacrifices, you continue to pollute yourselves with idols** to this day. (Ezekiel 20:23-31 NLT)

A few verses later, the Creator almost seems resigned to the fact that people will not stop their fraudulent customs, but He has one caveat:

> "As for you, O house of Israel," thus says the
> Lord GOD: "Go, serve every one of you his
> idols—and hereafter—if you will not obey Me;
> but profane My holy name no more with your
> gifts and your idols. (Ezekiel 20:39 NLT)

God realized people will keep rebelling in spite of His instructions. But He told people here that if they're going to continue in their presentation of "gifts" and their worship of idols, then He wants people to **not attach** His Name to it. "Profane My holy name no more with your gifts and your idols," He said. He does not want people to say they're doing these practices to worship Him, Jesus Christ! He urges them not to call it Christian! He doesn't want Christ to be "put back in Christmas," as is commonly broadcast today, because Christ was never in Christmas. In fact, you won't even find the word "Christmas" in the whole Bible. Jesus was simply never a part of these customs, and He does not wish to be associated with these vile practices He hates.

The end of the lie

In this chapter, we've seen quite a bit of bad, almost unspeakable news. But, as I said at the outset, there is a bright and glorious future. A happy ending is on its way, as the Bible is indeed a lengthy report of Good News.

The wonderful news is that the deception is coming to an end. The darkness of the devil shall be replaced by the light of the Creator who promised to return to Earth, and the ancient scam known today as Christmas will be gone forever, as Satan Himself will be destroyed.

The Bible reveals that Satan has wanted to be like the Most High God from a time before Adam and Eve were created. The Creator explained how the angel once known as Lucifer has said in his heart: "I will climb to the highest heavens and be like the Most High." (Isaiah 14:14 NLT)

But Satan will come to an end filled with irony. He himself will become a permanent member of the Coal Kids Club. Many students of Scripture already know that Satan will be tossed into what is called the lake of fire, also known biblically as "Gehenna" fire. This place called

"Gehenna" simply means "the Valley of Hinnom," and it still exists in the modern state of Israel. But what is surprising to some is that this Valley of Hinnom is the exact same location where the pagan sun god Baal was worshiped, and where so many families threw their children into the scorching arms of Molech! Recall how God complained:

> They have built pagan shrines to Baal in the valley of Ben-Hinnom, and there they sacrifice their sons and daughters to Molech. I have never commanded such a horrible deed; it never even crossed my mind to command such a thing. What an incredible evil, causing Judah to sin so greatly! (Jeremiah 32:35 NLT)

So God has a strong sense of irony, bringing about the end of the phony "king" known by many titles such as Molech and Satan in the very place in the Valley of Hinnom, the hotspot called Tophet (the fireplace), where countless children were terrorized by flames and ultimately murdered.

> For Tophet was established of old, Yes, for **the king** it is prepared. He has made it deep and large; Its pyre is fire with much wood; The breath of the LORD, like a stream of brimstone, Kindles it. (Isaiah 30:33 NKJV)

And the irony doesn't stop there. The Creator compares Satan to a tree that has been "cut down" and has "fallen," as He uses those precise terms to describe the devil's demise:

> "How you **are fallen** from heaven, O Lucifer, son of the morning! How you are **cut down to the ground**, You who weakened the nations! (Isaiah 14:12 NKJV)

And it gets even better:

> In that wonderful day when the LORD gives his people rest from sorrow and fear, from slavery and chains, you will taunt the king of Babylon. You will say, "The mighty man has been destroyed. Yes, your insolence is ended. For the LORD has crushed your wicked power and broken your evil

> rule. You struck the people with endless blows of rage and held the nations in your angry grip with unrelenting tyranny.
>
> But finally the earth is at rest and quiet. Now it can sing again!
>
> Even the trees of the forest—the cypress trees and the cedars of Lebanon—sing out this joyous song: 'Since you have been cut down, no one will come now to cut us down!' (Isaiah 14:3-8 NLT)

Are you appreciating the humor that God has inserted into the destruction of the devil? Once Jesus has returned to Earth to finally end Satan's long reign of tyranny, there will finally be "peace on Earth" year round, and the whole world will sing again. And it's not only people who will be singing, but apparently **the trees of the forest** will be singing for joy as well. Why? Because no one with a blade or chainsaw will be coming to chop them down for a Christmas tree anymore! That nonsense will finally be over!

Here is that comical verse again, this time from the King James Version:

> Yea, the **fir trees** rejoice at thee, and the cedars of Lebanon, saying, Since thou art laid down, **no feller** is come up against us. (Isaiah 14:8 KJV)

Go to Google right this second, and click on images. Then enter "fir tree" as your search term. You'll be stunned to see what a fir tree is. It's your typical Christmas tree! Yes, folks, what we call Christmas trees today are all over your Bible.

Now look up the word "feller" in any dictionary. A feller is someone who cuts down a tree. Thus, when Satan is personally cut down like the millions of green trees he prompted to be chopped down over thousands of years, then all the remaining fir trees on this planet will in essence be rejoicing, since the devil will no longer be around to inspire people to chop down trees for holiday decoration! This has been in Scripture for thousands of years, and now you're finally seeing it with your own eyes, perhaps even grasping its staggering meaning for the first time at this very second!

This notion of trees singing for joy when Jesus returns to Earth for the time of judgment is repeated elsewhere in Scripture, written in songs by King David:

> Then the trees of the woods shall rejoice before the LORD, For He is coming to judge the earth. (1 Chronicles 16:33 NKJV)

> Then all the trees of the woods will rejoice before the LORD. For He is coming, for He is coming to judge the earth. He shall judge the world with righteousness, And the peoples with His truth. (Psalm 96:12-13 NKJV)

Christmass hypnosis

It's at this time in the future when the vast majority of people will have their eyes opened to the truth, and they will finally understand how the devil has been tricking them with subtle suggestions all these years, through all generations since Adam and Eve. But Jesus has promised that people will snap out of this mass hypnosis, what I call "Christmass hypnosis":

> You will look back on all the ways you defiled yourselves and will hate yourselves because of the evil you have done. (Ezekiel 20:43 NLT)

He says people will finally get rid of all those gold and silver ornaments they've been hanging on their idols for centuries:

> Ye shall defile also the covering of thy graven images of silver, and the **ornament of thy molten images of gold**: thou shalt cast them away as a menstruous cloth; thou shalt say unto it, Get thee hence. (Isaiah 30:22 KJV)

All this absurdity of cutting down trees from groves and making them stand again for glamorous decoration will come to an end:

> Thy graven images also will I cut off, and thy **standing images** out of the midst of thee; and thou shalt no more worship the work of thine hands. And I will pluck up thy **groves** out of the midst of thee (Micah 5:13-14 KJV)

It is then that people will finally be taught by God Himself, without any interference from the devil. Again, that twentieth chapter of Ezekiel is key, for it explains how God will give people one final chance to learn the truth:

> "And I will bring you into the wilderness of the peoples, and there I will plead My case with you face to face. (Ezekiel 20:35 NKJV)

> I will judge you there just as I did your ancestors in the wilderness after bringing them out of Egypt, says the Sovereign LORD. I will examine you carefully and hold you to the terms of the covenant. I will purge you of all those who rebel and revolt against me. (Ezekiel 20:36-38 NLT)

This event has not happened yet. God has not pleaded face to face with millions of people in the wilderness since the Israelites left Egypt. It will take place in the future, one thousand years after Jesus returns, during what is described as the Second Resurrection (see my later chapter on "The resurrection no one talks about").

Jesus will be pleading with people one final time, because He doesn't want them to become members of the final incarnation of the Coal Kids Club. Because the Gehenna fire is not just intended for the devil. It is for anyone and everyone who refuses to repent and follow the laws of God that lead to eternal life:

> But the cowardly, the unbelieving, the vile, the murderers, the sexually immoral, those who practice magic arts, the idolaters and all liars— they will be consigned to the fiery lake of burning sulfur. This is the second death."
> (Revelation 21:8 NIV)

The Gehenna fire brings about the second death for sinful people, the eternal death from which there is no more resurrection. It's designed for the incorrigibly wicked, the people David sang about in the Psalms:

> Let **burning coals** fall upon them: let them be cast into the fire; into deep pits, that they rise not up again. (Psalm 140:10 KJV)

While there may be some super-wicked people who end up in this massive blaze, as they receive the wages of sin, extinguishing their life forever, the vast majority of people will likely be saved. Once again, the rescue has been written about in Ezekiel 20:

> For on my holy mountain, the great mountain of Israel, says the Sovereign LORD, the people of Israel **will someday worship me, and I will accept them**. There I will require that you bring me all your offerings and choice gifts and sacrifices. When I bring you home from exile, you will be like a pleasing sacrifice to me. And I will display my holiness through you as all the nations watch.

> Then when I have brought you home to the land I promised with a solemn oath to give to your ancestors, you will know that I am the LORD. **You will look back on all the ways you defiled yourselves and will hate yourselves because of the evil you have done**. You will know that I am the LORD, O people of Israel, when I have honored my name by treating you mercifully in spite of your wickedness. I, the Sovereign LORD, have spoken!" (Ezekiel 20:41-44 NLT)

The good news is amazingly great news. The paradise of the kingdom of God will not include any of the evil experienced by mankind for millennia, as the Divine Family leaves the unseen dimension of heaven and takes up residence here on Earth:

> I heard a loud shout from the throne, saying, "Look, God's home is now among his people!

> He will live with them, and they will be his
> people. God himself will be with them. He will
> wipe every tear from their eyes, and there will be
> no more death or sorrow or crying or pain. All
> these things are gone forever."
> (Revelation 21:3-4 NLT)

The grand illusion is now over. The curtain has been pulled back to expose the elaborate hoax, and your eyes have been opened to the truth. The deception will eventually die.

But how and when did this global deceit begin? And **why** is this trickery taking place even now? Get ready to have your eyes opened even more, as these questions and others will be answered in the chapters ahead. We'll start with three words of Jesus that will begin to unlock the mystery. They are three words that connect most of the dots in the Bible concerning our ultimate destiny. And, shockingly, they are three words from the Messiah that most Christians don't believe.

Chapter Two:
Three words of Jesus that most
Christians don't believe

M illions of people who call themselves Christian have a love affair with Jesus. They pray to Him and sing inspiring songs, lifting up praise on a regular basis. When they read the Bible, many put an extra focus on the words spoken by their Creator, in the Old Testament as well as the New. That's why red-letter Bibles are popular, because the words of Jesus are printed in bright color so they seem to jump off the page.

But there are three words found in two verses of the Bible, both of which were spoken by Jesus Himself, which many Christians go out of their way to avoid. To this day, some believers may not even know these verses are in Scripture, because their pastors have never given a sermon focusing on them, nor will they. Countless preachers avoid these passages like the plague. Maybe it's because they don't know what they mean or they don't how to deal with them. Worse yet, perhaps it's because some are suppressing the truth of God, a crime for which they'll be held accountable in the future.

While few people will ever hear these proclamations from Jesus in the churches they attend, the statements are among the most important and revealing in all of Scripture, for they declare in plain language who and what you really are, why you exist, and what your ultimate destiny is, should you decide to take hold of it. Life and the Bible will finally make sense when you merely agree with the words on the page.

One of these stunning statements is found in the New Testament, and one is in the Old, both having been spoken by the God whose name in Hebrew is Yeshua, that is Jesus the Christ. Both sections of the Bible contain the same, astonishing three-word phrase that drives so many self-proclaimed believers absolutely bonkers. It is quite possibly the most shocking statement in all of Scripture. Most people simply don't believe it, or don't want to believe it. They just can't handle it, and maybe they don't even wish to try. Therefore, the statement is left alone, as if it were not even in the Bible. Except it is there. The words are on the page. Twice.

So which three words uttered by the Creator of all things are so unnerving to those who say they worship Him? The phrase that sends many Christians over the edge is: "You are gods." Yes, folks, Jesus of Nazareth, God Almighty, has actually said more than once that "you are gods," and He meant what He said. Not only do I agree with it, but a few famous Christian champions including C.S. Lewis believe it to be true as well, as we'll see in a few moments. So buckle up, because you're finally going to learn where Jesus made such a startling declaration, and the tremendous meaning it holds for your personal future.

The frequent denial

I don't know about you, but there have been times in my life when, after I have informed a Christian person that Jesus said, "You are gods," he or she has a response of, "The Bible doesn't say 'You are gods.'" Believers are simply incredulous that God has indeed stated, "You are gods." They don't get it, and I think many don't even want to get it. Ignorance is bliss to them, and as long as they keep singing their worship songs, they think all is right in their walk with their Savior.

But I'm among those who believe every word spoken by Jesus, and I certainly don't think such an interesting and important declaration like this should be ignored or suppressed. Yeshua first uttered the words long before His human ministry. It's found in the book of Psalms, and should be featured in red letters, if Bible publishers would highlight God's spoken words in color in the Old Testament, as they often do in the New. But here is the stunning statement:

I said, "You are gods, And all of you are children of the Most High. **(Psalm 82:6 NKJV)**

It doesn't matter which Bible you open to check this verse. Please look it up in every one you can find because they all render it correctly and the same. The Hebrew word that is translated as "gods" in this sentence is "Elohim," the exact same word that is translated as "God" more than two thousand times in Scripture.

Our Creator is actually summing up who we all are and what we're intended to become in this one, underreported sentence. The Bible means what it says, and here God is telling us that we human beings are gods – that is, we are of God's family, the actual **children** of the Most High God, as the quote clearly says. It is not saying that we are the Creator God. It is merely telling us we are His children, His offspring. God is actually having kids, and we're the offspring of the divine God. Millions of Christians don't understand that "God" is actually a plural word in Hebrew. They don't comprehend that this one God is, in reality, a single family of divine beings, and that this one God family is reproducing, creating additional beings that have the potential to become part of the divine family!

I really don't know why so many people have a hard time grasping this. They go through their whole lives seeing families here on Earth, generation after generation, giving birth to children. The kids are obviously the same kind of physical life form as their parents with many of the same characteristics. People give birth to other people. They don't give birth to trees, or fish, or puppies.

It's the same situation in the animal kingdom. Creatures of all types give birth to offspring that are the same kind of animal. As I've said countless times in interviews, the children of cats are cats. The children of dogs are dogs. The children of giraffes are giraffes. And the children of God are gods! Your Bible already says so in Psalm 82:6. Isn't it time you finally agree with everything your Maker tells you?

Repeat performance

The second utterance of "You are gods" took place when the Creator left His existence in the spirit world of heaven and came to Earth to

temporarily dwell as a typical, physical, human being. It was during this
lifetime of thirty-three years that Jesus of Nazareth said from His own
mouth:

> "Is it not written in your Law, 'I have said you
> are "gods"'? (John 10:34 NIV)

Many don't realize that Yeshua was actually quoting Himself from the
Scripture in Psalms when He made this profound statement.

Now let's examine the remark in its full context so you will have no
doubt that Jesus meant exactly what He said. It came about during a walk
through the Holy Temple one winter in Jerusalem. The religious leaders of
Jesus' day were giving Him a hard time about whether or not He was the
Anointed One of God, known as the Messiah:

> The Jews who were there gathered around him,
> saying, "How long will you keep us in suspense?
> If you are the Messiah, tell us plainly."
>
> Jesus answered, "I did tell you, but you do not
> believe. The works I do in my Father's name
> testify about me, but you do not believe because
> you are not my sheep. My sheep listen to my
> voice; I know them, and they follow me. I give
> them eternal life, and they shall never perish; no
> one will snatch them out of my hand. My Father,
> who has given them to me, is greater than all; no
> one can snatch them out of my Father's hand. I
> and the Father are one."
>
> Again his Jewish opponents picked up stones to
> stone him, but Jesus said to them, "I have shown
> you many good works from the Father. For which
> of these do you stone me?"
>
> "We are not stoning you for any good work,"
> they replied, "but for blasphemy, because you, a
> mere man, claim to be God."
>
> Jesus answered them, "Is it not written in your
> Law, 'I have said you are "gods"'?

> If he called them 'gods,' to whom the word of
> God came – and Scripture cannot be set aside –
> what about the one whom the Father set apart as
> his very own and sent into the world? Why then
> do you accuse me of blasphemy because I said, 'I
> am God's Son'? (John 10:24-36 NIV)

Before we get to the remark about us being gods, I briefly wish to point out that Jesus confirmed He was indeed the long-awaited Savior, the Messiah, when He said in verse 25: "I did tell you, but you do not believe."

More importantly, He declared that He is, in fact, God:

> I give them eternal life, and they shall never
> perish (John 10:28 NIV)

He told everyone right then that He is a member of the divine Elohim, the family of God, bestowing everlasting life on people He calls His sheep. He goes on to say in verse 30 that "I and the Father are one."

The Jews who heard these statements knew precisely what Jesus was saying about Himself. It was crystal clear to them that Yeshua had just identified Himself as God, a member of the divine family. That's why they immediately picked up rocks in a frantic effort to stone him to death:

> "We are not stoning you for any good work,"
> they replied, "but for blasphemy, because you, a
> mere man, claim to be God." (John 10:33 NIV)

And that's when Jesus launched back with the three words that confounded not only the Jews of His day, but still perplex millions of Christians today: "You are gods."

> Jesus answered them, "Is it not written in your Law, 'I
> have said you are "gods"'? (John 10:34 NIV)

The first thing to note is that Jesus was referring to a law that was already on the books, a statement that He Himself had made during Old Testament times. That, of course, is found in Psalm 82:6, as we've seen. So He is confirming what He had previously said, just in case people had not understood it.

If you wish to know the root word in Greek from which the word "gods" is translated here in John, it is "theos." That's the precise term used all through the New Testament concerning the divine God, such as God the Father. "Theos" is where we get words like "theology," meaning "the study of God," or names such as "Theodore," which means "God's gift." So in Hebrew, Greek and English, when Jesus says "You are gods," He means exactly what He says.

Now let's read verses 34 and 35 together, as they're intended, so we can fully comprehend Jesus:

> Jesus answered them, "Is it not written in your Law, 'I have said you are "gods"'?
>
> If he called them 'gods,' to whom the word of God came – and Scripture cannot be set aside – what about the one whom the Father set apart as his very own and sent into the world? Why then do you accuse me of blasphemy because I said, 'I am God's Son'? (John 10:34-35 NIV)

I realize it's still shocking to many of you who may never have realized this is in the Bible. So, here's a simple way to understand what Jesus is saying when it's put into modern lingo:

"Come on, guys! It already says in your own unbreakable law that God has called **you yourselves gods**! So why are you getting on my case, accusing me of doing wrong just because I call myself God's Son?"

Jesus was telling these people they were clueless about their own Scripture, just as most Christian leaders remain today on this subject. He reminded them that human beings "are gods," that we are part of God's family, all children of the Most High as He previously indicated in Psalm 82:6. So how in the world could using the term "God's Son" be offensive to them, when God has already said that we ourselves are gods? There comes a time, folks, when we have to accept the words on the page, even when the words blow our minds with sheer magnificence.

The others who get it

At this point, some of you might be wondering if I've lost my bearings and have plunged off a cliff. It doesn't bother me if you think that, because I stand on the Holy Word of God, just reporting what it already says. But I'm certainly not the only one who thinks this way.

One of the greatest Christian champions in recent times is a Belfast-born author named C.S. Lewis. He is famous for books such as "Mere Christianity" and "The Weight of Glory" among more than thirty others. Even children are familiar with his work, as he wrote the well-known classic, "The Chronicles of Narnia," which was turned into major motion pictures in 2005 and 2010.

In Protestant churches across America today, Mr. Lewis, who died the same day U.S. President John F. Kennedy was assassinated in 1963, is still revered as one of the most respected Christian authors of all time. Pastors continue to base some of their sermons on the works of this man. But strangely, they never seem to quote Lewis concerning what is arguably his most important and intriguing assertion. By now, you can take an excellent guess at which statement that is, and probably be correct. Because C.S. Lewis believed and championed the three-word phrase of Jesus that most other Christians don't believe, and tremble at the thought of it being heard from their lips: "You are gods."

In the spring of 2000, Christianity Today magazine named 1952's "Mere Christianity" by Lewis the best religious book of the 20th century, calling it, "The best case for the essentials of orthodox Christianity in print." A review does not get more glowing than that.

(http://www.christianitytoday.com/ct/2000/april24/5.92.html)

Here is a staggering quotation from his book, positioned at the end of the "Counting the Cost" chapter, where Lewis referred to Jesus talking about our divine destiny as gods:

> The command *Be ye perfect* is not idealistic gas. Nor is it a command to do the impossible. He is going to make us into creatures that can obey that command. He said (in the Bible) that we were 'gods' and He is going to make good

His words. If we let Him – for we can prevent Him if we choose – He will make the feeblest and filthiest of us into a god or goddess, dazzling, radiant, immortal creature, pulsating all through with such energy and joy and wisdom and love as we cannot now imagine, a bright stainless mirror which reflects back to God perfectly (though, of course, on a smaller scale) His own boundless power and delight and goodness. The process will be long and in parts very painful; but that is what we are in for. Nothing less. He meant what He said.

(C.S. Lewis, Mere Christianity (New York: HarperCollins, 2001), pp. 205-206)

This is not the only time Lewis called men and women "gods and goddesses." Here's an excerpt from 1949's "The Weight of Glory:"

It is a serious thing, to live in a society of possible gods and goddesses, to remember that the dullest and most uninteresting person you talk to may one day be a creature which, if you saw it now, you would be strongly tempted to worship, or else a horror and a corruption such as you now meet, if at all, only in a nightmare. All day long we are, in some degree, helping each other to one or other of these destinations.

(C.S. Lewis. The Weight of Glory, HarperSanFrancisco, ©1949 C.S. Lewis Pte. Ltd., Copyright renewed © 1976, revised 1980 C.S. Lewis Pte. Ltd., pp. 45-46)

It boggles my mind sometimes how countless Protestant preachers who love to talk about the brilliant teachings of C.S. Lewis intentionally go out of their way to ignore his most uplifting, inspiring message about our destiny. That we can become gods. I surmise it's because these pastors just don't believe it's true. They don't believe their own Bibles. They don't believe their own God. But, just as Mr. Lewis has written, Jesus meant what He said.

Who else is out there that believes Jesus' statement that we are gods? How about one of the biggest groups of Jesus worshipers on the planet? The Roman Catholic Church! That's correct. Despite the fact that it's rarely brought up anymore, it is part of the official teaching of the Catholic Church that God became a physical human being so that we physical human beings can become god. It has been there since the earliest centuries after Jesus was resurrected back to life.

You can see this for yourself on the Internet right this second at the official Vatican website. The entire teaching of the Catholic Church, known as the catechism, is online at vatican.va. To save time, here's the portion we're discussing, teaching No. 460:

> The Word became flesh to make us "partakers of the divine nature."
>
> "For this is why the Word became man, and the Son of God became the Son of man: so that man, by entering into communion with the Word and thus receiving divine sonship, might become a son of God."
>
> "For the Son of God became man so that we might become God."
>
> "The only-begotten Son of God, wanting to make us sharers in his divinity, assumed our nature, so that he, made man, might make men gods."
> (http://www.vatican.va/archive/ENG0015/__P1J.HTM#-GY)

I am not Catholic. I don't belong to any denomination, for that matter. I just worship our Heavenly Father and his Divine Son, Jesus Christ. But as you can see from its own official teachings, the Catholic Church asserts what I am trumpeting in this chapter. That the whole purpose of God's departure from heaven to dwell with us on Earth was so He could show us the correct way to live, leading us to eventually share in his divinity and become gods, just like Jesus said!

The four statements from the catechism come from different people, but they all reach the same conclusion. The first is an excerpt from the New Testament itself, for the apostle Peter let everyone know that they can become "partakers of the divine nature."

Here's the entire verse in a modern version, so there's no confusion in your mind:

> And because of his glory and excellence, he has given us great and precious promises. These are the promises that enable you to share his divine nature and escape the world's corruption caused by human desires. (2 Peter 1:4 NLT)

Yes, we're going to share God's divine nature. If we keep the commandments to enter into life as Jesus said in Matthew 19:17, we're going to be divine. The Bible says so.

The three statements following that by Peter are comments from other ancient leaders in the Catholic Church, namely Irenaeus, Athanasius and Thomas Aquinas. While the wording is their own, it is abundantly clear they all completely understood the astounding reason God created humans: because the single family of God is reproducing, creating more divine beings in that growing family. Lots and lots of children of God!

The children of God

Now that you see that I'm not the only one championing this cause, let's jump back into the Bible, because your eyes may finally be opened to the glorious, shining truth that Satan and deceptive pastors in this world have done their best to keep hidden in darkness and prevent you from learning it.

Please pay attention now, because I'm going to present many Scriptures on the subject, and you can look them up in your own Bible to confirm it's the truth. Now that you've seen that Jesus taught we are intended to become gods, part of the divine God family, the verses may be energized with new life, leaping off the page so you'll understand them with total clarity.

You probably already know that believers are called by **family** terms such as "children of God" and "sons of God" numerous times in the Bible. Here are just a few:

> Blessed are the peacemakers: for they shall be called the children of God. (Matthew 5:9 KJV)

> For as many as are led by the Spirit of God, these are sons of God. (Romans 8:14 NKJV)

> The Spirit itself beareth witness with our spirit, that we are the children of God
> (Romans 8:16 KJV)

But you may not have known the Bible also calls us the offspring of God:
> "Therefore since we are God's offspring ...
> (Acts 17:29 NIV)

The Bible calls us the children and offspring of God because that is what we are. Our divine Father is fathering offspring, children in His family who are intended to become divine just like their Father. He is producing more of His glorious, immortal kind, the God kind. If we go back to the very beginning of the Book, we find confirmation of the purpose:

> Then God said, "Let us make mankind in our image, in our likeness, so that they may rule ...
> (Genesis 1:26 NIV)

Notice that God's family already has more than one person in it, because the command uses plural pronouns such as "us" and "our." This could have been God the Father conversing with Jesus very anciently, basically saying to one another, "Hey, let's have more people in our loving, divine family. Let's produce men and women to not only look like us, but become like us as well!" And why would this have been done? The very same verse has the answer: "so that they may rule."

From Genesis to Revelation, a main theme of the Bible is that people have been created by God so they can develop and perfect the proper know-how, temperament and righteous character to reign and rule alongside God, just as our Creator is ruling the universe this very moment.

Here are some jaw-dropping scriptural promises with emphasis added so you can finally comprehend the wonderful truth millions of Christians have never been told:

> If we endure, We shall also <u>reign</u> with Him.
> (2 Timothy 2:12 NKJV)

> And he that overcometh, and keepeth my works unto the end, to him will I give <u>power over the nations</u>: And he <u>shall rule</u> them with a rod of iron ... (Revelation 2:26-27 KJV)

> And have made <u>us</u> kings and priests to our God; And <u>we shall reign</u> on the earth."
> (Revelation 5:10 NKJV)

> Then I saw thrones, and the people sitting on them had been given the <u>authority to judge</u>. ... They all came to life again, and they <u>reigned with Christ</u> for a thousand years. ... they will be priests of God and of Christ and will <u>reign with him</u> a thousand years. (Revelation 20:4-6 NLT)

> <u>To him who overcomes I will grant to sit with Me on My throne</u>, as I also overcame and sat down with My Father on His throne.
> (Revelation 3:21 NKJV)

Are you finally understanding what the Bible has been shouting at you since it was originally written? Jesus Himself says true believers will sit down on God's own throne and rule over the nations with Him! This is precisely what God does right now, and we'll be joining Him to do the very same job in the future! How is this possible? Because of those three simple words from Jesus: "You are gods."

I know it blows your mind, because it blows my mind every time I think about what God has promised. Feel free to read this chapter and the Bible verses again and again to be sure, but I assure you, this is no joke. The words are on the page. Want more proof? Here we go:

> Don't you realize that someday <u>we believers will judge the world</u>? ... Don't you realize that <u>we will judge angels</u>? (1 Corinthians 6:2-3 NLT)

The Bible is point blank telling us that we believers will be judging the citizens of the world. This is something that God does. So how can we do it? Because we are gods, just like Jesus said. The Bible is outright telling us that we will be judging angels. How can we do this? Because, just as Jesus said, we are gods.

In the book of Psalms, David knew the truth about our destiny, but translators have obscured it slightly in this song:

> what is mankind that you are mindful of them, human beings that you care for them? You have made them a little lower than the angels and crowned them with glory and honor. You made them rulers over the works of your hands; you put everything under their feet ...
> (Psalm 8:4-6 NIV)

The phrase "a little lower than the angels" should actually be translated "a little lower than God," because the Hebrew word there is "Elohim," the ubiquitous word for God. The NIV Bible even has a footnote at the word "angels," saying it could be read as "God." The rest of the text makes it obvious, because it confirms the reason God made human beings to begin with: to be rulers over everything that God has made!

This verse from Psalm 8 is reiterated in the New Testament, making it absolutely clear that all created things will be under our control:

> and put everything under their feet." In putting everything under them, God left nothing that is not subject to them. Yet at present we do not see everything subject to them. (Hebrews 2:8 NIV)

It's pretty obvious to everyone that at this moment, in our human form, we only see the physical world in which we walk, eat and breathe. We don't see the entire scope of our dominion. That will come to fruition when Jesus returns to Earth and quickens us into our immortal bodies composed of His Spirit. That's when we'll be transformed from human beings to divine, spirit beings, just like our divine brother Jesus:

> Whatever is born of the flesh is flesh, and whatever is born of the Spirit is spirit.
> (John 3:6 HCSB)

Dear friends, we are God's children now, and

> what we will be has not yet been revealed. We know that when He appears, <u>we will be like</u> <u>Him</u> because we will see Him as He is.
> (1 John 3:2 HCSB)

> And since we are his children, we are <u>his heirs</u>. In fact, together with Christ we are <u>heirs of God's</u> <u>glory</u>. But if we are to <u>share his glory</u>, we must also share his suffering. (Romans 8:17 NLT)

Are you grasping what your Bible is saying? It says that we as God's own children are His heirs, equal inheritors with Jesus, and that we're eventually going to be just like Christ, born into the spirit world as spirit beings, sharing his divine glory! We're not going to be made up of flesh and blood when this happens. A miraculous metamorphosis will take place that changes our physical, human, mortal bodies into divine, spirit, immortal bodies. The Bible promises this will happen!

> What I am saying, dear brothers and sisters, is that our physical bodies cannot inherit the Kingdom of God. These dying bodies cannot inherit what will last forever. But let me reveal to you a wonderful secret. We will not all die, but <u>we will</u> <u>all be transformed</u>! It will happen in a moment, in the blink of an eye, when the last trumpet is blown. For when the trumpet sounds, those who have died will be raised to live forever. And we who are living will also be transformed. <u>For our</u> <u>dying bodies must be transformed into bodies</u> <u>that will never die; our mortal bodies must be</u> <u>transformed into immortal bodies.</u>
> (1 Corinthians 15:50-53 NLT)

This will be the consummate moment when we will "be filled with all the fullness of God." (Ephesians 3:19 NKJV)

Remember, the divine family of God is enlarging itself, having children of the very same kind, the same type of Beings that They are. This family is raising gods.

When are Christians going to stop this nonsense of thinking their ultimate destiny is to float around on a heavenly cloud, strumming a harp for all eternity, doing a bunch of nothingness but singing worship songs for millions upon billions upon trillions of years. We're not dogs gazing into our master's face. Just as Jesus said, we are gods, g-o-d-s, who will not only look upon our Master's face, but actually rule the entire universe with Him, sitting on His throne!

If you want more information on this subject, I wrote an in-depth book that explores this topic in extreme detail. It's called "The Divine Secret," and it explains our phenomenal destiny in terms that even people with no Bible experience can fully understand.

But now, you have no more excuses not to know who and what you really are, why you're here and what your future holds for you. As you've seen with your own eyes, the Bible says human beings are the children of God, the very offspring of God. All believers are right now being trained to live according to God's laws, not the ways of Satan in this sick, evil world the devil has shaped. Once Jesus returns, all the obedient servants of God will be transformed, given brand-new, immortal bodies composed of spirit, sitting down on God's own throne to rule the nations. All thanks to three words of Jesus that most Christians don't believe: "You are gods."

Chapter Three:
The conception of deception

As we continue the mission to reveal the glorious truth and expose the wicked lies that have pervaded the entire world, there's an important concept mentioned in the New Testament that sheds a tremendous amount of light on the dark ocean of deception in which we've all been drowning for millennia. It comes from the apostle Paul, and it should be taken to heart by everyone who truly wishes to learn and live the truth. Paul has revealed to believers in the true God:

> For we are not fighting against flesh-and-blood enemies, but against evil rulers and authorities of the unseen world, against mighty powers in this dark world, and against evil spirits in the heavenly places. (Ephesians 6:12 NLT)

This one statement speaks volumes, and it's key to unlocking the mystery of the conception of deception. We all need to realize that the battle we face on a daily basis is not a fight against things we can see, such as other human beings. It is a war against rulers who cannot be seen. They're invisible to the naked eye. Now, you may wonder, "How can this be? What do you mean they're invisible?" I mean exactly what I said, and it's what the Bible has been saying for many centuries.

The conflict in which we engage every day is one that pits flesh-and-blood human beings, like you and me, against nefarious beings who dwell in the unseen dimension of the spirit world. They are, as a point in fact, wicked entities who don't consist of flesh and blood, but spirit. Specifically, they are former angels who have rebelled against their

Maker, and are now trying their best to thwart God's plan of reproduction, the creation of billions of beings who are being instructed on how to gain eternal life in God's own family.

Once we agree with the words on the pages of the Bible, our view into this invisible dimension becomes much clearer, leading to a greater understanding of what's taking place not only at this moment in our lives, but what's soon to come in all our futures. It helps us grasp the ultimate origin of deception, and why the trickery is still taking place.

Before the beginning

As we have read in the Coal Kids Club chapter, the people of Earth have been engaging in astonishingly depraved behavior for quite a while, basically the entire time people have been hopping around on the ground from whence they came. Some of the evil that has taken place has been committed intentionally, and some has been brought about through lies and deceit passed from generation to generation of our closest family and friends. But the darkness did have a starting point. It was conceived long ago. And now we're going to probe the Bible to reveal the truth of the matter.

Let's take a journey far back in time, before God ever said, "Let there be light." We're going back to an age before our planet was created and Adam and Eve were planted in the Garden of Eden by the Creator. We're traveling to a point where only the God family existed, without the company of any other beings. Jesus referred to this time alone with His fellow Divine Being during His final prayer to God the Father just before the Savior was executed. Jesus urged:

> Now, Father, glorify Me in Your presence with that glory I had with You before the world existed. (John 17:5 HCSB)

Here, it's revealed that Jesus did share a glorious existence with His Father before Planet Earth was even created. Then at some point in the vast reaches of antiquity – we're not told precisely when – God decided to manufacture some company, and it was not human beings. He fashioned messengers that are known today as angels, and Scripture says these angels are actually made up of spirit:

In speaking of the angels he says, "He makes his angels spirits, and his servants flames of fire." (Hebrews 1:7 NIV)

The word "spirit" comes originally from the Hebrew word "ruwach," and it also means "wind." Many Bibles, in fact, translate "spirit" as "wind," such as:

He makes the winds His messengers, Flaming fire His ministers. (Psalm 104:4 NASB)

One very bright and beautiful angel fashioned by God was named Lucifer, coming from a Latin term meaning light-bearer. The specific word used in the Hebrew Old Testament for Lucifer is "heylel," which means the shining one. Two prophets of the Bible, Isaiah and Ezekiel, focus like a laser beam on this shining angel, and they shall be our starting point as we begin to probe why the world is now full of such dark deception.

Both of these prophets feature direct discourse from God to this angel, as the Maker lamented how the bright spirit being chose the wrong path despite initially being formed so wonderfully and given so much:

"You were the seal of perfection,
Full of wisdom and perfect in beauty.
You were in Eden, the garden of God;
Every precious stone was your covering:
The sardius, topaz, and diamond, Beryl, onyx, and jasper, Sapphire, turquoise, and emerald with gold.
The workmanship of your timbrels and pipes
Was prepared for you on the day you were created.
"You were the anointed cherub who covers;
I established you;
You were on the holy mountain of God;
You walked back and forth in the midst of fiery stones.
You were perfect in your ways from the day you were created,
Till iniquity was found in you.
(Ezekiel 28:12-15 NKJV)

These four verses explain much. The first point is that this angel was created at a certain time. "The day you were created" is how God twice stated it; so Lucifer had a birthday. He is not an eternal being like God who had no beginning. He was called "the anointed cherub who covers," meaning he was the cherub, another word for angel, selected by God to cover the divine throne of the Creator with his angelic wings. And, perhaps most interestingly, this angel was perfect in his ways. Perfect, that is, until something rotten was found inside his mind. And that rotten something is called iniquity.

The word "iniquity" here comes from the Hebrew term "evel," and it's obvious today's English word "evil" is almost a carbon copy of it. "Evel" also happens to rhyme with devil. (Imagine that!) Various Bibles translate "evel" as "evil," "wickedness," "sin," "wrong," "unrighteousness" and "perverseness." Thus, the guardian angel of God's throne was discovered to be the very first pervert, and an extremely wicked one at that. He essentially was found to be filled with sin, which the apostle John in the New Testament defines very simply: "sin is lawlessness." (1 John 3:4 NIV) Not to beat around the bush, John said plainly a few sentences later: "the devil has been sinning from the beginning." (1 John 3:8 NIV)

Satan was, and still is, evil because he's lawless, full of rebellion against his Maker. He doesn't follow, or even wish to follow, the divine laws of God revealed throughout the rest of Scripture and summed up in the famous Ten Commandments.

And what specifically was wrong with the character of this top angel? The Bible provides us some of his key traits:

> you declared, 'I am perfect in beauty.'
> (Ezekiel 27:3 HCSB)

> For you have said in your heart: 'I will ascend into heaven, I will exalt my throne above the stars of God; I will also sit on the mount of the congregation on the farthest sides of the north;
> (Isaiah 14:13 NKJV)

> I will ascend above the tops of the clouds; I will make myself like the Most High."
> (Isaiah 14:14 NIV)

In just a few verses, we see that the Creator of all things was able to read Lucifer's mind. The angel was so proud of his own beauty, that he became dangerously arrogant, secretly fantasizing about flying up above the clouds, reaching the place of God's heavenly throne located "on the farthest sides of the north," wherever that is in the unseen dimension of heaven. He would then place his own throne there above the thrones of the other angels, as he would **make himself like the Most High God**. The moment this iniquity was discovered in his character is the instant he became known as "Satan," which simply means enemy or adversary.

This enemy is not described as intellectually challenged. In fact, Scripture uses terms such as "great wisdom" and "full of wisdom" to help paint his portrait. At one point, God told him:

Yes, you are wiser than Daniel; no secret is hidden from you! (Ezekiel 28:3 HCSB)

Therefore, when we think of the devil, we have to admit we're dealing with a highly intelligent yet arrogant supernatural being originally created in the unseen spirit realm to be a top-ranking angel stationed at God's own throne. In the New Testament, Jesus revealed even more about the perverted nature of Satan, as He explained:

He was a murderer from the beginning, not holding to the truth, for there is no truth in him. (John 8:44 NIV)

Now keep in mind, someone doesn't actually have to kill someone for God to consider him a murderer. Here's how John defines the term:

Anyone who hates another brother or sister is really a murderer at heart. (1 John 3:15 NLT)

This single verse almost sums up the entire message of the Bible. If individuals have no outward care and concern for their fellow beings (this applies to spirit beings as well as human beings), it's equivalent to killing them in God's sight. Meanwhile, as Jesus continued his thought on the devil's nature in the eighth chapter of John, He hit the nail on the head with another title for Satan:

When he lies, he speaks his native language, for he is a liar and the father of lies. (John 8:44 NIV)

So, not only does Satan lust to be like the Most High God, he is a liar and the inventor of lying. Many people today don't realize how serious a violation it is to lie. They think in their own minds that if they can get away with fudging the truth now and then, they're fine with God. But here are two Scriptures that hopefully will change their mind:

> Lying lips are an abomination to the LORD, But those who deal truthfully are His delight. (Proverbs 12:22 NKJV)

> But the fearful, and unbelieving, and the abominable, and murderers, and whoremongers, and sorcerers, and idolaters, and <u>all liars</u>, shall have their part in the lake which burneth with fire and brimstone: which is the second death. (Revelation 21:8 KJV)

We know for sure that the Creator didn't invent lies, because Scripture tells us outright He has never lied, noting "God, who cannot lie" (Titus 1:2 NKJV) and "it is impossible for God to lie." (Hebrews 6:18 NASB)

Thus, it is absolutely clear that the origin of sin started in the mind of this brilliant archangel formerly known as Lucifer, the light-bearer. There was simply no deception until the powerful spirit named Lucifer abandoned the light of truth and literally went to the dark side. It happened a long time ago, in a place far, far away. We can finally see the conception of deception, the very commencement of lying and deceit, with Satan the liar, pegged as the **inventor of lying**. He has been filled with hatred ever since, and therefore, as Jesus said, "He was a murderer from the beginning."

Darkness caused the original 'Star Wars'

Satan's desire to be like the Most High apparently consumed him so much, he artfully sought assistance from his fellow angels, whom the Bible often refers to as "stars." Through his mastery of subtle suggestion, he eventually was able to convince a third of the other spirits to join him in his dark rebellion, actually going to war against God and the righteous angels who remained faithful to their Creator. Here's how your Bible talks about the original "Star Wars":

> Then war broke out in heaven. Michael and his
> angels fought against the dragon, and the dragon
> and his angels fought back.
> (Revelation 12:7 NIV)

> And the dragon lost the battle, and he and his
> angels were forced out of heaven. This great
> dragon – the ancient serpent called the devil, or
> Satan, the one deceiving the whole world – was
> thrown down to the earth with all his angels.
> (Revelation 12:8-9 NLT)

> His tail drew a third of the stars of heaven and
> threw them to the earth. (Revelation 12:4 NKJV)

Jesus once commented about the moment the devil and his band of rebel stars were ejected from heaven, noting in cinematic fashion: "I saw Satan fall like lightning from heaven." (Luke 10:18 NKJV)

And where did these lawless angels end up? As we just read, Satan "was thrown down to the earth with all his angels." And that's why this crafty character, the inventor of lying, was just waiting in a garden called Eden for the Creator to take a pile of dirt and transform it into a being in the image and likeness of God, the first man.

The end from the beginning

Although Adam was totally new to the scene, his unscrupulous company in the garden had longed for the moment he could work his craft once again, to engage in smooth-tongued sorcery to taint humanity.

He apparently was aware of the Master Plan to turn human beings into divine "children of God," because the Creator tells everyone the end of the story far in advance:

> I make known the end from the beginning, from
> ancient times, what is still to come. I say, 'My
> purpose will stand, and I will do all that I please.'
> (Isaiah 46:10 NIV)

I will tell you the future before it happens."
(Isaiah 42:9 NLT)

Knowing full well that divinity was something he could never attain because he was merely an angel, Satan became inflamed with jealousy. Hatred flowed through every inch of his mind, culminating in a devious scheme to have the first humans not only take away their immortality, but also place all of their progeny under an automatic death penalty. Remember, the devil "was a murderer from the beginning" (John 8:44 NIV). Satan, who is also called "the oppressor" in Scripture, became bent on destruction:

You are in constant dread all day long because of the <u>fury of the oppressor, who has set himself to destroy.</u> (Isaiah 51:13 HCSB)

He eagerly anticipated the creation of Adam and Eve so he could begin deceiving God's own offspring, hoping that they, too, would disobey their Maker just like he did. Why? Because, as we have seen, Satan wanted (and still wants) to be like the Most High. He is desperate to become God, the supreme Ruler of all things. He enjoys ultimate power. He wanted to be the one having dominion, which is rulership, over these human beings, supplanting the authority and sovereignty of the Creator.

At the same time, because his mind is twisted and perverse and filled with hatred, he is fully bent on seeing the lives of the children of God ended. What a masterful trick it would be if he could deceive people into disobeying the true God, and have them follow him (the false god), even if they believed they were doing the right thing and following the true God!

The world of two

The origin of deception on Earth is not difficult to determine. Satan was in the Garden of Eden having crafty conversations with the very first woman, deceiving "the whole world," as we've read in Revelation.

The whole world at that time had a population of just two people, namely Adam and Eve. If the enemy could subtly suggest that they should listen to his devious instructions, and willingly sin, that is go against the teaching of the true God, breaking His commandments, then Satan would succeed in murdering God's own children by causing them to die. He would prevent them from receiving the everlasting life intended for them. The devil was well aware that breaking God's law earns people death, since "the wages of sin is death" (Romans 6:23 KJV).

And not only did he seek the ultimate death of God's kids, he wanted to show the true Creator that he could convince people to follow his own unlawful instructions, so that he, the devil, would be the people's leader, the god of this world. This is the precise title the apostle Paul has bestowed upon the devil, referring to him as "the god of this world" (2 Corinthians 4:4 KJV).

Because Satan desperately wishes to be like the Most High, his motives for murder were evidently lust and jealousy. He was aware of God's glorious future for human beings, the very people who alone have the potential of being born into God's very own family as divine gods. He saw what men and women were going to receive, and he wanted it for himself. Badly. He was jealous of God's Master Plan to transform humans made of dirt into everlasting rulers who will sit on the throne of the Creator and rule the nations, while he, himself, would never get that opportunity. Remember, Satan is merely an angel; he is not the same type of being that God is. He is not in God's divine family and, unlike men and women, he does not have the potential to become part of that ruling family. How do we know? God says so:

> For to which of the angels did God ever say, "You
> are my Son; today I have become your Father"?
> Or again, "I will be his Father, and he will be my
> Son"? (Hebrews 1:5 NIV)

As this verse plainly states, no angel has ever heard the Creator God say that God has fathered him or will father him. But human beings – this includes ordinary people along with Jesus when He walked here as a human – have been given this tremendous declaration from God. The above verse from Hebrews is actually quoting several passages from the Old Testament, one of which is Psalm 2:

> I will proclaim the LORD's decree: He said to
> me, "You are my son; today I have become your
> father. (Psalm 2:7 NIV)

The astonishing statement continues:

> Ask me, and I will make the nations your
> inheritance, the ends of the earth your possession.
> You will break them with a rod of iron; you will
> dash them to pieces like pottery."
>
> (Psalm 2:8-9 NIV)

Not only does this statement apply to Jesus, it applies to you and me as well! The thought is repeated by the risen Jesus in the final book of Scripture, as He explains that **all** human beings who are obedient to His instructions will eventually be given the divinely ordained authority to rule over non-believing nations, even having the power to shatter them to pieces with an iron rod, the very same ability He has! Here is that amazing promise:

> To the one who is victorious and does my will
> to the end, I will give authority over the nations
> – that one 'will rule them with an iron scepter
> and will dash them to pieces like pottery' – just
> as I have received authority from my Father.
>
> (Revelation 2:26-27 NIV)

The other two Old Testament Scriptures quoted in Hebrews 1:5 list identical declarations:

> I will be his father, and he will be my son.
>
> (2 Samuel 7:14, 1 Chronicles 17:13 NIV)

Again, only Jesus and human beings obedient to His truth are the ones who are part of God's family. Angels are not. They were designed by God as a different type of being with a unique purpose, which is revealed in Scripture. All angels, including Satan, were created to actually serve **us**! They're designed to help human beings reach their destination, to become divine children in God's family:

> Therefore, angels are only servants – spirits sent
> to care for people who will inherit salvation.
>
> (Hebrews 1:14 NLT)

The fact that Satan slithered his way into the mind of Eve so he could take away the eternal life of humans is evidence that he knew in advance what they would become, and he did his fiendish best to thwart this marvelous end game. It has been driving him bonkers that these crummy clumps of clay would become divine beings, God's literal children, while he, the one-time golden boy, the shining star of the heavens, would be made to eventually serve what he felt were the scum of the Earth.

The first lie on Earth: What a crock!

The Bible describes the devil in the garden as "more cunning" than any other beast:

> Now the serpent was more cunning than any
> beast of the field which the Lord God had made.
> And he said to the woman, "Has God indeed said,
> 'You shall not eat of every tree of the garden'?"
> (Genesis 3:1 NKJV)

We're not told how long it was before this conversation took place. But Satan planted a wily seed of doubt in Eve's mind, prompting her to question the direct order from her Maker to avoid eating from the tree of knowledge of good and evil:

> The woman said to the serpent, "We may eat the
> fruit from the trees in the garden. But about the
> fruit of the tree in the middle of the garden, God
> said, 'You must not eat it or touch it, or you will
> die.'" (Genesis 3:2-3 HCSB)

And this is when Satan spoke the first recorded lie in all of Scripture:

> "You won't die!" the serpent replied to the
> woman. (Genesis 3:4 NLT)

This answer was in direct opposition to what God had previously taught the couple, as He had instructed:

> If you eat its fruit, you are sure to die."
> (Genesis 2:17 NLT)

The satanic deception that people won't really die remains with us today. The religions of men and women, courtesy of the devil's trickery, still teach the lie that people don't really die when they kick the bucket.

Whether it's a belief in reincarnation or mainstream Christianity, people simply have been fooled into thinking they instantly and automatically continue to exist somewhere else once their physical bodies expire. It is the opposite of what the Bible teaches. God personally said in the garden:

> You will eat bread by the sweat of your brow until you return to the ground, since you were taken from it. For you are dust, and you will return to dust." (Genesis 3:19 HCSB)

Now when God confronted Eve after she had eaten of the forbidden fruit, she admitted she had been tricked by this reptilian villain, who may have looked more like a crocodile than a snake. She confessed:

> The serpent deceived me, and I ate.
> (Genesis 3:13 NKJV)

If I may take the liberty of translating this into today's street lingo, what Eve really meant was: "That damn liar tricked me! And I actually bought the crapola he was shoveling!" Since that initial deception for mankind, little has changed for the world at large. This same scenario is echoing across the planet even now, as the devil continues singing his song of deception, and most of the world listens and buys into his bull.

Remember, this "great dragon" is "that old serpent, called the Devil, and Satan, which **deceiveth the whole world**." (Revelation 12:9 KJV) And "the whole world is under the control of the evil one" (1 John 5:19 NIV).

The whole world back in the original garden had a population of just two. As I write this, the global population has rocketed to well over seven billion. While that's a lot of minds in the devil's prison, Satan actually made it easy on himself for perpetuating his cunning fraud. He didn't have to get into the heads of seven billion individuals all at one time. He just expertly lied to the mother of everyone on the Earth, and she not only bought into his baloney, she passed the devil's message to her husband, and their kids, and their kids, all the way to our present generation. Every single one of us has merely inherited a string of lies from our parents and religious leaders over thousands of years:

For the leaders of the people have misled them.
They have led them down the path of destruction.
(Isaiah 9:16 NLT)

When people finally awake out of the "Matrix"-style dream world in which they've been living, they'll admit to God that they've been victims of non-stop, devious hooey that amounted to a pile of nothingness:

The Gentiles shall come to You
From the ends of the earth and say,
"Surely our fathers have inherited lies,
worthlessness and unprofitable things."
(Jeremiah 16:19 NKJV)

The cocktail of death

The devil's attractive lie about not dying was in effect like a fatal cocktail. It was a delicious mixed drink consisting of part truth and part deception. But it took away the immortality planned for mankind. Let me explain. After the devil told Eve the lie that she wouldn't die, in the very next statement he provided her some truth, which excited her, as the truth of God should always be exciting to our ears. Satan said:

"God knows that your eyes will be opened as
soon as you eat it, and you will be like God,
knowing both good and evil." (Genesis 3:4 NLT)

As stunning as it may seem, this was a completely true statement from Satan! Their eyes were opened as soon as they "ate" the fruit, as soon as they bought into his junk. They suddenly became aware of things they had not known previously. They would now know and experience both good and evil. We can even read this phrase spiritually to mean that human beings would now know and deal with both God and the devil. Incidentally, God Himself is well aware of both good and evil, because He and His righteous servants are good, and those in rebellion against Him are evil.

And last but not least, human beings actually **became like God**, at least in one respect. Your Bible says so. God the Father and Jesus confirmed that Adam and Eve actually became like them, suddenly being aware of both good and evil:

> Then the LORD God said, "Look, the human
> beings <u>have become like us</u>, knowing both good
> and evil. What if they reach out, take fruit from
> the tree of life, and eat it? Then they will live
> forever!" (Genesis 3:22 NLT)

This is why the tree of life had to be cut off from the first humans, because they would have attained eternal life had they eaten from it. After they had disobeyed God's instructions, these freshly sinning flesh-and-blood creations would have turned into wicked spirit beings, and God had already experienced enough of that garbage with Satan and his band of demons.

The deadly cocktail – the pattern of mixing a subtle lie with the truth – is very effective, and has been the modus operandi for all deceivers since Day One. Think about all the "trusted" politicians, "honest" lawyers, "faithful" spouses and "unbiased" journalists, and you'll undoubtedly agree. And yes, I'm laying on the cynicism pretty thick in that sentence.

We all need to consider this cocktail with every thought that we drink into our minds. If the drink we're swallowing is not 100 percent truth, but has some falsehood as a mixer, it can lead to death. We wouldn't consume a glass of fresh-squeezed orange or grapefruit juice if we knew that a few drops of poison were stirred into it, would we? Of course not.

But so many people have little problem accepting the deception that has been broadcast by the devil, as they march along like robots "according to the course of this world, according to the prince of the power of the air, the spirit who now works in the sons of disobedience." (Ephesians 2:2 NKJV)

Yes, the Bible says the devil is a spirit who rules the airwaves, incessantly coaxing people into disobeying their Maker. It's no wonder that billions of people gladly lie to their own children every December. They have been brainwashed by countless songs and movies suggesting it's perfectly fine to do so, especially when they do it "for the children." The devil presents his lies to the children of men as glamorous notions to which no one would object. These ideas include peace on Earth, love among friends and family, and a fun time for everyone.

The foundation of the world

The decision by Adam and Eve to rebel against God was the exact moment this world was actually founded. The foundation was not the moment the planet was created, it was the moment the current system of operation, the world as we know it, was instituted. It was when the entire world became a giant fraud. And the hoax has still not been shattered.

The first man and woman decided they would follow someone other than their Maker, and that's the moment the devil became their ruler, their king, the god of this world. The vast majority of men and women repeat this flawed pattern today, following someone other than their Creator, even if they're not cognizant of it. When anyone, be it Adam and Eve or their billions of children, does not stick to the truth of God, that person becomes "of the devil":

> The one who does what is sinful is of the devil, because the devil has been sinning from the beginning. (1 John 3:8 NIV)

For instance, Adam's very first child, Cain, is said to have "belonged to" the devil. He bought into the enemy's lies so much, that he ended up being the world's first human being who killed his fellow man, specifically his own literal brother, Abel. Thus, Cain, just like the devil, became a murderer from the beginning:

> We must not be like Cain, <u>who belonged to the evil one</u> and killed his brother. And why did he kill him? Because Cain had been doing what was <u>evil</u>, and his brother had been doing what was righteous. (1 John 3:12 NLT)

Centuries later, Jesus told some Jewish people during His earthly ministry that they, too, belonged to Satan, for the same reason:

> "You are of your father the devil, and the desires of your father you want to do. He was a murderer from the beginning, and <u>does not stand in the truth,</u> because there is no truth in him. (John 8:44 NKJV)

When Adam and Eve violated God's instructions after the deception of Eve, just as millions of self-professing believers today are tricked into disobeying the divine laws, the couple's transgression earned them the wages of sin, which is mortality. The New Testament says this is one of the reasons the Creator had to leave heaven temporarily and dwell on Earth as a human being, so he could fix the fatal mess the devil had created:

> The reason the Son of God appeared was to destroy the devil's work. (1 John 3:8 NIV)

Jesus is even referred to as "the Lamb slain <u>from the foundation of the world</u>." (Revelation 13:8 KJV)

Even though it would be thousands of years after Adam and Eve sinned that Jesus would pay the price for their infraction and be killed Himself, Scripture indicates He was "slain from the foundation of the world." That's because the original sin by the first couple was the exact moment of confirmation that the Creator would have to be slain. It became codified that He would personally accept the death penalty for every person who ever lived so He could save His own kids from eternal death.

The prison planet

An interesting point the Bible relates about the foundation of the world is that the initial rebellion by the first humans placed the world into a state of captivity. It made the planet one gigantic prison – a prison for our minds. We became slaves, placed under the control of the devil and his sinful agenda which have been polluting the world for thousands of years, even into our own time. Remember, "the whole world is under the control of the evil one." (1 John 5:19 NIV)

Although most may not realize it, we actually live day to day in a state of bondage. We're held captive to sin, death and the fear of death. We're prisoners of this fear, being reminded constantly of the mortal demise that awaits all of us, courtesy of the fallen angel. The New Testament states that people "lived their lives as slaves to the fear of dying." (Hebrews 2:15 NLT)

This fear dates back to that very first lie, when Satan suggested people wouldn't die. When we look back at this event with objective eyes, it's easy to see how they were drawn like a magnet to the falsity. After all, which of these statements sounds more attractive? The one from God stating that disobedience would bring about their death? Or the fib from the devil suggesting they would not die – that they were, in effect, immortal, even if they disobeyed? The answer is obvious.

People then and now really **want to believe the lie** that they can do anything they wish, and still not be dead forever. This is why millions of people today still hang on to this phony notion that they have an "immortal soul," despite the fact that this oft-spoken phrase appears nowhere in Scripture. It's a spellbinding idea that has mesmerized and plagued all of humanity since its inception. If you wish to know what God Himself has twice said about what really happens to disobedient souls, here it is: "The soul that sinneth, it shall die." (Ezekiel 18:4, 20 KJV). Once again, the end result of rebellion against the Creator is permanent death, not eternal existence somewhere.

But back to this idea of the prison planet. The full context of Hebrews 2:15 provides more insight into this captivity of our minds, and how Jesus is able to set us free from the prison of the mind, where the devil himself is the warden:

> Because God's children are human beings—made of flesh and blood—the Son also became flesh and blood. For only as a human being could he die, and only by dying could he break the power of the devil, who had the power of death. Only in this way could he set free all who have lived their lives as slaves to the fear of dying. (Hebrews 2:14-15 NLT)

As we can see, the Bible clearly states the devil has the power of death over us. He's the one who not only caused the original death penalty for Adam and Eve, but his perpetual lying over thousands of years has kept us unknowingly desiring death, as he has inspired the people of today to follow the sick beat of the enemy instead of the uplifting song of their true righteous Parents in heaven.

This notion that we're all prisoners who are enslaved is found numerous times in Scripture, including these portions:

they themselves are slaves of sin and corruption. For <u>you are a slave to whatever controls you.</u> (2 Peter 2:19 NLT)

The trouble is with me, for I am all too human, <u>a slave to sin</u>. (Romans 7:14 NLT)

I the LORD have called thee in righteousness, and will hold thine hand, and will keep thee, and give thee for a covenant of the people, for a light of the Gentiles; To open the blind eyes, to <u>bring out the prisoners from the prison</u>, and them that sit in <u>darkness</u> out of the <u>prison house</u>. (Isaiah 42:6-7 KJV)

But his own people have been robbed and plundered, <u>enslaved, imprisoned, and trapped</u>. (Isaiah 42:22 NLT)

The Spirit of the Lord GOD is on Me, because the LORD has anointed Me to bring good news to the poor. He has sent Me to heal the brokenhearted, to proclaim <u>liberty to the captives</u> and <u>freedom to the prisoners</u>; to proclaim the year of the LORD's favor, and the day of our God's vengeance (Isaiah 61:1-2 HCSB)

This is what the LORD says ... I will say to the <u>prisoners</u>, 'Come out in freedom,' and to <u>those in darkness</u>, 'Come into the light.' (Isaiah 49:8-9 NLT)

Fear factor

Despite the fact most people are indeed prisoners of fear, we don't have to be, and God actually has told us countless times through many books of the Bible not to be afraid. Here are just a few:

For I, the LORD your God, will hold your right hand, Saying to you, 'Fear not, I will help you.' (Isaiah 41:13 NKJV)

Be strong and courageous; don't be terrified or afraid of them. For it is the LORD your God who goes with you; He will not leave you or forsake you." (Deuteronomy 31:6 HCSB)

Fear not: for they that be with us are more than they that be with them. (2 Kings 6:16 KJV)

"Don't be afraid. Even though you have committed all this evil, don't turn away from following the LORD. Instead, worship the LORD with all your heart. (1 Samuel 12:20 HCSB)

Yea, though I walk through the valley of the shadow of death, I will fear no evil; For You are with me; Your rod and Your staff, they comfort me. (Psalm 23:4 NKJV)

Don't be afraid, little flock, because your Father delights to give you the kingdom.
(Luke 12:32 HCSB)

There is no fear in love; but perfect love casts out fear, because fear involves torment. But he who fears has not been made perfect in love.
(1 John 4:18 NKJV)

As you can see, from Old Testament times to the New, God has been urging His people to break free from the grip of the devil, to free our minds from all kinds of fear. In Psalm 23 mentioned above, David declared he wouldn't fear evil, even though he was walking through the valley of the shadow of death. If you ever wondered what he meant, he's talking about our entire planet. This whole world in which we live is the valley of the shadow of death, because the people of the world walk metaphorically in a giant valley, an extremely large pit, just waiting for our death penalty to arrive. David said he would not fear evil because his Maker, who happened to be packing an iron rod to punish the wicked, was protecting him.

When we're no longer filled with the fears, worries and stress caused by the devil, we can finally come to life, worshiping God in spirit and in truth, as Jesus instructed:

But the time is coming—indeed it's here now—
when true worshipers will worship the Father
in spirit and in truth. The Father is looking for
those who will worship him that way. For God is
Spirit, so those who worship him must worship
in spirit and in truth." (John 4:23-24 NLT)

The one thing to fear

Although the Bible is filled with messages telling us not to fear, there
is actually one fear that is very healthy in nature, providing us wisdom and
peace of mind. And that is "the fear of the LORD."

The phrases "fear the LORD," "fear of the LORD" and "fear of God"
are plentiful in Scripture, but they can be confusing to some people who
might wonder, "Should we really be **afraid** of our Maker?"

It's a good question because the Hebrew word for fear, "yira," does,
in fact, mean fear in a bad sense, like being terrified. But it also means
having the utmost respect and reverence for someone in a positive sense.
And in the case of our Creator, both hold true. As we look at some verses
mentioning this fear, the real meaning will become self-evident:

Do this so that you may fear the LORD your God
all the days of your life by keeping all His statutes
and commands I am giving you, your son, and
your grandson, and so that you may have a long
life. (Deuteronomy 6:2 HCSB)

Fear the LORD your God, serve him only and
take your oaths in his name. Do not follow other
gods, the gods of the peoples around you; for the
LORD your God, who is among you, is a jealous
God and his anger will burn against you, and
he will destroy you from the face of the land.
(Deuteronomy 6:13-15 NIV)

Now therefore fear the LORD, and serve him
in sincerity and in truth: and put away the gods
which your fathers served on the other side of

the flood, and in Egypt; and serve ye the LORD.
(Joshua 24:12 KJV)

Only fear the LORD, and serve him in truth with
all your heart (1 Samuel 12:24 KJV)

Fear the LORD, you his holy people, for
those who fear him lack nothing. ... Come, my
children, listen to me; I will teach you the fear of
the LORD. Whoever of you loves life and desires
to see many good days, keep your tongue from
evil and your lips from telling lies.
(Psalm 34:9-13 NIV)

The fear of the LORD is to hate evil: pride, and
arrogancy, and the evil way, and the froward
mouth, do I hate. (Proverbs 8:13 KJV)

Fear of the LORD is the foundation of true
wisdom. All who obey his commandments will
grow in wisdom. Praise him forever!
(Psalm 111:10 NLT)

And the spirit of the LORD shall rest upon him,
the spirit of wisdom and understanding, the spirit
of counsel and might, the spirit of knowledge
and of the fear of the LORD (Isaiah 11:2 KJV)

Do not be afraid of those who kill the body but
cannot kill the soul. Rather, be afraid of the One
who can destroy both soul and body in hell.
(Matthew 10:28 NIV)

Moses said to the people, "Do not be afraid. God
has come to test you, so that the fear of God will
be with you to keep you from sinning."
(Exodus 20:20 NIV)

As should be obvious from these Scriptures, there are both positive
and negative aspects to this fear. The positive aspects are overwhelmingly
good, for the fear of the LORD leads to wisdom, understanding, and
obedience to the commandments that produce eternal life. It is the hate of

evil, pride, arrogance and the "froward" mouth, which means habitually disposed to disobedience and opposition, the precise character of the adversary known as the devil. As Moses told the people, having a healthy fear of God in our minds is to keep us from sinning.

But as is demonstrated by several verses, there is also the notion of terror. If we choose not to obey the commandments of God, continuing in lies and deception, following the ways of other gods such as the devil, then God's anger will burn against us, and we'll be completely destroyed, body and soul, in the Gehenna fire. We simply won't exist any longer. We'll be dead forever. Now that should spark some fear into people to get with the program, stop their rebellion and follow the path that leads to everlasting life.

After reading this chapter, you should now understand the ancient origin of evil, the conception of the global deception that continues to this day, and the reason why the people of this world have been aimlessly wandering like mindless zombies. We're actually in an ongoing war against evil and the wicked spirit beings promoting rebellion against the Creator. But why is God even allowing evil in the first place? Will it continue to plague us forever? And what is the true destiny of Satan? For these questions, there are solid answers from the Bible, and they just may stun you.

Chapter Four:
The good in the bad

Why is there evil? Why does God allow evil to continue to exist? If God truly is love, then why doesn't He eliminate all evil from our lives right now?

These are some of questions that people have been wondering about for time immemorial. And the answers that are given are sometimes laughable, especially when they come from the leaders of today's mainstream religion that calls itself Christianity. I'm sure you've heard cop-out responses such as "God is a mystery" or "We're not meant to know such things."

The secret to understanding why there's evil and why God allows it to continue is not difficult to discover. All we need to do is to read the entire Bible, and actually believe the words on the page for what they say. God wasn't kidding when He had His servants write His thoughts. While accepting the words on the page seems like it should be an easy exercise, it can be difficult for many readers, since their minds have been so poisoned with confusion from their pastors and priests who have mixed in a lot of demonically inspired error with the truth of Scripture. Remember what we learned in the previous chapter about the deadly cocktail. Part truth and part deception is toxic, and we have to make sure we're dealing with 100 percent truth without any poison in the mix.

The answer is in the end game

When seeking to solve the mystery as to why evil exists, I think addressing another question first will make the answer more than obvious.

And that question is: What in the world is God doing with us? What's the **purpose** of our own, personal existence? Why are we all here? What's the end game?

Once we realize the reason for our own existence, then all becomes clear. The answer to that question has been revealed in the Bible as well. And it is probably not what you've been taught by thousands of deceived (or intentionally deceiving) ministers who have been suppressing the glorious, Biblical truth from you. You have not been created to get a winning ticket to heaven to float on a cloud for all eternity, doing a bunch of nothingness except playing a musical instrument and singing worship songs to God. I know that's what millions of people have been taught, and they believe it with all their heart through little fault of their own. So I don't blame them. They have simply not been instructed on the truth from their own Bibles. They've been tricked.

And if they ever do ask their pastors about the actual words they read in Scripture that do reveal the truth, they're often told something to the effect of, "I know the Bible says that, but it doesn't really **mean** that." Herein lies the problem, not believing the Word of God for what it plainly states.

It all goes back to the "three words of Jesus that most Christians don't believe," so if you haven't read that chapter yet, please do so right now, because it will greatly help you understand the reason for evil.

Those three words are "You are gods," which Jesus said twice in Psalm 82:6 and John 10:34. If people would only accept the fact that God is reproducing more members of his divine family, adult children of God to sit down on His own throne and rule the nations with Him just as He promised in Revelation, then they would finally wake up to the reason why evil exists:

> "To him who overcomes I will grant to sit with Me on My throne, as I also overcame and sat down with My Father on His throne.
> (Revelation 3:21 NKJV)

> And he that overcometh, and keepeth my works unto the end, to him will I give power over the nations: And he shall rule them with a rod of iron
> ... (Revelation 2:26-27 KJV)

> Don't you realize that someday <u>we believers will
> judge the world?</u> ... Don't you realize that <u>we
> will judge angels?</u> (1 Corinthians 6:2-3 NLT)

These are just a few of the verses which tell us outright of our glorious future if we get with the program to overcome evil. We, as members of God's family, will be above the angels, sitting on God's own throne, judging both the people of this world and angels, ruling them with a rod of iron, just like the disciplining rod that Jesus has. Why don't people ever talk about these Scriptures? The New Testament has been blaring them for centuries. We already know why, because Satan has been using every tool he can, including the leaders of today's religions to avoid any utterance of such amazing lines. They're the verses that countless ministers never dare to address in their sermons, because they either don't know what they indicate, they're afraid to speak the truth, or they do know the truth and don't wish to inform their flocks **why** people are born in the first place! We all need to accept the wondrously joyful Good News that God is having and raising children to be gods to reign in the divine family!

It's difficult for many people to accept the glorious truth because Satan has been holding people's minds in a prison since the beginning. He has convinced people the Bible doesn't mean what it says, and the mere suggestion that we could become gods who rule the universe under the authority of our Designer initially sounds over the top and arrogant beyond all measure. But it's there in the Bible, many times from start to finish, and, as we'll see, it's the very reason why evil exists and is allowed to continue, at least for now.

Previously, we read all about the conception of deception, how evil began a long time ago before the Earth was ever created. But now we're scouring through Scripture to find out why this evil was allowed. And a good place to start is in the Old Testament:

> I form the light, and **create darkness**: I make peace,
> and **create evil**: **I the LORD do all these things**.
> (Isaiah 45:7 KJV)

> The LORD has made everything for its own purpose,
> Even the wicked for the day of evil.
> (Proverbs 16:4 NASB)

Here we have direct statements from the Word which begin to answer the question in plain fashion. They say that the true God, Jesus, is actually responsible for the evil. As stunning as it sounds, God says He created evil! He says He has made everything for its own purpose, and that includes the wicked for the day of evil. As we all know, we are currently living in the day of evil, when rebellion against God's instructions rules the day and the ultimate wicked one, the devil, is perched as "the god of this world." (2 Corinthians 4:4)

It is not just the Old Testament that indicates God has created everything. Here's a well-known New Testament verse that attests to the same thing:

> For by Him all things were created, both in
> the heavens and on earth, visible and invisible,
> whether thrones or dominions or rulers or
> authorities—all things have been created through
> Him and for Him. (Colossians 1:16 NASB)

Again, the Bible declares that the Creator, who is Jesus Christ of Nazareth, has Himself made everything. This includes evil itself and wicked rulers both in the physical and spiritual worlds. You might not like this explanation, but it's the truth from the Bible, and we'll see much more of it in detail coming up.

If we go back to the first chapter of Genesis, we see that God and everything good are represented by light, and all that is evil is represented by darkness, and God went on a mission to separate the two:

> And God saw the light, that it was good: and God
> divided the light from the darkness.
> (Genesis 1:4 KJV)

Tragically, most men and women have been following the current ruler of this world, Satan, in the partial or complete rejection of God's instructions, as they plunge willingly into the darkness. Near the conclusion of the Bible, we're told:

> This is the verdict: Light has come into the
> world, but people loved darkness instead of light
> because their deeds were evil. (John 3:19 NIV)

So, at this point, we see the Biblical statement that God is the One responsible for evil's existence (along with the existence of everything else), and that for the most part, people have loved spiritual darkness more than light because their actions were evil.

This is where God's Master Plan comes in. When we accept what Scripture says about God having and raising children in the proper way of living, it's much easier to understand why He has created evil and is allowing it to continue.

The Maker is actually testing everyone to see if each person will be obedient to His laws, to His eternal way of life, or if they will choose the way of the devil, which is evil and sin. He wants to test and examine people over the course of time, to see if they're really properly prepared to become members of His family, to see if they can handle divine power. As we've seen in the previous chapter, apparently there are some spirit beings who can't handle it. They intentionally have chosen to follow the incorrect path, and that has resulted in catastrophic problems.

Testing one, two, three

There's no shortage of Scriptures explaining how people are being tested for obedience to God's instructions. We've already studied the very first test, a simple food test, where God had set evil within sight of the first humans. Remember, it was God who created the tree of knowledge of good **and evil**, and the wicked one, the devil, was placed in the garden as well.

In the wake of the fall from grace, God's examinations of us have only continued and gotten more pervasive into every aspect of our lives. For instance, many people don't realize that Jesus, in His pre-human existence, instructed the very first child of Adam and Eve about learning how to do what's right in life, to reject sin, which is the breaking of God's laws. Here God speaks directly with Cain:

> "Why are you so angry?" the LORD asked Cain. "Why do you look so dejected? You will be accepted if you do what is right. But if you refuse to do what is right, then watch out! Sin is crouching at the door, eager to control you. But you must subdue it and be its master."
> (Genesis 4:7 NLT)

This remark clearly indicates that God has etched out two paths for people to choose. One path is submitting to God and doing what is right. The other path is submitting to the devil, refusing to obey God's instructions and instead doing evil. In other words, sin. But He also noted that with God's assistance, people can resist the devil, master the evil and overcome the rebellion of sin:

> Submit yourselves therefore to God. Resist the devil, and he will flee from you. (James 4:7 KJV)

> Be serious! Be alert! Your adversary the Devil is prowling around like a roaring lion, looking for anyone he can devour. Resist him and be firm in the faith (1 Peter 5:8-9 HCSB)

Sadly for Cain, he failed his test, when he ended up murdering his own brother, Abel. But the tests have continued throughout time for everyone else. Some classic examples include the events when God brought His people out of Egypt and led them in the wilderness for four decades. There were no distractions in the desert, and He explained that He would be testing their obedience in numerous ways:

> Remember how the LORD your God led you through the wilderness for these forty years, humbling you and testing you to prove your character, and to find out whether or not you would obey his commands.
> (Deuteronomy 8:2 NLT)

> Then the LORD said to Moses, "I am going to rain bread from heaven for you. The people are to go out each day and gather enough for that day. This way I will test them to see whether or not they will follow My instructions.
> (Exodus 16:4 HCSB)

Immediately after God gave His people the Ten Commandments, the Israelites were shaking with fear due to heavy lightning and thunder, not to mention a heavenly trumpet blast and smoke coming from the mountain. But Moses tried to calm their fears by explaining it was all just part of a test:

"Don't be afraid," Moses answered them, "for God has come in this way to test you, and so that your fear of him will keep you from sinning!" (Exodus 20:20 NLT)

And the test from God throughout time has been simple. He is commanding people to make a choice between following good and following evil:

"See, I have set before you today <u>life and good, death and evil</u>, in that I command you today to love the LORD your God, to walk in His ways, and to keep His commandments, His statutes, and His judgments, that you may live and multiply; and the LORD your God will bless you in the land which you go to possess.

"But if your heart turns away so that you do not hear, and are drawn away, and worship other gods and serve them, I announce to you today that you shall <u>surely perish</u>; you shall not prolong your days in the land ...

"I call heaven and earth as witnesses today against you, that I have set before you life and death, blessing and cursing; therefore <u>choose life</u>, that both you and your descendants <u>may live</u> (Deuteronomy 30:15-19 NKJV)

This declaration is one of the most famous portions of the Bible, and yet somehow, millions of believers don't seem to realize that God Himself has intentionally set evil in front of people as a potential course of action, and has commanded them to make a personal choice on how to conduct themselves. And the direct order is not to choose evil and death, but to choose life! That's correct, we have been commanded by God to choose the path of life. And that's eternal life, folks, not the temporary existences that even wicked sinners enjoy at this moment.

God issued His instructions, explaining to people what is godly and good and what leads to everlasting life. Scripture explains that God "fed thee in the wilderness with manna, which thy fathers knew not, that he might humble thee, and that he might prove thee, to do thee **good at thy latter end**." (Deuteronomy 8:16 KJV) The good thing that God will do for obedient servants at their "latter end" is resurrect them from death and give them eternal life! But He also placed before His people what the devil promoted, and that is evil, the rejection of God's instructions. And the end result of such rebellion is the opposite of life. It is perishing. It is eternal death.

The testing ground

Here are a few more Scriptures about the testing process, so you're clear about why God allows evil to exist:

> What is man, that You think so highly of him and pay so much attention to him? You inspect him every morning, and <u>put him to the test every moment</u>. (Job 7:18 HCSB)

> You have <u>tested my heart</u>; You have examined me at night. You have tried me and found nothing evil; I have determined that my mouth will not sin. (Psalm 17:3 HCSB)

> <u>Test me</u>, LORD, and <u>try me; examine my heart and mind</u> ... I do not sit with the worthless or associate with hypocrites. I hate a crowd of evildoers, and I do not sit with the wicked. (Psalm 26:2-5 HCSB)

> Search me, O God, and know my heart; <u>test me</u> and know my anxious thoughts. Point out anything in me that offends you, and lead me along the path of everlasting life. (Psalm 139:23-24 NLT)

Here it's explained why God pays so much attention to people. There's a divine inspection taking place, with the test in effect at every single moment, according to Job. In the Psalms, David encouraged God to test and try him, to probe what was really going on in the deepest recesses of his mind. David explained how he hated evildoers, and he wanted his

Maker to see if anything in his own heart was offensive to God. And why? Because David knew the end game, and wanted eternal life! "Lead me along the path of everlasting life" is how he put it. He knew he had to resist and overcome evil to be on the path to immortality.

In the New Testament, this theme of being tested is again mentioned, with believers being told they should not be surprised by any trial or tribulation coming their way:

> Dear friends, don't be surprised when the fiery ordeal comes among you to test you as if something unusual were happening to you.
> (1 Peter 4:12 NASB)

> Instead, be very glad—for these trials make you partners with Christ in his suffering, so that you will have the wonderful joy of seeing his glory when it is revealed to all the world.
> (1 Peter 4:13 NLT)

> A man who endures trials is blessed, because when he passes the test he will receive the crown of life that God has promised to those who love Him. (James 1:12 HCSB)

Are you understanding the plan yet? Since the beginning of time, God has been testing people with good versus evil. People are tried with all sorts of evil to see if they will pass the test to receive the astounding gift of the crown of eternal life. This is the reason we're all here! To overcome evil and follow the good so we can gain life!

If God had not created evil for us to experience, we would have no idea what it was, and would not know how to reject it. He created this world to be the testing ground. It's the specific place where people could have the knowledge of both good and evil, to experience both, and then willfully choose to resist, reject and overcome the evil. As He told Cain, we have to subdue the sin and master it.

Remember the end game. God has intended His children to overcome evil so they can sit with Him on His throne and rule with Him! Here are those never-talked-about Scriptures again:

"To him who overcomes I will grant to sit with
Me on My throne, as I also overcame and sat
down with My Father on His throne.
(Revelation 3:21 NKJV)

And he that overcometh, and keepeth my works
unto the end, to him will I give power over the
nations: And he shall rule them with a rod of iron
... (Revelation 2:26-27 KJV)

Don't you realize that someday we believers will
judge the world? ... Don't you realize that we
will judge angels? (1 Corinthians 6:2-3 NLT)

We all need to understand that God is not making robots out of human
beings. He could have formed mindless individuals if He wished to, but He
instead is having and raising children who possess the freedom to choose,
and who have chosen life over death. These are the people who will
become divine members of God's own family, and will sit on the throne
of Yeshua, reigning over other people and even angels. When are people
going to wake up and start believing their Bibles for a change instead of the
deceptive hoax that they've fallen for since Garden of Eden days?

Practice makes perfection

It's important to realize that God's testing process is here for our
ultimate benefit. He is giving all of us a little bit of time in our temporary
lives here to learn **how** to overcome the evil. To learn that we should never
engage in it, and never want anything to do with it. Few people take to
heart the commandment from God to eliminate all evil and be **perfect**!
Yes, folks, we have been commanded by God Almighty to be perfect and
blameless in our thoughts and deeds, from the Old Testament to the New.
Here's just a sampling, all spoken by God Himself:

I am the Almighty God; walk before me, and be
thou perfect. (Genesis 17:1 KJV)

You must be blameless before the LORD your
God. (Deuteronomy 18:13 HCSB)

Be perfect, therefore, as your heavenly Father is
perfect. (Matthew 5:48 HCSB)

If you're a person who thinks we cannot be perfect, then you're calling God a liar. Because over and over, He tells us to be blameless and perfect! Sin can be overcome, especially when we have the power and presence of the Almighty dwelling inside us. He actually says He will eventually place His Spirit inside everyone so that we **can** be obedient:

> And I will put my Spirit in you and move you to follow my decrees and be careful to keep my laws. (Ezekiel 36:27 NIV)

> "I will put my law in their minds and write it on their hearts. I will be their God, and they will be my people. (Jeremiah 31:33 NIV)

And why does He want us little lumps of clay to become perfect? Because **He Himself** is perfect:

> He is the Rock; his deeds are perfect. Everything he does is just and fair. He is a faithful God who does no wrong; how just and upright he is! (Deuteronomy 32:4 NLT)

Remember, God is raising children, divine offspring of the Supreme Being, and He expects His children to act in the same mature way that He does. Just as you don't want your own kids to misbehave, God wants, expects and demands His own children to be obedient, because He is raising them to be **like Him**, to think and act in the same manner, to rule the universe as members of His family. Jesus clearly stated:

> If you want to enter into life, keep the commandments." (Matthew 19:17 HCSB)

An easy way to remember this concept is to sum up the entire Bible using the three words you often tell your own misbehaving children today as you raise them: "Knock it off!" God wants us to stop our nonsensical embrace of evil and choose the good way, the obedient way that leads to eternal life so we can reign with Him.

Want it shorter than three words? How about just one word? BEHAVE! Want it shorter than six letters? Here you go: OBEY.

The Calamityville Horror

There is a very common misconception about the God of the Bible, and it's heard incessantly in churches that call themselves Christian, and is broadcast on radio and television as well. And that is that God is so full of love, that He would never harm anyone or cause any sort of evil in someone's personal life. That, dear friends, is a fairy tale, and if you're hearing such pablum from your pastor or priest, maybe it's time to leave that church. The notion that God never causes evil, harm or suffering, particularly on people He cares for, is simply the opposite of what Scripture reveals. He is not so gentle and lovey-dovey all the time, as we're about to see.

Keep in mind that the Maker of all things is trying to bring everyone to eternal life, but He will not grant us that immortal status if we continue to willfully reject His commands during our temporary existence. In fact, God has uncorked the L-word, saying anyone professing to be a believer who doesn't follow His instructions is actually **a liar**:

> Whoever says, "I know him," but does not do
> what he commands is a liar, and the truth is not
> in that person. (1 John 2:4 NIV)

When people don't obey His commands for righteousness, God responds with all sorts of things, ranging from personal problems to national catastrophes. And the Bible is replete with the Almighty wreaking havoc and disaster on people. God is the author of what could be called "The Calamityville Horror." Here are some verses to warm you up to this fact:

> Is it not from the mouth of the Most High that
> both calamities and good things come?
> (Lamentations 3:38 NIV)

> When disaster comes to a city, has not the LORD
> caused it? (Amos 3:6 NIV)

> If you abandon the LORD and worship foreign
> gods, He will turn against you, harm you, and
> completely destroy you, after He has been good
> to you." (Joshua 24:20 HCSB)

Are you paying attention, all you "addicted to love" pastors and churchgoers out there? The God of the Bible, the One you claim to worship, says that He Himself is the cause of calamities and disasters. Even after He has provided people with all kinds of goodness and blessings, it is He who will cause people harm and completely destroy them if they reject His instructions. Here's another:

> "'But if you will not listen to me and carry out all these commands, and if you reject my decrees and abhor my laws and fail to carry out all my commands and so violate my covenant, then I will do this to you: I will bring on you sudden terror, wasting diseases and fever that will destroy your sight and sap your strength. You will plant seed in vain, because your enemies will eat it.
> (Leviticus 26:14-16 NIV)

And this is just scratching the surface. We're now going to see how God describes the wide array of evils He personally will bring about, and this is on those whom He **loves**! You may never have read the following list of curses or heard about it in a lovey-dovey church, because they actually don't want you to realize that God will severely punish and harm you if you don't abide by His demands. As you read it, remember that "Jesus Christ is the same yesterday and today and forever" (Hebrews 13:8 NASB).

Here's His big list of calamities:

> "But if you do not obey the LORD your God by carefully following all His commands and statutes I am giving you today, all these curses will come and overtake you:
>
> You will be cursed in the city and cursed in the country. Your basket and kneading bowl will be cursed. Your descendants will be cursed, and your land's produce, the young of your herds, and the newborn of your flocks. You will be cursed when you come in and cursed when you go out.

The LORD will send against you curses, confusion, and rebuke in everything you do until you are destroyed and quickly perish, because of the wickedness of your actions in abandoning Me.

The LORD will make pestilence cling to you until He has exterminated you from the land you are entering to possess.

The LORD will afflict you with wasting disease, fever, inflammation, burning heat, drought, blight, and mildew; these will pursue you until you perish.

The sky above you will be bronze, and the earth beneath you iron. The LORD will turn the rain of your land into falling dust; it will descend on you from the sky until you are destroyed.

The LORD will cause you to be defeated before your enemies. You will march out against them from one direction but flee from them in seven directions. You will be an object of horror to all the kingdoms of the earth.

Your corpses will be food for all the birds of the sky and the wild animals of the land, with no one to scare them away.

"The LORD will afflict you with the boils of Egypt, tumors, a festering rash, and scabies, from which you cannot be cured.

The LORD will afflict you with madness, blindness, and mental confusion, so that at noon you will grope as a blind man gropes in the dark. You will not be successful in anything you do. You will only be oppressed and robbed continually, and no one will help you.

You will become engaged to a woman, but another man will rape her. You will build a house but not live in it. You will plant a vineyard but not enjoy its fruit.

Your ox will be slaughtered before your eyes, but you will not eat any of it. Your donkey will be taken away from you and not returned to you. Your flock will be given to your enemies, and no one will help you.

Your sons and daughters will be given to another people, while your eyes grow weary looking for them every day. But you will be powerless to do anything.

A people you don't know will eat your land's produce and everything you have labored for. You will only be oppressed and crushed continually.

You will be driven mad by what you see.

The LORD will afflict you with painful and incurable boils on your knees and thighs—from the sole of your foot to the top of your head.

"The LORD will bring you and your king that you have appointed to a nation neither you nor your fathers have known, and there you will worship other gods, of wood and stone.

You will become an object of horror, scorn, and ridicule among all the peoples where the LORD will drive you.

"You will sow much seed in the field but harvest little, because locusts will devour it.

You will plant and cultivate vineyards but not drink the wine or gather the grapes, because worms will eat them.

You will have olive trees throughout your territory but not anoint yourself with oil, because your olives will drop off.

You will father sons and daughters, but they will not remain yours, because they will be taken prisoner.

Whirring insects will take possession of all your trees and your land's produce.

The foreign resident among you will rise higher and higher above you, while you sink lower and lower.

He will lend to you, but you won't lend to him. He will be the head, and you will be the tail.

"All these curses will come, pursue, and overtake you until you are destroyed, since you did not obey the LORD your God and keep the commands and statutes He gave you. These curses will be a sign and a wonder against you and your descendants forever.

Because you didn't serve the LORD your God with joy and a cheerful heart, even though you had an abundance of everything, you will serve your enemies the LORD will send against you, in famine, thirst, nakedness, and a lack of everything. He will place an iron yoke on your neck until He has destroyed you.

The LORD will bring a nation from far away, from the ends of the earth, to swoop down on you like an eagle, a nation whose language you don't understand, a ruthless nation, showing no respect for the old and not sparing the young.

They will eat the offspring of your livestock and your land's produce until you are destroyed. They will leave you no grain, new wine, oil, young of your herds, or newborn of your flocks until they cause you to perish.

They will besiege you within all your gates until your high and fortified walls, that you trust in, come down throughout your land. They will besiege you within all your gates throughout the land the LORD your God has given you.

"You will eat your children, the flesh of your sons and daughters the LORD your God has given you during the siege and hardship your enemy imposes on you.

The most sensitive and refined man among you will look grudgingly at his brother, the wife he embraces, and the rest of his children, refusing to share with any of them his children's flesh that he will eat because he has nothing left during the siege and hardship your enemy imposes on you in all your towns.

The most sensitive and refined woman among you, who would refinement and sensitivity, will begrudge the husband she embraces, her son, and her daughter, the afterbirth that comes out from between her legs and the children she bears, because she will secretly eat them for lack of anything else during the siege and hardship your enemy imposes on you within your gates.

"If you are not careful to obey all the words of this law, which are written in this scroll, by fearing this glorious and awesome name—Yahweh, your God— He will bring extraordinary plagues on you and your descendants, severe and lasting plagues, and terrible and chronic sicknesses.

He will afflict you again with all the diseases of Egypt, which you dreaded, and they will cling to you. The LORD will also afflict you with every sickness and plague not recorded in the book of this law, until you are destroyed.

Though you were as numerous as the stars of the sky, you will be left with only a few people, because you did not obey the LORD your God.

Just as the LORD was glad to cause you to prosper and to multiply you, so He will also be glad to cause you to perish and to destroy you. You will be deported from the land you are entering to possess.

Then the LORD will scatter you among all peoples from one end of the earth to the other, and there you will worship other gods, of wood and stone, which neither you nor your fathers have known.

You will find no peace among those nations, and there will be no resting place for the sole of your foot. There the LORD will give you a trembling heart, failing eyes, and a despondent spirit.

Your life will hang in doubt before you. You will be in dread night and day, never certain of survival.

In the morning you will say, 'If only it were evening!' and in the evening you will say, 'If only it were morning!'—because of the dread you will have in your heart and because of what you will see.

The LORD will take you back in ships to Egypt by a route that I said you would never see again. There you will sell yourselves to your enemies as male and female slaves, but no one will buy you." (Deuteronomy 28:15-68 HCSB)

Again, all this horror is what He does to those He loves. Just imagine what He has in store for His enemies! Oh wait, we don't need to imagine. The Bible provides us some answers, and they're not pretty. Here's what's in store for those nations who actually fight against Jerusalem at the time Jesus is returning to Earth:

> And the LORD will send a plague on all the nations that fought against Jerusalem. Their people will become like <u>walking corpses, their flesh rotting away. Their eyes will rot in their sockets, and their tongues will rot in their mouths.</u>
> (Zechariah 14:12 NLT)

What a horror! This sounds like what you'd see on "The Walking Dead." Maybe this is where the show's producers got the inspiration. Holy Scripture features people walking around like corpses with their flesh, eyes and tongues all rotted. Here's how the New King James Version translates this unnerving passage:

> Their flesh shall dissolve while they stand on their feet, Their eyes shall dissolve in their sockets, And their tongues shall dissolve in their mouths. (Zechariah 14:12 NKJV)

People's flesh will dissolve! This is sheer ghoulishness, and it's all caused by the loving God of your Bible! Please, for your own eternal benefit, I urge you to awake from the hypnosis you've been put under by all those smooth-talking, big-smiling preachers who never give you the whole story. Their mesmerizing discussions tend to focus solely on what's nice and easy. What's pleasant. What's palatable. The non-offensive. They rarely, if ever, inform you of the gruesomeness that God inflicts on people He has created while trying to rescue them from their eternal death!

I know what some Christians might already be thinking now: "Hey, those are all Old Testament quotes. But we worship the God of the New Testament!" I'm not sure they even know what they're saying when they make this absurd statement, since the God of the Bible is eternal, covering both Testaments, and they pray every night to "Our Father," not just to the New Testament Jesus, the Son of God. But that being said, here's what the **New** Testament says about some of the evil the God of the New Testament will inflict.

Let's dare to open the freshest, most recent book of the Bible. It's called Revelation. And I encourage you to read all of it on your own when you have time. The evils that God Himself will inflict on the families of this planet are appalling. I'll provide you just a small sampling, so you can see the anguish that's on its way:

> The fifth angel sounded his trumpet, and I saw a star that had fallen from the sky to the earth. The star was given the key to the shaft of the Abyss. When he opened the Abyss, smoke rose from it like the smoke from a gigantic furnace. The sun and sky were darkened by the smoke from the Abyss.
>
> And out of the smoke locusts came down on the earth and were given power like that of scorpions of the earth. They were told not to harm the grass of the earth or any plant or tree, but only those people who did not have the seal of God on their foreheads.
>
> They were not allowed to kill them but only to torture them for five months. And the agony they suffered was like that of the sting of a scorpion when it strikes. During those days people will seek death but will not find it; they will long to die, but death will elude them.
> (Revelation 9:1-6 NIV)

Yes, it's hideous. People will feel as if they've been stung by scorpions, and they'll be tortured for nearly half a year with excruciating pain. People will yearn to die, but won't be able to. And, as ugly as this sounds, it continues. Here's an example of another plague coming from the wrath of God:

> The sixth angel sounded his trumpet, and I heard a voice coming from the four horns of the golden altar that is before God. It said to the sixth angel who had the trumpet, "Release the four angels

who are bound at the great river Euphrates."

And the four angels who had been kept ready for this very hour and day and month and year were released to kill a third of mankind. The number of the mounted troops was twice ten thousand times ten thousand. I heard their number.

The horses and riders I saw in my vision looked like this: Their breastplates were fiery red, dark blue, and yellow as sulfur. The heads of the horses resembled the heads of lions, and out of their mouths came fire, smoke and sulfur.

A third of mankind was killed by the three plagues of fire, smoke and sulfur that came out of their mouths. The power of the horses was in their mouths and in their tails; for their tails were like snakes, having heads with which they inflict injury. (Revelation 9:13-19 NIV)

Indeed, an entire third of the men, women and children of Earth will be wiped out in this coming scenario. And one might think that the survivors would finally wake up to the need to stop their rejection of God's laws. But sadly, the answer is no:

The rest of mankind who were not killed by these plagues still did not repent of the work of their hands; they did not stop worshiping demons, and idols of gold, silver, bronze, stone and wood— idols that cannot see or hear or walk. Nor did they repent of their murders, their magic arts, their sexual immorality or their thefts.
(Revelation 9:20-21 NIV)

Notice in these verses that not only do people refuse to quit their stealing, killing, occult activity and fornication, they also do not stop using idols and worshiping demons. That means that all this sordid activity is already going on right now! It's the very reason God is coming to punish us! People don't even realize that when we reject His explicit instructions that lead to life, we're not filled with His presence, His Holy Spirit.

Our minds get consumed with all the worthless garbage of the world: astrology, desire for money, power, fame, vapid entertainment, and even the fraudulent religious practices that have become popular across the globe, such as senselessly setting up green trees and decorating them with silver and gold. We already know where all these customs originated, with the worship of demons and the devil himself! Remember, the Bible says the devil is the god of this world! And the True God of the Bible is using extremely severe punishment, urging us to knock it off!

> "I will punish the world for its evil, And the wicked for their iniquity; I will halt the arrogance of the proud, And will lay low the haughtiness of the terrible. **(Isaiah 13:11 NKJV)**

> For look, the LORD is coming from His place to punish the inhabitants of the earth for their iniquity. The earth will reveal the blood shed on it and will no longer conceal her slain.
> (Isaiah 26:21 HCSB)

If we profess that the Bible is true, which it is, we have to acknowledge the fact that God is a God of punishment and discipline. He is the Punisher:

> He punishes the nations – won't he also punish you? (Psalm 94:10 NLT)

Now we have all seen just a small fraction of the evil that God can cause. It's no thrill to read any of it, let alone experience it. But God does not look forward to punishing His children, any more than you as human parent look forward to disciplining your own children. He issues warnings about terrible consequences in the hope that people will listen to Him. If we don't listen and obey, that's when we're subject to His righteous anger.

All things for good

Now having taken you through a whole bunch of darkness, I don't wish your heart to be troubled in any way. Because the Bible is really about Good News. That's what the word "gospel" means. It doesn't mean bad news. But even though plenty of bad stuff, including horrific evil, takes place, it all works for the good purpose of God. Here's a New

Testament Scripture that many people already know, but it cannot be stressed enough:

> And we know that God causes all things to work together for good to those who love God, to those who are called according to His purpose. (Romans 8:28 NASB)

This remark about God causing "all things to work together for good" reminds us that all things include evil. It ties in perfectly with what we read near the beginning of this chapter:

> I form the light, and **create darkness**: I make peace, and **create evil**: **I the LORD do all these things**. (Isaiah 45:7 KJV)

> The LORD has made everything for its own purpose, Even the wicked for the day of evil. (Proverbs 16:4 NASB)

God can and does use all sorts of evil, whether it's deception from the devil, or disasters upon individual people or large nations, to work His phenomenal purpose. And that is to correct and save people from their rebellion against Him so He can quicken them into their immortal bodies as divine children of God to reign for all eternity with Him.

The story of Joseph from the book of Genesis confirms this very idea. The eleventh son of Jacob, famous for his coat of many colors (which may represent all the nations created by God) is a foreshadowing of the story of Jesus. He was the obedient son of his father who was betrayed by his own brothers and lived among slaves for years, actually being thrown into prison for a crime he did not commit, just as Jesus never committed a crime against God:

> So Joseph's master took him and put him into the jail, the place where the king's prisoners were confined; and he was there in the jail. (Genesis 39:20 NASB)

Now please think not only on the physical level, but on the spiritual level as well. Remember what we studied in depth in the last chapter. That this world in which we live is actually a giant spiritual prison, where the king of this world, the devil, is holding everyone's mind in captivity. We're in bondage to sin and the result of sin, which is death.

Joseph is a representation of Jesus, so when you read his story, try substituting the name of Jesus for Joseph, and you'll be taking another step into the spirit dimension:

> But the LORD was with Joseph and extended kindness to him, and gave him favor in the sight of the chief jailer. The chief jailer committed to Joseph's charge all the prisoners who were in the jail; so that whatever was done there, he was responsible for it. The chief jailer did not supervise anything under Joseph's charge because the LORD was with him; and whatever he did, the LORD made to prosper.
> (Genesis 39:21-23 NASB)

The analogy reveals that God the Father was with Jesus during the time Jesus spent living among the prisoners. Jesus performed His duties so well, He was elevated to be in charge of all the prisoners! Jesus was, in effect, raised to be put in a position where He was the real leader of the people.

Most people know the rest of Joseph's story, how he was freed from the prison and became the official second-in-charge in the kingdom of Egypt, just as Jesus was freed from this prison of Earth and became the second-in-charge to God the Father in the kingdom of God.

But the very end of Joseph's story is even more fascinating, and is often overlooked. After Joseph's father Jacob had died and was buried, his brothers who had betrayed him years earlier suddenly had fear coursing through their veins. Again, think on the spiritual level as you read the account, because Joseph's brothers represent you and me, the brothers of Jesus, who are filled with the same fears they had:

> When Joseph's brothers saw that their father was dead, they said, "Perhaps Joseph will hate us, and may actually repay us for all the evil which we did to him."

> So they sent messengers to Joseph, saying,
> "Before your father died he commanded, saying,
>
> 'Thus you shall say to Joseph: "I beg you, please
> forgive the trespass of your brothers and their
> sin; for they did evil to you."'" Now, please,
> forgive the trespass of the servants of the God of
> your father." And Joseph wept when they spoke
> to him.
>
> Then his brothers also went and fell down before
> his face, and they said, "Behold, we are your
> servants." (Genesis 50:15-18 NKJV)

Your eyes should be open to the metaphor by now. Just as Joseph's brothers who sinned against him feared for their own lives, we as human beings have fear that we won't be forgiven for our evil rebellion against God.

> Joseph said to them, "Do not be afraid, for am I
> in the place of God? (Genesis 50:19 NKJV)

Now the very next statement is one of the most important and uplifting Scriptures in the entire Bible, and it again confirms why God is allowing evil. Here's what Joseph (the representative of Jesus) told the evil members of his own family:

> But as for you, ye thought evil against me; but
> God meant it unto good, to bring to pass, as it is
> this day, **to save much people alive**.
> (Genesis 50:20 KJV)

Are you able to grasp what's being said here on the spiritual level? This goes infinitely beyond the physical man Joseph and his human brothers. This is a message for the ages. God is intentionally using evil, even wickedness against Himself, for a **good** purpose. And what is that purpose? **To save much people alive!** In other words, to save countless numbers of people eternally! God is using all the evil that has been committed since time immemorial, even evil against His own Person, to grant repentant people everlasting life as divine children of God!

This has been the message of God since the book of Genesis. It has been broadcast by the Creator since the very beginning!

> I declare the end from the beginning, and from long ago what is not yet done, saying: My plan will take place, and I will do all My will.
> (Isaiah 46:10 HCSB)

The glorious purpose of God is revealed even by means of the experience of evil. Throughout each of our lives, we all experience both good and evil, the result of our ancient parents eating from the tree of knowledge of good and evil. But now, after we know what evil is and how much pain and heartache it causes, we should realize which path is the better path to choose. We have been shown the way of life and good, or the way of death and evil. We have been ordered to stop our ridiculous march toward eternal death once and for all:

> 'As I live!' declares the Lord GOD, 'I take no pleasure in the death of the wicked, but rather that the wicked turn from his way and live. Turn back, turn back from your evil ways! Why then will you die ... ?" (Ezekiel 33:11 NASB)

It's time to choose. To choose life. To keep the commandments. To be perfect. To be sons and daughters of God! It is high time to get with the program, to come out of the devil's prison of death, and finally come to life! What are you waiting for?

Chapter Five:
The end of the wicked

Is the loving and merciful God of the Bible some kind of monster who will torture disobedient people and rebellious angels for all eternity? Will writhing pain and hideous shrieking continue for endless millennia? There are plenty of teachers who call themselves Christian who would have you believe such a thing. But the truth from the Bible is, as you might have suspected by now, the very opposite.

It was a very long time ago the devil deceived Eve by telling her, "You will not surely die." And here we are now, thousands of years later, with most people, including millions of devout Christians, still clinging to this nefarious lie with a relentless grip.

Not only do they believe it about themselves concerning the moment of physical death of faithful Christians, they also believe it concerning the destiny of the wicked. And when I say the wicked, I'm referring to both Satan the devil, whom the Bible calls the "wicked one" in at least half a dozen places including 1 John 5:18, as well as wicked people who have been following his instructions and committing evil deeds throughout their life.

When it comes to the ultimate fate of the devil and his minions, the common belief among Bible readers is that even these sinners "shall not die." Most are under the impression that Lucifer and all evildoers will indeed have eternal life, being alive and aware forever, although tortured with excruciating pain in a fiery place with no relief. But is this what the Bible itself teaches? That the wages of sin is eternal life? Even if it's in a place that's not pleasant? We're now going to look at many Scriptures to find out the true fate of the wicked, because the message of the Bible again will reveal the antithesis of the trending belief.

The world in a hurry

We live in an age where people want things very quickly. We have fast food, same-day delivery, instant messages, Twitter, Instagram, Snapchat, real-time stock quotes, electronic navigation for our cars, live tech help on the Internet, get-rich-quick schemes and speed dating, to name but a few. People want to know things, and to know them quickly. The same impetuous desire for knowledge and wisdom dates far back into antiquity to our first human parents in the garden, Adam and Eve. Impatience is part of our human nature, whereas God instructs us to be long-suffering: "You also must be patient." (James 5:8 HCSB)

Sometimes our impatience is evident even when it comes to a matter of Bible study. If we have a certain question about the Word of God, we want an answer, and we want an answer now. Right now. In a rush. Instantly. With only a single verse. Short and sweet. "Just tell me quickly, so I can move on to other things," is the attitude.

But this desire for an instant answer can be problematic on occasion. Because one verse of the Bible that many presume is self-evident does not always answer the question properly, especially when there are countless other Scriptures demonstrating the polar opposite. If we're really looking for the truth, the solid truth of God, then surely we need to investigate all that the Bible says on any given matter. So let's probe the Word of God to find out what it actually says concerning the fate of those it calls wicked.

The quick verse

Because people today are in such a hurry, they often rush to the end of the book to find out how the story ends. On the matter at hand, they open up the last book of the Bible, fast-forward the pages to one of its final chapters, and focus on the following verse, which has become quite well-known:

> And the devil, who deceived them, was thrown into the lake of burning sulfur, where the beast and the false prophet had been thrown. They will be tormented day and night for ever and ever. (Revelation 20:10 NIV)

At first glance, it seems pretty straightforward, and many people use this one verse to explain what they surmise will happen to the devil and his ilk. They suggest an eternal life of miserable torment and never-ending agony. This is what millions of Christians wholeheartedly believe: that God will be torturing the devil and all evil people who haven't repented of their sins for trillions of unending years. I'm not sure how that jives with the "God is love" mantra that's broadcast on all the Christian channels these days, but that's another story.

What I'm saying is that it's high time we look at the rest of the Bible. Because, as we shall see, there are scores of Scriptures revealing a very different outcome for the wicked one and all those who have chosen his pernicious path. Once we understand the ultimate destiny for the rebels, the confusion about Revelation 20:10 will vanish into nothingness, just like everything that is evil.

Life and death

Among the most famous Scriptures in the Bible is one that most Christians say they believe, but they actually don't. Or, to be more accurate, they believe only a portion of it. Here it is:

> For the wages of sin is death; but the gift of God
> is eternal life through Jesus Christ our Lord.
> (Romans 6:23 KJV)

While everyone is attracted to the second part of the verse about God granting us the gift of eternal life through Jesus, so many disregard the first seven words in that sentence: "For the wages of sin is **death**." It's quite perplexing that despite such a clear statement on the end result of sin, people generally don't believe it. They think that the wages of sin is the opposite of death. They believe instead that the wages of sin is eternal life, an endless life of being scorched in fire but somehow never being totally consumed. Ironically, they are actually holding on to the original lie from Satan who said, "You will not surely die." (Genesis 3:4 NKJV)

While the trick of the devil has been to convince people that they never die no matter how many rules of the Creator they may break, here's what the Word of God says:

> ... I say to the wicked, 'Wicked one, you will surely die' (Ezekiel 33:8 HCSB)

> Those far from You will certainly perish; You destroy all who are unfaithful to You.
> (Psalm 73:27 HCSB)

God has said to the devil, and to every wicked individual (human or spirit), "You will surely die." He uses the words "certainly perish" and "destroy" just in case someone has a thick head, as He wants to make sure they understand there is no more existence for sinners. They will be completely annihilated. And there is plenty more evidence.

What the hell?

There is a fiery place of destruction that is talked about in the Bible, and we have seen it previously in this book. It is called the Valley of Hinnom. The Greek word for that is "Gehenna." Most Bibles in English translate Gehenna as "hell." This Gehenna fire is commonly referred to as the lake of fire, because they're equated in Scripture:

> And if anyone's name was not found written in the book of life, he was thrown into the lake of fire. (Revelation 20:15 NASB)

This lake of fire called Gehenna is, in fact, the end-time appearance of the Coal Kids Club. Just as Satan has inspired countless human beings throughout many generations to burn their children to death, becoming heaps of ashes inside a blazing furnace, so God will use the same method of execution for the devil and his followers, in the very same location that the Original Coal Kids Club existed in ancient Israel. Gehenna. The Valley of Hinnom.

Jesus Christ warned people about this Gehenna fire many times in the New Testament, and He made it clear it was not a place where people would be alive forever in agony. He said both their body and soul would be completely destroyed:

> And fear not them which kill the body, but are not able to kill the soul: but rather fear him which is able to **destroy both soul and body** in hell [Gehenna]. (Matthew 10:28 KJV)

I know it's difficult for many to realize this hell fire brings about the complete death of someone. The reason is because we have been meticulously brainwashed over thousands of years through stories, songs and, in recent times, TV shows and movies, that all depict this fiery place as a place of eternal punishing that never ends, rather than one of *final* eternal punishment, which results in being dead forever. Again, the devil's lie that people don't really die when their physical life ends is still bouncing around inside the noggins of the vast majority, maybe even in your mind as you read this.

But the Word of God is very clear on this matter, as we shall see now with many more Scriptures revealing what happens to the wicked.

A fiendish surprise

Part of the reason why people mistakenly think the devil himself will be alive forever in the Gehenna fire is because they understand he is a spirit being, not currently made of flesh and blood as human beings are. Many will even cite a statement by Jesus suggesting that angels cannot die:

> But those who are counted worthy to take part in that age and in the resurrection from the dead neither marry nor are given in marriage. For they cannot die anymore, because they are like angels and are sons of God, since they are sons of the resurrection. (Luke 20:35-36 HCSB)

Thus, many Bible readers presume Satan is immortal and cannot ever die. But what does Scripture say about who is really immortal? Here's the answer:

> I urge you in the sight of God who gives life to all things ... who alone has immortality (1 Timothy 6:13-16 NKJV)

The Bible clearly states it is **God alone who is immortal** – not any angel and not any human being. All angels and all human beings have been created by God, and the duration of their life is at God's pleasure. He can and will take that life – even spirit life – away from any individual who continues to violate His instructions.

Regarding Jesus' statement in Luke about not dying anymore, it's important to focus on the first part of that verse where Jesus specifically mentions that eternal life is only for "those who are counted worthy to take part in that age." Angels who have rebelled against God are obviously not worthy for the age to come in the kingdom of God. Only angels and human beings who remain faithful to God's instructions are worthy. When that future age commences, the righteous human servants will be quickened into their new bodies made of spirit so they won't die anymore, just like the righteous angels won't be dying.

Now, I know there are some doubters on this point who think that since angels are currently spirit beings, they can't die. But God can do anything He wants, including end their existence:

Is any thing too hard for the LORD? (Genesis 18:14 KJV)

Is anything too difficult for Me? (Jeremiah 32:27 HCSB)

What I'm getting at is the notion that although the devil is at present a powerful spirit being who has been alive for a long time, perhaps many thousands or even millions of years, his status as a spirit being can and will be taken away from him. Astonishingly, the Bible declares that Satan will eventually be changed into a mortal, just like mortal men and women, and he will be executed, incinerated and turned into ashes in the Gehenna fire.

Perhaps you've never thought about the Bible this way, but the entire Good Book is actually the story of a powerful Spirit Being who intentionally left His immortal existence in the spirit dimension to come to Earth as a flesh-and-blood man for a brief time so that He could be killed for our everlasting benefit. That character is the Creator of all things, the Spirit named Jesus Christ.

Now here's the shocker. The enemy of the Creator, Satan the devil, who wanted to be like the Most High God, is also a spirit being who has dwelled in the unseen spirit dimension; and just like Jesus, this spirit will leave the unseen dimension in his final moments, becoming a mortal man (although against his will) so that he, too, can be killed by God for our benefit! The specific benefit to us is that evil will finally be gone from our presence forever! (Please go back and read the last two paragraphs again, and let this truth sink in.)

Let's now see the copious proof from the Bible of this jaw-dropping conclusion for the evil one bent on murdering us from the beginning.

As mentioned before, much of Satan's story appears in the writings of two major prophets of the Old Testament, Isaiah and Ezekiel. Both were inspired by God to write about the arrogant and blasphemous thoughts racing through the mind of Lucifer. Remember, Satan is the former guardian angel of God's throne who wanted to be like the Most High God and overthrow Him. He became God's adversary when this iniquity was discovered inside his character, and his ultimate end has been recorded by the prophets. Please also keep in mind what God has said about Himself: "I declare the end from the beginning." (Isaiah 46:10 HCSB) In other words, the Creator has told us from the beginning what's going to happen at the end, and that includes the end of Satan.

We'll start with Ezekiel, who not only reminds us about the devil's arrogance and pride, but reveals that **Satan will actually become a mortal man in his final moments**. Yes, the devil will actually have his status as a spirit entity taken away from him, and he'll be slain as a typical man. Here is the relevant passage:

> Thus saith the Lord GOD; Because thine heart is lifted up, and **thou hast said, I am a God, I sit in the seat of God**, in the midst of the seas; **yet thou art a man, and not God**, though thou set thine heart as the heart of God:
>
> Behold, thou art wiser than Daniel; there is no secret that they can hide from thee:
>
> With thy wisdom and with thine understanding thou hast gotten thee riches, and hast gotten gold and silver into thy treasures:
>
> By thy great wisdom and by thy traffick hast thou increased thy riches, and thine heart is lifted up because of thy riches:
>
> Therefore thus saith the Lord GOD; Because thou hast set thine heart as the heart of God;

> Behold, therefore I will bring strangers upon thee, the terrible of the nations: and they shall draw their swords against the beauty of thy wisdom, and they shall defile thy brightness.
>
> **They shall bring thee down to the pit**, and __thou shalt die the deaths of them that are slain__ in the midst of the seas.
>
> Wilt thou yet say before him that slayeth thee, I am God? but **thou shalt be a man, and no God, in the hand of him that slayeth thee**.
>
> __Thou shalt die the deaths of the uncircumcised__ by the hand of strangers: for I have spoken it, saith the Lord GOD. (Ezekiel 28:2-10 KJV)

Notice in the above verses that God, who declares the end from the beginning, has told the devil that he will eventually become a man, saying, __"thou shalt be a man,"__ and that he will die the death of an uncircumcised man. In this verse, the word "man" in Hebrew is "adam," the same word in Genesis and throughout Scripture referring to human beings. The proof gets even more detailed as the chapter continues:

> Thus saith the Lord GOD; Thou sealest up the sum, full of wisdom, and perfect in beauty.
>
> Thou hast been in Eden the garden of God; every precious stone was thy covering, the sardius, topaz, and the diamond, the beryl, the onyx, and the jasper, the sapphire, the emerald, and the carbuncle, and gold: the workmanship of thy tabrets and of thy pipes was prepared in thee in the day that thou wast created.
>
> Thou art the anointed cherub that covereth; and I have set thee so: thou wast upon the holy mountain of God; thou hast walked up and down in the midst of the stones of fire.
>
> Thou wast perfect in thy ways from the day that thou wast created, till iniquity was found in thee.

> By the multitude of thy merchandise they have filled the midst of thee with violence, and thou hast sinned: therefore I will cast thee as profane out of the mountain of God: and **I will destroy thee, O covering cherub**, from the midst of the stones of fire.
>
> Thine heart was lifted up because of thy beauty, thou hast corrupted thy wisdom by reason of thy brightness: I will cast thee to the ground, I will lay thee before kings, that they may behold thee.
>
> Thou hast defiled thy sanctuaries by the multitude of thine iniquities, by the iniquity of thy traffick; therefore will I bring forth **a fire from the midst of thee, it shall devour thee**, and **I will bring thee to ashes upon the earth** in the sight of all them that behold thee.
>
> All they that know thee among the people shall be astonished at thee: thou shalt be a terror, and **never shalt thou be any more**.
> (Ezekiel 28:12-19 KJV)

Some Bibles translate that final line as to say Satan "will be no more" (NIV), "will exist no more" (NLT), "will never exist again" (HCSB), "will cease to be forever" (NASB), "shall be no more forever" (NKJV), and "shalt nevermore have any being" (ASV).

It's truly eye-opening what happens when we just read and believe the words on the page. Because as we see in the above passage, it's more than obvious that the devil will become a physical, mortal being so he can be slain as a typical man. He will be tossed into the pit, the Gehenna fire, where he'll be completely burned up and turned into ashes while people watch this spectacle. It's a horrible end that will prevent him from existing anymore.

Now, let's take a look at what God has said through Isaiah concerning the wicked one:

> The LORD hath broken the staff of the wicked, and the sceptre of the rulers. He who smote the people in wrath with a continual stroke, he that ruled the nations in anger, is persecuted, and none hindereth. The whole earth is at rest, and is quiet: they break forth into singing.
>
> Yea, the fir trees rejoice at thee, and the cedars of Lebanon, saying, Since thou art laid down, no feller is come up against us. (Isaiah 14:5-8 KJV)

We spoke of this earlier in the chapter on the Original Coal Kids Club, as the evergreen trees will metaphorically rejoice at Satan's death, because no woodcutter will be chopping them down to serve as Christmas trees any longer. Now let's continue in this same chapter of Isaiah:

> How art thou fallen from heaven, O **Lucifer**, son of the morning! how art thou cut down to the ground, which didst weaken the nations!
>
> For thou hast said in thine heart, I will ascend into heaven, I will exalt my throne above the stars of God: I will sit also upon the mount of the congregation, in the sides of the north: I will ascend above the heights of the clouds; I will be like the most High.
>
> Yet thou shalt be brought down to hell, to the sides of the pit.
>
> They that see thee shall narrowly look upon thee, and consider thee, saying, **Is this the man that made the earth to tremble**, that did shake kingdoms;
>
> That made the world as a wilderness, and destroyed the cities thereof; that opened not the house of his prisoners? All the kings of the nations, even all of them, lie in glory, every one in his own house.

> But thou art cast out of thy grave like an abominable branch, and as the raiment of those that are slain, thrust through with a sword, that go down to the stones of the pit; as a **carcase trodden under feet**.

> Thou shalt not be joined with them in burial, because thou hast destroyed thy land, and slain thy people: the seed of evildoers shall never be renowned. (Isaiah 14:12-20 KJV)

In these red-letter quotes, God clearly states that Lucifer, also known as Satan, will be brought down to the pit, the realm of the dead, called Sheol in Hebrew, and the remains of his dead body will be in plain sight for people to see and even step upon. The prophet Malachi briefly mentioned this moment when human beings would stomp all over the remains of the wicked:

> Then you will trample on the wicked; they will be ashes under the soles of your feet on the day when I act," says the LORD Almighty.
> (Malachi 4:3 NIV)

And there's still more from Isaiah:

> And the LORD shall cause his glorious voice to be heard, and shall shew the lighting down of his arm, with the indignation of his anger, and **with the flame of a devouring fire**, with scattering, and tempest, and hailstones. (Isaiah 30:30 KJV)

> For **Tophet** is ordained of old; yea, **for the king** it is prepared; he hath made it deep and large: **the pile thereof is fire and much wood**; the breath of the LORD, like a stream of brimstone, doth kindle it. (Isaiah 30:33 KJV)

Once again, we see confirmation here that the devil's demise will occur at the very location of the ancient Coal Kids Club, which God called Tophet, the fireplace and drumming place. It will employ a devouring fire, prepared by one King (Jesus) and intended for another king, the king of this current world, Molech, also known as Satan.

An interesting point about the devil that we should keep in mind is that Satan is a king and all the kingdoms of this world are still under his control and authority until Jesus returns to give him the boot. Satan even had a discussion about this with the Creator, affirming this fact:

> So he took Him up and showed Him all the kingdoms of the world in a moment of time. The Devil said to Him, "I will give You their splendor and all this authority, because it has been given over to me, and I can give it to anyone I want. (Luke 4:5-6 HCSB)

I bring up this detail because Scripture is filled with prophecies about the kingdoms of this world, and the wicked rulers who run them. Not only do the prophecies refer to the human rulers at any given time in history, they can also refer to the true spiritual prince, the invisible prince of darkness who is pulling the strings of the human rulers through carnal possession or the art of suggestion. With this in mind, God directly spoke about the future of the devil, to whom he referred as the "arrogant one" and "the most proud," in prophecies about Babylon:

> Look, I am against you, you arrogant one — this is the declaration of the Lord GOD of Hosts — because your day has come, the time when I will punish you. (Jeremiah 50:31 HCSB)

> The most proud shall stumble and fall, And no one will raise him up; I will kindle a fire in his cities, And it will devour all around him." (Jeremiah 50:32 NKJV)

In similar fashion, the prophet Nahum described Satan's final stretch here on Earth, when he gave this prophecy concerning Nineveh:

> What do you conspire against the LORD? He will make an utter end of it. ... From you comes forth one Who plots evil against the LORD, A wicked counselor. (Nahum 1:9-11 NKJV)

The LORD has given a command concerning you: "Your name shall be perpetuated no longer. Out of the house of your gods I will cut off the carved image and the molded image. I will dig your grave, For you are vile."
(Nahum 1:14 NKJV)

Look to the mountains — the feet of one bringing good news and proclaiming peace! Celebrate your festivals, Judah; fulfill your vows. For the wicked one will never again march through you; he will be entirely wiped out.
(Nahum 1:15 HCSB)

The fire will devour you there; the sword will cut you down. (Nahum 3:15 HCSB)

Nothing can heal you; your wound is fatal. All who hear the news about you clap their hands at your fall, for who has not felt your endless cruelty? (Nahum 3:19 HCSB)

That's right, folks. People will be so overjoyed when the wicked one is "entirely wiped out," they'll be applauding and laughing like they've never laughed before. This is mentioned throughout the Bible, including Psalm 52:

God shall likewise destroy you forever; He shall take you away, and pluck you out of your dwelling place, And uproot you from the land of the living. The righteous also shall see and fear, And shall laugh at him, saying, "Here is the man who did not make God his strength, But trusted in the abundance of his riches, And strengthened himself in his wickedness."
(Psalm 52:5-7 NKJV)

The unforgivable sin

At this point, I'd like to take a moment to address why the devil is going to be destroyed. It is simply because he has committed the unforgivable or unpardonable sin. Jesus spoke about this during His human ministry:

> Whoever speaks a word against the Son of Man, it will be forgiven him. But whoever speaks against the Holy Spirit, it will not be forgiven him, either in this age or in the one to come. (Matthew 12:31 NIV)

The author of Hebrews expounded on the precise meaning of this blasphemy, explaining:

> If we deliberately keep on sinning after we have received the knowledge of the truth, no sacrifice for sins is left, but only a fearful expectation of judgment and of raging fire that will consume the enemies of God. (Hebrews 10:26-27 NIV)

As we can see, having the knowledge of God's truth is a key factor in whether we can be forgiven or not. The power and presence of God, which is the Holy Spirit, opens our minds to the truth. But once we're aware of the truth, we cannot continue to willfully break God's laws. Because, as this Scripture indicates, there is no sacrifice left that will remove our death penalty. All that remains is some serious fretting about the divine judgment that's on its way and the "raging fire that will consume the enemies of God."

Please notice the last part of the Scripture. It is specifically referring to the Gehenna fire. It's the raging fire that will **consume the enemies of God**. Well, who is the chief enemy of God? It's Satan, of course! Satan literally means "enemy." And Scripture says time and time again that he will be completely burned up in this raging blaze with no existence left. And why? Because Satan knows the truth of God. He knows it better than you and I know it. He knew God's plan from the very beginning, and was filled with jealousy and hate, becoming a murderer in his heart from ancient times. And despite his intimate knowledge of the truth, the dark angel has deliberately kept on sinning. Hence, there is no more sacrifice remaining to take away his death penalty, the final and fatal payment for his wages of sin.

Bakin' bacon

Now on to a Bible story that's a quick analogy for the future of those on the dark side. One of the most famous events in Scripture recounts a time when Jesus cast out a bunch of demons from people possessed by unclean spirits. He sent the fallen angels into a herd of pigs, which subsequently ran off a cliff and were killed in a lake. I'm presenting this account because it's a spiritual metaphor for the world in which we live, and it also reveals the ultimate destiny for the devil, his demons and all humans who are unclean in their minds, choosing the way of rebellion. Here we go:

> When He had come to the other side, to the country of the Gergesenes, there met Him two demon-possessed men, coming out of the tombs, exceedingly fierce, so that no one could pass that way.
>
> And suddenly they cried out, saying, "What have we to do with You, Jesus, You Son of God? Have You come here to torment us before the time?"
>
> Now a good way off from them there was a herd of many swine feeding.
>
> So the demons begged Him, saying, "If You cast us out, permit us to go away into the herd of swine."
>
> And He said to them, "Go." So when they had come out, they went into the herd of swine. And suddenly the whole herd of swine ran violently down the steep place into the sea, and perished in the water. (Matthew 8:28-32 NKJV)

On the physical level, this event is self-explanatory. The evil spirits whom Jesus evicted were sent into some unclean animals, which then ran off a cliff and drowned in a lake. But once again, it's time to put on our spiritual thinking caps, because there is much more to the story on the spirit plane.

In the unseen world where God and the angels live, there is a war going on, as we have mentioned previously in this book. The fierce demons in this story represent the angry angels who have rebelled against God. These demons even say to Him: "What have we to do with You, Jesus, You Son of God? Have You come here to torment us before the time?" They're admitting to their Creator that they have nothing to do with Him. They just don't like Him. And they also admit that they know that there's an appointed time in the future when they will face some kind of torment from Him.

The Scripture then notes that a good way off from them was a herd of swine feeding. The pigs that are a good way off from the spirits represent ungodly human beings! People who are not filled with the Spirit of God are the unclean creatures who dwell a good way off from the spirit dimension, living in this physical realm of Planet Earth.

> So the demons begged Him, saying, "If You cast us out, permit us to go away into the herd of swine." (Matthew 8:31 NKJV)

This statement alludes to the initial moment the evil spirits were kicked out of heaven and came to Earth. They would be present with us here in the physical world, even able to possess the minds of many people. Remember, "they went into the herd of swine."

> He said to them, "Go!" So they came out and went into the pigs, and the whole herd rushed down the steep bank into the lake and died in the water. (Matthew 8:32 NIV)

The climax of the story reveals how both the demons and the unclean animals (people who don't have the Spirit of God in them) are racing to kill themselves eternally. When we're filled with the spirit of Satan, his attitudes and the doctrines of his demons, we're all committing suicide. We're merely preparing our own eternal death. And where will this final death take place? The lake! The lake in the story represents the lake of fire, where all the spiritual swine – the devil, his angels and all human beings who follow the path of death – will end up. All this evil bacon will be bakin' in serious heat until completely consumed into ashes. It is **not** eternal life. It is eternal death. It is perishing, as the Bible says over and over.

The big list of Satan's death

Want more proof? No problem. Take a look now at this big list of what the Bible declares is the future for all wicked and ungodly individuals. It is by no means an exhaustive list, but the large number of verses provide a clear understanding of the end of the story for all rebels against God. It is complete destruction. Incineration into ashes. Everlasting death:

> And the God of peace will crush Satan under your feet shortly. (Romans 16:20 NKJV)

> Therefore the wicked will not survive the judgment, and sinners will not be in the community of the righteous. (Psalm 1:5 HCSB)

> the way of the ungodly shall perish. (Psalm 1:6 KJV)

> For our God is a consuming fire. (Hebrews 12:29 KJV)

> My breath will consume you like a fire. (Isaiah 33:11 NASB)

> You will throw them in a flaming furnace when you appear. The LORD will consume them in his anger; fire will devour them. (Psalm 21:9 NLT)

> For the sins of their mouths, for the words of their lips, let them be caught in their pride. For the curses and lies they utter, consume them in your wrath, consume them till they are no more. (Psalm 59:12-13 NIV)

> The Light of Israel will become a fire, their Holy One a flame; in a single day it will burn and consume his thorns and his briers. (Isaiah 10:17 NIV)

> The fire for Your adversaries will consume them! (Isaiah 26:11 HCSB)

So I will pour out my wrath on them and consume them with my fiery anger, bringing down on their own heads all they have done, declares the Sovereign LORD." (Ezekiel 22:31 NIV)

Later, God condemned the cities of Sodom and Gomorrah and turned them into heaps of ashes. He made them an example of what will happen to ungodly people. (2 Peter 2:6 NLT)

Not so the wicked! They are like chaff that the wind blows away. (Psalm 1:4 NIV)

Your people will be burned up completely, like thornbushes cut down and tossed in a fire. (Isaiah 33:12 NLT)

He will gather His wheat into the barn, but He will burn up the chaff with unquenchable fire." (Matthew 3:12 NASB)

"His winnowing fork is in His hand to thoroughly clear His threshing floor, and to gather the wheat into His barn; but He will burn up the chaff with unquenchable fire." (Luke 3:17 NASB)

let the wicked be ashamed, and let them be silent in the grave. Let the lying lips be put to silence (Psalm 31:17-18 KJV)

Behold, the whirlwind of the LORD goeth forth with fury, a continuing whirlwind: it shall fall with pain upon the head of the wicked. (Jeremiah 30:23 KJV)

the wicked perish in darkness (1 Samuel 2:9 HCSB)

The adversaries of the LORD shall be broken to pieces (1 Samuel 2:10 KJV)

You have made my enemies retreat before me; I annihilate those who hate me. (Psalm 18:40 HCSB)

By the wrath of the LORD Almighty the land
will be scorched and the people will be fuel for
the fire; they will not spare one another.
(Isaiah 9:19 NIV)

The fear of the LORD prolongs life, but the years
of the wicked are cut short.
(Proverbs 10:27 HCSB)

that though the wicked spring up like grass and
all evildoers flourish, they will be destroyed
forever. (Psalm 92:7 NIV)

For surely your enemies, LORD, surely your
enemies will perish; all evildoers will be
scattered. (Psalm 92:9 NIV)

"For God so loved the world, that He gave His
only begotten Son, that whoever believes in Him
shall not perish, but have eternal life.
(John 3:16 NASB)

through death He might destroy him who had the
power of death, that is, the devil
(Hebrews 2:14 NKJV)

You have rebuked the nations: You have
destroyed the wicked; You have erased their
name forever and ever. The enemy has come to
eternal ruin (Psalm 9:5-6 HCSB)

The wicked will go down to the grave.
(Psalm 9:17 NLT)

He will rain down blazing coals and burning
sulfur on the wicked, punishing them with
scorching winds. (Psalm 11:6 NLT)

For the terrible one is brought to nothing, The
scornful one is consumed, And all who watch for
iniquity are cut off (Isaiah 29:20 NKJV)

but the face of the LORD is against those who do evil, to blot out their name from the earth. (Psalm 34:16 NIV)

Everyone who hates his brother is a murderer; and you know that no murderer has eternal life abiding in him. (1 John 3:15 NASB)

O LORD our God, other lords beside thee have had dominion over us: but by thee only will we make mention of thy name. They are dead, they shall not live; they are deceased, they shall not rise: therefore hast thou visited and destroyed them, and made all their memory to perish. (Isaiah 26:13-14 KJV)

He will die because there is no discipline, and be lost because of his great stupidity. (Proverbs 5:23 HCSB)

In that day the LORD with his sore and great and strong sword shall punish leviathan the piercing serpent, even leviathan that crooked serpent; and he shall slay the dragon that is in the sea. (Isaiah 27:1 KJV)

But with righteousness He shall judge the poor, And decide with equity for the meek of the earth; He shall strike the earth with the rod of His mouth, And with the breath of His lips He shall slay the wicked. (Isaiah 11:4 NKJV)

He will put the wicked men to a horrible death (Matthew 21:41 NLT)

And then shall that Wicked be revealed, whom the Lord shall consume with the spirit of his mouth, and shall destroy with the brightness of his coming (2 Thessalonians 2:8 KJV)

For yet a little while and the wicked shall be no more; Indeed, you will look carefully for his place, But it shall be no more.
(Psalm 37:10 NKJV)

But the wicked shall perish, and the enemies of the LORD shall be as the fat of lambs: they shall consume; into smoke shall they consume away.
(Psalm 37:20 KJV)

You will watch when the wicked are destroyed.
(Psalm 37:34 HCSB)

But all sinners will be destroyed; there will be no future for the wicked. (Psalm 37:38 NIV)

As smoke is blown away, so You blow them away. As wax melts before the fire, so the wicked are destroyed before God. (Psalm 68:2 HCSB)

The LORD supports the humble, but he brings the wicked down into the dust.
(Psalm 147:6 NLT)

But the wicked shall be cut off from the earth, and the transgressors shall be rooted out of it.
(Proverbs 2:22 KJV)

The strongest among you will disappear like straw; their evil deeds will be the spark that sets it on fire. They and their evil works will burn up together, and no one will be able to put out the fire. (Isaiah 1:31 NLT)

His righteousness endures forever; His horn will be exalted with honor. The wicked will see it and be grieved; He will gnash his teeth and melt away; the desire of the wicked shall perish.
(Psalm 112:9-10 NKJV)

The righteous will never be shaken, but the wicked will not remain on the earth.
(Proverbs 10:30 HCSB)

The whole city celebrates when the godly succeed; they shout for joy when the wicked die. (Proverbs 11:10 NLT)

The wicked die and disappear, but the family of the godly stands firm. (Proverbs 12:7 NLT)

For there shall be no reward to the evil man; the candle of the wicked shall be put out. (Proverbs 24:20 KJV)

When the wicked rise to power, people go into hiding; but when the wicked perish, the righteous thrive. (Proverbs 28:28 KJV)

But it will not be well with the wicked; nor will he prolong his days, which are as a shadow, because he does not fear before God. (Ecclesiastes 8:13 NKJV)

he will give them that are wicked to the sword, saith the LORD. (Jeremiah 25:31 KJV)

"Do I have any pleasure at all that the wicked should die?" says the Lord GOD (Ezekiel 18:23 NKJV)

'As surely as I live, declares the Sovereign LORD, I take no pleasure in the death of the wicked (Ezekiel 33:11 NIV)

The soul that sinneth, it shall die ... and the wickedness of the wicked shall be upon him. (Ezekiel 18:20 KJV)

The oppressor will come to an end, and destruction will cease; the aggressor will vanish from the land. (Isaiah 16:4 NIV)

The merchants among the peoples will hiss at you; You will become a horror, and be no more forever. (Ezekiel 27:36 NKJV)

All those who know you among the nations are
appalled at you. You have become an object of
horror and will never exist again."
(Ezekiel 28:19 HCSB)

The revelation of Revelation

By now, it's clear what happens to Satan. He is going to lose his spirit
status, become a mortal man and eventually be killed for all time, just
like every other unrepentant sinner. But what about that one single verse
from Revelation we mentioned at the start, the one that causes so many
to think the devil's destiny is the opposite of what the scores of other
verses declare for him? Now that you know the rest of the story, here's
the explanation.

There is no question at all that the devil will eventually be thrown into
the lake of fire. Here is the verse in Revelation once again:

And the devil, who deceived them, was thrown
into the lake of burning sulfur, where the beast
and the false prophet had been thrown. They will
be tormented day and night for ever and ever.
(Revelation 20:10 NIV)

But it's this business about being "tormented day and night for ever and
ever" that confuses people. What millions of people fail to realize is that this
time of round-the-clock torment does not take place for endless days **after**
being tossed in the fire, it takes place **before** the incineration, in the days
leading up to the death penalty being imposed. Think of all the convicted
killers who are on death row at this moment. They are tormented day and
night by their impending punishment. They are figuratively sweating bullets
about their ultimate fate that they know is inevitable. They're tormented day
and night until the edge of extinction, the moment they vanish from the land
of the living and are no longer breathing. It's when they no longer exist. The
exact same thing holds true for Satan and his followers.

But why does the Bible say "for ever and ever?" To get to the truth of
the question, we need to look at the original terms in the Greek language.
The important root words in this sentence are "eis" and "aion." Let's deal
with "eis" first, which is rendered as "for" in this Scripture. The Greek

word "eis," which is pronounced just like "ice" in English, is a preposition that can mean to, toward, unto, into, for and even against. While it's translated as "for" 140 times in the King James Version, it's rendered as "into" 573 times, "to" 281 times, "unto" 207 times, and "toward" 29 times. In the case of this verse in Revelation, the proper usage should be "to," "unto" or "toward" instead of "for."

The next root word in Greek, "aion," appears twice in the text, and is translated as "ever and ever." The word "aion" means "age," "period of time," "perpetuity of time" and "eternity." It's precisely where we get our word "eon" from in English. It has been translated in Scripture not only as "ever," but also "world," "age" and "evermore." For instance, in this famous line from Jesus, it is rendered as "age":

> Therefore, just as the weeds are gathered and burned in the fire, so it will be at the end of the age. (Matthew 13:40 HCSB)

In the Old Testament, the word that's most often translated as "forever" is "olam," and it literally means "vanishing point."

So, here are three better translations of Revelation 20:10 I'm offering that will help you understand the finite nature of the torment for the devil and his followers:

"They will be tormented day and night up to the age of ages."

"They will be tormented non-stop until the eternal age."

"They will be tormented continuously up to the vanishing point."

Thus, when we read that the devil is going to be tormented day and night for ever and ever, Scripture is saying, in its original meaning, that he is going to be tormented day and night "up to" the time when the "age of ages" (referring to the age of eternity) begins. He won't be tormented all through eternity, because he won't exist any longer, as he will turn into ash once he's consumed.

He will be tormented around the clock "up to the vanishing point," the point where he is "erased from existence," as Doc Brown famously said in "Back to the Future." The eternal "age of ages" that is coming is the kingdom of God when Jesus returns, and it's intended for God's obedient servants only. The devil will not be allowed to participate in that glorious, everlasting reign.

Satan's torment may actually have begun already, but it will certainly take place and intensify once God has taken away his spirit status, and he experiences plenty of pain and anxiety as a human being. He'll actually see some of the newly quickened children of God who will have joined God on the divine plane, a state for which he himself has lusted for so long. He'll be able to physically feel every bit of fear and anguish while writhing in the agony of his impending doom. King David sang of this moment for the devil, stating, "All my enemies will be ashamed and shake with terror." (Psalm 6:10 HCSB)

When it comes to the devil and all breakers of God's laws, it's not going to be so brief for them on the edge of forever. God is going to make them sweat it out and shake with terror between the time of their death sentence and their execution. He wants them to think long and hard about why their existence is being extinguished. He wants every evildoer to reflect on their disobedience to His simple instructions, the laws that would have led them to eternal life.

As Revelation indicates, the sinners will be tormented day and night with plenty of mental anguish until they reach the edge of eternity, the vanishing point, the point of no return. We're not told how many days and nights the shaking with terror will last. But the rebels will eventually be thrown into the lake of fire, where they will finally feel the burn. There will be epic weeping and gnashing of teeth until they are completely consumed into ashes. It is not a process that will last trillions of years without end. It will last however long it takes to burn a body of flesh into ashes. Perhaps just minutes.

In conclusion, I wish to stress that God is not a monster. When it comes to His righteous punishment, He is not going to mercilessly torture anyone, including the devil and demons, for all eternity. Scripture says many times that He is merciful, and we should reflect that mercy:

> Be merciful, just as your Father is merciful.
> (Luke 6:36 NASB)

The most merciful thing God can do to those who know the truth and absolutely refuse to live by it is to put them out of their misery once and for all. He will pay the wicked the full amount of the wages they have earned when they opposed their Creator. They have all collected the wages of sin, which is not eternal existence in a scorching fire, but eternal death caused by an unquenchable fire. This is the ultimate end of the wicked, and the mere beginning of an eternal life of glory for all who break free from captivity and escape the devil's prison of death.

Chapter Six:
I AM hidden

Now that we know for sure the final destiny for Satan, does God actually tell us specifically **when** the devil will likely be destroyed? Is there a hint or a clue that gives us an indication of what precise date on the calendar the enemy will stop singing his song of rebellion and be slain once and for all? Is there a way to determine on which the day the satanic music dies?

While there is no outright declaration from Scripture stating something like, "Satan will cease to exist on this day of a certain month," there is a suggestion of the specific moment when Satan will sound like "American Pie" songwriter Don McLean and sing, "This'll be the day that I die."

The answer is not found in Revelation, nor is it located in any of the books of the big-name prophets such as Isaiah, Jeremiah, Ezekiel or Daniel. It's not even found in the gospels covering the human life of Jesus Christ. It's found in perhaps the last place anyone would ever suspect. It's in a book that some people don't even think should be included in the Bible, since the name of God is never even mentioned in it. But this book is one of the most interesting and revealing in all of Scripture, because it cinematically (and somewhat secretly) broadcasts the entire plan of God in just ten chapters. This highly overlooked and often maligned book of the Bible that reveals so much is none other than the book of Esther. Yes, folks, Esther.

Now, I'd like to admit to you that I'm one of those people who had read the book of Esther before and never thought much about its spiritual implications. What an oversight, because this small book in the

Old Testament tells us an astonishing amount about our soon-to-come future. When read with our spiritual eyes wide open, Esther not only depicts the rescue of God's chosen people from certain annihilation some five centuries before Jesus came to Earth, it also voices the Good News about the Master Plan for the kingdom of God. And, as an added bonus, it possibly pinpoints the final destruction of Satan the devil on a calendar day that just may blow your mind.

As I provide the highlights here, I urge you to read the entire book of Esther on your own, because over the course of just a few minutes, your mind will awaken to some stunning realizations you may never have previously considered. You may even think to yourself, "Oh my goodness! I can't believe I didn't see all these major points before! They've been on the pages of my own Bible all these years, and it's finally crystal clear to me now!" I can only hope that's the case for you, because that's the way it was for me as I prepared this book. I had not originally intended to write about Esther, but God apparently had His own plan to open my eyes and share the revelation with you.

To keep our study as simple as possible, I'm going to focus on just the main cast of characters in Esther, and the spiritual implications of their actions that echo through numerous ages of human history. Because, as will become self-evident, the story of Esther covers far more than just one ancient time period.

The main players

King Ahasuerus (some Bibles print his Greek name, which is King Xerxes). On the spiritual level, he represents God the Father

Queen Vashti, the first and disobedient bride of the king. She represents the physical, 12-tribed nation of Israel who refused to follow the royal commands

Esther, the ostensible star of the story who is the obedient replacement bride for the king. She represents spiritual Israel, all faithful followers of God, irrespective of their heritage

Mordecai, a man who lives by and teaches the divine instructions. He represents Jesus Christ

Haman, an arrogant character elevated to a high position under the king but who is full of hate and deception. He is the enemy who represents Satan the devil

The vast domain

The king in the story represents God the Father, for we're told at the outset that he reigned over a massive territory covering much of the known world:

> These events took place during the days of Ahasuerus, who ruled 127 provinces from India to Cush. (Esther 1:1 HCSB)

He is shown to be hosting extraordinary feasts, yet when he invited his first wife Vashti, who spiritually represents the original Israelites, to the banquet celebration, she didn't wish to take part:

> But Queen Vashti refused to come at the king's command that was delivered by his eunuchs. The king became furious and his anger burned within him. (Esther 1:12 HCSB)

The party she was invited to represents eternal life, but Vashti (the Israelites) wanted no part of it, being disobedient to the royal commandment. God gets furious whenever anyone, especially his beautiful, beloved bride, refuses to follow His divine commands. We must always remember that the relationship between God and His people is a marriage covenant, for He says, "I am married unto you." (Jeremiah 3:14 KJV)

The Scripture in Esther reveals concern over the insolence and rebellion spreading to others:

> For the queen's action will become public knowledge to all the women and cause them to despise their husbands and say, 'King Ahasuerus ordered Queen Vashti brought before him, but she did not come.'

Before this day is over, the noble women of Persia and Media who hear about the queen's act will say the same thing to all the king's officials, resulting in more contempt and fury.

"If it meets the king's approval, he should personally issue a royal decree. Let it be recorded in the laws of Persia and Media, so that it cannot be revoked: Vashti is not to enter King Ahasuerus's presence, and her royal position is to be given to another woman who is more worthy than she.

The decree the king issues will be heard throughout his vast kingdom, so all women will honor their husbands, from the least to the greatest." (Esther 1:17-20 HCSB)

The king divorced his wife, Vashti, just as God Himself formally divorced His first bride, ancient Israel, due to the nation's rebellious nature:

... it was because unfaithful Israel had committed adultery that I had sent her away and had given her a certificate of divorce."
(Jeremiah 3:8 HCSB)

A search was then undertaken for a replacement bride, one who would be obedient to the royal instructions. To make a long story short, the woman selected is the physical star of the story, an attractive Jewish woman whose original name was Hadassah (meaning myrtle), though she kept her ethnic roots hidden by going by the popular pagan name of Esther. On the spiritual level, she denotes all those who obey God.

The name Esther is very interesting and actually has three connotations, all having something to do with the meaning of this story, as we'll see later. The first meaning is "star," coming from the Persian word "stara." The second meaning is "the woman" or "the lady," derived from Easter or Ishtar, the famous pagan goddess of the dawn, sex and fertility. Today we still can hear the Esther connection to a woman inside the word "estrogen," the female hormone. Esther also derives from the Hebrew root "str" which means "to hide" or "conceal." Thus, her name sounds like "I am a hiding place" or "I am hidden."

In the Bible book starring her name, Esther was a relative of the faithful and godly man named Mordecai:

> Mordecai was the legal guardian of his cousin Hadassah (that is, Esther), because she didn't have a father or mother. The young woman had a beautiful figure and was extremely good-looking. When her father and mother died, Mordecai had adopted her as his own daughter.
> (Esther 2:7 HCSB)

As the representative of Christ in the story, Mordecai checked daily on the progress and well-being of his daughter:

> Every day Mordecai took a walk in front of the harem's courtyard to learn how Esther was doing and to see what was happening to her.
> (Esther 2:11 HCSB)

We're then introduced to the villain of the story. His name is Haman, and he represents Satan the devil, not because I personally think so, but because the Bible actually calls him "the adversary and enemy" as well as "wicked" later in the book:

> **The adversary and enemy is this wicked Haman.** (Esther 7:6 KJV)

The conflict in the story arises when the wicked Haman was elevated to a powerful position under the king, just as Satan has been elevated to be the god of this world:

> King Ahasuerus honored Haman, son of Hammedatha the Agagite. He promoted him in rank and gave him a higher position than all the other officials. (Esther 3:1 HCSB)

A brief comment on the fact that Haman was an Agagite. This simply means he was a descendant of Agag, who was an Amalekite king and enemy of ancient Israel. Agag and the Amalekites were known for their cruelty to the weak, and they were also demon worshipers who burned their children in the Original Coal Kids Club of Molech. In the days of

Israel's first king, Saul, the prophet Samuel chopped up this evil character with a sword:

> Samuel said, "Bring me Agag king of Amalek." Agag came to him trembling, for he thought, "Certainly the bitterness of death has come." Samuel declared: As your sword has made women childless, so your mother will be childless among women. Then he hacked Agag to pieces before the LORD at Gilgal. (1 Samuel 15:32-33 HCSB)

Haman, a direct descendant of the evil king Agag, was apparently extremely arrogant and filled with pride, just as we have seen the devil is filled with such traits. In the book of Esther, the conceit of Haman (Satan) was manifested in his desire to have people bow down to him:

> The entire royal staff at the King's Gate bowed down and paid homage to Haman, because the king had commanded this to be done for him. But Mordecai would not bow down or pay homage. (Esther 3:2 HCSB)

This illuminating scene was replayed in the New Testament gospels when Satan wanted Jesus to bow down before him during Yeshua's forty-day temptation in the wilderness. And just as Mordecai refused to bow down to Haman, so Jesus refused to pay homage to the devil:

> And he said to Him, "I will give You all these things if You will fall down and worship me." Then Jesus told him, "Go away, Satan! For it is written: Worship the Lord your God, and serve only Him." (Matthew 4:9-10 HCSB)

The refusal by both Jesus and Mordecai to bow down before the devil simply infuriated Satan:

> When Haman saw that Mordecai was not bowing down or paying him homage, he was filled with rage. (Esther 3:5 HCSB)

The next verse is enormously important, because it reveals the devil's true motivation, what's really taking place inside his twisted mind:

> And when he learned of Mordecai's ethnic
> identity, Haman decided not to do away with
> Mordecai alone. He planned to destroy all
> of Mordecai's people, the Jews, throughout
> Ahasuerus's kingdom. (Esther 3:6 HCSB)

Here, ladies and gentleman, is something you may have never realized. It is the fiendish intention of the devil himself to kill not only Jesus, but all of the children of God as well! Satan knows exactly who Jesus is. He's well aware that Jesus is the Creator of the universe, and he's jealous of the fact that the Maker of all things is reproducing Himself through human beings. He knows that he himself will never be God (though he desperately wants to be), so now it's his aching desire to destroy both Jesus and all of His children who are destined for greatness in the kingdom of God. Remember, the devil was a murderer from the beginning (John 8:44 KJV).

The jealous rage burned within Haman (Satan), and that's when he took measures into his own hands to map out the slaughter of God's representatives on Earth:

> In the first month, the month of Nisan, in King
> Ahasuerus's twelfth year, Pur (that is, the lot) was
> cast before Haman for each day in each month,
> and it fell on the twelfth month, the month Adar.

> Then Haman informed King Ahasuerus, "There
> is one ethnic group, scattered throughout the
> peoples in every province of your kingdom, yet
> living in isolation. Their laws are different from
> everyone else's and they do not obey the king's
> laws. It is not in the king's best interest to tolerate
> them. (Esther 3:7-8 HCSB)

Notice here the mention of one certain group which is scattered all through the kingdom, and yet living in isolation. This refers spiritually to all the believers who have separated themselves from the desires of this current pagan world in which we all live. They are the saints, simply meaning those people being sanctified or set apart. The apostle Paul urged the followers of God to set themselves apart, and not conform to the ways of this satanic world:

> Do not conform to the pattern of this world, but
> be transformed by the renewing of your mind.
> Then you will be able to test and approve what
> God's will is – his good, pleasing and perfect
> will. (Romans 12:2 NIV)

The story of Esther continues with the king (representing God the Father) allowing the death penalty for his own subjects, as the satanic schemer pushed for their demise:

> "If the king approves, let an order be drawn up
> authorizing their destruction, and I will pay 375
> tons of silver to the accountants for deposit in the
> royal treasury."
>
> The king removed his signet ring from his finger
> and gave it to Haman son of Hammedatha the
> Agagite, the enemy of the Jewish people.
>
> Then the king told Haman, "The money and
> people are given to you to do with as you see fit."
> (Esther 3:9-11 HCSB)

Once again, we need to realize we are witnessing the entire plan of God being acted out in the real-life events in the book of Esther. What we're seeing here is that Satan wants to see all of God's children receive the death penalty. And, as we've read earlier, the entire human race was given the death penalty at the foundation of the world, the moment when they chose to follow Satan as their god instead of their Creator. The enemy Satan has been the wealthy prince of this world since human beings rejected their Maker. Therefore, God told the devil, "The money and people are given to you to do with as you see fit." But although humans have been under the death penalty for thousands of years, there is still a day set in the future when their permanent execution, "the second death" as the Bible calls it in Revelation 20:6, takes place.

Next, Haman and Satan went public with their evil-minded plan on the day before Passover:

The royal scribes were summoned on the thirteenth day of the first month, and the order was written exactly as Haman commanded. It was intended for the royal satraps, the governors of each of the provinces, and the officials of each ethnic group and written for each province in its own script and to each ethnic group in its own language. It was written in the name of King Ahasuerus and sealed with the royal signet ring.

Letters were sent by couriers to each of the royal provinces telling the officials to destroy, kill, and annihilate all the Jewish people—young and old, women and children—and plunder their possessions on a single day, the thirteenth day of Adar, the twelfth month. (Esther 3:12-13 HCSB)

On the **thirteenth day** of the first month, just a day before the people of God held their annual Passover celebration of their freedom from the captivity of this worldwide prison, Satan began broadcasting the exact day that he intended for them to be destroyed. **The thirteenth day of the final month of the year**. Write that down somewhere. Because it may well be one of the most important dates ever, as we shall see.

Notice also that the Bible uses the word "annihilate" when it comes to destruction because, as we have seen from countless other verses, this is what happens to anyone who is thrown into the lake of fire. The second death is complete annihilation from existence. Death means death, not eternal life in a fire. Additionally, the Hebrew word for "annihilate" is "abad," and that word is most evident in the New Testament name of the angel who destroys:

Their king is the angel from the bottomless pit; his name in Hebrew is *Abaddon*, and in Greek, *Apollyon*—the Destroyer. (Revelation 9:11 NLT)

So, the one who sought to annihilate God's people, Abaddon the Destroyer, also known as Satan, will himself be annihilated.

fear of death

As we might expect, once word got out that everyone was suddenly under the death penalty, the joy of life evaporated and the fear of death set in:

> There was great mourning among the Jewish people in every province where the king's command and edict came. They fasted, wept, and lamented, and many lay on sackcloth and ashes. Esther's female servants and her eunuchs came and reported the news to her, and the queen was overcome with fear. (Esther 4:3-4 HCSB)

This corresponds with the fear of death that everyone experiences throughout their physical life, all courtesy of Satan the devil. We're all prisoners of death and the fear of death. The fact that the death penalty was announced in the first month of the year, but wouldn't be carried out until the final month of the year, emphasizes two important facts. One is that we as individuals are aware of our own mortality for virtually our entire lives, from childhood to the moment we conk out. We're all aware that we as flesh-and-blood human beings will expire at some point. Secondly, humanity as a whole has been aware of its collective death penalty from the very beginning, from the days of Adam and Eve. There is a permanent death penalty, the second death, coming in the future.

In an effort to save his people, Mordecai had a servant named Hathach (who represents a prophet of God) explain the details of the royal death decree to Esther so that she would jump into action:

> Mordecai also gave him a copy of the written decree issued in Susa ordering their destruction, so that Hathach might show it to Esther, explain it to her, and command her to approach the king, implore his favor, and plead with him personally for her people. (Esther 4:8 HCSB)

This reflects Jesus' numerous attempts over many centuries to warn His beloved people through prophets, apostles and godly teachers, to get people to wake up and take personal action – action that would save not just one's own personal life, but the lives of others as well. We have been instructed to make contact with the ultimate King, God the Father, to implore His favor on behalf of all people, to help them escape the death penalty and come to eternal life.

Esther was extremely hesitant to approach the king, just as many people today are hesitant about approaching and standing before God. But Mordecai (Jesus) sternly warned her of the fatal consequences if she did not take action:

> Mordecai told the messenger to reply to Esther, "Don't think that you will escape the fate of all the Jews because you are in the king's palace. If you keep silent at this time, liberation and deliverance will come to the Jewish people from another place, but you and your father's house will be destroyed. Who knows, perhaps you have come to your royal position for such a time as this." (Esther 4:13-14 HCSB)

The message here is quite plain. Believers won't escape the eternal death penalty just because we happen to be in the King's house, calling ourselves Christians and professing our love and allegiance to God. We all need to get it through our thick skulls that we need to overcome our fears, no matter how strong they are, and follow the instructions of God. We have to do whatever He says, getting off our bottoms and taking action, or else we will be destroyed and dead forever!

Esther was able to overcome her fear of death, and took decisive action, telling Mordecai:

> "Go and assemble all the Jews who can be found in Susa and fast for me. Don't eat or drink for three days, day or night. I and my female servants will also fast in the same way. After that, I will go to the king even if it is against the law. If I perish, I perish." (Esther 4:16 HCSB)

Esther eventually approached the king, and did not receive the death penalty:

> On the third day, Esther dressed up in her royal clothing and stood in the inner courtyard of the palace facing it. The king was sitting on his royal throne in the royal courtroom, facing its entrance.

> As soon as the king saw Queen Esther standing
> in the courtyard, she won his approval.
> (Esther 5:1-2 HCSB)

Esther's fasting represents our time here on Earth, abstaining from the lusts and pleasures of this world, denying ourselves so that we can get in harmony with God's plan, to do His will, instead of our own. She then put on her "royal clothing" to make herself presentable to the king. We as believers need to clothe ourselves properly with righteousness, and the New Testament actually describes an outfit that will help lead to eternal life. Because we are going up against dark, powerful forces in the unseen realm, Paul urges that we adorn ourselves with the armor of God:

> Put on all of God's armor so that you will be able to stand firm against all strategies of the devil. For we are not fighting against flesh-and-blood enemies, but against evil rulers and authorities of the unseen world, against mighty powers in this dark world, and against evil spirits in the heavenly places.
>
> Therefore, put on every piece of God's armor so you will be able to resist the enemy in the time of evil. Then after the battle you will still be standing firm. Stand your ground, putting on the belt of truth and the body armor of God's righteousness.
>
> For shoes, put on the peace that comes from the Good News so that you will be fully prepared. In addition to all of these, hold up the shield of faith to stop the fiery arrows of the devil.
>
> Put on salvation as your helmet, and take the sword of the Spirit, which is the word of God. Pray in the Spirit at all times and on every occasion. Stay alert and be persistent in your prayers for all believers everywhere.
> (Ephesians 6:11-19 NLT)

The story continues with the king's acceptance of Esther through an act of grace, and a conversation between the king and Esther, symbolizing a talk between God the Father and His bride:

> The king extended the gold scepter in his hand toward Esther, and she approached and touched the tip of the scepter.
>
> "What is it, Queen Esther?" the king asked her. "Whatever you want, even to half the kingdom, will be given to you." (Esther 5:2-3 HCSB)

Through His merciful grace, God the Father is letting His true believers know that once we properly prepare ourselves, we can approach His divine throne fearlessly, and ask whatever we want. This theme is repeated numerous times in the New Testament, including:

> You did not choose Me, but I chose you. I appointed you that you should go out and produce fruit and that your fruit should remain, so that whatever you ask the Father in My name, He will give you. (John 15:16 HCSB)

> And whatever we ask we receive from Him, because we keep His commandments and do those things that are pleasing in His sight. (1 John 3:22 NKJV)

The request from Esther was that the king and Haman enjoy a banquet together, but Haman (the devil) was far from content:

> "Still, none of this satisfies me since I see Mordecai the Jew sitting at the King's Gate all the time." (Esther 5:13 HCSB)

As long as Jesus is alive and in proximity to God the Father, the devil is not satisfied. Thus, Haman had gallows constructed, hoping to kill Mordecai upon them. But a tremendous twist of fate took place during a second banquet for the king and Mordecai. The king asked Esther what she truly wanted, and she gave this stunning response that spilled the beans on the wicked scheme:

> "For my people and I have been sold out to destruction, death, and extermination. If we had merely been sold as male and female slaves, I would have kept silent. Indeed, the trouble wouldn't be worth burdening the king."
>
> King Ahasuerus spoke up and asked Queen Esther, "Who is this, and where is the one who would devise such a scheme?"
>
> Esther answered, "The adversary and enemy is this evil Haman."
>
> Haman stood terrified before the king and queen. (Esther 7:4-6 HCSB)

Now it was known. The wretched plot of exterminating God's people was out in the open, and the enemy, which is the exact meaning of the name Satan, was identified. Not only that, he stood terrified before the king and queen, because in the future, Satan will be terrified again, tormented with anguish day and night up until the moment when he's thrown into the lake of fire.

The final moments of Haman's story in the book of Esther reveal him begging for his life:

> Haman remained to beg Queen Esther for his life because he realized the king was planning something terrible for him.
>
> Just as the king returned from the palace garden to the house of wine drinking, Haman was falling on the couch where Esther was reclining. The king exclaimed, "Would he actually violate the queen while I am in the palace?" As soon as the statement left the king's mouth, Haman's face was covered.
>
> Harbona, one of the royal eunuchs, said: "There is a gallows 75 feet tall at Haman's house that he made for Mordecai, who gave the report that saved the king."

The king commanded, "Hang him on it."

They hanged Haman on the gallows he had prepared for Mordecai. Then the king's anger subsided. (Esther 7:7-10 HCSB)

Thus, the wrath of God vanishes once the evil enemy gets extinguished from existence. The book continues, though, with more fun facts as the estate of Haman (which represents all the kingdoms of this world) was turned over to Esther, the faithful people of God. And she, in turn, put Mordecai (Jesus) in charge of it:

Mordecai the Jew was second only to King Ahasuerus, famous among the Jews, and highly popular with many of his relatives. He continued to seek good for his people and to speak for the welfare of all his descendants.
(Esther 10:3 HCSB)

Again, we obviously see Jesus here, as He is second only to God the Father, and He's very popular among His own relatives, the children of God, always seeking good for them.

Now what many regard as the highlight of the Esther story, the revenge of God's people on all their enemies, may provide a clue to the precise day in the future when Public Enemy Number One will face his own destruction.

Remember the date I told you to write down before. It's the thirteenth day of the twelfth month of the Hebrew calendar. The remaining chapters of Esther make a very big deal about this date. The king signed an order where the thirteenth would be the day that **all enemies of God's people** would be completely annihilated:

The king's edict gave the Jews in each and every city the right to assemble and defend themselves, to destroy, kill, and annihilate every ethnic and provincial army hostile to them, including women and children, and to take their possessions as spoils of war.

This would take place on a <u>single day</u> throughout all the provinces of King Ahasuerus, on <u>the thirteenth day</u> of the twelfth month, the month Adar.

A copy of the text, issued as law throughout every province, was distributed to all the peoples so the Jews could be ready to <u>avenge themselves against their enemies on that day</u>.
(Esther 8:11-13 HCSB)

This thirteenth day of the month of Adar is mentioned several times as the day all opposition to God will be terminated:

The king's command and law went into effect on <u>the thirteenth day</u> of the twelfth month, the month Adar. On the day when the Jews' enemies had hoped to overpower them, just the opposite happened. The Jews overpowered those who hated them.

In each of King Ahasuerus's provinces the Jews assembled in their cities to attack those who intended to harm them. Not a single person could withstand them; <u>terror of them fell on every nationality</u>.

All the officials of the provinces, the satraps, the governors, and the royal civil administrators aided the Jews because they were afraid of Mordecai.

For Mordecai exercised great power in the palace, and his fame spread throughout the provinces as he became more and more powerful.

<u>The Jews put all their enemies to the sword, killing and destroying them</u>. They did what they pleased to those who hated them.
(Esther 9:1-5 HCSB)

Got a hot date

There are famous events in history to which the Bible never attaches a date. For instance, we're never provided a clear, undisputable date for the birth of Jesus as a human being. But the Bible goes out of its way to make sure we understand the importance of other dates. We know for sure that Passover is always on the fourteenth day of the first month of the Hebrew calendar:

> The LORD's Passover begins at twilight on the fourteenth day of the first month.
> (Leviticus 23:5 NIV)

And in the book of Esther, the Bible appears to go out of its way to tell us the precise date in the future when all the enemies of God's people will be terminated: the thirteenth day of the final month.

It is not just some random day. It was specifically chosen by Jesus Himself. We read earlier that Haman cast lots to select the day of destruction. That means he held a lottery, choosing the day ostensibly at random. But Scripture tells us that all lotteries are determined by Jesus:

> The lot is cast into the lap,
> But its every decision is from the LORD.
> (Proverbs 16:33 NASB)

So this is what I am suggesting, because I cannot say it with absolute certainty. Scripture appears to hint strongly that the enemies of God, including the devil himself, will be tossed into the lake of fire on the thirteenth day of the final month of the Hebrew year for annihilation. If it's not the day of the devil's demise, it could be the day that all human beings who reject God are destroyed in the lake of fire. Perhaps this is the real origin of why so many people think the number thirteen is unlucky and that tragedy will strike on the thirteenth. From the thirteenth day of the first month in the days of Esther until the thirteenth day of the final month, Satan made God's people quiver with fear about the number thirteen for almost an entire year, and everyone else from all other regions knew the horror scheduled to take place on that date. Thus, the number thirteen became solidified in everyone's minds as a day of catastrophe because something really bad was going to take place then. And something dreadful did, in fact, take place at that time, when more than 75,000 people who were not Jews were slaughtered by the Jews.

For people today who regard thirteen as a lucky number, this could be the result of the tables having been turned, with God's people winning escape from the planned extermination on the thirteenth, and gaining victory over their enemies.

Interestingly, the Bible may also indicate the thirteenth of Adar in that year was a Friday. Could this be the true origin of the fear of Friday the 13th? I'm not kidding. The date that the people of God fought back and killed the forces of evil, the date that was originally intended for their destruction, was the thirteenth. And what took place the very next day on the fourteenth? Let's let the Bible speak for itself so you can see it with your own eyes:

> They fought on the thirteenth day of the month of
> Adar and <u>rested on the fourteenth,</u> and it became
> a day of feasting and rejoicing.
> (Esther 9:17 HCSB)

Thus, it is possible that the day following the intended slaughter of God's people was the Biblical day of rest, the day of feasting and rejoicing, the seventh day of the week, the Sabbath day. Saturday.

> "Work may be done for six days, but on the
> seventh day there must be a Sabbath of complete
> rest, a sacred assembly. (Leviticus 23:3 HCSB)

If this day of rest in Esther on the fourteenth were indeed a Saturday (and I am not saying with certainty that it was), that means the day Satan had intended for the killing of God's people but ended with the killing of God's enemies was a Friday. Friday the 13th!

You may be able to finally put aside all the confusion about the fear of Friday the 13th, because here we have solid evidence from the Bible that Satan planned to annihilate God's people from the face of the Earth on the thirteenth day of the month, with the next day possibly being a Sabbath, a day filled with rest, feasting and rejoicing on Saturday.

And wouldn't it be an amazing irony if Satan's own day of destruction in the future turns out to be a Friday as well? The notorious and much feared Friday the 13th would become "FRY-day the 13th," the day Satan will be broiled to death in the consuming fire of the glorious God.

Another possible clue can be seen when we examine God's spiritual plan involving the week itself. Many students of the Bible view the seven-day week as a microcosm for the time span of God's entire work. For instance, the first day of the week, Sunday, is when time as we know it began when God created light. It marks the beginning. The remainder of the week corresponds to all of human history, leading up to the seventh day of the week – the time of Sabbath rest representing the end of Satan's rule and the commencement of the paradise of the kingdom of God reigning on Earth. If Satan is allowed to exist up until the start of the eternal age, the Sabbath rest of God as we have discussed from Revelation 20:10, then this time frame suggests the devil's death will take place just prior to the Sabbath, and that would be on the sixth day of the week, Friday.

On his own head

It's worthy of noting that the annihilation Haman had plotted for God's people was to return on his own head, and will return on Satan's head in the future:

> For Haman ... the enemy of all the Jews, had plotted against the Jews to destroy them and had cast the pur (that is, the lot) for their ruin and destruction.
>
> But when the plot came to the king's attention, he issued written orders that the evil scheme Haman had devised against the Jews should come back onto his own head, and that he and his sons should be impaled on poles. (Esther 9:24-25 NIV)

Yes, the evil one's plot is going to come back on his own head, with his sons slain as well, a possible spiritual reference to the future death of all those following the devil. This theme of the wicked having evil coming back onto their own heads is repeated numerous times in Scripture, including:

> His trouble shall return upon his own head
> (Psalm 7:16 NKJV)

> All your evil deeds will fall back on your own heads. (Obadiah 1:15 NLT)

> I will return on your own heads what you have done. (Joel 3:7 NIV)

> ... judge Your servants, condemning the wicked by bringing his way on his own head ...
> (1 Kings 8:32 NASB)

The death of Satan is the final fulfillment of the original Genesis prophecy about the devil having his head crushed by Jesus, as the end has already been declared from the beginning:

> So the LORD God said to the serpent ... "I will put enmity between you and the woman, and between your offspring and hers; he will crush your head ..." (Genesis 3:14-15 NIV)

One more note on Satan's demise. The twelfth month of the Hebrew year is called Adar. When we understand the meaning of this word, we can see that even more dots get connected in this story and the picture becomes very clear.

The word Adar in Hebrew means "of glory" or "glorious," but it's derived from other ancient languages in which Adar means "fire." To this day, in the Zoroastrian religion, the Adar is the sacred fire. Interestingly, the word Zoroastrian literally means "seed of the woman" (zoro is seed, aster is woman), again echoing God's remark to Satan that he would create hostility between the devil and the Seed of the woman:

> And I will put enmity
> Between you and the woman,
> And between your seed and her Seed;
> He shall bruise your head,
> And you shall bruise His heel." (Genesis 3:15 NKJV)

Thus, it all makes perfect sense now. God, the one who declares the end from the beginning – in other words, the one who tells everyone right at the start how things are going to end up – has told us from the commencement of humanity's time on Earth about the ultimate blazing end of Satan and all enemies of God.

Jesus, who is the true Seed of the woman, will finally crush the head of the serpent, the fallen angel also known as Abaddon the Destroyer. He will bring the devil's own wicked scheme of annihilation of God's children upon his own head. This may take place on the thirteenth day of the twelfth month of the year, the month of the glorious fire, and it could possibly be on Friday the 13th. Satan and his evil minions will finally be thrown into God's fiery furnace, and be completely consumed into ashes in a magnificent, divinely ordained blaze of glory. This event will usher in the age of the ages, the everlasting kingdom of God, when Jesus takes over the estate of the devil and evil is vanquished forever!

I AM hidden in plain sight

Now that the story is wrapped up, there's one more fascinating and inspiring aspect that just may blow your mind. It may not have been evident at the outset of this chapter, but with everything we've learned here, it will become glaringly obvious as soon as I mention it. And that is that the entire theme of the Bible – focusing on God the Father and His Son Jesus, their marriage relationships to human beings, and the eventual destruction of the devil – has been secretly hiding in the book of the Bible whose name means the **star**, the **woman** and **I am hidden**! The hidden stars of the story of this woman named Esther are really God the Father and Jesus Christ!

Remember, folks, "Esther" not only means "star," it means "woman" and "I am hidden." So when we read the prophecy in Genesis about the Seed of the woman (Jesus) crushing the serpent (Satan), we need to realize that God orchestrated actual events thousands of years later to have history play out around this lady named Esther, meaning "the star," "woman," and "hiding place" to match His spiritual plan.

> • The story of God the Father and Jesus (the real, spiritual stars of the story) has been told through the physical, human star of this story, Esther, whose name means "star."

> • The story of Jesus, the Seed of the woman, has been planted inside Esther, whose name also means "the woman."

• The story of God the Father and Jesus has been hiding all along in the Scriptures of Esther, whose name also means "I am hidden."

• Though the name of the LORD – YHWH in Hebrew, which means I AM in English – is never mentioned in Esther, the Almighty God named I AM is hidden in both the name and events of Esther, which means "I am hidden." God is telling us that He is hiding in Esther. **I AM hidden!**

The truth about God's Master Plan and the kingdom of God has been hiding inside the book of Esther for thousands of years, and now it is finally coming to light right this second in your hands as you read the words on the pages of this book! Can you feel the light of God's Spirit entering your mind, opening up your spiritual eyes to this glorious truth?

Now consider this: God was not only hidden in "the woman" who was his bride in the Old Testament story of Esther. He's still hiding right at this moment in "the woman" who is the bride of Christ. The entire New Testament focuses upon God's personal presence, His Spirit, dwelling inside His new bride, His obedient followers:

> And this is the secret: Christ lives in you. (Colossians 1:12 NLT)

> Or do you not know that your body is a temple of the Holy Spirit within you, whom you have from God? (1 Corinthians 6:19 ESV)

The final book of the Bible confirms that all people truly faithful to God actually marry their Creator, who is the Lamb of God:

> Let us be glad and rejoice, and give honour to him: for the marriage of the Lamb is come, and his wife hath made herself ready. (Revelation 19:7 KJV)

The Spirit of Jesus Christ, who is called in Genesis the Seed of the woman, is living now as the Seed (the personal presence of God) inside the woman who belongs to Him, His bride. In other words, Jesus Himself is dwelling inside all true believers. While we don't see Him with our physical eyes, we know He's present by the fruit of the Spirit and gifts of the Spirit:

> But the fruit of the Spirit is love, joy, peace,
> patience, kindness, goodness, faith, gentleness,
> self-control. (Galatians 5:22-23 HCSB)

There is a variety of gifts of the Spirit mentioned in Scripture, including wisdom, knowledge, faith, healing, miracle-working, prophecy and speaking in other languages, all recorded in 1 Corinthians, chapter 12. And once we are quickened into our divine bodies, the divine Seed of Christ will become a permanent fixture within us:

> Whoever has been born of God does not sin, for
> His seed remains in him; and he cannot sin ...
> (1 John 3:9 NKJV)

The spiritual story of God sending away His first, disobedient bride (rebellious Israel) and marrying an obedient bride (all faithful followers of Christ in whom He lives), while confronting and defeating the devil and his dark forces once and for all at the end of the year, the end of humanity's reign before the arrival of the everlasting age, was secretly embedded in the book of Esther all along, and now it has finally come to light! It has been made spectacularly clear in these latter days in which we're living! We all can and should understand it perfectly just as prophecy tells us:

> In the latter days you will understand it perfectly.
> (Jeremiah 23:20 NKJV)

Are we going to believe our Bibles or not? We are living now in the last days before the return of Jesus to Earth. You've just been provided an extremely clear explanation using many Bible Scriptures to explain the past, present and future. It should enable all of us looking for truth to understand God's plan perfectly. He **wants** us to understand it perfectly. He has **promised** that we'll understand it perfectly. So let's now take Him up on that promise. Let's forget the unprofitable nonsense with which we've been brainwashed all these years and remove ourselves from the lies of Opposite World so we can live with a complete understanding of the Word of God. Let's receive God's gift of freedom from our prison, freedom from our fear of death. Let's finally overcome the wicked ways that lead to permanent annihilation and come to the blissful and euphoric path of eternal life, worshiping God in spirit and in truth!

Chapter Seven:
The resurrection no one talks about

"It is amazing." The voice on the radio was completely shocked. During the middle of the interview, the broadcaster admitted he was thoroughly astonished.

"It's amazing that nobody talks about this," he continued.

The radio host could not get over the fact that there was something clearly indicated in the Bible, and yet most congregations that call themselves Christian never utter a word about it.

"This is quite fascinating," he said. "In all my years in church, I have never heard the minister talking about it, and it's so important and it's so inspiring really to hear about it."

The voice on the radio who was so astounded was that of Ken Hancock, host of a Christian broadcast in Scotland called "Stained Glass Radio," and his guest on the air in the spring of 2012 was yours truly.

Hancock is not the only person who has never heard his minister discuss one of the most monumental and resplendent events in all of Holy Scripture. Millions of Christians across America and the world have never even heard of it, nor will they. Because, unfortunately, the pastors of most churches either don't know what's in their own Bibles, or they do know the content, and they're suppressing the magnificent truth. I say magnificent because it really does lift an enormous weight and it puts your mind at ease when you understand that people who don't follow God in this lifetime will have another chance in the future to learn and follow the truth so that they, too, might receive the glorious gift of eternal life. In other words, if they don't repent now, there's still one more shot later, thank God.

The time has finally come for you to understand what the ministers never bring up in church. It's time to find out what's so amazing, fascinating, and inspiring, as Hancock put it. Knowledge of this concept is one of the keys that will open up the minds of many who are seriously looking to worship God in spirit and in truth. It is the resurrection that no one talks about: the Second Resurrection.

In the dark

I used to be unsure as to why so many people in the Christian world are completely in the dark when it comes to the Second Resurrection, along with many other truths in the Bible. And then it hit me. They're in the dark simply because ... they are "in the dark." What I mean is, they're walking in the way of darkness, not letting the complete light of truth illuminate their path. They've been taught only portions of the light of truth in the Bible, and often very small portions at that. Thus, without the brightness of clarity, they walk in some dark locations that cause them to stumble.

One of these dark strongholds for self-professed believers concerns what really happens after our physical lives expire. Millions think that faithful people are instantly alive in the paradise of heaven looking down upon everyone on Earth, while those who never came to the truth are in an eternal frying pan, howling in unspeakable pain as the dial on the stove burner has been turned up to maximum heat. The Bible teaches no such thing. That belief is the mistaken perception of Opposite World. Its origin is the satanic suggestion of the serpent, the one who planted that long-lasting lie in the minds of our first human parents when he said, "You surely will not die!" (Genesis 3:4 NASB) People of all faiths still believe the demonic deception that they have an immortal soul that keeps on living when their heart stops beating. Try finding the phrase "immortal soul" in your Bible. You won't be able to because it's simply not there in any Scripture.

The first edition of this book has an in-depth proof of what really happens at death, so please read that if you haven't done so already. I don't wish to overwhelm you by repeating it all here, except to note that just as the Bible says, on the day of our death, we all go back to the ground from whence we came and we have no thoughts or knowledge of any kind:

for dust you are and to dust you will return."
(Genesis 3:19 NIV)

His breath goeth forth, he returneth to his earth;
in that very day his **thoughts perish**.
(Psalm 146:4 KJV)

for there is no work or device or knowledge
or wisdom in the grave where you are going.
(Ecclesiastes 9:10 NKJV)

The point of this chapter is not to focus on death, but, rather, to highlight the fact that we all **come back** from the dead. The concept is known as resurrection, and it's actually a main theme of the Bible that there are **two** major resurrections ahead in our future. Yes, I know it's a surprise to most people, but there are indeed two separate and distinct resurrections.

We all realize that our bodies are mortal and we eventually die, but the good news is that we all shall live again at some point in the future. But that return to life does not happen the moment our physical lives expire. It happens at two different times, for two different groups of people, and for two different reasons, all for a wondrous purpose that will have you dancing and shouting for joy.

Jesus said there are two

It's not always an easy task to explain the truth to someone, especially when he or she has been completely tricked into believing a lie; and that's the case when it comes to the idea that there is more than one resurrection coming. But we're going to examine many different Scriptures now that all attest to this surprising fact. Let's start with a red-letter quote from Jesus:

Do not be amazed at this, because a time is coming when all who are in the graves will hear His voice and come out—those who have done good things, to the resurrection of life, but those who have done wicked things, to the resurrection of judgment. (John 5:28-29 HCSB)

This one statement tells us several points of truth that need to be stressed. First, people who are dead are still **in their graves** at the moment when they hear God's voice waking them up. They're neither alive nor aware of a single thing. They are neither floating on a cloud in heaven nor sporting a giant grin as they look down on everyone. And they are not boiling in a fiery cauldron somewhere. They are completely unaware, asleep in darkness and oblivious to everything. Even Jesus Himself was completely unaware when He was dead for three days and three nights. Like everyone else in the grave, His thoughts perished until He was raised back to life by God the Father.

Jesus also mentioned that the collective wake-up happens **in the future**, and not at the time of someone's death. He said specifically that "a time is coming" when resurrection would take place. It has not happened yet for any human being since Jesus rose. "No one has ever gone into heaven," as Jesus told Nicodemus the Pharisee (John 3:13 NIV). So if you're a pastor who preaches funerals and you tell people who are in mourning that their deceased loved ones are in a much better place right now, alive and smiling in heaven at the moment they passed away, please stop this satanic deception immediately. Because you yourself will be held accountable for perpetuating this lie of the devil.

Now onto the meat of what Jesus said about people being raised in the future:

> all who are in the graves will hear His voice and come out—those who have done good things, to the resurrection of life, but those who have done wicked things, to the resurrection of judgment.
> (John 5:28-29 HCSB)

Notice, there are **two separate resurrections** mentioned here. The first is specifically called the **"resurrection of life,"** and it's for "those who have done good things." The second is called **"the resurrection of judgment,"** and that one is for "those who have done wicked things."

Here's another Bible version of the same two verses, so you can grasp the concept a little better:

> Don't be so surprised! Indeed, the time is coming when all the dead in their graves will hear the voice of God's Son, they will rise again. Those who have done good will rise to <u>experience eternal life</u>, and those who have continued in evil will rise to <u>experience judgment</u>.
>
> (John 5:28-29 NLT)

It could not be clearer. All dead people are still in their graves at present. But in the future, they will be awakened by the voice of Jesus, and they will rise again. The folks who have obeyed God's instructions are in the first resurrection, the "resurrection of life," and will experience eternal life. This is the reward for which we all should be striving, to be quickened into our new bodies made of spirit, to be alive forever as divine children of God.

But there is also a second resurrection, and it will revive the people who did not follow the divine instructions for whatever reason. Maybe they never heard of the true God or His laws. Maybe they were aware of God, but deliberately chose not to fully follow the path that leads to life. Or perhaps they presumed they were worshiping God correctly, but had been cleverly deceived by the powers that be, and were worshiping in error. The reason is irrelevant. They still "continued in evil."

And what will happen to these people who are raised in the Second Resurrection? As the Scripture says, they will "experience judgment." That makes sense, because, after all, it's called "the resurrection of judgment." They are going to be **judged**. They are going to be **tested**. They are going to be **evaluated**. They are going to be **examined**. They are going to be **coached**. This is what God says He does with everyone. He gets inside their inward parts to examine what kind of thoughts are really bouncing around in their head:

> But I, the LORD, search all hearts and <u>examine secret motives</u>. I give all people their due rewards, according to what their actions deserve."
>
> (Jeremiah 17:10 NLT)

And why will God be examining people who have not followed his instructions? Because, as we shall see, God is merciful and doesn't wish anyone to be dead forever. He is going to give folks a final chance at getting it right. Without the deception. And without the devil, who will have been annihilated in the lake of fire by then. God is not going to raise up rebellious people from the dead just to make them dead again in an instant. They were already dead. He could easily just leave them dead. He is going to raise them up for potential glory. He will forgive their previous sins and provide them a clear shot at learning the ways that lead to life everlasting, the same reward given to those who were raised in the First Resurrection.

The order of resurrections

The First Resurrection is mentioned countless times in the Bible, and it takes place not at the instant a person dies, but rather when Jesus Christ returns to Earth. This is explained well in what many Christians call the Resurrection Chapter of the Bible, which is the fifteenth chapter of Paul's First Letter to the Corinthians. Here's what Paul stated:

> Just as everyone dies because we all belong to Adam, everyone who belongs to Christ will be given new life. But there is an order to this resurrection: Christ was raised as the first of the harvest; then all who belong to Christ will be raised when he comes back.
> (1 Corinthians 15:22-23 NLT)

Many Bibles translate the last part of that verse to say that those who belong to Christ will be raised "at His coming." So, if we're going to believe our Bibles instead of the nonsense being broadcast in church or at funerals, the Word of God clearly says that the true believers, the saved, the elect, the called-out ones, the brethren – however you wish to label the faithful followers of Jesus – will all be raised in the First Resurrection at His coming, when He comes back to Earth at the end of this evil age.

And despite the widespread belief that virtually everyone is going to take part in this much-sought-after First Resurrection, the truth from Jesus is that comparatively few will succeed in the first round:

> "Enter through the narrow gate; for the gate is
> wide and the way is broad that leads to destruction,
> and there are many who enter through it. For the
> gate is small and the way is narrow that leads to
> life, and there are few who find it."
> (Matthew 7:13-14 NASB)

But if only a small fraction of all humanity who has existed since Adam and Eve are given eternal life in the First Resurrection, where does that leave everyone else? What about all those billions of people who never heard God's truth? What about your friends and relatives who didn't believe? What about the people who were confused about God? Or were lied to? Are they destined for eternal destruction because they were tricked by the devil and proceeded through the wide gate, the very popular path of this world?

The rest of the dead

One of the most ignored and suppressed phrases in the Bible provides the answer to the above questions, and the answer from Scripture shows they are not forever done for. The phrase that is virtually never uttered in most Christian churches is paramount to understanding this business about the Second Resurrection. That phrase is "the rest of the dead." It's found in Revelation 20:5, and it specifically pinpoints what will happen to every single person who did not get raised to eternal life in the First Resurrection. The individuals who did not get revived in Round One are called "the rest of the dead." The Bible talks about the rest of the dead people in a section that also mentions the faithful folks who had been raised to life previously in the First Resurrection at the return of Jesus. Here it is, as the apostle John was shown a vision of what's to come:

> Then I saw thrones, and the people sitting on
> them had been given the authority to judge. ...
> They came to life again, and they reigned with
> Christ for a thousand years. This is the first
> resurrection. (The rest of the dead did not come
> back to life until the thousand years had ended.)
> Blessed and holy are those who share in the first

> resurrection. For them the second death holds
> no power, but they will be priests of God and of
> Christ and will reign with him a thousand years.
> (Revelation 20:4-6 NLT)

Let's go through this slowly now so you can finally understand what many preachers do not want you to know, despite the fact it's part of the climax of the Good News. Understanding what "the rest of the dead" means will explode the enormous pile of hooey the religions of this world have been shoveling for centuries.

John is witnessing what is called the First Resurrection. There's no mystery there because he uses that exact term. He sees people who have come to life again in "the resurrection of life" which Jesus mentioned earlier. He says these newly quickened people were sitting on thrones, and they were given the authority to judge, reigning with Christ for a thousand years. We'll discuss much more about that divine authority to judge later in this chapter, but for now, I wish to focus just on who is being raised, and when they're coming back to life.

So far, it's quite evident that the people raised in the First Resurrection are those who have been obedient to God, for they're said to be blessed and holy, meaning they are sanctified and set apart for God. The Scripture also indicates that for these believers, "the second death holds no power," meaning they have now made the jump from mortal to immortal.

The second death is the eternal death from which there is no more resurrection, as we discussed in "The end of the wicked" chapter. So with the second death holding no power over them, these believers will have reached the spirit level. They will have become part of God's divine family, and they simply cannot die.

But now comes that all-important phrase that most ministers of the Christian faith hope you never discover: the rest of the dead. Let's read it from another Bible version just so you can see it's the same:

> But the rest of the dead did not live again until
> the thousand years were finished.
> (Revelation 20:5 NKJV)

We have already established that it's the people faithful to God who are raised to eternal life in the First Resurrection. But Scripture plainly says that the rest of the dead, the remainder of all of the people who ever existed, do not come back to life **until the thousand years were finished**! This is the time of the Second Resurrection! A thousand years after the First Resurrection!

This is not difficult to understand, friends. We're merely reading the words on the page, and we're believing them. I know that for some students of Scripture, it's difficult to extract yourself from the lies that have been presented as truth to you all these years. But if we all just believed what the Bible says in its own words, then all your misconceptions would vanish instantly.

The apostle John has informed us that the rest of the dead – whether it's Benedict Arnold, Billy the Kid or Elvis Presley – will be brought back to life in the Second Resurrection, if they did not get raised to life a thousand years earlier in the First Resurrection. It's easy to understand if you can just count to two.

When Jesus returns to Earth, that is Resurrection Number One. That's when the people who have followed the call to glory will come back to life, transformed as divine children of God. And then, a thousand years after that moment, the rest of the dead – all those people who did not answer God's call in the first round – will be brought back to existence in Resurrection Number Two.

First is spirit life

But there is a difference in the resurrections beyond the time disparity of a thousand years. Those people raised in the Second Resurrection will not be immortal like those raised in the First Resurrection. They will not be made of spirit like those who passed Round One. They are going to be raised into their flesh-and-blood, physical bodies, all for a wonderful purpose. We're now going to connect the dots from a number of Scriptures so you can understand what will take place, so you can grasp what is certain to happen in the future.

The believers who are raised in the First Resurrection will no longer have a body that is made up of flesh and blood. How do we know? Because the Resurrection Chapter of the Bible tells us this important fact:

> Now this I say, brethren, that **flesh and
> blood cannot inherit the kingdom of God**
> (1 Corinthians 15:50 KJV)

Paul tells us that it's simply impossible for people to inherit immortal, imperishable life if we're still in bodies that consist of flesh and blood, not to mention all those bones, tendons, nerves, etc. But he goes on to explain the big metamorphosis that will occur to our bodies at Jesus' return:

> But let me reveal to you a wonderful secret. We will not all die, but we will all be transformed! It will happen in a moment, in the blink of an eye, when the last trumpet is blown. For when the trumpet sounds, those who have died will be raised to live forever. And we who are living will also be transformed. For our dying bodies must be transformed into bodies that will never die; our mortal bodies must be transformed into immortal bodies. (1 Corinthians 15:51-53 NLT)

Notice again here that dead believers are not in heaven at Jesus' return. They are still unconscious in their graves, not aware of anything. But when they hear the trumpet call of God, they are awakened to life that cannot end. People will put on immortality since they did not have immortality previously. Only God has it. But believers will be transformed at the First Resurrection, becoming born of God's own Spirit, so that their bodies will actually consist of spirit, and not flesh and blood any longer. You'll finally understand now what Jesus meant when he said:

> Whatever is born of the flesh is flesh, and whatever is born of the Spirit is spirit.
> (John 3:6 HCSB)

Jesus meant that the faithful servants of God will finally be consummate members of God's family, being made up of the same stuff that composes God. And that substance is called spirit. And once they're made up of spirit, they can't die anymore. Remember what we read about the people coming back to life in Round One:

> Blessed and holy is the one who shares in the
> first resurrection! The second death has no power
> over them (Revelation 20:6 HCSB)

So that's the fantastic news for the believers. But what about all those other people, "the rest of the dead" who are raised to life in Round Two, the Second Resurrection that takes place a thousand years later? Are they going to be revived into a spirit body that doesn't die? In a word, no. They are going to be given bodies made of flesh and blood once again. This part of the Bible's jigsaw puzzle is found in the book of Ezekiel. The prophet explained the nature of the Second Resurrection, as God said He would take piles of dead bones and reanimate them with muscles, skin, breath and physical life:

> This is what the Sovereign LORD says: Look!
> I am going to put breath into you and make you
> live again! I will put flesh and muscles on you
> and cover you with skin. I will put breath into
> you, and you will come to life. Then you will
> know that I am the LORD.'"
> (Ezekiel 37:5-6 NLT)

God is going to bring all the people who rebelled against Him back to life in their physical bodies with flesh and muscles, covered with skin once again. He has told us this well in advance. It is at the time of the Second Resurrection far into the future that rebellious people will finally understand who He is. That **He** is their Maker.

And why would God give these evildoers who are raised in the Second Resurrection physical, mortal bodies instead of immortal, spirit bodies? So they can be judged. So they can be tested. So they can be examined. So they can be evaluated. So they can be coached. God will give these people another chance to get with the program. His program. And at the end of their coaching and judgment, they can either receive the glorious gift of eternal life if they've passed the test, or be killed in the lake of fire, annihilated into ashes, receiving the final wages of sin, which is the second and permanent death. He is not going to tolerate people with bad attitudes who can never die. He is not creating immortal sinners. He is raising divine, immortal children who are obedient to Him!

A world without Satan

The book of Revelation provides more details on what happens to the rest of the dead, but before the Second Resurrection takes place, Scripture indicates that Satan will have been destroyed. Remember, there is a period of a thousand years between the time of the First and Second Resurrections:

> When the thousand years are completed, Satan will be released from his prison, and will come out to deceive the nations ... to gather them together for the war; the number of them is like the sand of the seashore. And they came up on the broad plain of the earth and surrounded the camp of the saints and the beloved city, and fire came down from heaven and devoured them. And the devil who deceived them was thrown into the lake of fire (Revelation 20:7-10 NASB)

After Satan is killed, the apostle John immediately describes the Second Resurrection, when the rest of the dead will finally come out of their graves:

> Then I saw a great white throne and Him who sat upon it, from whose presence earth and heaven fled away, and no place was found for them. And I saw the dead, the great and the small, standing before the throne, and books were opened; and another book was opened, which is the book of life; and the dead were judged from the things which were written in the books, according to their deeds. And the sea gave up the dead which were in it, and death and Hades gave up the dead which were in them; and they were judged, every one of them according to their deeds. Then death and Hades were thrown into the lake of fire. This is the second death, the lake of fire. And if anyone's name was not found written in the book of life, he was thrown into the lake of fire. (Revelation 20:11-15 NASB)

The dead were judged

This event, my friends, will be a momentous occasion. Every person who has ever existed and who was not given eternal life in the First Resurrection will be revived out of their graves, even if his or her grave were in the sea, to stand before the Creator once again. They will exist in their own physical, flesh-and-blood bodies, and Scripture says they will be "judged." But this time of judgment is not a time of sentencing or an instant death penalty. It is a time of examination and evaluation. God is going to examine people and judge them, test them, evaluate them based on their deeds, what they do, how they act **after** they have been raised from the dead! Their actions will be compared to what was written in the books, which are the books of the Bible! People need to realize that Judgment Day in the future is not just to inform people that they're guilty of sinning. Everyone is already guilty of breaking God's laws right now, and the Bible makes no secret about that:

> For all have sinned, and come short of the glory of God (Romans 3:23 KJV)

> As it is written: "There is no one righteous, not even one; there is no one who understands; there is no one who seeks God. All have turned away, they have together become worthless; there is no one who does good, not even one."
> (Romans 3:10-12 NIV)

So when the rest of the dead are raised to temporary existence in physical bodies, there's going to be much more taking place than merely informing them that they've sinned against God. It is a time when they are going to be taught, judged and examined by the family of God to see if they will finally repent and act as they should according to what has been written in the books of the Bible, to see if they can finally come to eternal life! This is the future time of judgment. It's the final chance for people to ditch the way of darkness that has encompassed their whole lives and learn instead to follow the light, the way to everlasting life, the way that God Almighty lives!

Raising the dead is not just to kill 'em again

Unfortunately, when millions of people read their own Bibles, they don't read the whole thing, or they don't believe every Scripture. Because, as we'll see, there are countless verses that describe this judgment in the future, which will last for years. I realize the twentieth chapter of Revelation condenses the events into just a few sentences, so a fast read makes it appear that people who are raised in the Second Resurrection are judged and then rapidly thrown into the lake of fire if their names were not found in the book of life. But most people miss the true point of what's being described. Remember, these people were **already dead**, most of them for thousands of years! God is not going to raise them to physical life just to inform them, "Oh, by the way. You broke My laws. You're guilty. Now I'm going to throw you in a lake of fire to make you dead again. Good-bye, suckers!"

God is bringing them back to temporary life to give them a chance at finally knowing the truth, **without Satan there to deceive them**, so they may at last become members of God's family, just like the believers who were raised in the First Resurrection:

> For the terrible one is brought to nothing,
> The scornful one is consumed (Isaiah 29:20 NKJV)

With the terrible one Satan having finally been eliminated from the scene, there will be no more deceiver-in-chief. People will finally be taught what is right without any confusion added to the mix. They will discover the truth that God Himself has actually kept them from learning during their initial lifetimes for their own protection:

> As the Scriptures say, "God has put them into a deep sleep. To this day he has shut their eyes so they do not see, and closed their ears so they do not hear." (Romans 11:8 NLT)

You're reading that right. The New Testament is confirming what was written in previous Scriptures, that **God** is the one who has put most people's understanding in a state of slumber, intentionally **hiding** the truth from them. It was stated at least twice in the Old Testament:

> But to this day the LORD has not given you a
> mind that understands or eyes that see or ears
> that hear. (Deuteronomy 29:4 NIV)
>
> For the LORD has poured over you a spirit of
> deep sleep, He has shut your eyes
> (Isaiah 29:10 NASB)

Now why, you might ask, would God intentionally hide his marvelous truth from people? The answer is simple. Because if they knew the real truth about Him, not the deceptive falsehood that is passed off as truth in most Christian churches, then God would have to kill them if they didn't follow Him. That's correct. He would have no choice but to end their lives permanently, because they would have committed the unpardonable sin. They would have been touched by the Spirit of God, and would have known the glorious truth. But their continued rebellion of not following His divine laws, the instructions that lead to eternal life, would be their downfall. No matter the excuse for not following the instructions, they would still be guilty of blasphemy against the Holy Spirit. As mentioned before, there's only one thing left for people who know God's truth and willingly reject it. And it's not pretty:

> Dear friends, if we deliberately continue sinning
> after we have received knowledge of the truth,
> there is no longer any sacrifice that will cover
> these sins. There is only the terrible expectation
> of God's judgment and the raging fire that will
> consume his enemies. (Hebrews 10:26-27 NLT)

When we become aware of God's truth and deliberately reject it, that's when we're in serious trouble and can expect to be killed in the raging lake of fire. This is the message of the Bible from start to finish. But, because God is merciful and doesn't wish anyone to perish, He has actually hidden His truth from the vast majority of humanity since the foundation of this world. God Himself has kept most of us asleep. He has kept us in the devil's prison of disobedience to the truth! It is not I who is saying this. It's the Word of God! Here's another example from the New Testament:

> For God has imprisoned all in disobedience, so
> that He may have mercy on all. Oh, the depth of
> the riches both of the wisdom and knowledge of
> God! How unsearchable are His judgments and
> unfathomable His ways!
> (Romans 11:32-33 NASB)

Are you finally waking up and smelling the truth? Your Bible says **God** is the one who has kept people in the dark. Your Bible says that **He** is the one that has hidden the truth from most people. Your Bible says the **Creator** is the one who has concluded people to be in unbelief, imprisoning them in disobedience. Why? "So that He may have mercy on all!" Yes, friends, God is full of mercy and is going to give all those billions of people who have ever lived a clear, Satan-free chance of learning and living the truth once they are raised in the Second Resurrection, the resurrection no one talks about! Do you finally see why this event is so important for "the rest of the dead"?

It means your family and friends who never came to understand the truth are not doomed for destruction! Unbelievers will still have a chance to gain eternal life and become members of God's family, which is what God has intended for them all along. God did not create billions of human beings in His own image just to have them tricked by the devil and see them roast in a fire until they become nothing but a pile of ashes. God the Father and Jesus Christ are having and raising beings just like Themselves to rule and reign with Them as Christ's own brothers and sisters in the never-ending kingdom of God! This is the Master Plan!

And because God knows that most people living in this current evil age will not come to the truth to be saved from the eternal death penalty, He is saving people in two separate stages. He is rescuing relatively few people in this current age of Round One, and then He'll save the vast majority of everyone else, "the rest of the dead," in Round Two. From the very beginning, He created a future time of judgment for the rebels, and that takes place **after** the Second Resurrection, when Satan no longer exists, and only the family of God is there to be the teachers of the future!

The judges of the future

The Bible is filled with prophecies about what will take place during the time after the Second Resurrection, the resurrection of judgment, when people will be examined to see if they'll make it into the kingdom. Let's start with some basics. It will be Jesus Christ, the Son of God who Himself is God, in charge of all the judging:

> The Father, in fact, judges no one but has given all judgment to the Son (John 5:22 HCSB)

> But the LORD abides forever; He has established His throne for judgment, And He will judge the world in righteousness; He will execute judgment for the peoples with equity. (Psalm 9:7-8 NASB)

> "And I will set My glory among the nations; and all the nations will see My judgment which I have executed and My hand which I have laid on them. (Ezekiel 39:21 NASB)

From the Old Testament to the New, it is clear that Jesus will be the top Judge of the future. And just as He led His rebellious people in the wilderness when they made their famous exodus from Egypt, Jesus will again lead all the people raised in the Second Resurrection into the wilderness where He'll have their full attention. He'll plead face to face with them to let them know this is their final chance to attain eternal life:

> "And I will bring you into the wilderness of the peoples, and there I will plead My case with you face to face. (Ezekiel 20:35 NKJV)

> I will judge you there just as I did your ancestors in the wilderness after bringing them out of Egypt, says the Sovereign LORD. I will examine you carefully and hold you to the terms of the covenant. I will purge you of all those who rebel and revolt against me. (Ezekiel 20:36-38 NLT)

"Come, let us discuss this," says the LORD.
"Though your sins are like scarlet, they will be as
white as snow; though they are as red as crimson,
they will be like wool. If you are willing and
obedient, you will eat the good things of the land.
(Isaiah 1:18 HCSB)

The promises made by God thousands of years ago will have their ultimate fulfillment in a time still ahead of us, this second round of judgment. God has said He will forgive everyone's previous sins, and He'll plead with them face to face so they will hold to the terms of the covenant. That covenant is the agreement that He began with Abraham, the end result of which is eternal life for obedience.

God will examine people carefully, and if they don't obey His laws, He said He will purge out all those who rebel. In other words, if they don't get with the program, they'll be killed in the Gehenna fire. Remember what Revelation states:

And if anyone's name was not found written in
the book of life, he was thrown into the lake of
fire. (Revelation 20:15 NASB)

This highly misunderstood Scripture **does not say everyone raised in the Second Resurrection is going to be thrown into the fire**. It says only those whose names are not found in the book of life will be annihilated. That means that the vast majority of people who have rejected God in Round One, this current age, will have a chance to keep their names written in the book of life in Round Two, after the Second Resurrection. Their names won't be erased from its pages automatically. God has said He'll plead with them face to face, urging them to stop their worthless shenanigans and receive the free gift of eternal life.

More than one judge

But it won't be just Jesus doing the judging, which is another surprise to most Christians. While Jesus will be the top official in charge of the exam, Scripture indicates He won't be doing the job alone. He'll employ the help of the rest of His family. And who are they? They're the children of God who were raised in the First Resurrection, and now have their own divine thrones from which to examine, coach and judge people. This is where many more dots of prophecy finally get connected. Here are some that should finally make sense to you in light of the Second Resurrection and its subsequent time of judgment:

> Don't you realize that someday we believers will judge the world? (1 Corinthians 6:2 NLT)

> And Jesus said to them, "Truly I say to you, that you who have followed Me, in the regeneration when the Son of Man will sit on His glorious throne, you also shall sit upon twelve thrones, judging the twelve tribes of Israel.
> (Matthew 19:28 NASB)

> Behold, a king shall reign in righteousness, and princes shall rule in judgment. (Isaiah 32:1 KJV)

> Then the sovereignty, power and greatness of all the kingdoms under heaven will be handed over to the holy people of the Most High. His kingdom will be an everlasting kingdom, and all rulers will worship and obey him.'
> (Daniel 7:27 NIV)

> Then I saw thrones, and the people sitting on them had been given the authority to judge.
> (Revelation 20:4 NLT)

> 'He who overcomes, I will grant to him to sit down with Me on My throne, as I also overcame and sat down with My Father on His throne.
> (Revelation 3:21 NASB)

Are you getting the picture? The obedient servants of God who were quickened into their spirit bodies in the First Resurrection will be members of God's own family by this point. They will be sitting on their own thrones, and sometimes even on the throne of Jesus! Why? Because they will "rule in judgment" with the "authority to judge." They will be testing, judging and evaluating the citizens of this world! They will be helping all their friends and relatives who didn't make it in the first round to finally make it in the second round. All these Scriptures will finally be fulfilled when the divine brothers and sisters of Jesus are part of the kingdom, the literal government and family of God!

The Bible calls Jesus the "KING OF KINGS, AND LORD OF LORDS." (Revelation 19:16 KJV) Have you ever wondered who those kings are that Jesus is the king of? Have you ever wondered who those lords are that Jesus is lord of? The kings and lords are **us**! You and me! The true believers who have been given the divine authority to judge the nations of this world!

> Now therefore, be wise, O kings; Be instructed, you judges of the earth. (Psalm 2:10 NKJV)

Jesus has personally guaranteed our power to judge and rule over these nations that are brought back to life in the Second Resurrection:

> To all who are victorious, who obey me to the very end, To them I will give authority over all the nations. They will rule the nations with an iron rod and smash them like clay pots.
> (Revelation 2:26-27 NLT)

Note that Jesus said we as rulers of the future will be equipped with a rod of iron, with which we'll have the authority to discipline the nations if need be. This is because Jesus Himself will be ruling during this future time of judgment with an iron rod:

> I will take note of you as you pass under my rod, and I will bring you into the bond of the covenant.
> (Ezekiel 20:37 NIV)

> You will break them with a rod of iron; you will dash them to pieces like pottery."
> (Psalm 2:9 NIV)

> if they violate my decrees and fail to keep my commands, I will punish their sin with the rod, their iniquity with flogging
> (Psalm 89:31-32 NIV)

But none of this has happened yet. We are not sitting on our thrones reigning over the nations. We have not been given a rod or scepter of iron with which to discipline. But we will during this second round of judgment. We will be the judges, rulers and coaches of the future, doing our best under the direction of Jesus to get the rebels to finally repent and become children of God. The divine teachers of the future will no longer be invisible or hidden from the populace as God currently hides Himself with invisibility:

> your teachers will be hidden no more; with your own eyes you will see them. Whether you turn to the right or to the left, your ears will hear a voice behind you, saying, "This is the way; walk in it." (Isaiah 30:20-21 NIV)

> And I will give you shepherds after my own heart, who will guide you with knowledge and understanding. (Jeremiah 3:15 NLT)

And don't forget what we learned in the Coal Kids Club chapter. This is the precise time that people who finally learn the truth will hate themselves for having engaged in all those ridiculous holiday traditions that God says He hates. The absurd customs such as hanging silver and gold Christmas ornaments on a green tree standing upright in the living room:

> You will also defile the <u>covering of your images of silver</u>, And the <u>ornament of your molded images of gold</u>. You will throw them away as an unclean thing; You will say to them, "Get away!" (Isaiah 30:22 NKJV)

Most will finally repent

The good news is that most people will finally get with the program. That's right, the atheists of the world and those who did not properly follow God during their initial life on Earth will actually see the light, hate themselves for their sins, and come to the path that leads to eternal life. Here's another prophecy from Ezekiel predicting the same future:

> "For on My holy mountain, on the high mountain of Israel," declares the Lord GOD, "there the whole house of Israel, all of them, will serve Me

> in the land; there I will accept them and there I will seek your contributions and the choicest of your gifts, with all your holy things.
>
> As a soothing aroma I will accept you when I bring you out from the peoples and gather you from the lands where you are scattered; and I will prove Myself holy among you in the sight of the nations.
>
> And you will know that I am the LORD, when I bring you into the land of Israel, into the land which I swore to give to your forefathers.
>
> There you will remember your ways and all your deeds with which you have defiled yourselves; and you will loathe yourselves in your own sight for all the evil things that you have done.
>
> Then you will know that I am the LORD when I have dealt with you for My name's sake, not according to your evil ways or according to your corrupt deeds ... **(Ezekiel 20:40-44 NASB)**

The judgment after the Second Resurrection will be a time when people actually desire to learn the laws of God, and will finally accept the instruction in righteousness:

> Those who are confused will gain understanding, and those who grumble will accept instruction. (Isaiah 29:24 HCSB)
>
> Many peoples will come and say, "Come, let us go up to the mountain of the LORD, to the temple of the God of Jacob. He will teach us his ways, so that we may walk in his paths." The law will go out from Zion, the word of the LORD from Jerusalem. (Isaiah 2:3 NIV)

They'll want to learn the ways of God because the Creator says He'll change the rebellious spirit within them. He'll give them a change of heart, causing them to pull a 180-degree turn:

> "I will give you a new heart and put a new spirit within you; I will take the heart of stone out of your flesh and give you a heart of flesh. I will put My Spirit within you and cause you to walk in My statutes, and you will keep My judgments and do them. Then you shall dwell in the land that I gave to your fathers; you shall be My people, and I will be your God. I will deliver you from all your uncleannesses. ... Then you will remember your evil ways and your deeds that were not good; and you will loathe yourselves in your own sight, for your iniquities and your abominations.

(Ezekiel 36:26-31 NKJV)

What a wonderful time this will be after the Second Resurrection, as people will have a change of heart (thanks to God), and they will **want** to learn His laws! It's the exact opposite of what's taught in most Christian churches today – that God's laws don't matter, or that the laws were done away with by Jesus, being nailed to the cross. If you're hearing in church that we're not supposed to follow God's laws, then it's high time you bolt as fast as you can out the door. I'm serious.

Now, how long will people who are raised in the Second Resurrection be given as a time of testing? I can't say for sure, because there is no outright declaration in Scripture. However, there is a very strong hint that it will be one hundred years. It's a red-letter quote from God in the book of Isaiah:

> "For behold, I create new heavens and a new earth; And the former shall not be remembered or come to mind. ... I will rejoice in Jerusalem, And joy in My people; The voice of weeping shall no longer be heard in her, Nor the voice of crying. No more shall an infant from there live but a few days, Nor an old man who has not fulfilled his days; For the child shall die one hundred years old, But the sinner being one hundred years old shall be accursed. (Isaiah 65:17-20 NKJV)

Why does God seem to suggest a hundred-year life span during this future paradise when there's no more crying? And why will sinners be accursed when then they reach the age of one hundred? Because that could very well be the end of the line for the two opposing destinies for human beings. For those who will have passed the test and are judged worthy of eternal life, their human bodies will die, probably just for a fraction of a second, the "blink of an eye" as happened for those in the First Resurrection (1 Corinthians 15:52 NLT). They will then be instantaneously quickened into their new, immortal, spirit-composed bodies.

Dust busters

But for those people who do not get with the program and instead keep on with their deliberate rejection of God's laws, then they will be accursed, with only one punishment left for them, the death penalty in the lake of fire, where they'll be turned into ashes and dust. It's reminiscent of what God told Adam at the very beginning of the Bible:

> For you are dust, And to dust you shall return."
> (Genesis 3:19 NASB)

It also gives new insight as to why Jesus told His disciples to shake the dust from their feet if stubborn people refuse to accept God's truth:

> If any household or town refuses to welcome you or listen to your message, shake its dust from your feet as you leave. I tell you the truth, the wicked cities of Sodom and Gomorrah will be better off than such a town on the judgment day.
> (Matthew 10:14-15 NLT)

Here we have Jesus talking about the judgment day of the future, the time after the Second Resurrection, and He has told His students to shake the dust off their feet as a witness against the obstinate people alive during His human ministry. Why might He have used this seemingly odd phrase of shaking the dust off their feet? Scripture provides the answer. Because those who are granted eternal life in the future will, in fact, be trampling with their feet upon the dust and ashes of the wicked! God has said so:

> You will trample the wicked, for they will be
> ashes under the soles of your feet on the day I am
> preparing," says the LORD of Hosts.
> (Malachi 4:3 HCSB)

So when the disciples of Jesus shook dust off their feet, they were issuing a dire warning to the people who refused to accept the truth. The message was, in effect: "If you sinners don't repent, you're going to be incinerated into ashes and dust, and we're going to trample on your ashes! So get with the program!" It's simply another way of saying this more direct warning that Jesus issued twice: "Unless you repent, you too will all perish." (Luke 13:3,5 NIV)

Now you know the true conclusion of the Bible, and the glorious hope that is out there for all those who are not in compliance at this moment with God's laws. They're not doomed to be dead forever.

There is a First Resurrection, the resurrection of life, for the obedient servants of God. And then a thousand years later, there is a Second Resurrection, the resurrection of judgment, for "the rest of the dead." It will be followed by a time of coaching and judgment, perhaps a hundred years long, when people will experience a change of heart and a fresh willingness to obey the ways that will lead them to eternal life. Will most choose life instead of death? I personally think so, because Scripture has inspiring prophecies such as these:

> And when I am lifted up from the earth, I will
> draw everyone to myself." (John 12:32 NLT)

> And so all Israel will be saved. As the Scriptures
> say, "The one who rescues will come from
> Jerusalem, and he will turn Israel away from
> ungodliness. And this is my covenant with them,
> that I will take away their sins."
> (Romans 11:26-27 NLT)

> But this is the new covenant I will make with the
> people of Israel on that day, says the LORD: I will
> put my laws in their minds, and I will write them
> on their hearts. I will be their God, and they will
> be my people. And they will not need to teach

> their neighbors, nor will they need to teach their relatives, saying, 'You should know the LORD.' For everyone, from the least to the greatest, will know me already. (Hebrews 8:10-11 NLT)

> I have sworn by my own name; I have spoken the truth, and I will never go back on my word: Every knee will bend to me, and every tongue will confess allegiance to me. (Isaiah 45:23 NLT)

The statement from Jesus that He would draw all men to Himself has obviously not been fulfilled yet, because at the present moment, not everyone is being drawn to Him. Only a select few are. But He indicated every person will be drawn to Him in the future. Why? So He can offer everyone the chance to become His divine children after the Second Resurrection, the resurrection no one talks about, takes place! There is that future opportunity to join God's family!

Not only will "all Israel" be saved and have their sins forgiven, there won't be any more need to evangelize and try to get people to convert in the future because everyone will eventually know God. And Jesus has sworn by His own holy name, indicating He'll never go back on His promise that every knee will bow before Him, and every tongue will confess allegiance to Him, the King of kings and Lord of lords. Thank God that the vast majority of formerly rebellious people will ultimately understand the truth, and choose to receive life everlasting. Those are the words on the page, and I believe them.

Chapter Eight:
The unknown sin

W e have talked a lot about Satan in this book, and for good reason, because the devil is the driving force responsible for Opposite World, the rebellious society in which we all operate on a daily basis. Shockingly, this relentless enemy has even infiltrated today's Christianity in a very devious way, so that believers in God don't even recognize the presence of darkness. The devil has used all his brilliance to create what I call "the unknown sin."

It's a sin that most people who call themselves believers are not even aware of. It's a sin that many pastors and priests are themselves guilty of, and guilty of spreading. And if someone ever has the courage to bring the matter to light, especially in the presence of a member of the clergy, then all hell might break loose, with people getting called a variety of vicious names, merely for pointing out what the words in the Bible actually say.

But we're not supposed to be in fear of anyone's reaction, especially when speaking God's truth, so I'm going to address it in detail for you here. I won't keep you in suspense any longer, because the subject matter is very serious. In fact, it's a matter of life and death. Your life and death. The big deception that has infiltrated modern Christianity is not knowing what "sin" actually is, and rejecting its Bible definition. For countless people who profess faith in Jesus today, the true essence of sin remains unknown.

Sin-cere Christians

At the outset, I'd like to stress that I don't hold anything personal against people who proclaim the love of Jesus and call themselves Christians. After all, I'm one of them, and I hope to see everyone on this planet repent to gain eternal life in the coming kingdom of God. But in recent years, there has been a growing problem that is putting many people's relationship with their Creator in a threatened condition.

People who call themselves Christian talk all the time about how Jesus came to save sinners, and they're often very willing to admit how they themselves were sinners before coming to know Jesus. They might even quote Jesus telling a woman who was caught in adultery to "go, and sin no more" (John 8:11 KJV). That's all very well and good.

But try sometime to ask a believer what the Bible definition of "sin" is. If you don't get a concert of crickets chirping, you might hear some nervous babbling about sin consisting of harmful activities such as smoking, drinking, carousing, doing drugs or just being a mean person. But none of those is the exact definition of sin, at least not in Scripture. You may be surprised that the Bible itself does define what sin is, and you may not like its description, because it could put you at odds with your own pastor. Why? Because, unfortunately, many pastors today seem to be working overtime to convince you the Bible doesn't mean what it says on this subject. They, too, have been seduced by the devil.

While the Word of God talks about sin in both the Old and New Testaments, the Bible definition of sin is found in the New Testament. Thank goodness for that, because I know some people who call themselves "New Testament believers," and they presume anything in the Old Testament is either done away with, or somehow not intended for them to follow.

The definition of sin comes from John, the apostle whom Jesus loved, and it's found in his first letter, in 1 John 3:4 to be specific. I'm providing numerous Bible translations of this little-discussed verse, just so there's no mistaking what the actual meaning is. Here now is the official definition from Scripture of sin:

> Whoever commits sin also commits lawlessness, and sin is lawlessness. (1 John 3:4 NKJV)
>
> Whosoever committeth sin transgresseth also the law: for sin is the transgression of the law. (KJV)
>
> Everyone who sins breaks the law; in fact, sin is lawlessness. (NIV)
>
> Everyone who sins is breaking God's law, for all sin is contrary to the law of God. (NLT)
>
> Everyone who commits sin also breaks the law; sin is the breaking of law. (HCSB)
>
> Everyone who practices sin also practices lawlessness; and sin is lawlessness. (NASB)
>
> Everyone who makes a practice of sinning also practices lawlessness; sin is lawlessness. (ESV)

So, finally, sin is no longer unknown. As is obvious from all these renderings of 1 John 3:4, sin simply means **lawlessness**, the breaking of God's law. Yes, folks, I realize many of you may never have actually heard that from your pastor, but it's right there in your Bible. Sin is breaking any law of the Creator. Many people don't wish to focus on the true nature of sin, because it means that God's laws, His divine instructions and commandments, are still in force.

Sinful excuses

I bring this up because there has been a strong movement in the ostensible Christian faith over many years to obscure what sin is, to get believers thinking that God's laws are somehow not meant for us at this time. All kinds of excuses are proffered, and you've probably heard statements such as:

> "God's commandments were only for those people in the **Old** Testament. But we are **New** Testament believers!"
>
> "Jesus nailed the law to His cross, so the law is done away with."
>
> "Jesus obeyed and fulfilled the law for us, so we don't have to."
>
> "The law was created by that harsh, old God the Father. But we worship His loving Son."

"If we try to obey God's commandments, we're wrongly trying to earn our salvation, but salvation is a free gift from God."

"Following God's laws is being 'legalistic.'"

"Jesus forgives us for breaking God's laws, so we shouldn't even bother trying to keep the commandments."

"God is glorified by forgiving our sins, so the more we sin and are forgiven, the more God is glorified."

"We don't have to do anything to be saved, except believe in Jesus."

All of the above thoughts have been spoken so many times that millions of Christians absolutely believe them. They parrot these claims not only to each other, but also to potential converts to the faith. No matter how they phrase it, they convey the message that it's somehow wrong or not necessary to keep God's commandments. Once again, we're living in Opposite World. Because from start to finish, the Bible is filled with Scriptures telling us the polar opposite, urging us all to keep the commandments, to follow God's laws, which are described as truth, a delight and eternal:

And Your law is truth. (Psalm 119:42 NKJV)

For Your law is my delight. (Psalm 119:77 NKJV)

All your words are true; all your righteous laws are eternal. (Psalm 119:160 NIV)

The notion that God's laws are not meant to be followed is the intentional deception of the devil himself. Remember, Satan is a liar and wants to see all of us dead. He was a murderer from the beginning. He knows the New Testament says "the wages of sin is death" (Romans 6:23), so he has tricked an immeasurable number of Christians into thinking it's perfectly fine to disregard or disobey God's laws. Thus, many Christians don't even realize they are committing suicide. Yes, they're killing themselves! They are voluntarily taking away their eternal life, because they don't know what sin is, nor do they know the result of sin. That's why I say this issue is a matter of life and death.

As we have just seen, sin is the breaking of God's laws. So if we think those laws are not meant to be followed when they really are still in effect, then we are earning the payment for sin, which is eternal death!

Countless people of devotion who say they love and worship Jesus with all their heart are actually following the dark and destructive path of their archenemy, Satan the devil!

The divine code

Let's see now what the Bible itself says about God's laws, and if we're still intended to follow the instructions from the Maker of all things. The word "law" in its original Hebrew is "torah," and it means "instruction" or "teaching" as well as "law." It's important to remember that, because, I think for some strange reason, people are more willing to follow an instruction or a teaching rather than a law, even though they mean the exact same thing. We can see that all the way back in Genesis, the patriarch Abraham obeyed God's torah, which are His laws and instructions:

> Because Abraham obeyed my voice, and kept my charge, my commandments, my statutes, and my laws [torah]. (Genesis 26:5 KJV)

> because Abraham listened to My voice and kept My mandate, My commands, My statutes, and My instructions." (Genesis 26:5 HCSB)

Even before the Ten Commandments were etched into stone tablets at Mount Sinai, God tested the Israelites in the wilderness to see if they would follow His instructions. After His people failed the test for resting on the Sabbath day, the seventh day of the week, the Creator asked this important question:

> And the LORD said to Moses, "How long do you refuse to keep My commandments and My laws? (Exodus 16:28 NKJV)

The instructions from God are the code by which we are meant to live. And when I say that, I mean two things. The first is that they are the teachings we should follow here in this physical world for our own benefit. When we don't lie, steal, murder and cheat other people, we tend to have fewer problems through the years.

But secondly, and infinitely more importantly, obedience to God's instructions are a substantial part of the code to receive the reward of eternal life! So many people are surprised when they find out that Jesus Himself in the New Testament said that people must keep the commandments if they wish to enter everlasting life:

> if you want to receive eternal life, keep the commandments (Matthew 19:17 NLT)

I did not make that statement. Jesus did. Feel free to read it again, and read it in your own Bible, because it says the same thing. When pressed on which commandments we should keep, Jesus then began recounting the instructions found in the **Old** Testament:

> "'You shall not murder, you shall not commit adultery, you shall not steal, you shall not give false testimony, honor your father and mother,' and 'love your neighbor as yourself.'"
> (Matthew 19:18-19 NIV)

The above response from Jesus should alone prove that the Old Testament commandments are still in force. And if we, as believers, love our Savior, what are we instructed to do? Again, Jesus has the answer to this question:

> "If you love Me, keep My commandments.
> (John 14:15 NKJV)

When God led His people out of slavery in Egypt, He explained to them what was really going on. He was presenting them two choices: eternal life versus eternal death, and the key to obtaining eternal life was obeying His instructions:

> "Now listen! Today I am giving you a choice between life and death, between prosperity and disaster. For I command you this day to love the LORD your God and to keep his commands, decrees, and regulations by walking in his ways. If you do this, you will live and multiply, and the LORD your God will bless you and the land you are about to enter and occupy.
> (Deuteronomy 30:15-16 NLT)

"Take to heart all the words of warning I have
given you today. Pass them on as a command
to your children so they will obey every word
of these instructions. These instructions are not
empty words—they are your life!
(Deuteronomy 32:47 NLT)

Dozens of times, the great names of the Bible, whether Jesus Christ
or other well-known figures, have urged us to knock off our disobedience
and obey the divine instructions. They're not empty words. They are
our very life. If we refuse to obey the instructions, we will end up dead
forever. We seem to have no problem understanding that children should
obey our human parents, but apparently God the Father and Jesus Christ,
our Parents in heaven, are less worthy of respect by many Christians.
Because many believers are under the impression we can (or even should)
disobey God. This line of thinking is absurd and lethal. The laws are
commandments, not suggestions.

Here's a very brief rundown of some of the many Scriptures in both
the Old and New Testaments which tell us to obey God's instructions:

But the mercy of the LORD is from everlasting
to everlasting upon them that fear him, and his
righteousness unto children's children; To such
as keep his covenant, and to those that remember
his commandments to do them.
(Psalm 103:17-18 KJV)

Depart from me, you evil ones, so that I may obey
my God's commands. (Psalm 119:115 HCSB)

Keep my commands and live, And my law as the
apple of your eye. (Proverbs 7:2 NKJV)

Let us hear the conclusion of the whole matter:
Fear God, and keep his commandments: for this is
the whole duty of man. (Ecclesiastes 12:13 KJV)
I prayed to the LORD my God and confessed and
said, "Alas, O Lord, the great and awesome God,
who keeps His covenant and lovingkindness for
those who love Him and keep His commandments
(Daniel 9:4 NASB)

When you obey my commandments, you remain in my love, just as I obey my Father's commandments and remain in his love.
(John 15:10 NLT)

This is how we are sure that we have come to know Him: by keeping His commands.
(1 John 2:3 HCSB)

And whatever we ask we receive from Him, because we keep His commandments and do those things that are pleasing in His sight.
(1 John 3:22 NKJV)

So the dragon was enraged with the woman, and went off to make war with the rest of her children, who keep the commandments of God and hold to the testimony of Jesus.
 (Revelation 12:17 NASB)

Here is the patience of the saints: here are they that keep the commandments of God, and the faith of Jesus. (Revelation 14:12 KJV)

Blessed are they that do his commandments, that they may have right to the tree of life, and may enter in through the gates into the city.
(Revelation 22:14 KJV)

For it is not those who hear the law who are righteous in God's sight, but it is those who obey the law who will be declared righteous.
(Romans 2:13 NIV)

This is how we know that we love God's children when we love God and obey His commands. For this is what love for God is: to keep His commands. Now His commands are not a burden
(1 John 5:2-3 HCSB)

I hope you noticed just how many **New** Testament quotes are included there. Because all those folks who call themselves New Testament believers never seem to mention them. I especially like the last one that defines what "love for God" actually is. Love for God does not mean having some romantic feeling for the Creator or belting out your favorite worship song in church. Scripture says love for God is "to keep His commands." This is ironic because so many people will, in one breath, proclaim their love for God, but in the next breath, happily claim His laws and commands have been done away with or are not intended to be followed any longer. It is Opposite World at its best, and it comes from the people who are supposed to be closest to the truth.

Here's another New Testament verse you may never hear in a Christian church, despite it being written by the apostle John:

> He that saith, I know him, and keepeth not his commandments, **is a liar**, and the truth is not in him. (1 John 2:4 KJV)

Are you seeing it with your own eyes? You might want to highlight that verse in your own Bible. Scripture calls self-professed Christians "liars" if they don't obey God's commandments. I know that calling someone a liar sounds harsh, but this is the Holy Word of God making the statement. Our Creator wants us to stop our insane disobedience to the instructions that lead to eternal life.

The lawbreaker lists

At times, the Bible provides listings of people who will not make it into God's kingdom. When we take the time to read the lists slowly, we see that those who are excluded are the ones who break the laws of God. Here are just two of those lists:

> Do you not know that the unrighteous will not inherit the kingdom of God? Do not be deceived. Neither fornicators, nor idolaters, nor adulterers, nor homosexuals, nor sodomites, nor thieves, nor covetous, nor drunkards, nor revilers, nor extortioners will inherit the kingdom of God. (1 Corinthians 6:9-10 NKJV)

"But cowards, unbelievers, the corrupt, murderers, the immoral, those who practice witchcraft, idol worshipers, and all liars—their fate is in the fiery lake of burning sulfur. This is the second death." (Revelation 21:8 NLT)

Notice how, in the list from Corinthians, Paul urges fellow believers not to be deceived on this matter of God's law. Because the deception was already spreading in the years immediately following the death and resurrection of Jesus. And today in the 21st century, the deception is so widespread, it has actually become what most people think Christianity is. There are many millions of believers across the planet who have been tricked into thinking they're in perfectly good shape with God if they continue to ignore the divine commands. Many of these people will get the biggest, mind-blowing shock ever when they find out God is not going to give them eternal life, all because they practiced lawlessness.

Here's another quote from Jesus not often heard in church:

"Not everyone who says to Me, 'Lord, Lord,' will enter the kingdom of heaven, but he who does the will of My Father who is in heaven will enter. Many will say to Me on that day, 'Lord, Lord, did we not prophesy in Your name, and in Your name cast out demons, and in Your name perform many miracles?' And then I will declare to them, 'I never knew you; DEPART FROM ME, YOU WHO PRACTICE LAWLESSNESS.' (Matthew 7:21-23 NASB)

You're reading that correctly. People who call themselves Christian and who say they've been able to perform miracles and cast out demons are actually not known by God. Jesus will tell them to get out of His presence. Why? Because they practice **lawlessness**. They break God's laws, and they tell other people the laws of God are void:

It is time for You to act, O LORD, For they have regarded Your law as void. (Psalm 119:126 NKJV)

Paul urges everyone to stop their disobedience to the divine laws, because that's the reason why God is so angry with human beings, actually calling them "sons of disobedience":

> Therefore put to death your members which are on the earth: fornication, uncleanness, passion, evil desire, and covetousness, which is idolatry. Because of these things the wrath of God is coming upon the sons of disobedience
> (Colossians 3:5-6 NKJV)

If the law were done away

Here are some important questions to ask all those folks in churches who think God's law is somehow not meant to be followed. Presuming the law is done away with, are we now allowed to murder other people? Does God permit us to lie, steal, lust for things, fornicate and commit adultery? If God's law is not meant to be followed, we can break the very first commandment and worship other gods, right? If the law were done away with, is it not perfectly fine to bow down and worship Satan the devil?

But few ever dare to ask themselves such obvious questions. Programmed by the dark forces of Opposite World, they mindlessly walk around repeating the same rebellious excuses, urging other people to believe in Jesus, while suggesting they don't have to do anything else once they profess that belief! Their new converts don't give up their sin, because they think a nominal belief in Jesus is all that's necessary to attain eternal life. Hence, from the beginning of their conversion, people are not told what the Bible definition of sin is. This idea of all that's needed for salvation is a belief or faith in God is the opposite of what the Bible teaches. Here's how the apostle James, the brother of Jesus, put it:

> You say you have faith, for you believe that there is one God. Good for you! Even the demons believe this, and they tremble in terror.
> (James 2:19 NLT)

That's right. The rebellious angels all have a belief and faith in God. In fact, it's beyond just faith for them. They know with absolute certainty God exists and that Jesus is their Boss. They are fully aware of God's

Master Plan. And yet, they tremble in terror because they know He is going to punish them for their disobedience to His laws! So people need to wake up to the fact that faith in God is not enough to get us the reward of eternal life. We actually have to do His will and obey His instructions.

The preparation for eternal life

It is crucial for us to remember what God's Master Plan is, what He's really doing with people. He is not creating pets who will just gaze at His face and sing worship songs for all eternity. He is enlarging the divine family. He is having and raising adult children to rule and reign with Him in the coming kingdom of God, so He has to teach us the rules by which we will live and govern in the future kingdom.

With this is mind, when we read the Old Testament accounts of God training His people in the wilderness before they entered the Promised Land, we should think spiritually, because it is also talking about **our** training right now, at this very moment. We are being trained and tested in our modern wilderness, the pagan world into which we've all been born. We all in this 21st century are still dwelling in spiritual Egypt, and we're commanded to come out of it. Our Creator is now training us with His laws, preparing us for entry into the ultimate Promised Land, the coming kingdom of God!

Here's a very brief section of Deuteronomy, revealing that God's laws are eternal, and they are the way that we'll be living in the future Promised Land:

> If only they had such a heart to fear Me and keep all My commands <u>always,</u> so that they and their children will prosper <u>forever</u>. ... I will tell you every command—the statutes and ordinances—you are to teach them, <u>so that they may follow them in the land I am giving them to possess</u>.'
>
> "Be careful to do as the LORD your God has commanded you; you are not to turn aside to the right or the left. Follow the whole instruction the LORD your God has commanded you, so that you may <u>live</u>, prosper, and have a <u>long life in the land you will possess</u>.

(Deuteronomy 5:29-33 HCSB)

Everyone realizes that these instructions were given to Moses and the Israelites before they entered the physical Promised Land way back in the day. But what I'm trying to get you to realize is that God's law is spiritually active forever, and is meant to be learned right now by all of us because these are the laws we'll be living by, teaching and enforcing in the **real** Promised Land. The **eternal** Promised Land. The kingdom of God which we're about to possess! The instructions to obey God were not just a one-time thing, for "those people back then." They are for you and me right now and for our eternity! Deuteronomy is telling the same story as the rest of the Bible, because "Jesus Christ is the same yesterday and today and forever" (Hebrews 13:8 NASB). God is not going to put up with all those excuses from self-professing "Christians" about why His laws are done away with, because **none** of them are!

The buried statement of Jesus

It is nothing short of shocking to see how many of today's Christians completely bury, ignore or rebel against the direct teaching of Jesus about this very matter. It's Opposite World. The fifth chapter of Matthew contains the clearest teaching from Jesus about the laws of God, as He directly addressed the issue of the divine instruction allegedly being destroyed or done away with:

> "Don't assume that I came to destroy the Law or the Prophets. I did not come to destroy but to fulfill.
>
> For I assure you: Until heaven and earth pass away, not the smallest letter or one stroke of a letter will pass from the law until all things are accomplished.
>
> Therefore, whoever breaks one of the least of these commands and teaches people to do so will be called least in the kingdom of heaven. But whoever practices and teaches these commands will be called great in the kingdom of heaven.
>
> For I tell you, unless your righteousness surpasses that of the scribes and Pharisees, you will never enter the kingdom of heaven.

(Matthew 5:17-20 HCSB)

Why are these red-letter sentences from Jesus rarely uttered in thousands of churches that call themselves Christian? Because the folks who operate and attend these churches cannot stand to hear from their Savior's own lips that He intends for them to keep the laws of God! He says to practice the law at least five different ways in the above text. Let's list them:

- Jesus urged everyone not to think the law has been abolished. Yet millions of Christians today believe the opposite, thinking the law is abolished.

- Jesus said until heaven and Earth disappear, not the slightest bit of the law is done away with. Yet millions of Christians today believe the opposite, despite the fact that heaven and Earth have not passed away.

- Jesus said whoever breaks one of the least of the divine commands and teaches other people to break them will be called least in God's kingdom. Yet millions of Christians today believe the opposite, thinking that forgiveness trumps obedience, and that there's no possible way human beings can keep God's instructions, even though Scripture says they're not a burden.

- Jesus said whoever practices and teaches these commands will be called great in God's kingdom. Yet millions of Christians today believe the opposite and go so far as to impugn, mock and persecute believers who obey God's instructions and teach them to others. Chances are, you've heard self-professed believers putting fellow Christians in a bad light by calling them "legalistic" or "Judaizers" for merely trying to obey the direct instructions of their Creator.

- Jesus said unless your righteousness surpasses that of the scribes and Pharisees, you'll **never** enter God's kingdom. Yet millions of Christians believe the opposite, thinking righteousness (obeying the law) has little, if anything, to do with salvation. To them, merely believing that Jesus is God or their Savior is all that's needed to give them that golden entry ticket to the kingdom.

If we continue reading the fifth chapter of Matthew, we can easily see that Jesus was actually making it tougher to follow God's laws. For instance, we don't have to kill someone to be guilty of murder. Just being angry with someone or calling them an idiot makes us guilty of murder, and puts us in danger of being turned into ashes in the Gehenna fire:

> "You have heard that it was said to our ancestors, Do not murder, and whoever murders will be subject to judgment. But I tell you, everyone who is angry with his brother will be subject to judgment. And whoever says to his brother, 'Fool!' will be subject to the Sanhedrin. But whoever says, 'You moron!' will be subject to hellfire. (Matthew 5:21-22 HCSB)

And we don't even have to have sex with someone who is not our spouse for us to be guilty of adultery. Merely lusting after that person is the same as committing the physical crime:

> "You have heard that it was said, Do not commit adultery. But I tell you, everyone who looks at a woman to lust for her has already committed adultery with her in his heart.
> (Matthew 5:27-28 HCSB)

Jesus is expecting us to live our lives righteously. It's actually a commandment to do that:

> Seek the Kingdom of God above all else, and live righteously, and he will give you everything you need. (Matthew 6:33 NLT)

Interestingly, just as "sin" is one of those words for which people don't know the Bible definition, so is "righteous" or "righteousness." The reason why will become obvious as soon as you see it right now:

> And if we are careful to obey all this law before the LORD our God, as he has commanded us, that will be our righteousness."
> (Deuteronomy 6:25 NIV)

As is very plain, righteousness is defined as obeying all of God's laws. It is no coincidence that these Biblical meanings are obscured by the powers that be in today's Christianity. Many of its leaders are deliberately encouraging people to abandon the commands of their Maker. When confronted on the matter, they break out that list of excuses I mentioned earlier, none of which have the firm support of Scripture.

Nailed to the cross?

One of the most popular excuses on the list is the claim that the law of God has been "nailed to the cross." There have been countless sermons over hundreds of years with many Christian pastors broadcasting the message that Jesus nailed His own law to the cross when He was put to death in the first century. These ministers take a snippet of a statement from the book of Colossians where the phrase "nailing it to his cross" appears, and have turned it into a monstrosity that demonstrates how Satan is still the god of this world by twisting the Scripture into the antithesis of what it says.

Let's look at this section now from a variety of Bible translations to see if Jesus really nailed the law to the cross so that we're no longer under any obligation to abide by it. Let's start with the King James Version:

> And you, being dead in your sins and the un-
> circumcision of your flesh, hath he quickened
> together with him, having forgiven you all tres-
> passes; Blotting out the handwriting of ordinanc-
> es that was against us, which was contrary to us,
> and took it out of the way, nailing it to his cross
> (Colossians 2:13-14 KJV)

It is the use of the word "ordinances" in verse 14 that people generally get stuck on. Many try to claim that every single ordinance of God was somehow against us and has been done away with. If that's the case, then we can lie, cheat, steal, murder and worship other gods. But if we look at this passage in other translations of the Holy Bible, the real meaning becomes clear. I personally think the New Living Translation is one of the best versions on this matter, as it states:

> You were dead because of your sins and because

> your sinful nature was not yet cut away. Then
> God made you alive with Christ, for he forgave
> all our sins. <u>He canceled the record of the charges</u>
> <u>against us</u> and took it away by nailing it to the
> cross. (Colossians 2:13-14 NLT)

Notice here that what was canceled and nailed to the cross was not the law of God, but the record of the charges against us – in other words, our **sins** were nailed to the cross! It even says that specifically: "he forgave all our sins." And with our sins nailed to the cross, that means our eternal death penalty has been taken away! So, in effect, our **death penalty** was nailed to the cross, because Jesus paid our legal debt in our stead!

Here are some more translations of verse 14 that shine a truthful light on what has been canceled:

> having canceled the charge of our legal indebt-
> edness, which stood against us and condemned
> us; he has taken it away, nailing it to the cross.
> (Colossians 2:14 NIV)

> He erased the certificate of debt, with its obliga-
> tions, that was against us and opposed to us, and
> has taken it out of the way by nailing it to the
> cross. (Colossians 2:14 HCSB)

> having canceled out the certificate of debt con-
> sisting of decrees against us, which was hostile
> to us; and He has taken it out of the way, having
> nailed it to the cross.
> (Colossians 2:14 NASB)

Are you seeing the pattern here? It is not any law of God that has been nailed to the cross (because Jesus Himself said not the slightest bit of any law is done away with), but it is our own personal sins and the result of our sins that's been abolished, and that's **death**! Remember, "the wages of sin is death; but the gift of God is eternal life through Jesus Christ our Lord" (Romans 6:23 KJV).

By allowing Himself to be nailed to a piece of wood and die a horrible death, our Maker has paid our debt, the wages of sin for all of humanity. He has paid the death penalty for you, for me and for everyone the world has ever known or will know. If people would just glance at the very next verse, they'd get the complete thought on the matter:

> In this way, he disarmed the spiritual rulers and authorities. He shamed them publicly by his victory over them on the cross.
> (Colossians 2:15 NLT)

Jesus disarmed Satan and his evil demons by taking away the death penalty for billions of people! The devil, who was "a murderer from the beginning," has been on a mission to see all of God's children end up eternally dead. But with Jesus having paid the wages of sin in our stead, Satan's wretched plan of killing us all has been thwarted, with God providing the way to everlasting life for all men and women who take Him up on His offer. Thus, the devil's devious hold on humanity has been broken, and his captives have been set free from the prison of death. The dark forces of this world have therefore been smacked down and put to shame publicly.

Unfortunately, despite his being shamed, the devil is still around today, and he does not give up easily. He knows his ultimate fate is to be thrown in the lake of fire as we have discussed at great length in this book already. So now, he is still trying to kill as many of God's people as he can, and that's why he continues his deception through many churches, tricking Christian believers into thinking God's laws have been abolished, so they will eventually perish for eternity. All those excuses I listed previously that Christian pastors and believers have been pushing concerning the laws of God being no longer in force are nothing short of satanic deception. Remember, the former archangel Lucifer was perfect in his ways until iniquity, which is lawlessness, was found in him. And he is the chief promoter of every excuse not to follow the divine code.

The enemy doesn't care how he kills you. He just wants you dead. And he knows that if you continue to break God's laws willingly, the end result will be a searing trip into the lake of fire where sinners will be turned into ashes and dust. The New Testament clearly says if we continue to break God's laws after coming to the truth, the only thing we can expect is a trip into the fire that will annihilate us from existence:

> If we deliberately keep on sinning after we have
> received the knowledge of the truth, no sacrifice
> for sins is left, but only a fearful expectation of
> judgment and of raging fire that will consume the
> enemies of God. (Hebrews 10:26 NIV)

This is why it's so important for all of us to wake up out of this deception of Opposite World and get a firm grip on what sin actually is. It is the breaking of God's law! The law has not been nailed to the cross. Only our transgressions and the penalty for disobedience have been nailed there, as long as we start obeying the law and the God who wrote it with His own finger.

The ultimate fulfillment

Now, I know there are plenty of folks who tell themselves there's no possible way to keep God's laws, so they don't even bother trying. They also never ask themselves why God would in one breath say that if we love Him, we have to keep His commandments, but in the next breath, do away with them. Though many complain about the hundreds of instructions in the Old Testament, I try to get people to focus on just ten, the famous Ten Commandments. People have little problem today joining all kinds of ten-step programs to lose weight or quit smoking, drugs and alcohol, but they have a big objection to following a ten-step program that leads to eternal life. Go figure.

The key to understanding how people can (and will) follow the divine instructions is found in a series of three overlooked prophecies by Jesus Himself. Once we connect the statements together, a lightbulb will be switched on in your mind so you can finally see the process. The first one is a statement we've already read:

> "Do not think that I have come to abolish the
> Law or the Prophets; I have not come to abolish
> them but to fulfill them. (Matthew 5:17 NIV)

Now, as mentioned earlier, Jesus here is plainly stating that the laws written in the Torah are not done away with. They're very much in effect. But there's something more in this statement that most people miss, perhaps because they're not thinking spiritually. In the final words of this sentence, Jesus said He came to **fulfill** the laws. This means not only will He obey and perform the laws in His own personal life, but He is going to personally prompt millions of **other** people to be able and willing to follow the code as well. That's correct. He's going to get inside their hearts and minds and personally compel people to be obedient.

The other two statements from Jesus on this will help you understand what I mean. Here they are:

> "But this is the covenant that I will make with the house of Israel after those days, says the LORD: <u>I will put My law in their minds, and write it on their hearts</u>; and I will be their God, and they shall be My people.
> (Jeremiah 31:33 NKJV)

> I will give you a new heart and put a <u>new spirit within you</u>; I will remove your heart of stone and give you a heart of flesh. <u>I will place My Spirit within you and cause you to follow My statutes and carefully observe My ordinances</u>.
> (Ezekiel 36:26-27 HCSB)

Feel free to read those two portions of Scripture again, because you likely won't hear them discussed in church. Jesus is telling us that He will fulfill the law by putting His own Holy Spirit into people's minds and hearts so they'll no longer have any objection to obeying divine instructions. With God's own presence living inside them, they will **want** to obey the rules, and will gladly seek to learn and follow the laws of their Maker. This is already taking place now for the elect, those chosen by God to receive His Spirit before His return to Earth. But the verses in Jeremiah and Ezekiel are perhaps more directly focused on the future that's still ahead of us, after people have been raised in the Second Resurrection, the resurrection of judgment. It is after Jesus has returned to Earth to rule in person that people of all backgrounds will journey to Him, finally desiring to learn His instructions:

Many peoples will come and say, "Come, let
us go up to the mountain of the LORD, to the
temple of the God of Jacob. He will teach us his
ways, so that we may walk in his paths." The law
will go out from Zion, the word of the LORD
from Jerusalem. (Isaiah 2:3 NIV)

At that time, people will have their rebellious heart of stone removed, and in its place be given a heart that's responsive to the laws of God. Jesus said He will put His law in their minds and write it on their hearts. He said He will personally **cause** people to desire obedience to the instructions. Does this in any way sound like Jesus has done away with His own laws? Of course not. He wants **everyone** to eventually keep His instructions. He's so bent on it, that He is going to make it happen, despite the nonsense of "the laws are not meant for Christians" being shoveled on most churchgoers from countless deceivers in the pulpits.

When the presence of the Almighty is dwelling inside everyone, it will provide the ultimate fulfillment to the Ten Commandments. What I mean is that the instructions are not just rules by which we're meant to abide in this life, they are **promises** from God that we will actually be able to follow His laws in the future.

So, for example, when God says, "You shall not steal" in Exodus 20:15, Jesus is not merely telling us not to steal. He is promising us that, eventually, we won't be stealing anything or even wanting to steal, because His own Spirit will be dwelling inside us, preventing us from stealing!

It's like a father teaching his child to ride a bike. As the dad walks or jogs alongside his child who is learning to ride, he might say, "Don't worry, kiddo, you shall not fall." He's assuring his child that he or she won't fall, because he's there to prevent it from happening. "You shall not fall."

In the very same way, when God says that we shall not steal, murder or commit adultery, He is actually making a solemn promise to us that we won't be doing any of that kind of lawbreaking, because His Spirit, His divine presence, will be living inside us, prompting us to obey the eternal code! That is really what Jesus meant when He said He came to fulfill the law. It is He who is fulfilling it by putting His own divine presence inside us so that we **want** to obey Him, and can actually do so!

Another Jesus

Before closing this chapter, there's one final point that needs to be stressed. And that is how God views the many pastors who go to extraordinary lengths to convince people that the eternal laws are no longer in force, when Jesus said the opposite is true.

Readers should know that any minister who provides some excuse about the instructions of God being abolished are outright lying to you, and, in the words of the apostle Paul, are preaching "another Jesus:"

> But I fear that, as the serpent deceived Eve by his cunning, your minds may be seduced from a complete and pure devotion to Christ. For if a person comes and preaches another Jesus, whom we did not preach, or you receive a different spirit, which you had not received, or a different gospel, which you had not accepted, you put up with it splendidly! (2 Corinthians 11:3-4 HCSB)

How true that is today. Millions of churchgoing believers happily go along with the spirit of disobedience, the promotion of lawlessness, from their own ministers. Most don't even think twice about it. Paul gives a scathing indictment of these teachers and preachers, calling them "false apostles" who are actually working – knowingly or unknowingly – for Satan the devil:

> For such are false apostles, deceitful workers, transforming themselves into apostles of Christ. And no wonder! For Satan himself transforms himself into an angel of light. Therefore it is no great thing if his ministers also transform themselves into ministers of righteousness, whose end will be according to their works. (2 Corinthians 11:13-15 NKJV)

That's correct. Your Bible talks about ministers who claim to be representing the forces of light, the living Jesus, but they are, in reality, working for the dark angel who pretends to be an angel of light. When are believers going to wake up to this bold statement in Holy Scripture? The so-called "Christian" pastors who say the laws of God are done away with are actually doing the devil's work! They don't want people understanding the true purpose of their existence, and are actually promoting the ways that lead to death instead of life, the opposite of what God has intended.

It's not just the apostle Paul who blasted lawless ministers. Here's what Peter warned about deceivers infiltrating the true believers in Jesus:

> But false prophets also arose among the people, just as there will also be false teachers among you, who will secretly introduce destructive heresies ... (2 Peter 2:1 NASB)

And God Himself takes them to task repeatedly. Here's what the Creator said about deceptive pastors and priests, calling them His enemies, shepherds who actually feed on their own flock:

> "Therefore, <u>you shepherds,</u> hear the word of the LORD: As surely as I live, says the Sovereign LORD, you abandoned my flock and left them to be attacked by every wild animal. And though you were my shepherds, you didn't search for my sheep when they were lost. <u>You took care of yourselves and left the sheep to starve</u>. Therefore, you shepherds, hear the word of the LORD.
>
> This is what the Sovereign LORD says: <u>I now consider these shepherds my enemies</u>, and I will hold them responsible for what has happened to my flock. I will take away their right to feed the flock, and I will stop them from feeding themselves. I will rescue my flock from their mouths; the sheep will no longer be their prey. (Ezekiel 34:7-10 NLT)

And through the prophet Jeremiah, God squarely places the blame on the pastors for making His people turn into lost sheep:

> Woe be unto **the pastors** that **destroy and scatter the sheep of my pasture!** saith the LORD. (Jeremiah 23:1 KJV)

"My people have been lost sheep. Their shepherds have led them astray and turned them loose in the mountains. They have lost their way and can't remember how to get back to the sheepfold. All who found them devoured them. Their enemies said, 'We did nothing wrong in attacking them, for they sinned against the LORD, their true place of rest, and the hope of their ancestors.' (Jeremiah 50:6-7 NLT)

And to this day, pastors across the world are lying to the congregants in their churches by promising them eternal life by just believing in Jesus, without ever having to obey the laws that Jesus wrote:

You have discouraged the righteous with your lies ... . And you have encouraged the wicked by promising them life, even though they continue in their sins. (Ezekiel 13:22 NLT)

It should be more than clear by now. What is being taught by thousands of pastors who claim to be Christian is simply not Biblical. It is the opposite of what's revealed in God's Holy Word.

As we now know, the Bible says God's laws are truth, a delight and not a burden. It says all the laws are eternal. It says obedience to the laws is your very life. Jesus said if you wish to enter into life, "keep the commandments." He also said, "If you love me, keep my commandments." Scripture says anyone who claims to know God but doesn't obey God's commandments is a liar and the truth is not in him. The New Testament says it is not people who hear the law who are righteous in God's sight, but it's those who obey the law who will be declared righteous. It says those who practice lawlessness will be told by God to get away from Him, because He never knew them.

Here's the bottom line: God is not lawless. He's a Being who obeys the laws that He Himself wrote. He's not illegal in any sense of the word. It is the enemy, Satan the devil, who keeps broadcasting the opposite message that we no longer should keep God's law because the deceptive lawbreaker wants you dead. It is the Creator's holy law which reveals the difference between right and wrong, good and evil, light and darkness, righteousness and sin, life and death. Now that we finally know that the Bible defines sin as the breaking of God's law, it is high time that all of us looking to enter into life to do what Jesus instructed: "Keep the commandments."

Chapter Nine:
A time to hate

"Don't be a hater." I can't tell you how many times I've seen that phrase on television and the Internet recently. Celebrities say it frequently and the message is often emblazoned on T-shirts. Perhaps it's so popular because we live in a politically correct age when we're supposed to be accepting and even supportive of every idea under the sun, no matter how perverse and disturbing it may be.

There are even some people who make a big show about raising their children not to hate anything at anytime. While that may sound nice at first, there is a huge problem with it. I'll demonstrate my point by discussing a woman with whom I used to work at a TV news station. I'll call her Carolyn. Not because I'm trying to protect her identity, but because her name is actually Carolyn. On one afternoon, the staff of the station was treated to a buffet lunch, and all employees were lined up with plates in hand, selecting our favorite foods from the choices on the table.

I happened to be standing next to Carolyn, who was chattering on and on with pride about how she was raising her children not to hate **anything** in life. It was at that moment I asked her a three-word question that froze her in her tracks.

"What about evil?" I humbly suggested.

Carolyn was stunned. She just stood there silently with her eyes popping out of their sockets. She stared at me with a look of bewilderment, her jaw dropping as far as it could go. It was as if she had never heard of the word "evil," or the concept that it was perfectly OK to hate something – in this case, evil. Who knows? Maybe she herself was never taught that such a thing as evil even exists, and therefore she blew a gasket, unable to grasp what I was saying. Nevertheless, that simple question brought an end to the conversation.

I bring this up because there are millions of people who remain ignorant about what the Bible says about hate. They simply don't know, or intentionally don't wish to know, that God Himself despises many things and even hates certain people, declaring as much countless times throughout Scripture. Today's Christians in particular just don't want to deal with the fact that God Almighty is, at times, a hater. We all need to recognize that the Word of God boldly declares there indeed is "A time to love, and a time to hate." (Ecclesiastes 3:8 KJV)

Now, before I get into the meat of this chapter, I don't wish to mislead anyone. The Bible clearly has many verses describing the love of God. Here are just a few from John, the apostle whom Jesus loved:

> The one who does not love does not know God, for God is love. (1 John 4:8 NASB)

> If we love one another, God remains in us and His love is perfected in us. (1 John 4:12 HCSB)

> For the Father Himself loves you, because you have loved Me and have believed that I came from God. (John 16:27 HCSB)

And John also instructs us not to hate our brothers:

> If someone says, "I love God," and hates his brother, he is a liar; for the one who does not love his brother whom he has seen, cannot love God whom he has not seen. (1 John 4:20 NASB)

But, despite what is often preached in many churches today, the Bible never says God's love for us is unconditional, or that He loves all people at all times. In fact, as we shall see, God is a hater of many things. Scripture uses a variety of words to express this idea. In addition to "hate," we see terms including "abhor," "despise," "detest," "detestable" and "abomination" sprinkled throughout both the Old and New Testaments to describe the Creator's personal disgust for a wide variety of matters. So let's begin.

Hating evil

If you happen to be like my TV colleague Carolyn, you might be astonished to learn that in numerous instances, Scripture says it's OK to hate evil. As a matter of fact, it's beyond OK. We're actually commanded by the Almighty to despise it:

Hate evil and love good (Amos 5:15 HCSB)

The fear of the LORD is to hate evil (Proverbs 8:13 KJV)

Hate what is evil; cling to what is good.
(Romans 12:9 NIV)

You who love the LORD, hate evil! (Psalm 97:10 NKJV)

As we can see, hating evil is good and godly. If we're not hating evil, we stand in opposition to the divine instruction, and, thus, we are sinning, breaking the commandment. But what constitutes evil? What does God hate, and what should we be hating? The Bible provides the answers in extreme specificity:

The LORD hates six things; in fact, seven are detestable to Him: arrogant eyes, a lying tongue, hands that shed innocent blood, a heart that plots wicked schemes, feet eager to run to evil, a lying witness who gives false testimony, and one who stirs up trouble among brothers.
(Proverbs 6:16-19 HCSB)

Don't scheme against each other. Stop your love of telling lies that you swear are the truth. I hate all these things, says the LORD."
(Zechariah 8:17 NLT)

"You shall not eat any detestable thing.
(Deuteronomy 14:3 NASB)

"You must not sacrifice to the LORD your God an ox or sheep with a defect or any serious flaw, for that is detestable to the LORD your God.
(Deuteronomy 17:1 HCSB)

A detestable thing has been committed in Israel and in Jerusalem: Judah has desecrated the sanctuary the LORD loves by marrying women who worship a foreign god. (Malachi 2:11 NIV)

"If a man or woman among you in one of your towns that the LORD your God will give you is discovered doing evil in the sight of the LORD your God and violating His covenant and has gone to worship other gods by bowing down to the sun, moon, or all the stars in the sky—which I have forbidden— and if you are told or hear about it, you must investigate it thoroughly. If the report turns out to be true that this detestable thing has happened in Israel, you must bring out to your gates that man or woman who has done this evil thing and stone them to death.
(Deuteronomy 17:2-5 HCSB)

You must burn up the carved images of their gods. Don't covet the silver and gold on the images and take it for yourself, or else you will be ensnared by it, for it is abhorrent to the LORD your God. (Deuteronomy 7:25 HCSB)

In the Book of Proverbs, wisdom is personified by Scripture, and is shown to hate a variety of activities and characteristics:

I hate pride and arrogance, evil behavior and perverse speech. (Proverbs 8:13 NIV)

Often, the Bible juxtaposes what God hates with what He loves for the effect of highlighting the contrast:

"For I, the LORD, love justice; I hate robbery and wrongdoing. (Isaiah 61:8 NIV)

You love righteousness and hate wickedness (Psalm 45:7 NIV)

The LORD detests the use of dishonest scales, but he delights in accurate weights.
(Proverbs 11:1 NLT)

Lying lips are abomination to the LORD: but
they that deal truly are his delight.
(Proverbs 12:22 KJV)

The LORD detests the sacrifice of the wicked,
but the prayer of the upright pleases him.
(Proverbs 15:8 NIV)

The LORD detests the way of the wicked, but he
loves those who pursue righteousness.
(Proverbs 15:9 NIV)

The thoughts of the wicked are an abomination to
the LORD: but the words of the pure are pleasant
words. (Proverbs 15:26 KJV)

What comes as a surprise to many is that not only are wicked thoughts
and actions hateful to God, so are the people who engage in them:

The LORD examines the righteous, but the
wicked, those who love violence, he hates with
a passion. (Psalm 11:5 NIV)

Those with twisted minds are detestable to the
LORD, but those with blameless conduct are His
delight. (Proverbs 11:20 HCSB)

… for the devious are detestable to the LORD,
but He is a friend to the upright.
(Proverbs 3:32 HCSB)

He who justifies the wicked and he who
condemns the righteous, Both of them alike are
an abomination to the LORD.
(Proverbs 17:15 NASB)

A woman must not wear men's clothing, nor a
man wear women's clothing, for the LORD your
God detests anyone who does this.
(Deuteronomy 22:5 NIV)

... for you hate all who do evil. You will destroy
those who tell lies. The LORD detests murderers
and deceivers. (Psalm 5:5-6 NLT)

And God has placed in both the Old and New Testaments the fact that he hates one person in particular by name and his descendants:

> I have loved Jacob, and I hated Esau, and laid his mountains and his heritage waste for the dragons of the wilderness. (Malachi 1:2-3 KJV)

> They will be called a wicked country and the people the LORD has cursed forever.
> (Malachi 1:4 HCSB)

> As it is written, Jacob have I loved, but Esau have I hated. (Romans 9:13 KJV)

God's decision to hate certain individuals immediately brings up the question if the Creator is somehow unfair or unjust. And Scripture provides the answer:

> Are we saying, then, that God was unfair? Of course not! For God said to Moses, "I will show mercy to anyone I choose, and I will show compassion to anyone I choose." So it is God who decides to show mercy. We can neither choose it nor work for it. (Romans 9:14-16 NLT)

For those unfamiliar with the Bible, Esau is the twin brother of Jacob and grandson of Abraham. And Scripture says God had good reason to hate him:

> See that no one is sexually immoral, or is godless like Esau, who for a single meal sold his inheritance rights as the oldest son.
> (Hebrews 12:6 NIV)

Now, before you start feeling too sorry for Esau, God has plenty of hatred and disgust for His own rebellious people with whom He originally chose to have a loving relationship:

> My inheritance has become to me like a lion in the forest. She roars at me; therefore I hate her.
> (Jeremiah 12:8 NIV)

> Again and again I sent my servants the prophets, who said, 'Do not do this detestable thing that I hate!' But they did not listen or pay attention; they did not turn from their wickedness or stop burning incense to other gods. (Jeremiah 44:4-5 NIV)

Through the prophet Isaiah, God got so fed up with His people, He called them a smoke or a stench in his nostrils, depending on which translation of Scripture you're reading:

> All day long I opened my arms to a rebellious people. But they follow their own evil paths and their own crooked schemes. All day long they insult me to my face by worshiping idols in their sacred gardens. They burn incense on pagan altars. At night they go out among the graves, worshiping the dead. They eat the flesh of pigs and make stews with other forbidden foods. Yet they say to each other, 'Don't come too close or you will defile me! I am holier than you!' These people are a stench in my nostrils, an acrid smell that never goes away. (Isaiah 65:2-5 NLT)

He also slammed them for their pride:

> The Sovereign LORD has sworn by his own name, and this is what he, the LORD God of Heaven's Armies, says: "I despise the arrogance of Israel, and I hate their fortresses. I will give this city and everything in it to their enemies."
> (Amos 6:8 NLT)

God has even made it a divine promise that He will **hate us** if we don't follow His commands:

> "If in spite of all this you still refuse to listen and still remain hostile toward me ... I will destroy your pagan shrines and knock down your places of worship. I will leave your lifeless corpses piled on top of your lifeless idols, and I will despise you. (Leviticus 26:30 NLT)

When the Israelites were ending their forty years in the wilderness and were about to march into the Promised Land, God warned them numerous times not to adopt the pagan customs of the people who were already dwelling there, because He hates the practices fiercely:

> "When you enter the land the LORD your God is giving you, do not imitate the detestable customs of those nations. No one among you is to make his son or daughter pass through the fire, practice divination, tell fortunes, interpret omens, practice sorcery, cast spells, consult a medium or a familiar spirit, or inquire of the dead. Everyone who does these things is detestable to the LORD, and the LORD your God is driving out the nations before you because of these detestable things. You must be blameless before the LORD your God. (Deuteronomy 18:9-13 HCSB)

Unfortunately, the Israelites were true to their rebellious nature and went ahead with their abominations, including burning their own children in the Original Coal Kids Club, as we discussed earlier:

> They have built the high places of Baal in the Valley of Hinnom to make their sons and daughters pass through the fire to Molech— something I had not commanded them. I had never entertained the thought that they do this detestable act causing Judah to sin!
> (Jeremiah 32:35 HCSB)

Even Solomon, one of the wisest people ever, wasn't so smart when it came to enflaming God's disgust:

> On the Mount of Olives, east of Jerusalem, he even built a pagan shrine for Chemosh, the detestable god of Moab, and another for Molech, the detestable god of the Ammonites.
> (1 Kings 11:7 NLT)

Among the most revolting actions to God since the beginning of human existence has been the worship of the sun. People actually conducted (and many Christians today still conduct) "sunrise services," something which the Creator calls an abomination:

> Then he brought me into the inner courtyard of the LORD's Temple. At the entrance to the sanctuary, between the entry room and the bronze altar, there were about twenty-five men with their backs to the sanctuary of the LORD. They were facing east, bowing low to the ground, <u>worshiping the sun</u>!
>
> "Have you seen this, son of man?" he asked. "Is it nothing to the people of Judah that they commit these detestable sins, leading the whole nation into violence, thumbing their noses at me, and provoking my anger? Therefore, I will respond in fury. <u>I will neither pity nor spare them. And though they cry for mercy, I will not listen</u>."
> (Ezekiel 8:16-18 NLT)

The final portion of the above passage is worth highlighting. God has clearly said that when He pours out His anger to punish His people, He will neither pity nor spare them. And despite any cries for mercy, He won't be listening. Interestingly, it's not just in a time of disaster that God shuts off His hearing. Any and all prayers that we offer up on a daily basis are actually hated by the Almighty if we disregard His instructions:

> God detests the prayers of a person who ignores the law. (Proverbs 28:9 NLT)

That is not a misprint. You're reading it correctly. God can't stand our prayers if we refuse to obey His laws. Here's the same verse from another Bible version, just so you can see how consistent the thought is:

> One who turns away his ear from hearing the law,
> Even his prayer is an abomination. (Proverbs 28:9 NKJV)

What may be even more shocking to today's religious crowd is that God actually hates religious gatherings, even church services, when people are not obeying Him. Yes, folks, it's in your Bible:

"I hate, I despise your religious festivals; your
assemblies are a stench to me. ... Away with the
noise of your songs! I will not listen to the music
of your harps. But let justice roll on like a river,
righteousness like a never-failing stream!
(Amos 5:21-24 NIV)

The New Testament calls people who claim to know God but who
disobey His instructions not only detestable, but worthless as well:

They profess to know God, but by their deeds
they deny Him, being detestable and disobedient
and worthless for any good deed.
(Titus 1:16 NASB)

In condemning the religious leaders of His day, Jesus noted that what
people value highly in this world is strongly hated by God:

And He told them: "You are the ones who justify
yourselves in the sight of others, but God knows
your hearts. For what is highly admired by people
is revolting in God's sight.
(Luke 16:15 HCSB)

By now it should be abundantly clear to everyone that God's hatred
is sparked by our disobedience to His commands. He did not devise His
instructions just so that we can make every possible excuse to disregard
them.

Everyone should read the entirety of Psalm 119 to get the flavor of how
important it is to keep the instructions. The word "hate" appears numerous
times in this ancient song, compelling us to stick to the Maker's rules:

From Your precepts I get understanding;
Therefore I hate every false way.
(Psalm 119:104 NASB)

I hate those who are double-minded,
But I love Your law. (Psalm 119:113 NASB)

Therefore I esteem right all Your precepts
concerning everything,
I hate every false way. (Psalm 119:128 NASB)

> I hate and despise falsehood,
> But I love Your law. (Psalm 119:163 NASB)

The prophet Ezekiel has provided one of the most stinging indictments direct from God on the activities He really hates, for the Creator was fed up with the actions of His own people. God had this prophet go public to spill the beans on their wretched sins, which resulted in their destruction:

> "Son of man, are you ready to judge Jerusalem? Are you ready to judge this city of murderers? Publicly denounce her detestable sins, and give her this message from the Sovereign LORD: O city of murderers, doomed and damned—city of idols, filthy and foul—you are guilty because of the blood you have shed. You are defiled because of the idols you have made. Your day of destruction has come! You have reached the end of your years. I will make you an object of mockery throughout the world.
>
> O infamous city, filled with confusion, you will be mocked by people far and near.
>
> "Every leader in Israel who lives within your walls is bent on murder. Fathers and mothers are treated with contempt. Foreigners are forced to pay for protection. Orphans and widows are wronged and oppressed among you.
>
> You despise my holy things and violate my Sabbath days of rest. People accuse others falsely and send them to their death. You are filled with idol worshipers and people who do obscene things.
>
> Men sleep with their fathers' wives and have intercourse with women who are menstruating. Within your walls live men who commit adultery with their neighbors' wives, who defile their daughters-in-law, or who rape their own sisters. There are hired murderers, loan racketeers, and extortioners everywhere. They never even think

of me and my commands, says the Sovereign LORD.

"But now I clap my hands in indignation over your dishonest gain and bloodshed. How strong and courageous will you be in my day of reckoning? I, the LORD, have spoken, and I will do what I said. I will scatter you among the nations and purge you of your wickedness. And when I have been dishonored among the nations because of you, you will know that I am the LORD." (Ezekiel 22:2-16 NLT)

All those despicable actions – from financial and sexual sins to religious crimes such as idol worship and working on the Sabbath – were committed in ancient times, and, sadly, all of them are being committed today. It's why God is filled with rage and is coming back to punish the disobedient. Remember, the Bible is a timeless book, and Jesus Christ is the same yesterday, today and forever. The reason why our Designer has filled Scripture with what He hates is to prompt us to stop doing those reprehensible actions so we can come to receive the gift of God, which is eternal life! We must never forget the command of Jesus:

if you want to receive eternal life, keep the commandments (Matthew 19:17 NLT)

Again through the prophet Ezekiel, Jesus made it clear what would happen to wicked people who repent and follow the instructions, as well as the outcome for righteous people who abandon obedience:

"Now if the wicked person turns from all the sins he has committed, keeps all My statutes, and does what is just and right, he will certainly live; he will not die. None of the transgressions he has committed will be held against him. He will live because of the righteousness he has practiced.

Do I take any pleasure in the death of the wicked?" This is the declaration of the Lord GOD. "Instead, don't I take pleasure when he turns from his ways and lives?

But when a righteous person turns from his righteousness and practices iniquity, committing the same detestable acts that the wicked do, will he live? None of the righteous acts he did will be remembered. He will die because of the treachery he has engaged in and the sin he has committed.

"But you say, 'The Lord's way isn't fair.' Now listen, house of Israel: Is it My way that is unfair? Instead, isn't it your ways that are unfair?

When a righteous person turns from his righteousness and practices iniquity, he will die for this. He will die because of the iniquity he has practiced.

But if a wicked person turns from the wickedness he has committed and does what is just and right, he will preserve his life. He will certainly live because he thought it over and turned from all the transgressions he had committed; he will not die.

But the house of Israel says, 'The Lord's way isn't fair.' Is it My ways that are unfair, house of Israel? Instead, isn't it your ways that are unfair?

"Therefore, house of Israel, I will judge each one of you according to his ways." This is the declaration of the Lord GOD. "Repent and turn from all your transgressions, so they will not be a stumbling block that causes your punishment. Throw off all the transgressions you have committed, and get yourselves a new heart and a new spirit. Why should you die, house of Israel? For I take no pleasure in anyone's death." This is the declaration of the Lord GOD. "So repent and live! (Ezekiel 18:21-32 HCSB)

The above passage sums up the message of the Bible. If we continue to disobey God's instructions, we will be dead forever. But if we repent of the sins that God hates, all those vile actions not only listed in this chapter but in the entire Bible, we will live forever. It's that simple, and the choice is yours. So please remember, it's absolutely fine to hate, when we're hating that which God despises. As the Maker of all things has commanded us: "Hate evil and love good." (Amos 5:15 HCSB) God is a hater of the thoughts and actions that result in our eternal death. He's begging us to choose life. Everlasting life.

Chapter Ten:
Light up the darkness

At this point, I would like to take you to a place in your Bible study and your life to which you may never have ventured, or even thought about going. It is a shining place of peace and comfort, beaming with all the brilliance and foreknowledge of the Creator Himself. It is a place of glorious light and also one of thick darkness, both physical and spiritual.

It's a subject that will shed divine light on the entire plan of God, especially why He takes certain actions, helping you to further understand and appreciate what God intended to do not only with His original creation, but what He is actively doing right now on a daily basis in your personal life and in the lives of every human being.

The subject matter is of deep significance, revealing the reasons behind the actions of God from the beginning to the end. They become clear with the daily appearance of light, and the daily appearance of darkness. I have never written about this before, but have thought about it and studied it extensively. I'm finally putting the words on the page now, and I pray you'll stick with this entire chapter so you can finally see the light.

We are going to examine a region of God's creation that I believe does not receive its deserved attention. We are going to probe God's creation of light, the separation of light from the darkness, and how the Bible deals with light and darkness from Genesis through Revelation. It will open your eyes to matters as simple as when a day really begins, to more significant issues such as what God has in store for you in your very own future. What you learn here may explode the strongly held views that have held your mind in captivity for years. And I say this to all those who call themselves Christian, myself included. So take a deep breath, and be patient as we light up the darkness.

The initial part of this study will focus on something that ostensibly seems very simple, but it has been turned upside down by this world, and continues to remain in confusion at this very moment. And that, my friends, is a three-letter word found originally in Genesis. The word I'm referring to is **day**.

When people see or hear the term "day," they probably give little thought to it, because they think they already understand what a day is – when it begins, when it ends, and what takes place during a day. But what I'm about to show you from scores of Bible references is that the time period that we call day is something very different than we're all used to. Its true spiritual significance can only become clear when we understand not only when a day begins, but what it represents concerning God's ultimate plan for a time coming very soon when only the light of day exists, and night does not. Yes, there will be an everlasting age where there is no more darkness, no more death, no more sorrow, no more crying, no more pain and no more evil of any kind. That time is called the kingdom of God.

So let's jump into this thing that most of us take for granted: the day.

The beginning and the end

The first issue I'd like to address is the beginning and end of a day. After all, when does a day really commence? And when is it completed?

For billions of people on the planet now, the day officially starts sometime in the dead of the night, when it's very dark. We call it midnight, and it's twelve hours before or after the time when the sun is at its highest point in the sky, which, of course, is called noon.

For many others who claim to follow the Bible, the day starts at sunset, when the sun goes down below the horizon in the late afternoon. In our modern world, millions of Jews and even some Christians reckon each day from sunset to sunset. So their Sabbath day observances, for example, actually begin on Friday evening at sunset, and conclude the following evening, Saturday evening, at sunset.

But is this marking of the passage of days the way it began in the Bible? Is it the way intended by God?

As shocking as this may sound, the answer is a resounding **no**. If you want to know the Bible truth of the matter and you have the gonads to investigate what God's Word plainly says – even if it goes against what your personal belief and church tradition have been for countless years – then please continue reading, because the answer will become overwhelmingly obvious when we just accept the words that are on the pages of the Bible. This is going to take some time, because millions of people hold an opposite view, and I want to make sure I don't gloss over any concern they might have. So please make yourself comfortable.

At the very outset, we all need to admit that the Bible does not contain any explicit statement from God declaring something to the effect of: "You shall start each day at such and such a time." It's just not there. Thus, the only way we can determine the intended starting point and ending point for each day is to examine the entire scope of Scripture to see what the Bible says for itself on matters relating to the day. And when I say the entire scope, I mean the whole enchilada of the Bible, because far too many people try to base a whole doctrine on a few ambiguous verses.

When we just read the words on the pages of the Old and New Testaments and actually believe them, it becomes as clear as day that days begin neither at midnight nor at sunset. That's correct. Not at sunset. As astonishing as it may sound, each new day, according to the Word of God, actually begins and ends with **light**, not darkness. As you read this entire chapter, especially the New Testament references, this will be proven beyond the shadow of a doubt.

Let there be light

The best place to start looking into this matter is right in the beginning. And by the beginning, I mean the Beginning. The very start of the Bible where the first words tell us:

> "In the beginning, God created the heavens and
> the earth." (Genesis 1:1 NLT)

What we know from the next verse is that the situation was very dark, without a sliver of light over our planet:

The earth was formless and empty, and darkness covered the deep waters. And the Spirit of God was hovering over the surface of the waters. (Genesis 1:2 NLT)

But then things suddenly changed for the brighter.

Then God said, "Let there be light," and there was light. (Genesis 1:3 NLT)

Here, just three verses into the Bible, an illumination of divine proportions changed the whole scene from one of darkness to one of light, as God Himself commenced His work by making light shine.

And God saw that the light was good. Then he separated the light from the darkness. (Genesis 1:4 NLT)

This fourth verse is one of the most important and overlooked Scriptures in the entire Bible concerning the revealing of God's spiritual plan, and I'll explain why in-depth later in this chapter. But for now, I wish to focus on the creation of the day itself. Divine action was taken by the Creator to separate the light from the darkness, and that's when God attached a name to both the light as well as the darkness.

God called the light "day" and the darkness "night." (Genesis 1:5 NLT)

Here in easy-to-understand language is the very first indicator that a day starts with the light, because God actually slapped a name on the light, labeling it "**day**." Notice He did not call evening "day" and he did not call the dark time of midnight "day." He called the **light** "day." So even if we had no other verses of the Bible discussing the matter, the obvious answer to the question of when does a day begin would have to be with "the light." All the time when God was creating this light and giving it a name is when time and days as we know them began.

Not only does God call the light "day," we also see that darkness has its own, very different name, and that, of course, is "night." The end of the light is actually the beginning of "night." I know it sounds simple, and that's because it truly is simple. God means what He says. And He calls light "day," and darkness He calls "night."

As the story of the first week of creation continues to unfold through the first and second chapters of Genesis, we see a pattern emerging that confirms days start with light, and not with darkness.

From the rest of that very same verse 5 in which God was working, calling the light by the name of day and darkness by the name of night, we discover the demarcation point for the first day.

> And evening passed and morning came, marking
> the first day. (Genesis 1:5 NLT)

Here we have one of the clearest, yet most grossly misunderstood, statements in Scripture concerning the divine timetable of days.

The Scripture says, "And evening passed and morning came, marking the first day." It means exactly what it says, folks. After God spent His time creating by saying, "Let there be light," the Bible says that evening passed and then morning came, marking the first day. Evening came **after** God had created the light. Therefore, the clock here on Planet Earth started ticking the moment God created the light which He called "day." The daylight hours faded into evening. That's when evening passed and "night" began with the darkness. Finally, when the next morning arrived at first light, that signified the completion of the very first 24-hour day. The morning light marked the completion of Day One and the dawn of Day Two.

Though the precise wording of Genesis 1:5 varies slightly from one Bible translation to another, the meaning is very clear when we keep in mind that evening came after God spent His initial time creating light. Here are some of the translations of the verse:

> And evening passed and morning came, marking
> the first day. (Genesis 1:5 NLT)
>
> Evening came and then morning: the first day.
> (Genesis 1:5 HCSB)
>
> And there was evening, and there was morning –
> the first day. (Genesis 1:5 NIV)
>
> And there was evening and there was morning,
> one day. (Genesis 1:5 ASV)
>
> and there is an evening, and there is a morning –
> day one. (Genesis 1:5 YLT)

> And the evening and the morning were the first
> day. (Genesis 1:5 KJV)

The pattern and wording in each Bible translation remain consistent through the second, third, fourth, fifth and sixth days of the week. They are found respectively in verses 8, 13, 19, 23 and 31. By the time the seventh day is mentioned at the start of Genesis Chapter Two, the mentions of the evening and morning are no longer included in Scripture.

Now to be fair, I have heard from some people who read the King James or New King James Version of the Bible, both of which state "the evening and the morning were the first day." And they claim that such wording demonstrates that days start in the evening, and not in the morning. Their thinking is that the Bible mentions evening before morning, and indicates the first day commenced at evening. I can certainly understand this line of thinking, so let's delve into this suggestion.

Here it is again from the most popular Bible translation, the King James Version:

> And God called the light Day, and the darkness
> he called Night. And the evening and the morning
> were the first day. (Genesis 1:5 KJV)

Let's first notice what the verse does **not** say. It does not say, "And the evening and the morning **and all afternoon** were the first day."

I bring this up because many people somehow (probably unintentionally) alter the meaning of the word "morning" in their mind, morphing it into a very long time period that lasts all day long, some twelve hours, all the way until darkness arrives again. Perhaps they think that any presence of light, even at three o'clock in the afternoon, means "morning." It doesn't mean that at all. Morning means morning, commencing at first light. It does not mean afternoon, and it does not last twelve hours.

It starts with the arrival of light at dawn and lasts until noon, when the sun reaches its highest point in the sky at any given longitude. Morning is translated from the Hebrew word "boqer." There is a very different Hebrew word that means day or daytime, and that word is "yom." In English we have separate words for "morning" and "day," and there are separate words for them in Hebrew as well, since they don't mean the same thing. The word "evening" comes from the Hebrew word "ereb."

So upon close inspection, what the King James Version is saying actually agrees with all the other translations. It is telling us that "morning" is the cutoff time, specifically designating the end of the 24-hour day.

Remember, the first half of Genesis 1:5 talks about God calling the light "day" and the darkness "night." Yet, almost inexplicably, the people who suggest days start with the darkness ignore this crucial first part of the verse. They somehow blot out of their head all the time that God created the light, the time He saw that it was good, and that He named the light "day." They simply don't account for that time of light that God called "day," even though it's prominently displayed right there at the very start of the Bible.

This is important to remember: God began His time of working by making light shine. Later on, evening came **after the light of day** that God had just created.

And, **after hours of darkness** that God Himself called "night," there was **morning** when the light returned, marking the completion of Day One, the very first day. Yes, it's really this simple. A day does not begin with twelve hours of darkness. It begins with the light, just as God instituted at creation.

As creation week continued, note that on the fourth day:

> Then God said, "Let lights appear in the sky to separate the day from the night. Let them be signs to mark the seasons, days, and years. Let these lights in the sky shine down on the earth." And that is what happened.
>
> God made two great lights – the larger one to govern the day, and the smaller one to govern the night. He also made the stars. God set these lights in the sky to light the earth, to govern the day and night, and to separate the light from the darkness. And God saw that it was good. And evening passed and morning came, marking the fourth day. (Genesis 1:14-19 NLT)

In these verses, notice how days are always mentioned before night, and light is mentioned before darkness! This is the pattern of how days are to be measured. Verse 14 even specifies that point, saying that not only are the two lights in the sky (the sun and moon) to mark seasons and years, but it also puts the words "days" in the same sentence! And the larger light, the sun, is mentioned to govern the day before the smaller light, the moon, governs the night. So many people miss this.

Now, I suspect a few of you may think I've gone off the deep end with this "morning day" notion, but some of the world's most respected Bible scholars have stated the same thing long before I ever came on the scene.

Among the most famous proponents of the morning day is Roland de Vaux, the highly acclaimed French archaeologist who led the team that initially worked on the Dead Sea Scrolls in the 1950s. He was director of the Ecole Biblique (Biblical School) in East Jerusalem, and oversaw research on the scrolls. He subsequently wrote the Biblical classic "Ancient Israel," in which he described the details of everyday life among God's people. In his book, de Vaux makes it very plain that the day starts at dawn:

> In Israel, the day was for a long time reckoned from morning to morning. When they wanted to indicate the whole length of a day of twenty-four hours, they said 'day and night' or some such phrase, putting the day first: Scores of references could be quoted ... This suggests that they reckoned the day starting from the morning, and it was in fact the morning, with the creation of light, that the world began; the distinction of day and night, and time too, began on a morning ... The opposite conclusion has been drawn from the refrain which punctuates the story of Creation: 'There was an evening and there was a morning, the first, second, etc., day'; this phrase, however, coming after the description of each creative work (which clearly happens during the period of light), indicates rather the vacant time till the morning, the end of a day and the beginning of the next work.
>
> (Roland de Vaux, "Ancient Israel" (McGraw-Hill, 1961), p. 181.)

The morning after

Beyond the pattern of days beginning at dawn found in the first week of creation, the book of Genesis also contains the famous story of Abraham's nephew, Lot, having sex with his two daughters. Perhaps because the theme of incest is so startling, many people overlook that this event also suggests a morning day. The events took place shortly after God had firebombed the family's city of Sodom, and the three survivors fled to the region to live inside a cave in the mountains without Lot's wife, who had been turned into a pillar of salt. Here are the relative verses of the story:

> So they made their father drink wine that night.
> And the firstborn went in and lay with her father,
> and he did not know when she lay down or when
> she arose. It happened on the <u>next day</u> that the
> firstborn said to the younger, "Indeed I lay with
> my father <u>last night</u>; let us make him drink wine
> <u>tonight</u> also, and you go in and lie with him,
> that we may preserve the lineage of our father."
> (Genesis 19:33-34 NKJV)

The phrase "the next day" is translated in other Bibles as "on the following day," "on the morrow" and "the next morning." It seems obvious from this story, no matter how disturbing it may be, that the "next day" began with the morning light, not at sundown.

A similar reckoning of time is found in the Old Testament story of a Levite who took a concubine in the book of Judges. At some point, the concubine became unfaithful to the man and went back home to live with her father. Four months later the man came to visit the gal's dad, hoping to reconcile with his woman. As you read the following verses, please pay close attention to the references of time, and when the next day actually begins:

> Now his father-in-law, the young woman's father,
> detained him; and he stayed with him <u>three days</u>.
> So they ate and drank and lodged there.

Then it came to pass <u>on the fourth day that they arose early in the morning</u>, and he stood to depart; but the young woman's father said to his son-in-law, "Refresh your heart with a morsel of bread, and afterward go your way." So they sat down, and the two of them ate and drank together. Then the young woman's father said to the man, "Please be content to stay <u>all night</u>, and let your heart be merry." And when the man stood to depart, his father-in-law urged him; so he lodged there again.

Then he <u>arose early in the morning on the fifth day</u> to depart, but the young woman's father said, "Please refresh your heart." So they delayed until <u>afternoon</u>; and both of them ate.

And when the man stood to depart – he and his concubine and his servant – his father-in-law, the young woman's father, said to him, "Look, <u>the day is now drawing toward evening</u>; please <u>spend the night</u>. See, <u>the day is coming to an end</u>; lodge here, that your heart may be merry. <u>Tomorrow</u> go your way <u>early</u>, so that you may get home." (Judges 19:4-9 NKJV)

Later in the same chapter, some wicked men actually gang-raped the concubine, and the account leans toward a day beginning in the morning:

... and they knew her, and abused her all the night <u>until the morning</u>: and <u>when the day began to spring</u>, they let her go. Then came the woman in the <u>dawning of the day</u>, and fell down at the door of the man's house where her lord was, till it was <u>light</u>. (Judges 19:25-26 KJV)

And in the early days of Israel's monarchy, King Saul actually tried to hunt down and kill David, the man who would succeed him as the nation's ruler. As we see in the following verse, "tomorrow" begins in the morning:

> Saul also sent messengers to David's house to
> watch him and to kill him <u>in the morning</u>. And
> Michal, David's wife, told him, saying, "If you
> do not save your life tonight, <u>tomorrow</u> you will
> be killed." (1 Samuel 19:11 NKJV)

These accounts more than suggest that each next day commences early in the morning at daybreak. Remember, the Bible does agree with itself, and we'll see that as we continue to read the overwhelming evidence proving morning days in the rest of Scripture.

Moses, manna, and the Sabbath

One of the most instructive parts in the Old Testament demonstrating how days begin with the morning light instead of sunset is found in Exodus, shortly after the Israelites made their great escape from Egyptian slavery.

You may already know that God miraculously fed His people each day for forty years with a mysterious bread-like food called "manna." This word "manna" is Hebrew and literally means "what is it?" While no one today knows for sure what exactly it was, the Bible notes, "it was like white coriander seed, and the taste of it was like wafers made with honey." (Exodus 16:31 NKJV)

God used this manna and the time of its collection each morning to test the Israelites to see if they were going to follow His laws. In this case, it was whether or not they would obey the instruction to rest on the Sabbath day.

There in the barren wilderness, out in the middle of nowhere when God had their full attention without any distractions, Moses informed them of when their day of rest was scheduled to take place. He quoted God Himself, so it was not the personal opinion of Moses. Here's how Scripture records it:

> So they gathered it <u>every morning</u>, every man
> according to his need. And when the sun became
> hot, it melted.

> And so it was, on the sixth day, that they gathered twice as much bread, two omers for each one. And all the rulers of the congregation came and told Moses.
>
> Then he said to them, "This is what the LORD has said: 'Tomorrow is a Sabbath rest, a holy Sabbath to the LORD. Bake what you will bake today, and boil what you will boil; and lay up for yourselves all that remains, to be kept until morning.'"
>
> So they laid it up till morning, as Moses commanded; and it did not stink, nor were there any worms in it.
>
> Then Moses said, "Eat that today, for today is a Sabbath to the LORD; today you will not find it in the field.
>
> "Six days you shall gather it, but on the seventh day, the Sabbath, there will be none."
> (Exodus 16:21-26 NKJV)

So, here we have Moses initially talking to the people on the sixth day of the week, what we call Friday on our modern calendar. He told them that God said **tomorrow** is the day of rest called the Sabbath, so get all the baking and boiling done today, to be kept until **morning**.

Please notice that God did not say anything about evening, sunset, darkness or tonight in this instruction. He did **not** say, "Get all your baking and boiling done today, because tonight at evening starts the Sabbath."

The quote specifically says for them to get all their baking and boiling done that day, and for them to store it all up until the **morning**. Why the morning? Because dawn is the moment when the next day, the Sabbath, was starting, and they were not permitted to do any more work.

That Saturday morning, when the Sabbath commenced, Scripture says the manna still smelled fresh and had no worms in it. Not only that, the Bible outright declares through the mouth of Moses that once morning dawned, that moment was the start of the Sabbath day, not the night before.

Read this portion again:

> So they laid it up till <u>morning</u> ... . Then Moses said, "Eat that <u>today</u>, for <u>today</u> is a Sabbath to the LORD; today you will not find it in the field. (Exodus 16:24-25 NKJV)

Remember, the people had gathered a double portion of manna on Friday, because there would be zilch on Saturday. So they consumed half of that stockpile on Friday, the sixth day of the week. As for the remainder of their collected food, they baked or boiled it throughout that sixth day of the week to be their meals for Saturday, the Sabbath day. And the Bible specifically says God had commanded the people eat the leftovers, the second half of their Friday collection of manna on Saturday, **after the light of morning** had broken. The light of morning is the cutoff point for when each day ends and a new one begins.

Day of sacrifice

When it comes to sacrificing animals, many people today are surprised that the ancient Israelites actually grilled and ate most of the meat from the slain animals. But beyond that, the Torah provides more evidence of days beginning in the morning, with red-letter quotes from God concerning eating the meat. Here's an example:

> "If you bring an offering to fulfill a vow or as a voluntary offering, the meat must be eaten on the same day the sacrifice is offered, but whatever is left over may be eaten on the <u>second day</u>. (Leviticus 7:16 NLT)

And just when does this second day begin? Compare what God Himself says in this same book of Leviticus concerning a thanksgiving offering:

> When you bring a thanksgiving offering to the LORD, sacrifice it properly so you will be accepted. Eat the entire sacrificial animal on the day it is presented. Do not leave any of it until the <u>next morning</u>. I am the LORD. (Leviticus 22:29-30 NLT)

If the Bible is consistent, and it is, "the second day" apparently begins at the "next morning," otherwise the text would have stated something to the effect of, "Do not leave any of the meat until evening," or "until sunset."

Samuele Bacchiocchi, Ph.D., a Seventh-day Sabbath-keeping author and professor at Andrews University in Michigan before his death, noted concerning these instructions:

> What the two laws are saying is that while the flesh of the thanksgiving sacrifice was to be eaten only on the same day the sacrifice was made, that is, until the morning when the new day began, the flesh of the votive sacrifice could be eaten also "on the morrow," that is, after the morning which marked the end of the day in which the sacrifice was made. Both laws, then, suggest that the morning marked the end of a day and the beginning of a new day.
> (Samuele Bacchiocchi, "The Time of the Crucifixion and the Resurrection" http://www.biblicalperspectives.com/books/crucifixion/4.html)

Annual holy days

Now, I know what many of you might be wondering at this point: "What about some of God's annual holy days? Doesn't the Bible specifically state that they are to be observed from evening to evening?" Indeed it does for a couple of the celebrations, but certainly **not all** of them, and there are a variety of possible explanations for the evening-to-evening exceptions.

In the springtime, during the first month of the Hebrew calendar, the Passover and adjacent Feast of Unleavened Bread take place, and followers of God are instructed:

> 'In the first month, on the fourteenth day of the month at evening, you shall eat unleavened bread, until the twenty-first day of the month at evening. (Exodus 12:18 NKJV)

In the fall, in the seventh month, the Day of Atonement (called Yom Kippur in Hebrew) takes place, and the Bible specifically instructs:

> "It shall be to you a sabbath of solemn rest, and
> you shall afflict your souls; on the ninth day of
> the month at evening, from evening to evening,
> you shall celebrate your sabbath."
> (Leviticus 23:32 NKJV)

I can certainly understand why many people rush to these two verses and assert something like, "See?! The words on the page show us that every single day starts in the evening!"

But do they actually say that? As a matter of fact, they don't. Let's be clear. These two verses do not say anything specifying when days in general begin or end. They are ambiguous at best. They are merely telling when to observe two of God's festivals. The very fact that they mention evening here while other annual Sabbaths such as Pentecost or the Feast of Tabernacles (or even typical calendar days) do not mention evening suggest they're an exception to the pattern of the morning day which had long been established since creation week!

Day of Atonement

Let's look at the Day of Atonement to help you understand what I mean. Here's what the Bible says about it in the Torah:

> "Also the <u>tenth day</u> of this seventh month shall
> be the Day of Atonement. It shall be a holy
> convocation for you; you shall afflict your souls,
> and offer an offering made by fire to the LORD.

> "And you shall do no work on that same day, for
> it is the Day of Atonement, to make atonement
> for you before the LORD your God.

> "For any person who is not afflicted in soul on
> that same day shall be cut off from his people.

> "And any person who does any work on that
> same day, that person I will destroy from among
> his people.

"You shall do no manner of work; it shall be a statute forever throughout your generations in all your dwellings.

"It shall be to you a sabbath of solemn rest, and you shall afflict your souls; on the <u>ninth day</u> of the month <u>at evening, from evening to evening,</u> you shall celebrate your sabbath."
(Leviticus 23:27-32 NKJV)

God places the Day of Atonement on the tenth day of the month, but interestingly, it's commanded to be observed from the ninth day of the month at sunset, to the following evening, the evening of the tenth. Many people think this is saying the ninth day of the month ends at sundown and that's when the tenth day of the month begins. But those words are simply not on the page. Again, the very fact that two different calendar days – the ninth and the tenth – are mentioned instead of one calendar day is more proof that there's a calendar-day change between the start and end of this Atonement festival.

To put this in modern perspective, if you're renting a car or a moving truck for a 24-hour period, you actually rent it over two calendar days. Let's say you need a rental vehicle from 6 p.m. on the ninth day of the month until the following evening, 6 p.m., on the tenth day of the month. That's a one-day, 24-hour period, but there is a change in the calendar day from the ninth to the tenth of the month in the midst of the rental. In our modern age, the day change takes place at midnight. But in ancient Israel, the calendar-day change for the Day of Atonement would have been at sunrise!

Again, there are **two** calendar days mentioned for this holy day. The ninth and the tenth! If every single day truly started at sunset in the evening, there would be absolutely no need to tell us to observe the day from evening to evening, since everyone would already be aware that **all** days began at sundown. If such were the case, Scripture would just say to observe it on the tenth of the month, without any extra language about observing it from evening to evening. The reason the evening is mentioned for Atonement and not for the Feast of Tabernacles, for instance, is because Tabernacles follows the general rule of days beginning at sunrise, and the time of Atonement observance is something out of the norm.

Now, why might God be instructing the Day of Atonement to be observed from evening to evening instead of morning to morning? Let's remember that God commands His people to afflict their souls, and this is understood to mean going without eating and drinking for 24 hours. It's a full day's worth of fasting. The New Testament even refers to this holy day as "the fast" in Acts 27:9.

So, by having this holy day begin on the previous calendar day of the ninth day of the month at sundown, it means by the next morning, when people are awake, they would already be hungry. For this annual Sabbath, God actually wants people to have some sense of hunger, afflicting their souls, during the time they're awake. By commanding them to stop eating at sunset from the previous day is a guarantee they'd be afflicted with hunger pangs all through their waking hours on the tenth day. Otherwise, if the festival started at sunrise, people could have eaten all through the night and then not be quite as famished throughout that tenth day.

Passover and Unleavened Bread

What about the festivals of Passover and Unleavened Bread? Why are they commanded to be observed with an evening start time? Let's look again at what the Bible actually says:

> 'In the first month, on the fourteenth day of the month at evening, you shall eat unleavened bread, until the twenty-first day of the month at evening. (Exodus 12:18 NKJV)

First of all, nowhere here does it state that days either begin or end "at evening." Those words are not on the page. It specifically notes that the fourteenth day of the month at evening is when we are to begin eating unleavened bread. And we're supposed to continue eating the unleavened bread until evening time on the twenty-first day of the month. It's as simple as that. Again, when we just read the words on the page, without injecting anything else into it, it's only telling us when we're supposed to eat unleavened bread. It has nothing to do with when days begin or end, and there'd be no need for that information if every single day started at sundown.

If God gave us this command this very year for the first time, you'd understand Him clearly if He said, "On the fourteenth day of the month at 6 p.m., you shall eat unleavened bread, until the twenty-first day of the month at 6 p.m." You would easily understand that God is not telling you when to start or end calendar days. You'd realize He is merely telling you the time of day and the duration of time that He wants you to eat unleavened bread. From 6 p.m. on the fourteenth, until 6 p.m. on the twenty-first.

Regarding the Passover lamb itself, Scripture says: "And ye shall keep it up until the fourteenth day of the same month: and the whole assembly of the congregation of Israel shall <u>kill it in the evening</u>" (Exodus 12:6 KJV). The time frame is repeated in Leviticus 23:5: "In the fourteenth day of the first month at even is the LORD'S passover." (KJV)

While God in the Old Testament does not specify the reason why the Passsover lamb is slain in the evening of the fourteenth day of the month and the unleavened bread is to be eaten starting that same day "on the fourteenth day of the month at evening," it all becomes clear in the New Testament. Jesus, who is the true Passover Lamb of God (1 Corinthians 5:7), was slain in the late afternoon on that very same fourteenth day of the first month!

And we're to begin eating the unleavened bread at evening to commemorate the time frame when Jesus was slain and subsequently placed in the grave. The Feasts of Passover and Unleavened Bread actually focus on the events of Jesus' death in the first century, and how the sins of all humanity became forgiven during this very important time in history. It has nothing to do with the starting time of calendar days or dates.

Jesus, like the Passover lamb of ancient Israel, was slain on the fourteenth day of the first month of the Hebrew calendar at the time, not in the morning, but in the later part of the day, estimated by most people to be about 3 p.m.

Here are two Bible versions of a single verse in the gospel of Matthew concerning the approximate time of day in the moments before Jesus died:

> And about the ninth hour Jesus cried out with a loud voice, saying, "Eli, Eli, lama sabachthani?" that is, "My God, My God, why have You forsaken Me?" (Matthew 27:46 NKJV)

> About three in the afternoon Jesus cried out
> in a loud voice, "Eli, Eli, lemasabachthani?"
> (which means "My God, my God, why have you
> forsaken me?"). (Matthew 27:46 NIV)

It's important to note that the ninth hour of the day is "about three in the afternoon." And why on Earth is the ninth hour actually 3 p.m.? Because time itself was **reckoned from sunrise!** People in the time of Jesus were still counting the hours from the rising of the sun, which is yet more proof that days themselves begin with the light, not darkness!

One final note concerning the mentions of the Day of Atonement and the Feast of Unleavened Bread. There is another theory why the Bible mentions that their observances start in the evening, and it comes from the expert Bible scholar Roland de Vaux, who says:

> These two passages belong to the final redaction
> of the Pentateuch. This method of reckoning is
> used in New Testament times and under later
> Judaism for the sabbath, the religious feasts
> and civil life. The change of reckoning must
> therefore have taken place between the end of the
> monarchy and the age of Nehemias [Nehemiah].
> (de Vaux, p. 182.)

In other words, de Vaux is suggesting that the words concerning "the evening" observances were **added** as part of the final editing of the Torah by the likes of Ezra and/or Nehemiah. These two champions of God, both of whom have books of the Bible named for them, are thought by scholars to have edited the first five books of Scripture – known famously as the Torah, Pentateuch or the five books of Moses – to include extra, updated information on these books that were originally written by Moses.

As a simple example to help you understand what I mean, the books written by Moses contain specific details about the death of Moses. Here's one text:

> Moses was 120 years old when he died, yet his
> eyesight was clear, and he was as strong as ever.
> (Deuteronomy 34:7 NLT)

So you might ask yourself, "How could this be accomplished? How could a man who's dead write down the details about his own death?" The answer is simple. Moses didn't write that verse. The original book of Deuteronomy written by Moses was actually redacted – that is to say, edited, at a later point in time, by other God-fearing men such as Ezra or Nehemiah. They merely included the extra information about the prophet's death to this fifth book of Moses.

Thus, at least according to de Vaux, the two verses that mention Passover and the Day of Atonement being celebrated on an evening-to-evening timetable "belong to the final redaction of the Pentateuch." He thinks it was sometime after the Israelites were exiled for seventy years in Babylon and had adopted the pagan, Babylonian custom of starting days at sunset that this evening-day notion was first placed into Scripture for the Bibles you hold in your hand today.

Though it wasn't how days were originally marked from sunrise, an evening day was a heathen custom that Jews had eventually adopted (just like the Jews named one of their calendar months after the pagan god Tammuz) and were observing by the time they left their exile in Babylon and headed back to Jerusalem. This pagan custom of commencing the day at sundown is still observed in modern Judaism today, and even some Christians who are trying to get back to the roots of the Bible go along with the evening-day reckoning, not realizing the full measure of what the Bible has to say about the day truly starting at morning instead of evening. And there is plenty more. Are you ready?

Five easy pieces of the puzzle

Do you like Bible trivia? I do, so here's a quick quiz of five extremely simple questions for you. I'm confident even the most scripturally challenged contestants on the TV game show "Jeopardy!" could answer these correctly.

Question one: For how long did God Himself say it would rain when he was talking to Noah who built the ark? The answer: "Forty days and forty nights."

> "I will cause it to rain upon the earth forty days and forty nights" (Genesis 7:4 KJV)

Question two: For how long did Moses go without food and water when he was on Mount Sinai receiving the Ten Commandments from God? Answer: "Forty days and forty nights."

> And he was there with the LORD forty days and
> forty nights; he did neither eat bread, nor drink
> water. And he wrote upon the tables the words of
> the covenant, the ten commandments.
> (Exodus 34:28 KJV)

Question three: For how long did Jesus go without food and water leading up to His temptation by Satan the devil? Answer: "Forty days and forty nights."

> And when He had fasted forty days and forty
> nights, afterward He was hungry.
> (Matthew 4:2 NKJV)

Question four: For how long was Jonah inside a fish that swallowed him? Answer: "Three days and three nights."

> And Jonah was in the belly of the fish three days
> and three nights. (Jonah 1:17 KJV)

Question five: For how long did Jesus say He would be in the heart of the earth as He predicted His death? Answer: "Three days and three nights."

> "For as Jonah was three days and three nights in
> the belly of the great fish, so will the Son of Man
> be three days and three nights in the heart of the
> earth. (Matthew 12:40 NKJV)

Are you beginning to sense a pattern here? Your very own Bible in both the Old and New Testaments has all these very famous events recorded with the days mentioned before the nights! Why? Because days obviously start in the morning with the light of day, and not the darkness of night.

If days were to actually begin at sundown, as so many people presume, the text would say "forty nights and forty days" or "three nights and three days." But it doesn't. Remember, Jesus Himself, the God of the Old Testament, personally told Noah: "I will cause it to rain upon the earth forty days and forty nights" (Genesis 7:4 KJV). And Jesus Himself in the

New Testament personally said He would "be three days and three nights in the heart of the earth." (Matthew 12:40 NKJV)

This is God Almighty, the Creator of the universe, talking in these verses, and here's a news flash for you: God **always** mentions days before nights when talking of them in the plural. It may come as a shock, but there is not a single instance in the entire Bible where it mentions any amount of "nights and days" in that order. Not one. There is never any listing of "forty nights and forty days," "three nights and three days," or **any number** of nights and days with nights being mentioned before days! That's a fact. And why is this so? Because days start with the light of day, and not the darkness of night!

While we're on the subject of Jesus' time in the grave, as I previously demonstrated in the first edition of "Shocked by the Bible," Jesus actually died on a Wednesday, and as He predicted, He spent a full "three days and three nights" in the grave until He was resurrected by His Father sometime around sunset on what we would call Saturday evening. He died in the late afternoon, and His body was put in the grave just at the sun was setting.

So, technically speaking, Jesus remained dead in the grave for three nights and three days in that exact order: Wednesday night, Thursday daytime, Thursday night, Friday daytime, Friday night, Saturday daytime. He was then raised from death around sundown Saturday night and the women found His empty tomb at first light Sunday morning, the first day of the week.

I stress this because, although Jesus in actuality spent three nights and three days in the earth, He Himself uses the phrase "three days and three nights" when referring to His time in the ground. Why does Jesus mention days before nights? Because that's the way He created it from the beginning! The true counting of days starts with the light of day, not the darkness of night.

But wait. There's more. The gospel of Matthew provides a detailed account of the timetable of Jesus' death and resurrection. And here's what Matthew's report says about the moment when the women who followed Jesus first arrived at His tomb:

> In the end of the sabbath, **as it began to dawn toward the first day of the week**, came Mary Magdalene and the other Mary to see the sepulchre. (Matthew 28:1 KJV)

Notice, the New Testament plainly states that the Sabbath, the seventh day of the week, **was ending as it began to dawn toward** the first day of the week. This is unmistakable, folks. As dawn was breaking in Jerusalem, sometime between 5 and 6 a.m., the women came to the tomb. Holy Scripture says the Sabbath day was just ending, and it was beginning to dawn **toward** the first day of the week, which had not actually begun yet!

This is absolute proof that the change in the numeric day of the week from the seventh day of the week to the first of the week happens at "dawn." If days actually began at sunset, then the first day of the week would have been half over by dawn. But this verse tells us the Sabbath, the seventh day of the week, was **ending** as dawn was breaking **toward** the first of the week. People need to stop dancing around this Scripture, and believe what the Word of God is telling them. The day starts with the light of day, not with the darkness of night!

The resurrection clincher

If you still had any doubt as to when days really begin, this Scripture will knock it out of the park. As we all know, Jesus began presenting himself alive to numerous people on that famous first day of the week after He rose from the dead. Let's take a look at how the apostle John recorded it in his gospel:

> But Mary stood outside by the tomb weeping, and as she wept she stooped down and looked into the tomb. And she saw two angels in white sitting, one at the head and the other at the feet, where the body of Jesus had lain.
>
> Then they said to her, "Woman, why are you weeping?" She said to them, "Because they have taken away my Lord, and I do not know where they have laid Him."

Now when she had said this, she turned around and saw Jesus standing there, and did not know that it was Jesus.

Jesus said to her, "Woman, why are you weeping? Whom are you seeking?" She, supposing Him to be the gardener, said to Him, "Sir, if You have carried Him away, tell me where You have laid Him, and I will take Him away."

Jesus said to her, "Mary!" She turned and said to Him, "Rabboni!" (which is to say, Teacher).

Jesus said to her, "Do not cling to Me, for I have not yet ascended to My Father; but go to My brethren and say to them, 'I am ascending to My Father and your Father, and to My God and your God.'"

Mary Magdalene came and told the disciples that she had seen the Lord, and that He had spoken these things to her.

Then, <u>the same day at evening, being the first day of the week,</u> when the doors were shut where the disciples were assembled, for fear of the Jews, Jesus came and stood in the midst, and said to them, "Peace be with you."
(John 20:11-19 NKJV)

I hope you're paying attention to that last verse, because it says it all. It was that very same day in the evening, still the first day of the week, when Jesus appeared to his assembled disciples. It was Sunday night, and your Bible calls it "the same day" and "the first day of the week."

If you don't like the New King James Version, let's look how other Bibles render that all-important verse of John 20:19:

Then the same day at evening, being the first day of the week (KJV)

That Sunday evening (NLT)

On the evening of that first day of the week (NIV)

In the evening of that first day of the week (HCSB)

When therefore it was evening, on that day, the first day of the week (ASV)

So when it was evening on that day, the first day of the week (NASB)

If you're still not understanding the profound significance of this, it's that the Holy Bible is outright shouting that the time after sunset on Sunday night is still "the first day of the week." Please absorb this in your mind. If days truly began at sunset, which millions of Jews and some Christians believe, then this verse would have said it was the **second** day of the week. But it doesn't. It says it was the *same day*, the *first day* of the week!

Roadtrip to Emmaus ... and BACK!

And now, ladies and gentlemen, the proof positive.

After Jesus made His identity known to Mary, he spent the rest of the daylight hours on that first day of the week making personal guest appearances with other believers, proving to them He was indeed alive again. Two of those followers are specifically mentioned in the gospel of Luke, when the pair was walking to a village called Emmaus during the daylight hours of Sunday, the first day of the week.

Jesus appeared to these gentlemen, at first incognito, to find out what they were talking about. Here's their conversation, and there are important clues which reveal the precise timetable of events they were discussing:

> That same day two of Jesus' followers were walking to the village of Emmaus, seven miles from Jerusalem. As they walked along they were talking about everything that had happened.
>
> As they talked and discussed these things, Jesus himself suddenly came and began walking with them. But God kept them from recognizing him.
>
> He asked them, "What are you discussing so intently as you walk along?" They stopped short, sadness written across their faces.

Then one of them, Cleopas, replied, "You must be the only person in Jerusalem who hasn't heard about all the things that have happened there the last few days."

"What things?" Jesus asked.

"The things that happened to Jesus, the man from Nazareth," they said. "He was a prophet who did powerful miracles, and he was a mighty teacher in the eyes of God and all the people. But our leading priests and other religious leaders handed him over to be condemned to death, and they crucified him. We had hoped he was the Messiah who had come to rescue Israel. This all happened three days ago.

"Then some women from our group of his followers were at his tomb <u>early this morning</u>, and they came back with an amazing report. They said his body was missing, and they had seen angels who told them Jesus is alive! Some of our men ran out to see, and sure enough, his body was gone, just as the women had said." (Luke 24:13-24 NLT)

Jesus then spent time that Sunday afternoon giving these believers an in-depth explanation from the Word of God what all the events meant:

Then Jesus took them through the writings of Moses and all the prophets, explaining from all the Scriptures the things concerning himself. (Luke 24:27 NLT)

This discussion between Jesus and His believers on the road to Emmaus extended into the very late hours of Sunday afternoon, and the gospel thankfully provides the time frame in a play-by-play description:

By this time they were nearing Emmaus and the end of their journey. Jesus acted as if he were going on, but they begged him, <u>"Stay the night</u> with us, since it is <u>getting late</u>." So he went home with them. (Luke 24:28-29 NLT)

Once again, in plain language, we have the Bible telling us it's very late in the afternoon, with other translations using the phrase "nearly evening" as the men begged Jesus to stay the night with them. As sundown was approaching, Jesus indeed went on walking with the men to Emmaus and ate dinner with them after their arrival there:

> As they sat down to eat, he took the bread and blessed it. Then he broke it and gave it to them. Suddenly, their eyes were opened, and they recognized him. And at that moment he disappeared! (Luke 24:30-31 NLT)

So here we have Jesus eating an evening meal with the men. When they recognized that their guest was, in fact, their Savior with whom they were dining, Jesus instantly vanished, dematerializing by His divine power. And the story continues with even more revealing details:

> And within the hour they were on their way back to Jerusalem. There they found the eleven disciples and the others who had gathered with them, who said, "The Lord has really risen! He appeared to Peter."
>
> Then the two from Emmaus told their story of how Jesus had appeared to them as they were walking along the road, and how they had recognized him as he was breaking the bread.
>
> And just as they were telling about it, Jesus himself was suddenly standing there among them. "Peace be with you," he said.
> (Luke 24:33-36 NLT)

After the men had broken bread with Jesus, Scripture says "within the hour" they headed back toward Jerusalem. Maybe that was 15 minutes, a half hour, or 45 minutes. Now it's important to remember how far Emmaus is from Jerusalem geographically. The New Living Translation mentions "seven miles," but it actually is more like seven and a half miles, if we use the King James Translation of "threescore furlongs" in verse 13. A furlong is an eighth of a mile, so sixty furlongs means seven and a half miles.

In either case, my point is that these men who dined with Jesus in the early part of the evening on Sunday night then hoofed it at least seven, but more likely seven and a half, miles back to Jerusalem. This is after they had already completed the long walk getting there, probably originating from Jerusalem to begin with, since they were well aware of what the women had said to fellow believers in the city that very morning, and they even told Jesus He must be the only person in Jerusalem not to be aware of what had happened.

And this is crucial to remember. The journey back had to take at least two hours, but probably closer to three. So the time frame of their arrival back in Jerusalem would have been well after sundown, somewhere between 8 to 9 p.m. local time, which certainly cannot be considered daylight hours. It is, in fact, several hours into the night of Sunday night!

We know the time of year this was taking place. It was springtime, during the week of Passover and Unleavened Bread. In Israel at this time of year, sunset is about 6 p.m. Standard Time. So by the time the two men traveled back to Jerusalem to meet the other disciples, it was most likely at least 8 or 9 o'clock at night.

The Bible does agree with itself. And when these men came back to Jerusalem from Emmaus, and Jesus instantly materialized in front of everyone to say "Peace be with you," it was after dark on Sunday night, and your very own Bible you've been reading all these years still calls it "the first day of the week" and not the second day of the week. If days really begin at sundown, the Bible would have said the appearance by Jesus to his gathered disciples took place on the second day of the week.

But as we've read already in the gospel of John:

> Then, the <u>same day at evening, being the first day of the week</u>, when the doors were shut where the disciples were assembled, for fear of the Jews, Jesus came and stood in the midst, and said to them, "Peace be with you."
> (John 20:19 NKJV)

Why does your Bible call Sunday night after dark "the first day of the week" and not the second day of the week? Because – say it with me, folks – days start with the light of day, and not the darkness of night!

The not-so-silent majority

I mentioned earlier the importance of examining the whole scope of Scripture when investigating this matter of when days start. This holds true for any question you have. But because so many people have longstanding preconceived notions, sometimes it's impossible to boot out the erroneous ideas that have taken up permanent residence in their minds. These people may cite a few Bible verses that could be understood in more than one way, and they attempt to make an impregnable fortress of doctrine out of them.

The big list of days and nights

With this in mind, I wish to show you now that a vast majority of Bible verses place days before nights, sunrise before sunset, etc., not only in English, but in the original languages of Hebrew and Greek as well. This following gigantic list is certainly not exhaustive, but the sheer number of verses mentioning the light of day before the darkness of night may surprise you.

> While the earth remaineth, seedtime and harvest, and cold and heat, and summer and winter, and day and night shall not cease. (Genesis 8:22 KJV)

> That which was torn of beasts I brought not unto thee; I bare the loss of it; of my hand didst thou require it, whether stolen by day, or stolen by night. (Genesis 31:39 KJV)

> Thus I was; in the day the drought consumed me, and the frost by night; and my sleep departed from mine eyes. (Genesis 31:40 KJV)

> And Moses stretched forth his rod over the land of Egypt, and the LORD brought an east wind upon the land all that day, and all that night; and when it was morning, the east wind brought the locusts. (Exodus 10:13 KJV)

> And the LORD went before them by day in a pillar of a cloud, to lead them the way; and by night in a pillar of fire, to give them light; to go by day and night: (Exodus 13:21 KJV)

He took not away the pillar of the cloud by day, nor the pillar of fire by night, from before the people. (Exodus 13:22 KJV)

For the cloud of the LORD was upon the tabernacle by day, and fire was on it by night, in the sight of all the house of Israel, throughout all their journeys. (Exodus 40:38 KJV)

Now stay at the entrance of the Tabernacle day and night for seven days, and do everything the LORD requires. If you fail to do this, you will die, for this is what the LORD has commanded." (Leviticus 8:35 NLT)

Sometimes the cloud stayed only from evening till morning, and when it lifted in the morning, they set out. Whether by day or by night, whenever the cloud lifted, they set out.
(Numbers 9:21 NIV)

And the people stood up all that day, and all that night, and all the next day, and they gathered the quails (Numbers 11:32 KJV)

Now if you destroy them, the Egyptians will send a report to the inhabitants of this land, who have already heard that you live among your people. They know, LORD, that you have appeared to your people face to face and that your pillar of cloud hovers over them. They know that you go before them in the pillar of cloud by day and the pillar of fire by night. (Numbers 14:14 NLT)

And there shall be no leavened bread seen with thee in all thy coast seven days; neither shall there any thing of the flesh, which thou sacrificedst the first day at even, remain all night until the morning. (Deuteronomy 16:4 KJV)

"Your life shall hang in doubt before you; you shall fear day and night, and have no assurance of life. (Deuteronomy 28:66 NKJV)

This book of the law shall not depart out of thy mouth; but thou shalt meditate therein day and night (Joshua 1:8 KJV)

And he stripped off his clothes also, and prophesied before Samuel in like manner, and lay down naked all that day and all that night.
(1 Samuel 19:24 KJV)

Then Saul fell straightway all along on the earth, and was sore afraid, because of the words of Samuel: and there was no strength in him; for he had eaten no bread all the day, nor all the night.
(1 Samuel 28:20 KJV)

Then Rizpah daughter of Aiah, the mother of two of the men, spread burlap on a rock and stayed there the entire harvest season. She prevented the scavenger birds from tearing at their bodies during the day and stopped wild animals from eating them at night. (2 Samuel 21:10 NLT)

"And may these words of mine, with which I have made supplication before the LORD, be near the LORD our God day and night, that He may maintain the cause of His servant and the cause of His people Israel, as each day may require (1 Kings 8:59 NKJV)

And these are the singers, chief of the fathers of the Levites, who remaining in the chambers were free: for they were employed in that work day and night. (1 Chronicles 9:33 KJV)

That thine eyes may be open upon this house day and night, upon the place whereof thou hast said that thou wouldest put thy name there; to hearken unto the prayer which thy servant prayeth toward this place. (2 Chronicles 6:20 KJV)

Let thine ear now be attentive, and thine eyes open, that thou mayest hear the prayer of thy servant, which I pray before thee now, day and night, for the children of Israel thy servants, and confess the sins of the children of Israel, which we have sinned against thee: both I and my father's house have sinned. (Nehemiah 1:6 KJV)

Nevertheless we made our prayer unto our God, and set a watch against them day and night, because of them. (Nehemiah 4:9 KJV)

So we continued the work with half the men holding spears, from the first light of dawn till the stars came out. (Nehemiah 4:21 NIV)

By day you led them with a pillar of cloud, and by night with a pillar of fire to give them light on the way they were to take. (Nehemiah 9:12 NIV)

"Because of your great compassion you did not abandon them in the wilderness. By day the pillar of cloud did not fail to guide them on their path, nor the pillar of fire by night to shine on the way they were to take. (Nehemiah 9:19 NIV)

Let the day perish wherein I was born, and the night in which it was said, There is a man child conceived. (Job 3:3 KJV)

He created the horizon when he separated the waters; he set the boundary between day and night. (Job 26 :10 NLT)

But his delight is in the law of the LORD, And in His law he meditates day and night.
(Psalm 1:2 NKJV)

Day after day they pour forth speech; night after night they reveal knowledge. (Psalm 19:2 NIV)

My God, I cry out by day, but you do not answer, by night, but I find no rest (Psalm 22:2 NIV)

For day and night Your hand was heavy upon me (Psalm 32:4 NKJV)

My tears have been my food day and night, while people say to me all day long, "Where is your God?" (Psalm 42:3 NIV)

But each day the LORD pours his unfailing love upon me, and through each night I sing his songs, praying to God who gives me life.
(Psalm 42:8 NLT)

Day and night they prowl about on its walls; malice and abuse are within it.
(Psalm 55:10 NIV)

The day is Yours, the night also is Yours; You have prepared the light and the sun.
(Psalm 74:16 NKJV)

In the day of my trouble I sought the Lord: my sore ran in the night, and ceased not: my soul refused to be comforted. (Psalm 77:2 KJV)

In the daytime also he led them with a cloud, and all the night with a light of fire.
(Psalm 78:14 KJV)

O LORD God of my salvation, I have cried day and night before thee (Psalm 88:1 KJV)

The sun will not harm you by day, nor the moon at night. (Psalm 121:6 NLT)

When I applied my mind to know wisdom and to observe the labor that is done on earth – people getting no sleep day or night–
(Ecclesiastes 8:16 NIV)

Then the LORD will create over all of Mount Zion and over those who assemble there a cloud of smoke by day and a glow of flaming fire by night; over everything the glory will be a canopy.
(Isaiah 4:5 NIV)

Then he cried, "A lion, my Lord! I stand continually on the watchtower in the daytime; I have sat at my post every night. (Isaiah 21:8 NKJV)

Like a shepherd's tent my house has been pulled down and taken from me. Like a weaver I have rolled up my life, and he has cut me off from the loom; day and night you made an end of me. (Isaiah 38:12 NIV)

I waited patiently till dawn, but like a lion he broke all my bones; day and night you made an end of me. (Isaiah 38:13 NIV)

Your gates will stay open day and night to receive the wealth of many lands. The kings of the world will be led as captives in a victory procession. (Isaiah 60:11 NLT)

O Jerusalem, I have posted watchmen on your walls; they will pray day and night, continually. (Isaiah 62:6 NLT)

If only my head were a pool of water and my eyes a fountain of tears, I would weep day and night for all my people who have been slaughtered. (Jeremiah 9:1 NLT)

So I will throw you out of this land and send you into a foreign land where you and your ancestors have never been. There you can worship idols day and night – and I will grant you no favors!' (Jeremiah 16:13 NLT)

It is the LORD who provides the sun to light the day and the moon and stars to light the night, and who stirs the sea into roaring waves. (Jeremiah 31:35 NLT)

"This is what the LORD says: 'If you can break my covenant with the day and my covenant with the night, so that day and night no longer come at their appointed time (Jeremiah 33:20 NIV)

This is what the LORD says: 'If I have not made my covenant with day and night and established the laws of heaven and earth (Jeremiah 33:25 NIV)

Therefore this is what the LORD says about Jehoiakim king of Judah: He will have no one to sit on the throne of David; his body will be thrown out and exposed to the heat by day and the frost by night. (Jeremiah 36:30 NIV)

Cry aloud before the Lord, O walls of beautiful Jerusalem! Let your tears flow like a river day and night. (Lamentations 2:18 KJV)

You stumble day and night, and the prophets stumble with you. So I will destroy your mother (Hosea 4:5 NIV)

It will be a unique day – a day known only to the LORD – with no distinction between day and night. When evening comes, there will be light. (Zechariah 14:7 NIV)

And Jesus saith unto him, Verily I say unto thee, That this day, even in this night, before the cock crow twice, thou shalt deny me thrice. (Mark 14:30 KJV)

And will not God bring about justice for his chosen ones, who cry out to him day and night? Will he keep putting them off? (Luke 18:7 NIV)

Each day Jesus was teaching at the temple, and each evening he went out to spend the night on the hill called the Mount of Olives (Luke 21:37 NIV)

"I must work the works of Him who sent Me while it is day; the night is coming when no one can work. (John 9:4 NKJV)

But their plot became known to Saul. And they watched the gates day and night, to kill him. (Acts 9:24 NKJV)

This is the promise our twelve tribes are hoping to see fulfilled as they earnestly serve God day and night. (Acts 26:7 NIV)

You are all children of the light and children of the day. We do not belong to the night or to the darkness. (1 Thessalonians 5:5 NIV)

Each of the four living creatures had six wings and was covered with eyes all around, even under its wings. Day and night they never stop saying: "'Holy, holy, holy is the Lord God Almighty,' who was, and is, and is to come."
(Revelation 4:8 NIV)

"That is why they stand in front of God's throne and serve him day and night in his Temple. And he who sits on the throne will give them shelter. (Revelation 7:15 NLT)

The fourth angel sounded his trumpet, and a third of the sun was struck, a third of the moon, and a third of the stars, so that a third of them turned dark. A third of the day was without light, and also a third of the night. (Revelation 8:12 NIV)

Then I heard a loud voice saying in heaven, "Now salvation, and strength, and the kingdom of our God, and the power of His Christ have come, for the accuser of our brethren, who accused them before our God day and night, has been cast down. (Revelation 12:10 NKJV)

There will be no rest day or night for those who worship the beast and its image, or for anyone who receives the mark of its name."
(Revelation 14:11 NIV)

And the devil, who deceived them, was thrown into the lake of burning sulfur, where the beast and the false prophet had been thrown. They will be tormented day and night for ever and ever. (Revelation 20:10 NIV)

"I will cause it to rain upon the earth forty days and forty nights" (Genesis 7:4 KJV)

And Moses was on the mountain forty days and forty nights. (Exodus 24:18 NKJV)

And he was there with the LORD forty days and forty nights; he did neither eat bread, nor drink water. And he wrote upon the tables the words of the covenant, the ten commandments.
(Exodus 34:28 KJV)

And when He had fasted forty days and forty nights, afterward He was hungry.
(Matthew 4:2 NKJV)

So when he had eaten, his strength came back to him; for he had eaten no bread nor drunk water for three days and three nights.
(1 Samuel 30:12 NKJV)

So he got up and ate and drank. Strengthened by that food, he traveled forty days and forty nights until he reached Horeb, the mountain of God.
(1 Kings 19:8 NIV)

Then they sat on the ground with him for seven days and nights. No one said a word to Job, for they saw that his suffering was too great for words. (Job 2:13 NLT)

And Jonah was in the belly of the fish three days and three nights. (Jonah 1:17 KJV)

For forty days and forty nights he fasted and became very hungry. (Matthew 4:2 NLT)

"For as Jonah was three days and three nights in the belly of the great fish, so will the Son of Man be three days and three nights in the heart of the earth. (Matthew 12:40 NKJV)

The next day Moses took his seat to serve as judge for the people, and they stood around him from morning till evening. (Exodus 18:13 NIV)

"This is the offering of Aaron and his sons, which they shall offer to the LORD, beginning on the day when he is anointed: one-tenth of an ephah of fine flour as a daily grain offering, half of it in the morning and half of it at night.
(Leviticus 6:20 NKJV)

For forty days, every morning and evening, the Philistine champion strutted in front of the Israelite army. (1 Samuel 17:16 NLT)

They sacrificed the regular burnt offerings to the LORD each morning and evening on the altar set aside for that purpose, obeying everything written in the Law of the LORD, as he had commanded Israel. (1 Chronicles 16:40 NLT)

I am about to build a Temple to honor the name of the LORD my God. It will be a place set apart to burn fragrant incense before him, to display the special sacrificial bread, and to sacrifice burnt offerings each morning and evening, on the Sabbaths, at new moon celebrations, and at the other appointed festivals of the LORD our God. He has commanded Israel to do these things forever. (2 Chronicles 2:4 NLT)

Every morning and evening they present burnt offerings and fragrant incense to the LORD.
(2 Chronicles 13:11 NIV)

The king contributed from his own possessions for the morning and evening burnt offerings and for the burnt offerings on the Sabbaths, at the New Moons and at the appointed festivals as written in the Law of the LORD.
(2 Chronicles 31:3 NIV)

Even though the people were afraid of the local residents, they rebuilt the altar at its old site. Then they began to sacrifice burnt offerings on the altar to the LORD each morning and evening. (Ezra 3:3 NLT)

They are destroyed from morning to evening: they perish for ever without any regarding it. (Job 4:20 KJV)

They also who dwell in the farthest parts are afraid of Your signs; You make the outgoings of the morning and evening rejoice.
(Psalm 65:8 NKJV)

In the morning it springs up new, but by evening it is dry and withered. (Psalm 90:6 NIV)

To declare Your lovingkindness in the morning, And Your faithfulness every night
(Psalm 92:2 NKJV)

They arranged to meet Paul on a certain day, and came in even larger numbers to the place where he was staying. He witnessed to them from morning till evening, explaining about the kingdom of God, and from the Law of Moses and from the Prophets he tried to persuade them about Jesus. (Acts 28:23 NIV)

The mighty God, even the LORD, hath spoken, and called the earth from the rising of the sun unto the going down thereof. (Psalm 50:1 KJV)

From the rising of the sun unto the going down of the same the LORD'S name is to be praised. (Psalm 113:3 KJV)

For from the rising of the sun even unto the going down of the same my name shall be great among the Gentiles; and in every place incense shall be offered unto my name, and a pure offering: for my name shall be great among the heathen, saith the LORD of hosts. (Malachi 1:11 KJV)

The small list of nights and days

Meanwhile, here's a listing of verses where night is mentioned before day in the original Hebrew and Greek, as well as English.

At that time I also said to the people, "Have every man and his helper stay inside Jerusalem at night, so they can serve us as guards by night and as workers by day." (Nehemiah 4:22 NIV)

"Go and gather together all the Jews of Susa and fast for me. Do not eat or drink for three days, night or day. (Esther 4:16 NLT)

Evening, and morning, and at noon,* will I pray, and cry aloud: and he shall hear my voice.
(Psalm 55:17 KJV)

* The New Living Translation of this verse, which is a thought-for-thought translation, has: Morning, noon, and night I cry out in my distress, and the LORD hears my voice.
(Psalm 55:17 NLT)

It will not be quenched night or day; its smoke will rise forever. From generation to generation it will lie desolate; no one will ever pass through it again. (Isaiah 34:10 NIV)

"They were a wall to us both by night and day,* all the time we were with them keeping the sheep. (1 Samuel 25:16 NKJV)

* The NLT has this verse: In fact, day and night they were like a wall of protection to us and the sheep. (1 Samuel 25:16 NLT)

May your eyes be open toward this temple night and day, this place of which you said, 'My Name shall be there,' so that you will hear the prayer your servant prays toward this place.
(1 Kings 8:29 NIV)

I the LORD do keep it; I will water it every moment: lest any hurt it, I will keep it night and day.* (Isaiah 27:3 KJV)

* The NLT and the NIV render the last portion of this verse "day and night"

Now, Jeremiah, say this to them: "Night and day my eyes overflow with tears. I cannot stop weeping, for my virgin daughter – my precious people – has been struck down and lies mortally wounded. (Jeremiah 14:17 NLT)

Night and day, whether he sleeps or gets up, the
seed sprouts and grows, though he does not know
how. (Mark 4:27 NIV)

and this woman was a widow of about eighty-
four years, who did not depart from the temple,
but served God with fastings and prayers night
and day.* (Luke 2:37 NKJV)

* The NLT renders it as "day and night"

So be on your guard! Remember that for three
years I never stopped warning each of you night
and day with tears. (Acts 20:31 NIV)

Timothy, I thank God for you – the God I serve
with a clear conscience, just as my ancestors did.
Night and day I constantly remember you in my
prayers. (2 Timothy 1:3 NLT)

Adding it up

When we count up both lists, there are more than 90 verses specifically
listing the light of day before darkness of night, and only a dozen showing
the reverse. Why do millions of people completely ignore this jaw-
dropping fact?

Analyzing the few verses where night happens to be mentioned first,
there are logical explanations why they were written that way, without
having anything to do with the start time of a day. Here's the first verse
on the small list:

At that time I also said to the people, "Have
every man and his helper stay inside Jerusalem
at night, so they can serve us as guards by night
and as workers by day." (Nehemiah 4:22 NIV)

When we examine the text closely, the reason why night is mentioned
before day here is more than obvious. Nehemiah is one of the leaders
overseeing the reconstruction of Jerusalem after the Jews were freed from
their 70-year exile in Babylon. This fourth chapter of his book talks about
military threats from foreign enemies looking to stop the building project.
The ninth verse declares:

> But we prayed to our God and posted a guard day
> and night to meet this threat.
> (Nehemiah 4:9 NIV)

Notice, Nehemiah himself uses the phrase "day and night" in this sentence, suggesting days start at morning. And as the chapter unfolds, he explains how there was a combination of construction work and guarding the walls taking place simultaneously:

> So we continued the work with half the men
> holding spears, from the first light of dawn till
> the stars came out. (Nehemiah 4:21 NIV)

Even in this verse 21, again we see light mentioned before darkness: "from the first light of dawn till the stars came out." But then comes verse 22, which, as we have read, states:

> At that time I also said to the people, "Have
> every man and his helper stay inside Jerusalem
> at night, so they can serve us as guards by night
> and as workers by day." (Nehemiah 4:22 NIV)

Remember that Nehemiah was recounting the history of how Jews rebuilt Jerusalem, and the sentence prior to verse 22 explains the time frame. Let's put them together so you can understand the proper context.:

> So we continued the work with half the men
> holding spears, from the first light of dawn
> till the stars came out. At that time I also said
> to the people, "Have every man and his helper
> stay inside Jerusalem at night, so they can serve
> us as guards by night and as workers by day."
> (Nehemiah 4:21-22 NIV)

In this section, Nehemiah is simply giving a detailed account of the time frame, showing how the Jews were building all day long "from the first light of dawn till the stars came out." And then when the stars came out, Nehemiah mentions the phrase, "At that time." He was specifically telling the workers, once night had arrived, to stay inside the city walls through the night. Why? "So they can serve us as guards by night and as workers by day." He is merely informing us of the time frame that the builders and their helpers could be guarding the city through that very night and then get back to work on the construction project the next day.

There are also some Bible readers who believe that since this reconstruction was right after the Babylonian exile, many of the Jews had already adopted the pagan Babylonian system of days commencing at evening. So this could account for the mention of "night and day." While this may be true, I personally have some doubt about it being the prime factor, since Nehemiah did mention "day and night" instead of "night and day" in verse 9.

Esther: Fast and furious

Another popular citation of those promoting evening days is an urgent action by Esther. She is the Jewish woman believed to have lived in Persia perhaps a century after the Babylonian exile. As we have read, Esther became a well-known heroine in Scripture for rescuing her fellow Jews from complete annihilation. Here's one verse from her eponymous Biblical book where she mentions night before day.

> "Go and gather together all the Jews of Susa and
> fast for me. Do not eat or drink for three days,
> night or day. My maids and I will do the same.
> And then, though it is against the law, I will go in
> to see the king. If I must die, I must die."
> (Esther 4:16 NLT)

Once again, there are those who (rightly or wrongly) believe that since this event took place many years after Jewish leaders had ostensibly adopted the Babylonian practice of starting days in the evening, then of course the text would place night before day. That's certainly a possibility and has to be taken into account.

But there are other options to be considered as well. One is the time of day that Esther made this statement to her Jewish cohort Mordecai. For example, if she were talking to him in the afternoon before dinner was served, then this could be a logical reason why she mentioned night first. The evening meal had not yet taken place. So in effect, she might have meant something like: "Don't eat dinner or anything for three days, non-stop night or day, starting immediately tonight!" The danger was so pressing, she did not want the fasting to wait until the next morning. She urged people to get with the program as soon as possible, with night being imminent.

Another simple possibility is the fact that millions of people in ordinary conversation use the phrase "night and day" virtually interchangeably with "day and night" to mean "continuously," and it has nothing to do with the start time of any given day. For instance, when you tell your spouse that you love him or her night and day, it just means that you love that person continuously, non-stop, around the clock.

One of the most famous songs in American history, in fact, is called "Night and Day." Written by Cole Porter in 1932, the tune has since has been recorded by dozens of artists including Frank Sinatra, Bing Crosby, Fred Astaire, Eartha Kitt, Billie Holiday, Dionne Warwick, Ella Fitzgerald, Shirley Bassey, Doris Day, Etta James, The Temptations, Chicago, Rod Stewart, U2, and Ringo Starr on his first solo album after the break-up of the Beatles. I won't sing it for you here, but you can go to YouTube on the Internet and listen to various versions.

The song is about someone who thinks constantly about the person who sparks his or her romantic desire. In fact, the end of the song shows how interchangeable the terms day and night are, as the singer longs to be making love "day and night, night and day." This phraseology is very likely how it could be understood in the Bible. In that light, here's a New Testament example of night preceding day in a sentence spoken by Jesus:

> He also said, "This is what the kingdom of God is like. A man scatters seed on the ground. Night and day, whether he sleeps or gets up, the seed sprouts and grows, though he does not know how. (Mark 4:26-27 NIV)

Please note that there's nothing here outright declaring that a day starts at night. In fact, when you read the phrase directly after "night and day," the answer to why night is stated first becomes clear. Jesus said, "Whether he sleeps or gets up." Obviously, if someone is talking about sleeping before getting up, that person should mention night before day. And, just as we saw in the song example from above, this appears to refer to a continuous action, in this case the non-stop growing and sprouting of a seed. This sense of continuity is plainly evident in the remainder of verses on the small list.

A day in the life

When we stop and think about it for a moment, the day itself, especially its daylight portion, is actually an analogy for life and the divine plan of God.

The day commences at dawn, when we wake up, symbolizing birth. The temperature is cool in the morning, and birds sing, heralding the beginning of a brand-new day, our brand-new life.

As the sun begins to rise in the sky, we use the expression, "the day is young." Everyone looks at the day ahead as quite a long time. In like fashion, life is still young for us when we're children or teenagers, thinking there's plenty of time left to live.

Then it gets warmer as the sun climbs high in the sky. Correspondingly, life heats up and gets more complicated as we grow up and enter the workforce, try to earn a living, engage in relationships with others and raise a family.

In the afternoon hours, we hurry to finish all our work, because we know the day is now far spent, sundown is near and night is on its way. This is the knowledge or even fear of death that many people experience as adults.

At sunset, the day is old and we're physically worn out, symbolizing our advancing into our senior years in life. Once the sun is down, the twilight of the day is the twilight of our lives. The temperature drops, yet there's still a glimmer of light left in the sky. These are the final moments of mortal life.

At night, when there is darkness and no more light of life, we go to sleep, representing death. Darkness reigns for a time, but then all of a sudden, we awake at the dawn of a new day! We are resurrected from daily slumber to live once again!

This pattern of life has been taking place every single day since creation week. God is showing you His divine plan with every cycle of twenty-four hours, even on your own biological clock. You awake refreshed in the morning with the light, not at the darkness of night. You work all day, representing your lifespan, and then you go to sleep at night, the time of death. But you're not meant to fear death at all, because the pattern always shows that an awakening occurs after your time of slumber, whether it's in your bed or in your grave. You are born again when you're raised from death, finally receiving the gift of eternal life!

Spirit in the sky

Finally, after the mountain of proof we've seen thus far about days starting with the light of morning and not the darkness of night, there's still one more extremely important angle that will shed even more light on this subject.

As you have become well aware by now, there is not just a single, physical meaning to many of the Scriptures. There is very often a secondary, spiritual meaning that provides deeper, profound insight into the unseen world where God lives and where He has planned out His divine destiny for us as the immortal children of God. And on this matter of light and darkness, there are extremely important spiritual implications.

I'll warm you up with some key Scriptures that reveal what light and darkness represent:

> And God saw **the light**, that **it was good**
> (Genesis 1:4 KJV)

In very clear language, right in the very first chapter of the Bible, we learn that light itself represents goodness.

The Creator also says:

> I form the light, and create darkness: I make peace, and create evil: I the LORD do all these things. (Isaiah 45:7 KJV)

Here, we see God saying that not only does He personally make good things such as light and peace, He also creates things which are the antithesis of goodness, including darkness and evil. In fact, much of the remainder of the Bible goes out of its way to inform us that darkness itself represents wickedness and evil. Here's just a small sampling to give you an idea:

> But the way of the wicked is like total darkness.
> (Proverbs 4:19 NLT)

Woe to those who call evil good and good evil, who put darkness for light and light for darkness (Isaiah 5:20 NIV)

But if thine eye be evil, thy whole body shall be full of darkness. If therefore the light that is in thee be darkness, how great is that darkness! (Matthew 6:23 KJV)

Now throw this useless servant into outer darkness, where there will be weeping and gnashing of teeth.' (Matthew 25:13 NLT)

And the light shines in the darkness, and the darkness did not comprehend it. (John 1:5 NKJV)

And the judgment is based on this fact: God's light came into the world, but people loved the darkness more than the light, for their actions were evil. (John 3:19 NLT)

Then Jesus spoke to them again, saying, "I am the light of the world. He who follows Me shall not walk in darkness, but have the light of life." (John 8:12 NKJV)

I have come into the world as a light, so that no one who believes in me should stay in darkness. (John 12:46 NIV)

'to open their eyes, in order to turn them from darkness to light, and from the power of Satan to God, that they may receive forgiveness of sins and an inheritance among those who are sanctified by faith in Me.' (Acts 26:18 NKJV)

This is the message we heard from Jesus and now declare to you: God is light, and there is no darkness in him at all. (1 John 1:5 NLT)

Obviously, light represents all that is good, and darkness represents all that is evil. As we see in the above verse, the Bible indicates "God is light."

Jesus, who called Himself "the light of the world," verbally scorched the evil Jewish leaders who arrested Him late at night shortly before He was put to death, as He said to them:

> Why didn't you arrest me in the Temple? I was there every day. But this is your moment, the time when the power of darkness reigns."
> (Luke 22:53 NLT)

Additionally, there may be more to the "darkness for light" prophecy in Isaiah than just equating good with light and darkness with evil. Here it is again:

> Woe unto them that call evil good, and good evil; **that put darkness for light**, and light for darkness (Isaiah 5:20 KJV)

Not only is God blasting people who call evil actions "good" and righteous actions "evil," but He also indicates that people "put darkness for light and light for darkness." Is this a veiled reference to people who have erroneously changed the start time of the day, making darkness (what God has labeled night) as if it were the light (what He calls day)? Just something to think about.

And here's a verse that may surprise you, because it relates directly to the subject of this entire chapter.

> The night is far spent, the day is at hand. Therefore let us cast off the works of darkness, and let us put on the armor of light. (Romans 13:12 NKJV)

Again, spiritually speaking, the night represents evil. The apostle Paul is telling believers that the current age of evil in which we live, what he calls night, is mostly spent. Although this age began with light, it turned to darkness, but that dark time is nearly over, and the next day, the time of the reign of God and His goodness, is at hand, about to begin. So Paul urges Christians to knock off anything that could be considered works of darkness (evil), and instead to put on the armor of light, which is all that is godly and good. He repeats this call to action in his other letters using similar phrases that mention light, darkness, day and night:

You are all children of the light and children of the day. We do not belong to the night or to the darkness. (1 Thessalonians 5:5 NIV)

For once you were full of darkness, but now you have light from the Lord. So live as people of light! (Ephesians 5:8 NLT)

Many points of light

In the big list of Bible quotes showing day preceding night, God said twice that He actually has a covenant (a contract or an agreement) with day and night, and that these agreements come at their appointed time. Here they are again:

"This is what the LORD says: 'If you can break my covenant with the day and my covenant with the night, so that day and night no longer come at their appointed time (Jeremiah 33:20 NIV)

This is what the LORD says: 'If I have not made my covenant with day and night and established the laws of heaven and earth
(Jeremiah 33:25 NIV)

The very fact that God mentions day before night multiple times in that covenant is hard evidence that days come before nights in the timetable of our Maker.

Moreover, as many devout Christians already know, Jesus declared Himself to be "the beginning and the end." His exact statement is:

I am Alpha and Omega, **the beginning and the end**, the first and the last. (Revelation 22:13 KJV)

He also declared that He is "the bright Morning Star."
(Revelation 22:16 NIV)

Thus, it makes perfect spiritual sense that the God named Yeshua, who is light with no darkness in Him at all, who is this bright Morning Star, who is the beginning and the end, who created His covenant with day and night, actually reveals His own godly character and the divine plan of God by marking the beginning and end of every single day with the appearance of a bright morning star in the sky!

Jesus, who is the beginning and the end, is also the bright Morning Star. Therefore, the bright morning star is, by definition, the beginning and the end – of the day! Are you finally getting this?

Remember, when Jesus began creating, everything was said to be good. Then mankind, through rebellion against God's instructions, turned this world to darkness. But now that darkness is nearly spent, and the new day, the day of everlasting light and everlasting life for all who repent and truly follow God, is about to dawn.

Right from the very beginning, "God saw that the light was good, and he separated the light from the darkness" (Genesis 1:4 NIV). Have you ever thought about the spiritual implication of this sentence? What I mean is this: Spiritually speaking, why did God separate the light from the darkness? Was it merely to create day and night in our physical world? The answer is no. As stunning as this may sound, the entire spiritual plan of God is actually summed up in this one, extremely overlooked verse!

In this fourth verse of the Bible, God equates light with goodness. As we've seen in many other verses, darkness represents evil, and it has always been associated with nefarious actions and deception (keeping us in the dark) since time immemorial. The plain and simple message of the Bible is that God has embarked on a divine mission to separate the light from the darkness. He is in the process of separating everyone who is good (represented by the light) from everyone who is evil (represented by the darkness). We are even commanded to separate ourselves from those who don't believe in our Creator:

> "Therefore, come out from among unbelievers,
> and separate yourselves from them, says the
> LORD." (2 Corinthians 6:17 NLT)

God is a brilliant Author when it comes to the Bible. He tells us His whole plan right at the beginning of the Book, and he repeats it at the end. He Himself is our beginning and end, our Maker and our Destiny, who authored our creation and salvation.

This is the deeper meaning of why Genesis talks about light being separated from darkness. It's not just the establishment of days and nights. It is telling us specifically when the divine mission began (in the beginning), and what the divine mission has been all along – to separate the light from the darkness, the good from the evil.

At the conclusion of the Bible in Revelation, the members of spiritual "darkness" such as Satan and all others who have refused to stop breaking God's laws, are finally separated from life itself, and are brought to destruction because they have earned "the wages of sin," which is eternal death (Romans 6:23).

The end of darkness forever

Here's a stunning news flash of the future that countless people, especially those who currently begin their days at night, may not even realize. In the coming kingdom of God, at least in the city of Jerusalem where God the Father and Jesus will personally dwell, there won't be any more night! That's right, no darkness. And not only does night come to an end forever, there won't be any more sunsets or sunlight visible throughout the day! Here's how the Bible describes the glorious illumination of the New Jerusalem once the Father and Jesus have left heaven and are both residing on this planet:

> The sun will no more be your light by day, nor will the brightness of the moon shine on you, for the LORD will be your everlasting light, and your God will be your glory. Your sun will never set again, and your moon will wane no more; the LORD will be your everlasting light, and your days of sorrow will end. (Isaiah 60:19-20 NIV)

> The city had no need of the sun or of the moon to shine in it, for the glory of God illuminated it. The Lamb is its light. (Revelation 21:23 NKJV)

> There shall be no night there: They need no lamp nor light of the sun, for the Lord God gives them light. And they shall reign forever and ever. (Revelation 22:5 NKJV)

Yes, folks, there's going to be bright light there forever, with no nighttime. This confirms the total abolition of evil, with physical and spiritual darkness completely eliminated forever. A city filled with the light of goodness and righteousness, without any darkness of evil, is wondrously fantastic news. The end of the Bible confirms this in unmistakable fashion, stating:

> "And God will wipe away every tear from their eyes; there shall be no more death, nor sorrow, nor crying. There shall be no more pain, for the former things have passed away."
> (Revelation 21:4 NKJV)

For those who have read to this point, I sincerely and humbly thank you for staying with me and learning what the Holy Word of God has to say on this issue. While it may not be a crucial matter for a person's individual salvation, we all should seek to be in complete harmony with the ways of our Designer, living our daily lives according to His design. The Bible does tell us to "prove all things" (1 Thessalonians 5:21 KJV).

I have just provided you the spirit-filled truth directly out of the Scriptures. And, as I'm sure you've read countless times, God says He wants you to worship Him in spirit and in truth:

> But the time is coming – indeed it's here now – when true worshipers will worship the Father in spirit and in truth. The Father is looking for those who will worship him that way. (John 4:23 NLT)

If you really do wish to worship God in spirit and in truth, then it's time to finally wake up out of this nightmare fascination with evil and death and its adherence to darkness in all respects. We all need to believe what our Bibles proclaim from Genesis to Revelation, from beginning to end. The day, which represents God, goodness and life, starts and ends with the light, not the darkness. Amen.

Chapter Eleven:
The mystery of Enoch

Did a famous character from Old Testament times simply vanish from the face of Planet Earth and go immediately to heaven, where he's still alive today, monitoring all events in our physical world?

Millions of devout Christians believe this, and suggest there's evidence in Scripture to back up the claim. I am referring to the well-known champion of God named Enoch. Many people are under the impression that Enoch escaped death and was zoomed alive to heaven because of his faithful obedience to God.

In the first edition of "Shocked by the Bible," I discussed another Old Testament figure who purportedly cheated death and went to dwell with God for all eternity. That person is Elijah, and when we examined all the Scriptures concerning his flight to heaven, we learned that the Bible clearly shows that this prophet was merely picked up into the atmosphere, the first heaven – not the third heaven where God resides – and was plopped back down on the ground at an undisclosed location. Years after his supernatural ride in the sky, Elijah even wrote a letter to the evil King Jehoram of Judah, castigating him for all the wicked deeds the monarch had committed. (2 Chronicles 21:12-15)

But since publication of the first book, I have received questions from readers wanting to know what happened to this other mysterious figure, Enoch. Why is there such interest? Because in a couple of instances, the Bible uses cryptic, ambiguous language that leads many to think Enoch never physically died, and that he was miraculously transported to heaven to live eternally with his Maker.

So let's put an end to this mystery once and for all. We're going to let the entire Bible speak for itself, and when we do, we'll discover there is a clear, unmistakable solution to the riddle of what really happened to Enoch.

Who is Enoch?

Right off the bat, I need to point out that there are two different people named Enoch mentioned in consecutive chapters of the book of Genesis.

The first Enoch in Scripture is the son of Cain, after whom his father named a city:

> Cain made love to his wife, and she became pregnant and gave birth to Enoch. Cain was then building a city, and he named it after his son Enoch. (Genesis 4:17 NIV)

But Cain's son Enoch is not the person we're going to focus on in this chapter. It is the other Enoch who appears in the very next chapter of Genesis. We're told he is the son of Jared:

> And Jared lived an hundred sixty and two years, and he begat Enoch (Genesis 5:18 KJV)

The Bible doesn't provide a whole lot of information about Enoch's life, but it does give a few details, so we're going to examine every single morsel. We see that as an adult, Enoch became a father at age 65:

> And Enoch lived sixty and five years, and begat Methuselah (Genesis 5:21 KJV)

The next few verses indicate Enoch lived another three hundred years, raising boys and girls while walking faithfully with God. And it is his final mention in Genesis that sparks the mystery:

> And Enoch walked with God after he begat Methuselah three hundred years, and begat sons and daughters (Genesis 5:22 KJV)

> And all the days of Enoch were three hundred sixty and five years (Genesis 5:23 KJV)

> And Enoch walked with God: and he was not; for God took him. (Genesis 5:24 KJV)

At this point, what we know for sure is that Enoch lived a total of 365 years, and that he raised children of both sexes. But many people are seriously confounded by verse 24, which notes that Enoch "walked with God," that "he was not" and that God "took him."

I will address this cryptic verse in a few moments, but I want to let you know there are two other places in Scripture that shed direct light on Enoch. These other verses, combined with what the Bible says elsewhere on the subject matter of death and whether anyone has gone to heaven will leave no doubt in your mind as to what truly happened to Enoch.

While the original appearances of Enoch are found at the start of the Bible, we have to travel nearly to the end of the Good Book for the rest of his story.

The Bible All-Star Team

In the New Testament book of Hebrews, we're given a list of people I like to call Bible All-Stars. They are some of the greatest champions of God who ever lived, and they're all mentioned by name, receiving praise for their unwavering faith. I think you'll instantly recognize these names. They include Noah, Abraham, Sarah, Abel, Moses, Jacob and Joseph. And guess who also makes the All-Star list. Yes, our good friend Enoch. And when we read the entire eleventh chapter of Hebrews, we learn Enoch's actual fate, and discover he did **not** cheat death by getting whisked away alive to heaven.

The first mention of Enoch appears in verse 5:

> By faith Enoch was translated that he should not
> see death; and was not found, because God had
> translated him: for before his translation he had
> this testimony, that he pleased God.
> (Hebrews 11:5 KJV)

At first glance, this statement sounds just as cryptic as what was stated in Genesis 5:24, which noted, "And Enoch walked with God: and he was not; for God took him."

Again, I will explain what these puzzling verses likely mean momentarily, but first we need to keep reading the rest of Hebrews 11, because it lists each of these heroes of faith, and actually tells us what eventually became of them.

Abel is the first Bible All-Star in the list:

> By faith Abel offered unto God a more excellent
> sacrifice than Cain, by which he obtained witness
> that he was righteous, God testifying of his gifts:
> and by it he **being dead** yet speaketh.
> (Hebrews 11:4 KJV)

Notice, Scripture plainly tells us that Abel is long dead, but he still speaks to us through his example of faith. Then comes the mention of Enoch, which, as we noted, states:

> By faith Enoch was translated that he should not
> see death; and was not found, because God had
> translated him: for before his translation he had
> this testimony, that he pleased God.
> (Hebrews 11:5 KJV)

The list continues with Noah cited in verse 7, Abraham mentioned in verses 8 through 10, and then Sarah, Abraham's wife, is honored in verse 11.

With five people including Enoch mentioned so far in this list of faithful champions, the Bible then takes a moment to reveal in clear, unmistakable terms what happened to all of them. Are you ready? Drumroll please ...

> These **all died** in faith, not having received the
> promises ... (Hebrews 11:13 KJV)

Are you seeing this, friends? Your very own Bible – in fact, all Bibles – agree on this. They all state that **all** these Bible heroes – and that includes Enoch – **died**!

Thus, the mystery of what happened to Enoch is not really a mystery, because the Bible already tells us that Enoch died! He did not cheat death and get snatched alive to heaven. If you're thinking verse 13 is some sort of mistranslation in the King James Version, here is the same sentence from other popular versions:

> These all died in faith, not having received the
> promises (Hebrews 11:13 NKJV)

All these people died still believing what God
had promised them. (Hebrews 11:13 NLT)

All these people were still living by faith when
they died. (Hebrews 11:13 NIV)

These all died in faith without having received
the promises (Hebrews 11:13 HCSB)

I have searched every Bible I can possibly find, and they all plainly
declare that **all these people died**! So then, without a doubt, Enoch died,
because he's in this big list of dead people!

And not only did Enoch die, verse 13 also tells us something else.
It says that Enoch, along with these other champions of faith, **did not
receive the promises**!

Here is the entirety of verse 13:

These all died in faith, **not having received the
promises**, but having seen them afar off, and
were persuaded of them, and embraced them, and
confessed that they were strangers and pilgrims
on the earth. (Hebrews 11:13 KJV)

The Bible tells us plainly that Noah, Abraham, Sarah, Abel, and Enoch
all died, and they did not receive what they were promised. The rest of
the Bible informs us the promise is eternal life in the coming kingdom of
God. The Scripture here in Hebrews reveals that these faithful heroes were
persuaded they would eventually receive the promise of eternal life, but
they knew it was "afar off," for sometime later, which will be **after** they
are all resurrected from the grave at the return of Jesus to Earth. So Enoch,
along with all the others, is not alive eternally right now, because the Bible
says he was among those who died and did not receive the promises!

'No one has ever gone into heaven'

Now beyond the plain statements from Hebrews that Enoch did, in
fact, die and did not receive the promise of eternal life, there is an arsenal
of Biblical evidence providing absolute proof he did not go to heaven to
dwell with God.

The first point is the clear declaration from Jesus Himself that **no one has ever gone to heaven except Himself**. You're reading that correctly. Just three verses before the most famous line of the Bible which is John 3:16, we see Jesus telling Nicodemus the Pharisee that no one has ever gone to heaven except Himself. Here it is:

> No one has ever gone into heaven except the one who came from heaven – the Son of Man
>
> (John 3:13 NIV)

It is quite ironic that people often open up their Bibles to read the well-known John 3:16, but their eyes never seem to catch this stunning truth spoken by Jesus just three verses prior. "No one has ever gone into heaven except the one who came from heaven." "No one" means exactly what it says; therefore, Enoch did **not** go to heaven, because Jesus said so. And Jesus is a speaker of truth. To even suggest that Enoch went to heaven is calling Jesus a liar.

Not only that, but keep in mind that Enoch lived thousands of years before Jesus came to physically dwell on Earth as a human being. Enoch lived and died thousands of years before Jesus became the atoning sacrifice for sins that actually enables us to be given eternal life in the first place!

> He is the atoning sacrifice for our sins, and not only for ours but also for the sins of the whole world. (1 John 2:2 NIV)

> But he has appeared once for all at the culmination of the ages to do away with sin by the sacrifice of himself. (Hebrews 9:26 NIV)

How could Enoch have gone to heaven when Jesus had not even paid the death penalty yet for the sins of Enoch and everyone else? Answer: Enoch did not go to heaven, because the atoning sacrifice had not even been made at that ancient time in Genesis.

Additionally, the very next verse in Hebrews declares that all people (and this, of course, includes Enoch) are destined to die once:

> And as it is appointed for men to die once, but after this the judgment (Hebrews 9:27 NKJV)

Finally, to drive this point home, here's a well-known verse:

> For as in Adam all die, so also in Christ all will
> be made alive. (1 Corinthians 15:22 HCSB)

Every single human being, from Adam and Eve all the way down to people in our time, have already died or will die. This, of course, includes Enoch, who has already died. But through the power of Jesus Christ, all people who have ever lived will be made alive through a series of resurrections that are still to come in the future.

The cryptic verses

With the Bible's clear declaration that Enoch and all those other people died, what's the real deal about his walking with God, the fact that "God took him," and that he "was translated" so he should not "see death?" Here again are the two verses that cause readers so much confusion:

> And Enoch walked with God: and he was not; for
> God took him. (Genesis 5:24 KJV)

> By faith Enoch was translated that he should not
> see death; and was not found, because God had
> translated him: for before his translation he had
> this testimony, that he pleased God.
> (Hebrews 11:5 KJV)

The first issue is this business about walking with God. Many people who read that Enoch "walked with God" like to claim that this is evidence that Enoch simply walked off this planet and stepped right into heaven to live with God forever, because we're told that "God took him."

It means nothing of the kind, as we can see from the exact same phrase used for someone else, specifically Noah:

> Noah was a just man and perfect in his generations,
> and Noah walked with God. (Genesis 6:9 KJV)

The phrase "walked with God" just means to live righteously and faithfully according to God's instructions. Modern Bible translations confirm this, as they render the phrase "walked with God" as:

> walking in close fellowship with God
> (Genesis 5:24 NLT)

> Enoch walked faithfully with God
> (Genesis 5:24 NIV)

And did walking with God mean that Noah stepped off the planet to join God forever in heaven? Of course not. Everyone knows that Noah died at a very ripe old age:

> And all the days of Noah were nine hundred and
> fifty years: and he died. (Genesis 9:29 KJV)

Now that we know what "walked with God" means, there are still some confusing terms in Hebrews 11:5 dealing with the fact that Enoch "was not found," for God "took him" and "translated" him. What can these possibly mean? We already know for sure that Enoch died at age 365, so let's turn our attention to what else the Bible says about this man to deduce alternatives for these ambiguous terms.

Beyond Enoch's appearance in the list of Bible All-Stars, there is one other section of the New Testament that mentions him. It reveals how Enoch was a tough-talking preacher of righteousness who fearlessly eviscerated sinners and those who spoke defiantly against God:

> And Enoch also, the seventh from Adam,
> prophesied of these, saying, Behold, the Lord
> cometh with ten thousands of his saints, To
> execute judgment upon all, and to convince all
> that are ungodly among them of all their ungodly
> deeds which they have ungodly committed, and
> of all their hard speeches which ungodly sinners
> have spoken against him. (Jude 1:14-15 KJV)

In case the King James English of 1611 sounds too archaic for you, here is the same section from a more modern Bible version:

> Enoch, the seventh from Adam, prophesied
> about them: "See, the Lord is coming with
> thousands upon thousands of his holy ones to
> judge everyone, and to convict all of them of all
> the ungodly acts they have committed in their
> ungodliness, and of all the defiant words ungodly
> sinners have spoken against him."
> (Jude 1:14-15 NIV)

Unfortunately, there are no other mentions of Enoch that provide further insight into his curriculum vitae, or how he spent his 365 years of life. But with what we know thus far, I believe we can paint a biblically accurate picture to help us figure out the cryptic verses and learn what likely became of him.

Scripture already says Enoch "walked with God," meaning he was walking in close fellowship with his Creator, being obedient to God's instructions. But he was not just an ordinary guy who happened to be faithful. He was also a fearless and vocal prophet living in an extremely wicked time. As we just read from the book of Jude, Enoch actually predicted the Second Coming of Jesus to Earth, thousands of years before Jesus even came the first time as a human being.

We need to remember that Enoch was not only the father of Methuselah, he was the great-grandfather of Noah. So Enoch was living in one of the most godless, evil ages in history – a time so wicked and vile that it prompted God to kill every human being with the exception of Noah and his seven other family members aboard Noah's ark:

> And GOD saw that the wickedness of man was
> great in the earth, and that every imagination of
> the thoughts of his heart was only evil continually.
> And it repented the LORD that he had made man
> on the earth, and it grieved him at his heart. And
> the LORD said, I will destroy man whom I have
> created from the face of the earth
> (Genesis 6:5-7 KJV)

Enoch lived 365 years amid this horrific time of darkness and rebellion against God's laws. When we look at the genealogy list in Genesis, we can do the math and see that Enoch was 252 years old when his grandson Lamech was born, and he still lived 113 more years. He did not get to see the birth of his great grandson Noah, however. Noah was born 69 years after Enoch died.

My point, though, is that these last generations leading up to Noah saw absolute lawlessness, with virtually everyone bent on committing disturbingly sordid actions. Other books of the Bible describe the filthy actions of wicked people at various times throughout history, committing murders, fornication, sex with animals, cannibalism, lying, stealing, worship of other gods and even sacrificing babies to demons!

It's no wonder an obedient servant such as Enoch almost sounded over the top when he blasted his fellow citizens in his end-time prophecy. Here it is again, and note how many times he mentions "ungodly":

> "Behold, the Lord came with many thousands
> of His holy ones, to execute judgment upon all,
> and to convict all the ungodly of all their ungodly
> deeds which they have done in an ungodly way,
> and of all the harsh things which ungodly sinners
> have spoken against Him." (Jude 1:14-15 NASB)

Now, with all that ungodliness going on and Enoch's apparent fearlessness in confronting those wretched sinners, I think it's fair to infer from the text that Enoch was probably not a popular character among the vile populace. And when he got in their faces with all his talk about the Lord returning to Earth to judge everyone for all their ungodly actions and their defiant words against God, he probably made more than a few enemies.

Remember, while the Bible does say that Enoch died, it does not give us any more information regarding his death. It merely says he was "not found," that he was "translated," and that "God took him."

Now, I wish to suggest some possibilities about what these mysterious terms might be saying. Here are the verses again:

> And Enoch walked with God: and he was not; for
> God took him. (Genesis 5:24 KJV)

> By faith Enoch was translated that he should not
> see death; and was not found, because God had
> translated him: for before his translation he had
> this testimony, that he pleased God.
> (Hebrews 11:5 KJV)

Notice how similar some portions of the sentences are, specifically:

> he was not; for God took him.

> was not found, because God had translated him

I suggest these two portions are actually saying the same thing. They both indicate Enoch was not found, because God had taken him somewhere. Notice, incidentally, that the word "heaven" does not appear in English as his destination, and it's not there in the original languages of Hebrew and Greek either.

I realize the word "translated" that appears twice in this verse is a confusing word for many people, but when you know the meaning of the Greek word from which it comes and see how other Bibles render it here and elsewhere in the Bible, it becomes quite easy to understand.

The original Greek word is "metatithemi," and its root means to transport, transfer, remove, take away or carry over. Here is how three popular, modern versions of the Bible have it in Hebrews 11:5:

> NKJV: "was taken away" and "had taken him"
>
> NLT: "was taken up" and "took him"
>
> NIV: "was taken" and "had taken him away"

I find all these to be an accurate rendering of the verb. It certainly does not mean going to heaven, and the word "heaven" does not appear in the original language. It just means to move from one place to another, even if that place is a belief in something. For instance, in Galatians 1:6, metatithemi is rendered as "removed" or "turning away":

> I marvel that ye are so soon removed from him that called you into the grace of Christ unto another gospel (Galatians 1:6 KJV)
>
> I marvel that you are turning away so soon from Him who called you in the grace of Christ, to a different gospel (Galatians 1:6 NKJV)

This verse demonstrates that metatithemi does not involve any mystical transformation from living on Earth to dwelling in heaven.

Now back to Hebrews 11:5. As the New King James Version puts it:

> By faith Enoch was taken away so that he did not see death, "and was not found, because God had taken him"; for before he was taken he had this testimony, that he pleased God.
> (Hebrews 11:5 NKJV)

As we have proven beyond any doubt, Enoch died. So the fact that he was **taken away** and did not **see death** and was **not found** has a very obvious and logical implication.

When we add up everything we know, Hebrews 11:5 is quite possibly saying that Enoch was **taken away (removed)** by God to some other location on Earth, so that he would not **see death (be murdered)** at the hand of his enemies who hated his message about God judging them, and that he was **not found** afterward by the wicked people still intent on killing him! It is certainly no stretch to reach this conclusion when we just let the Bible speak for itself.

However, this is not the only possibility concerning Enoch's fate. Here's another, and this scenario involves the actual death of Enoch.

Again, we know for sure that Enoch died, because Hebrews 11:13 says he died. This second theory (and I stress, it's just a theory) will focus on the phrase "for God took him." The idea of being "taken by God" has been understood by many to mean the death of someone. Even in today's English, when people refer to a loved one dying, they often avoid the word "death" by saying, "God took him."

Here's a New Testament example where Jesus was predicting the conditions on Earth at the time of His return, explaining how they'd be similar to the time of Noah:

> But as the days of Noah were, so also will the coming of the Son of Man be. For as in the days before the flood, they were eating and drinking, marrying and giving in marriage, until the day that Noah entered the ark, and did not know until the flood came and took them all away, so also will the coming of the Son of Man be. Then two men will be in the field: one will be taken and the other left. Two women will be grinding at the mill: one will be taken and the other left.
> (Matthew 24:37-41 NKJV)

Please notice in Jesus' words that all three uses of the words **took** and **taken** refer to the people being **killed**. It has nothing to do with any type of "rapture" that many people think. In Noah's day, the flood **took them**

all away, killing nearly the entire population of the world, perhaps into the millions. Only Noah and his relatives were left. When Jesus returns, it will be a similar situation. Two people will be working in the field, with one **taken (killed)** and the other left alive. Two women will be grinding at a mill, and one will be **taken (killed)** and the other left alive.

So in this light, Hebrews 11:5 could mean something different than simply being moved by God to another location to prevent him from being murdered. Here's the verse again, but this time let's read it from the New International Version:

> By faith Enoch was taken from this life, so that he did not experience death: "He could not be found, because God had taken him away." For before he was taken, he was commended as one who pleased God. (Hebrews 11:5 NIV)

Under the theory that being taken by God means to die, then this could easily be telling us that God mercifully put Enoch to death, and no one was able to find Enoch once he was no longer alive. This version of the Bible uses the phrase "did not experience death." That could mean that he did not experience a typical, natural cause of death, such as a heart attack. In other words, God may have euthanized him, putting him to sleep in the same loving manner He put Moses to death despite the fact Moses was in perfect health at age 120.

Just to remind you, God showed Moses the Promised Land from a mountain top, but He would not allow Moses to enter:

> Then the LORD said to Moses, "This is the land I promised on oath to Abraham, Isaac, and Jacob when I said, 'I will give it to your descendants.' I have now allowed you to see it with your own eyes, but you will not enter the land." So Moses, the servant of the LORD, died there in the land of Moab, just as the LORD had said. The LORD buried him in a valley near Beth-peor in Moab, but to this day no one knows the exact place. Moses was 120 years old when he died, yet his eyesight was clear, and he was as strong as ever. (Deuteronomy 34:4-7 NLT)

Scripture goes out of its way to tell us Moses was as strong as ever, that he had perfect eyesight and his natural vigor was not diminished. It informs us that although Moses was in terrific physical condition, God would not let Moses go with the rest of the Israelites into the land. So Moses was mercifully put to death by God, and Scripture says the Creator then personally buried the prophet in a secret location so no one would find him.

This scenario sounds hauntingly familiar to what we've been told about Enoch. For instance, although Enoch was 365 years old when he died, he was probably in excellent health, not yet having reached middle age. The typical life span for human beings in the time of Enoch was in the neighborhood of 900 years. His father Jared lived to age 962 (Genesis 5:20). His son Methusaleh died at 969 (Genesis 5:27).

So if criminals were looking to slay Enoch and there was no safe place to hide, God may have taken the same action He did with Moses. When the Bible says "God took him," it could mean that God mercifully ended Enoch's life by putting him to sleep, so that he wouldn't "experience death." Enoch merely entered his mortal slumber much sooner than his immediate family who lived more than 900 years.

Interestingly, there is a very important and overlooked prophecy in the book of Isaiah that deals directly with this subject. Here it is from two Bible versions, so its meaning is unmistakable:

> The righteous perisheth, and no man layeth it to heart: and merciful men are **taken away**, none considering that the righteous is **taken away** from the evil to come. (Isaiah 57:1 KJV)

> Good people pass away; the godly often die before their time. But no one seems to care or wonder why. No one seems to understand that God is protecting them from the evil to come. (Isaiah 57:1 NLT)

Here we have a red-letter quote with God Himself speaking, telling us that good, righteous people often die (they're taken away), and the survivors don't even understand the real reason why. And what is that real reason? God plainly says it's to protect that righteous person from the evil to come.

If indeed this were the case involving Enoch's demise, then it makes perfect sense why Enoch died at such a relatively young age. It explains why he did not "see" or "experience" death in the typical fashion that most others would experience death. And it also explains why Enoch was not found.

In case you don't understand, here's what I'm getting at. Because Enoch was such a vocal opponent of the wicked ways of the world during his life, he likely had enemies who desperately and relentlessly sought to kill him. God, of course, was aware of their nefarious plans, so He, in his boundless mercy, decided to "take him away" or, as a modern-day assassin might say, "take him out" in advance. Thus, according to this scenario, God may have put Enoch to death in the prime of his life, just as He put Moses to death in perfect health. If Enoch were indeed euthanized, he did not "see" or "experience" death like everyone else usually experiences. He merely went to sleep and never woke up. God then hid Enoch's grave from everyone, just as He hid Moses' burial place, and this is why Enoch was "not found."

Again, I stress that these two scenarios are merely possibilities of what may have happened to Enoch, but as we have just seen, there is more than enough evidence from Holy Scripture to make them plausible.

The words not on the page

Before closing the book on the mystery of Enoch, I feel the need to advise my fellow lovers of God and His truth about a serious problem that has crept into a wide variety of Bibles, perhaps even your own.

Some of you might be reading something called a "study Bible." These are Bibles that not only have a translation of the ancient Scriptures, they also have a section of notes where an editor or editors provide personal opinions about any given verse or subject, ostensibly to help you understand the Scriptures better.

I have no problem with the concept of a study Bible, nor the editors' desire to help readers comprehend what Scripture is saying. In fact, I'm all for it. But what I do object to is when the study notes don't get it right and contradict the clear meaning of what the Bible says in the actual Holy Scriptures. Sadly, this happens too often, and the story of Enoch is a prime example of how some of today's Bibles may mix the truth of God with erroneous ideas.

Here's an example of a problematic study note from a brand-new Bible I purchased recently in a Christian bookstore. Regarding the puzzling verse of Genesis 5:24, which we have examined thoroughly in this chapter, the study note focuses on the portion of the verse which states: "then he was no more, because God took him away."

The study note goes on to explain: "The phrase replaces 'and then he died' in the other paragraphs of the chapter. Like Elijah, who was 'taken' (2 Kings 2:10) to heaven, Enoch was taken away (cf. Psalm 49:15; 73:24) to the presence of God without experiencing death (Hebrews 11:5)."

Obviously, such a note helps perpetuate the myth that both Elijah and Enoch avoided typical, physical deaths and were taken away immediately to God's side in heaven. Now we all know how non-scriptural such a notion is, especially since Jesus said "No one has ever gone into heaven" except Himself.

But it gets worse. Not only are personal opinions getting into the study notes that appear below or beside the Bible verses, they are now sometimes finding their way into the actual English translations of the Scriptures themselves.

Here's an example from a verse we've read extensively, Hebrews 11:5. The King James Version has:

> By faith Enoch was translated that he should not
> see death; and was not found, because God had
> translated him (Hebrews 11:5 KJV)

But a more modern Bible – in this case, the New Living Translation – has the same verse saying:

> It was by faith that Enoch was taken up to heaven
> without dying – "he disappeared, because God
> took him." (Hebrews 11:5 NLT)

Now, I freely admit that I often enjoy the New Living Translation, and I think overall, it provides excellent insight into what the ancient languages are saying. But the NLT, just like all other versions of the Bible, are merely approximate translations by experts in Hebrew and Greek.

This is why one Bible version differs from another, since the linguists are providing you their best estimate of the meanings from Hebrew and Greek. Usually, thank God, the translators get it spot-on correct, or very close. But every once in a while, they may add a word or two that is not found in the ancient languages, and sometimes even a small addition can drastically change the meaning of the original text.

In the above citation of Hebrews 11:5, you need to be aware that the words "to heaven" do **not** appear in the original Greek language. And in countless Bibles in English, the translators get that fact correct by not including any mention of heaven. But so many people cling to this erroneous idea that Enoch went immediately to be with God in heaven without ever dying. And we have just read how that concept has now found its way into the actual words on the page of Scripture, not just the study notes. Do you understand the seriousness of this problem? It's now appearing in an actual Bible verse!

I'm not trying to censor anyone's belief or freedom of speech or worship. People are completely free to believe whatever they wish. But when translators add words to Scriptures that are not there in the original language, they have to be very careful not to go overboard and change the original intent. Because someone reading that translation today can now say: "See! My Bible says it right here! I'm reading the words on the page and they indicate 'Enoch was taken up to heaven without dying.' So you can't convince me that he didn't go to heaven because my Bible outright states that he did!" Such a reader usually is unaware that the word "heaven" is nowhere to be found in the original language, because he or she doesn't take the time to investigate, and many pastors don't wish to admit the lie about Enoch they have been teaching for years.

The Word of God contains serious warnings about mishandling God's instructions:

> See that you do all I command you; do not add to it or take away from it
> (Deuteronomy 12:32 NIV)

> "'How can you say, "We are wise because we have the word of the LORD," when your teachers have twisted it by writing lies?
> (Jeremiah 8:8 NLT)

> For I testify to everyone who hears the words of
> the prophecy of this book: If anyone adds to these
> things, God will add to him the plagues that are
> written in this book (Revelation 22:18 NKJV)

With this in mind, I encourage everyone to read and compare a variety of Bible versions. They're free online these days, so it's not as if you need to spend a fortune buying up printed Bibles. A number of Bible websites even allow you to see the actual Hebrew and Greek words that were written down by God's holy people, meaning you no longer have to wonder which words originally appeared on the page.

So now you know. The big mystery about Enoch has been solved. We can say with complete certainty from the Bible that this great man of faith, the great grandfather of Noah, did, in fact, die at age 365, just as the other Biblical heroes died without receiving the promise of eternal life. Jesus said no one has ever gone to heaven except Himself, and that includes Enoch. It has been appointed for all of us to die once, but the good news is that all people, including Enoch, you, and all your friends and family, will be made alive again in the future!

Chapter Twelve:
That's so gay

The teens and young adults of every generation always seem to be on the cutting edge of new expressions that push the envelope. Among their popular catchphrases these days is, "That's so gay."

They voice it to describe something they think is wrong, stupid, or just not to their liking. For instance, if young guys are hanging out together, and one of them does something silly or absurd, another might tell him, "That's so gay." The phrase can also be heard in shorter forms such as, "So gay," or just the ultra-brief and ever-popular, "Gay!"

The saying has become so widespread in recent years that numerous public-service TV ads have been produced to try to convince young people not to use it at all, because homosexual groups view it as a slur against them.

But irrespective of the intent behind the saying, there is no doubt that America – and much of the world, for that matter – have become "so gay" in recent times, and it's accelerating at a rapid rate.

We've seen the word "gay" itself morph from meaning "happy" to "homosexual."

We've seen massive parades with seas of people walking hand in hand, publicly declaring their gay pride, flying rainbow-colored flags, said to represent inclusiveness.

We've seen people fined, sued, and jailed in the U.S. and around the world for not accepting the entire gay agenda.

We've seen the U.S. Supreme Court discover a new right to same-sex marriage, though many were hard-pressed to find it in the Constitution.

We've seen a fast-food giant offer burgers wrapped in rainbow colors with secret messages that could be considered pro-gay hidden inside.

We've seen churches that call themselves Christian suddenly proclaim that homosexual sex is no longer sinful activity, with some even using lesbians to represent the Holy Family of Jesus in their live Nativity displays.

We've seen well-known news organizations publish stories about the Bible's alleged case for gay marriage, and a famous movie star admitting he desecrates Bibles because certain Scriptures describe what God really thinks of homosexual acts.

Because of such events, I wish to set the record straight – no pun intended – on what the Bible actually says about same-sex relations.

I do this out of godly love and concern for the well-being of all people, with no animus in my heart toward anyone and no desire to cause controversy. I want people to know how much God wishes to give everyone everlasting life, and He is urging every single person – even liars, murderers, thieves, homosexuals and heterosexuals – to stop any disobedient behavior so He can save them from the certain penalty of eternal death.

This chapter focuses on the sin of homosexual sex, as some of you may not realize the extent to which the Good Book addresses the subject, because it's a lot more than a verse or two in the Old Testament. The Bible is filled with Scriptures in both Testaments that will leave you with no doubt about what the Divine Family thinks about this practice. You'll realize how events on Planet Earth are actually coded by the Bible, as verses from thousands of years ago describe the news of today. You'll discover that many Christians who claim to follow God are actually blatant hypocrites when it comes to their obedience to His instructions.

And you'll learn that there is surprisingly good news for homosexuals that should make them quite gay, as in joyful, if they take one certain action. So be sure to read the entire chapter, because millions of people, including Christians, have never heard the stunning, tremendous reality.

The Gaylord of the Rings

I don't know about you, but I'm a big movie fan. I've seen hundreds of films throughout my life, being impressed by some and disappointed by many others. When I was younger, I tended not to know the beliefs of the stars on the silver screen. But in recent years, it's very difficult to be unaware of the viewpoints of the actors and actresses, for they seem to have an urgent desire to voice their personal opinions in public.

Take British actor Ian McKellen, for example. He's the well-known, handsome thespian born in 1939 who is best known for his roles as Gandalf the bearded wizard in "The Lord of the Rings" and "The Hobbit" trilogies as well as Magneto in the "X-Men" films. When I saw him in the first "Lord of the Rings" movie, I had no idea he was homosexual in real life. That changed when I read some newspaper interviews with the actor, in which he divulged a bizarre hobby in which he engages.

According to the reports, Mr. McKellen spends time tearing pages out of Bibles in every hotel room in which he stays. Not just any pages, but the pages of Scripture specifically condemning homosexual relations. I'm not kidding. The verse that sends McKellen over the edge is Leviticus 18:22. Here it is from a couple of versions:

> Thou shalt not lie with mankind, as with womankind: it is abomination.
> (Leviticus 18:22 KJV)

> "Do not practice homosexuality, having sex with another man as with a woman. It is a detestable sin. (Leviticus 18:22 NLT)

McKellen admits that he, like countless others, is shocked by the Bible.

"I think it's rather obscene and pornographic, and shouldn't be there, so I remove it," McKellen has said. "I'm not proudly defacing the book, but it's a choice between removing that page and throwing away the whole Bible."

When asked how many Bibles he has personally damaged, McKellen said, "I have no idea, but other people do it as well. People send me evidence that they have been removing that [page]."

The actor noted how some friends of his once sent him the Scripture in bulk: "I got delivered a package of forty of those pages – Leviticus 18:22 – that had been torn out by a married couple I know. They put them on a bit of string so that I could hang it up in the bathroom."

The reason I bring up McKellen's shredding habit is because he'd have to do a lot more vandalism if he truly knew how often the Bible talks about homosexuality. As we are about to see, the Good Book is simply replete with the subject matter, without a shred of tolerance for it.

Two chapters after the verse we just focused on comes a harsher decree from the Creator, declaring the death penalty for gay offenders:

> "If a man practices homosexuality, having sex with another man as with a woman, both men have committed a detestable act. They must both be put to death, for they are guilty of a capital offense. (Leviticus 20:13 NLT)

Now, for those who like to complain that the Bible is filled with venom and hate for homosexuals because of such an instruction, please be aware that God is an equal-opportunity offender. Just three verses earlier, He also mandates the death penalty for heterosexuals who have illicit sex:

> "'If a man commits adultery with another man's wife – with the wife of his neighbor – both the adulterer and the adulteress are to be put to death. (Leviticus 20:10 NIV)

It's even repeated later in another book:

> If a man is found sleeping with another man's wife, both the man who slept with her and the woman must die. You must purge the evil from Israel. (Deuteronomy 22:22 NIV)

Echoes of Sodom

There is a word in the English language whose origins stem from a homosexual hotbed often cited in the Bible. That word is "sodomy," and it's based on the decadent activities from the ancient city of Sodom. The Merriam-Webster Dictionary defines sodomy as "anal or oral copulation with a member of the same or opposite sex; also: copulation with an animal." The dictionary's editors correctly feature the origin of the term. As they explain, it's derived "from the homosexual proclivities of the men of the city in Genesis 19:1-11."

(http://www.merriam-webster.com/dictionary/sodomy)

These eleven verses in Genesis are quite illuminating, as they recount how the men of Sodom were so degenerate, they actually sought to gang-rape a pair of angels who were appearing on Earth in the physical form of ordinary human men:

> The two angels arrived at Sodom in the evening, and Lot was sitting in the gateway of the city. When he saw them, he got up to meet them and bowed down with his face to the ground.

> "My lords," he said, "please turn aside to your servant's house. You can wash your feet and spend the night and then go on your way early in the morning." "No," they answered, "we will spend the night in the square."

> But he insisted so strongly that they did go with him and entered his house. He prepared a meal for them, baking bread without yeast, and they ate.

> Before they had gone to bed, all the men from every part of the city of Sodom – both young and old – surrounded the house.

> They called to Lot, "Where are the men who came to you tonight? Bring them out to us so that we can have sex with them."

> Lot went outside to meet them and shut the door behind him and said, "No, my friends. Don't do this wicked thing. Look, I have two daughters who have never slept with a man. Let me bring them out to you, and you can do what you like with them. But don't do anything to these men, for they have come under the protection of my roof."

> "Get out of our way," they replied. "This fellow came here as a foreigner, and now he wants to play the judge! We'll treat you worse than them." They kept bringing pressure on Lot and moved forward to break down the door.
>
> But the men inside reached out and pulled Lot back into the house and shut the door. Then they struck the men who were at the door of the house, young and old, with blindness so that they could not find the door. (Genesis 19:1-11 NIV)

The story of Sodom culminates with the angels leading Lot and his immediate family to safety outside the city, and God firebombing the region into oblivion.

As you can see, the men of this city were extremely warped, being bold enough to pound on Lot's door, demanding to have homosexual relations with the two fresh faces who had just arrived in town. That goes far beyond what happens in the gay populace today. We haven't seen in the news entire populations of a city surround people's homes, trying to bash in the doors to have sex with its occupants. At least, not that I know of.

But this event in Genesis is not the only place the sordid actions of Sodom's citizens are mentioned. The depraved character of these people becomes absolutely clear when we look at numerous Scriptures. Even before the attempted gang rape of the angels, the Bible says:

> But the men of Sodom were exceedingly wicked
> and sinful against the LORD.
> (Genesis 13:13 NKJV)

Jesus Himself, in one of His pre-human appearances on Earth in the Old Testament, had a discussion with Abraham about the vileness of the people there:

> Then the LORD said, "The outcry against Sodom and Gomorrah is so great and their sin so grievous (Genesis 18:20 NIV)

Abraham tried bargaining with God. Would You not destroy the city if there are fifty righteous people dwelling there? The number got reduced during the haggling:

> Then he said, "May the Lord not be angry, but let
> me speak just once more. What if only ten can be
> found there?" He answered, "For the sake of ten,
> I will not destroy it." (Genesis 18:32 NIV)

The point is, in this large, cosmopolitan city, there were not even ten people who could be described as righteous, living in harmony with God's instructions. Virtually every person in the entire city was highly immoral.

The New Testament provides some more information about Sodom, explaining that the divine destruction of the area is intended to act as a stern warning for people disobedient to the Creator's laws:

> Later, God condemned the cities of Sodom and
> Gomorrah and turned them into heaps of ashes.
> He made them an example of what will happen
> to ungodly people. (2 Peter 2:6 NLT)

> … as Sodom and Gomorrah, and the cities around
> them in a similar manner to these, having given
> themselves over to sexual immorality and gone
> after strange flesh, are set forth as an example,
> suffering the vengeance of eternal fire.
> (Jude 1:7 NKJV)

Note how Jesus' brother Jude in the above verse mentions that the sinners had gone after "strange flesh." This term literally means "different flesh" or "other flesh," as in having sex with animals, which we have seen is echoed in the modern dictionary definition of sodomy.

Booting the sodomites

Those who followed the debased practices of Sodom became known as "sodomites" in Scripture, and that term is still with us today. The Old Testament reveals the Israelites did not put to death homosexuals as they were commanded, so sodomites ended up living in their midst, corrupting fellow citizens. That is, until some kings of Judah had the fortitude to kick them out:

> And there were also sodomites in the land: and
> they did according to all the abominations of
> the nations which the LORD cast out before the
> children of Israel. (1 Kings 14:24 KJV)

> And Asa did that which was right in the eyes of the LORD, as did David his father. And he took away the sodomites out of the land
> (1 Kings 15:11-12 KJV)

> And the remnant of the sodomites, which remained in the days of his father Asa, he [King Jehoshaphat] took out of the land.
> (1 Kings 22:46 KJV)

> And he [King Josiah] brake down the houses of the sodomites, that were by the house of the LORD (2 Kings 23:7 KJV)

The parade of pride, hand in hand

The citizens of Sodom were not just sexual deviants, they were proud of their behavior. They felt there was absolutely nothing wrong with their actions, and flaunted them openly. In recent years, there have been countless gay-pride parades across America and the world. Those thrusting the homosexual agenda on others are very public with their perversion. This attitude is not new. It was encoded in the Bible thousands of years ago:

> Behold, this was the iniquity of thy sister Sodom, **pride** ... (Ezekiel 16:49 KJV)

> The look on their faces testifies against them; they parade their sin like Sodom; they do not hide it. Woe to them! They have brought disaster upon themselves. (Isaiah 3:9 NIV)

It's fascinating how Scripture uses key words such as "pride" and "parade" when it comes to describing the sinful nature of the gay metropolis of ancient Sodom, the place that gave birth to "sodomy." The exact same words are used in our present day when we see news coverage about a "gay-pride parade." This is the actual term homosexuals use for their events – the very same words initially inked in Holy Scripture!

Here's another eye-opening example of what I mean:

> Every one that is **proud in heart** is an abomination to the LORD: though **hand join in hand**, he shall not be unpunished.
> (Proverbs 16:5 KJV)

Not only does Scripture declare that being proud in heart is an abomination – something God hates intensely – notice the second part of the verse. It says, "though hand join in hand." The Hebrew word for hand (yad) appears in the original language of Scripture twice in this verse, though some of today's Bibles don't even print the word hand for some strange reason. But the words hand in hand are there for an important reason, and it concerns two high-profile activities that are taking place right now in today's world.

The first is the aforementioned gay-pride parades. You've probably seen news coverage of these boastful marches on television or in your local newspaper. But you may not have paid attention to the fact that many of the participants are holding hands with each other as they walk. Just as the Bible says, they join hand in hand! Sometimes, they even join their hands over their heads, in a collective show of pride, which can be seen as a demonstration of defiance to their Maker.

On a quick side note, I'd like to point out that people who commit other sins, such as murder, stealing, lying, and adultery, are not usually proud and boastful in public about their transgressions. There are no pride parades for killers, thieves and those who cheat on their spouses.

The second, and perhaps more significant, manifestation of the "hand join in hand" statement from Scripture has to do with what was legalized nationally by the U.S. Supreme Court in 2015, and that is same-sex marriage. Recall what couples do at virtually all wedding ceremonies. They join hands, holding each other "hand in hand," just as was etched in the Bible code thousands of years ago. When you have a moment, go to Google Images, and search for "gay hands" or "gay wedding hands." You'll see what I'm talking about.

But the proud people who hold hands as they march in their gay-pride parades and boastfully hold same-sex wedding ceremonies will not go unpunished, according to the Bible. The proverb specifically noted, "he shall not be unpunished." And, as we read from Isaiah, God said, "Woe to them! They have brought disaster upon themselves" (Isaiah 3:9 NIV). This punishment also applies to the original person who was proud in his heart, Satan the devil, who has brought disaster upon himself and will be punished at the return of Jesus to Earth. You may recall this well-known proverb, which alludes to the future destruction of Satan and all others who are filled with pride and arrogance:

> Pride comes before destruction, and an arrogant
> spirit before a fall. (Proverbs 16:18 HCSB)

Telling 'whoppers'

In today's society, the prideful attitude seems boundless, going far beyond what happens in anyone's bedroom. Major companies have embraced the gay agenda in recent years, giving their collective stamp of approval to same-sex relations and providing financial benefits for the partners of homosexual employees. They include the biggest names in business, such as Coca-Cola, Campbell Soup, Kellogg, Ford, Chrysler, Toyota, eBay, Gap, Google, Kraft Foods, Nike, Microsoft, MillerCoors, Walt Disney and Kodak. There are scores more.
(Full list: http://www.wnd.com/2012/11/the-big-list-of-gayest-companies-in-america/)

In 2014, fast-food giant Burger King crafted a sandwich called the Proud Whopper, and sold it in San Francisco, with a shrewd publicity campaign on the Internet. For those unaware, a Proud Whopper is simply a regular Whopper hamburger that has been wrapped in rainbow-colored paper. It declares on the outside of the wrapper that it's a Proud Whopper, and when consumers unwrap the sandwich, there's a secret, slick message displayed on the paper's interior, stating: "We are all the same inside."
(https://www.youtube.com/watch?v=KLao1_JA2uE)

In the same vein, Burger King also tweaked its well-known slogan from "Have It Your Way" to "Be Your Way." The implication of self-pride is obvious. In an interview with BurgerBusiness.com*, Fernando Machado, Burger King's senior vice president, admitted the Proud Whopper campaign might not fit everyone's taste.

"But I am more excited that we are making this statement in support of self-expression," Machado said. "I would like to believe we are uniting people behind this message that I hope all can support. This is exactly what 'Be Your Way' means."

(http://burgerbusiness.com/proud-whopper-defines-burger-kings-be-your-way/)

A Christian dilemma

Now, it is no secret that many Christian groups today have been standing up against the homosexual agenda. But there's just one problem: Many of these believers are guilty of blatant hypocrisy and have given homosexuals some justification for their unnatural deeds.

The problem is that the same Bible (and even the same book of Leviticus) that shows God proclaiming homosexuality to be an abomination also declares in no uncertain terms that the very foods many Christians so eagerly toss down their gullets these days have also been prohibited by the Creator who uses the same word – abomination – to describe them:

> 'They shall be an abomination to you; you shall not eat their flesh, but you shall regard their carcasses as an abomination. 'Whatever in the water does not have fins or scales – that shall be an abomination to you.
>
> (Leviticus 11:11-12 NKJV)

Yes, folks, all those succulent lobsters, crabs, mussels, oysters, shrimp and clams that people enjoy, along with pork chops, pepperoni and the ever-popular bacon, are all detestable to your Maker, and He tells us all throughout the Bible not to eat them. A whole chapter is devoted to this subject in the prequel to this book.

But the point I'm making here is: There are homosexuals who cleverly cite the Bible to show how Christians are hypocrites when they eat popular foods such as pork and shellfish, while at the same time decrying gay sex as an abomination. The same God whose eternal law prohibits homosexual activity in Leviticus also bans the eating of unclean foods like bacon, ham and lobster. The homosexuals claim that if Old Testament food laws have somehow been done away with, as many Christians loudly suggest they have been, then the Old Testament laws on sex should be ancient history as well!

While at first that may seem like an excellent argument, there is a definitive Biblical answer to this dilemma. And that is that all of God's laws are still in effect. Many Christians hate to admit that Jesus plainly said in the New Testament that not a single one of His laws was being done away:

> "Do not think that I have come to abolish the Law or the Prophets; I have not come to abolish them but to fulfill them. For truly I tell you, until heaven and earth disappear, not the smallest letter, not the least stroke of a pen, will by any means disappear from the Law until everything is accomplished. Therefore anyone who sets aside one of the least of these commands and teaches others accordingly will be called least in the kingdom of heaven, but whoever practices and teaches these commands will be called great in the kingdom of heaven. (Matthew 5:17-19 NIV)

Thus, according to Jesus, we are to practice and teach His commands. It is still a sin to eat unclean animals and fish, and it is still a sin to engage in illicit sex.

The deception of Newsweek

For those who keep up with current events, it's astonishing sometimes to see how low some in the news media will sink to pervert the message of the Bible. In one egregious case, Newsweek published an in-depth story in December 2008, with the magazine's cover shouting: "The Religious Case for Gay Marriage."* The artwork on the front page featured a Holy Bible with a rainbow-colored bookmark protruding from its pages.
(http://www.newsweek.com/gay-marriage-our-mutual-joy-83287)

In the article, the reporter explained: "The Bible does condemn gay male sex in a handful of passages. Twice Leviticus refers to sex between men as 'an abomination' (King James version), but these are throwaway lines in a peculiar text given over to codes for living in the ancient Jewish world ..."

Wait. What?! Did Newsweek just label the two verses from Leviticus banning homosexual sex as "throwaway lines?" As a matter of fact, it did. The reporter casually states that Bible readers today are meant to throw away these verses. Perhaps Newsweek has heard of Ian McKellen ripping out hotel Bible pages and literally throwing them away. The article, though, demonstrates that many people are well aware what the Word of God teaches, but if they object to the content, their solution is to yank out and throw away passages unappealing to their taste.

Here's the big problem with that: Once people start tearing out and throwing away sentences from Scripture, where should they stop? Can they pick and choose which verses to keep and which ones to trash?

Let me ask you this: What's the very next verse after the ban on gay sex in Leviticus 18:22? Does anyone know what it is? (Yes, it's Leviticus 18:23. People never seem to tire of that joke.) The next instruction from God right after telling men not to engage in sex with other men is a command for people of both genders never to have sex with animals!

> "Do not have sexual relations with an animal and defile yourself with it. A woman must not present herself to an animal to have sexual relations with it; that is a perversion. (Leviticus 18:23 NIV)

Remember, Newsweek magazine and potentially millions of homosexuals and gay sympathizers believe and promote the deception that Leviticus 18:22, which bans gay sex, is a "throwaway line," and people should completely disregard it, since it's a "peculiar text" intended only for a certain people, the Israelites who lived during that time of antiquity. So if we follow this twisted line of thinking, then the very next verse must be a throwaway line as well, right? In other words, by Newsweek's logic, having sex with animals must be considered perfectly fine today, since Leviticus 18:23 would likely be a throwaway line as well.

These geniuses of journalism don't even realize that if they kept reading just one more sentence in the Bible, to verse 24, God explains that all people who engage in acts of homosexuality and bestiality become defiled by them:

> "'Do not defile yourselves in any of these ways, because this is how the nations that I am going to drive out before you became defiled.

(Leviticus 18:24 NIV)

People of many different races and creeds were spewed out of the Holy Land like throw-up because they engaged in these perverted actions inspired by Satan the devil. The Creator Himself was so disgusted and fed up with the pagan degenerates for their homosexual practices and sex with animals, He said He was personally kicking them out before the Israelites ever set foot in the area. So, the divine rules are not intended for God's chosen people alone, they're meant to be followed by everyone. These verses are not some "peculiar text" or code solely for living in the ancient Jewish world, as Newsweek claims. The Bible does not contain "throwaway lines."

The New Testament view

While the Old Testament has plenty to say about matters of homosexuality, I've heard many people claim that the New Testament doesn't even address the subject, and that Jesus never condemned the practice. Once again, they're wrong on both counts.

Regarding Jesus, millions of people don't comprehend that this man who walked the Earth performing astonishing miracles, including walking on water, giving sight to the blind and raising dead people back to life, is the same God, the very same Divine Person, who spoke the original instructions about sex to Moses, who then wrote them down in Leviticus! It was not God the Father conversing with Moses, since Jesus said <u>no one has ever seen the Father or heard His voice at any time</u>:

> "And the Father Himself, who sent Me, has testified of Me. You have neither heard His voice at any time, nor seen His form. (John 5:37 NKJV)

> No one has seen God at any time
> (1 John 4:12 NKJV)

Yes, the God of the Old Testament is Yeshua, Jesus the Christ. See the first "Shocked by the Bible" as well as "The Divine Secret" for an in-depth explanation on this. Once we understand this vital truth, we realize that Jesus actually condemned homosexuality numerous times, as we have just seen in this chapter. Through the books of Genesis, Leviticus, Kings, Isaiah and Ezekiel, Jesus made it perfectly clear He is disgusted by the practice. And, as mentioned before, we must not forget what Jesus said about His divine law during His human ministry in the New Testament:

> For truly I tell you, until heaven and earth disappear, not the smallest letter, not the least stroke of a pen, will by any means disappear from the Law until everything is accomplished. Therefore anyone who sets aside one of the least of these commands and teaches others accordingly will be called least in the kingdom of heaven, but whoever practices and teaches these commands will be called great in the kingdom of heaven. (Matthew 5:18-19 NIV)

Thus, by this plain statement, Jesus made it crystal clear in the New Testament that He still thinks same-sex relations are sickening, that they are just another abominable lie from the inventor of lying, Satan the devil.

His apostles felt the same, and one in particular, Paul, brought up gay sex several times, urging people not to be deceived, because homosexuals will not be among those who will be granted eternal life in God's coming kingdom:

> Do you not know that the unrighteous will not inherit the kingdom of God? Do not be deceived. Neither fornicators, nor idolaters, nor adulterers, nor homosexuals, nor sodomites, nor thieves, nor covetous, nor drunkards, nor revilers, nor extortioners will inherit the kingdom of God. (1 Corinthians 6:9-10 NKJV)

> We know that the law is good when used correctly. For the law was not intended for people who do what is right. It is for people who are lawless

and rebellious, who are ungodly and sinful, who consider nothing sacred and defile what is holy, who kill their father or mother or commit other murders. The law is for people who are sexually immoral, or who <u>practice homosexuality</u>, or are slave traders, liars, promise breakers, or who do anything else that contradicts the wholesome teaching that comes from the glorious Good News entrusted to me by our blessed God.
(1 Timothy 1:8-11 NLT)

Paul's grandest speech about homosexual relations is found in the first chapter of the book of Romans:

But God shows his anger from heaven against all sinful, wicked people who suppress the truth by their wickedness. They know the truth about God because he has made it obvious to them.

For ever since the world was created, people have seen the earth and sky. Through everything God made, they can clearly see his invisible qualities – his eternal power and divine nature. So they have no excuse for not knowing God.

Yes, they knew God, but they wouldn't worship him as God or even give him thanks. And they began to think up foolish ideas of what God was like. As a result, their minds became dark and confused. Claiming to be wise, they instead became utter fools. And instead of worshiping the glorious, ever-living God, they worshiped idols made to look like mere people and birds and animals and reptiles.

So God abandoned them to do whatever shameful things their hearts desired. As a result, <u>they did vile and degrading things with each other's bodies</u>. They traded the truth about God for a lie. So they worshiped and served the things

God created instead of the Creator himself, who is worthy of eternal praise! Amen.

That is why God abandoned them to their shameful desires. Even the women turned against the natural way to have sex and instead indulged in sex with each other.

And the men, instead of having normal sexual relations with women, burned with lust for each other. Men did shameful things with other men, and as a result of this sin, they suffered within themselves the penalty they deserved.

Since they thought it foolish to acknowledge God, he abandoned them to their foolish thinking and let them do things that should never be done. (Romans 1:18-28 NLT)

The information provided in the above text is very telling about human beings who intentionally don't follow God. Paul calls them "sinful, wicked people who suppress the truth by their wickedness." This sounds like a spot-on description of the wicked devil and what he does to God's truth. Paul says people knew the truth about God and refused to obey their Creator, or even say thanks to Him. Just like the devil. Once people had conjured up their own false ideas about what God is like, "their minds became dark and confused" and they became fools. Just like the devil. So God abandoned them, letting their own shameful desires run amok, just like the devil. Here is the money quote about the deviant sex again:

Even the women turned against the natural way to have sex and instead indulged in sex with each other. And the men, instead of having normal sexual relations with women, burned with lust for each other. Men did shameful things with other men, and as a result of this sin, they suffered within themselves the penalty they deserved. (Romans 1:26-27 NLT)

How is it that so many people in today's world claim the New Testament doesn't address same-sex relations? It's right there on the page. They either can't read it, don't want to read it, or they do, in fact, know that it's there, and, like the Scripture says, they "suppress the truth by their wickedness. They know the truth about God because he has made it obvious to them." (Romans 1:18-19 NLT)

The apostle Paul doesn't stop there, though. He goes on to provide a detailed list, describing the character qualities of many gay men and women. Here we go:

> Their lives became full of every kind of wicked-ness, sin, greed, hate, envy, murder, quarreling, deception, malicious behavior, and gossip.

> They are backstabbers, haters of God, insolent, proud, and boastful. They invent new ways of sinning, and they disobey their parents.

> They refuse to understand, break their promises, are heartless, and have no mercy.

> They know God's justice requires that those who do these things deserve to die, yet they do them anyway. Worse yet, they encourage others to do them, too. (Romans 1:29-32 NLT)

The queerest deception

Not only does Paul include "deception" on his list of gay attributes, but the final portion of the apostle's description gets into another serious matter evident in today's society. Again, here's how he wrapped it up:

> They know God's justice requires that those who do these things deserve to die, yet they do them anyway. Worse yet, they encourage others to do them, too. (Romans 1:32 NLT)

First, Paul explains that homosexuals are well aware that they deserve God's eternal death penalty for engaging in such lurid sexual activity, but they continue to take part nonetheless.

He then goes on to mention something even worse. He says homosexuals encourage other people to commit the same disgusting acts. In other words, they try to recruit people from the normal ranks of society, i.e. heterosexuals, persuading them not only to embrace homosexuality as normal, but engage in gay sex, too! They actually want those people who were originally obedient to the laws governing sex to switch sexual teams and violate the divine instructions, resulting in their exclusion from the kingdom of God!

This is nothing short of the personal attitude of Satan himself, because the devil wants to prevent as many people as possible from becoming a member of God's immortal family.

We see his fiendish deception at work in today's world with the pro-gay agenda in a variety of ways: children are taught from the earliest ages in public schools to question their gender and that being gay is completely natural, just an alternate lifestyle; some medical journals no longer call homosexuality a disorder; lawmakers pass rules giving rights and special protections to homosexuals; iconic corporations jump on the same-sex bandwagon; big-name celebrities come out of the closet to proclaim their sexual orientation or at least declare their support for the cause; movies and TV shows glorify the gay lifestyle, receiving awards for "courageous," pro-gay themes; and the rest of the print and electronic media create an atmosphere where anyone opposing the gay agenda is branded a bigot or a homophobe.

All these combine to broadcast a zeitgeist, a spirit of the times, where young people in particular think it's perfectly fine to engage in gay sex. They don't even realize they have been nudged, influenced, or "encouraged," as Paul said, (I think brainwashed is also fitting), into adopting this perverted way of thinking.

Remember, as we have seen earlier in the chapter titled "Three words of Jesus that most Christians don't believe," God's ultimate reason for creating human beings is to grow God's family, to have potentially billions and billions of immortal spirit beings, reigning according to His eternal laws. With Satan deceiving and encouraging people to be gay, then not only are homosexuals on the track toward eternal death, they're also not engaging in natural heterosexual relations, and thus, they're not producing more people who could eventually become immortal, divine children of God.

Good news after all

Finally, despite the negative tone we've seen in many Scriptures, there is actually some fantastic news for homosexuals. There is hope for them, and as long as they repent of their sins, just like everyone else needs to stop rebelling against God's laws, they can receive the wondrous reward of eternal life in God's very own family. Let's revisit this important warning:

> Do you not know that the unrighteous will not inherit the kingdom of God? Do not be deceived. Neither fornicators, nor idolaters, nor adulterers, nor homosexuals, nor sodomites, nor thieves, nor covetous, nor drunkards, nor revilers, nor extortioners will inherit the kingdom of God.
> (1 Corinthians 6:9-10 NKJV)

Please note that it's not just homosexuals who will be excluded from the kingdom of God. It's all those other violators, too. But the next verse provides the jaw-dropping good news:

> Some of you were once like that. But you were cleansed; you were made holy; you were made right with God by calling on the name of the Lord Jesus Christ and by the Spirit of our God.
> (1 Corinthians 6:11 NLT)

Paul explained that some people in the group of believers in Corinth, in their lives before repenting and coming to the truth of God, had been homosexuals, sodomites and all those other lawbreakers! Yet they were able to stop their demonically inspired transgressions with the assistance of God Himself.

Not only that, but Paul plainly says these people were cleansed of their sin, and were set apart by the Spirit, the very presence and power of God Himself! They were no longer guilty and waiting for the eternal death penalty. They were considered clean, walking on the path leading to everlasting life!

As stunning as this may sound, God does not want homosexuals to die! The Bible truth of the matter is that God wants <u>no one</u> to die. He gets no pleasure at all from it. Here's what the Creator urged through the prophet Ezekiel:

> I don't want you to die, says the Sovereign LORD. Turn back and live! (Ezekiel 18:32 NLT)

> As surely as I live, says the Sovereign LORD, I take no pleasure in the death of wicked people. I only want them to turn from their wicked ways so they can live. Turn! Turn from your wickedness ... Why should you die? (Ezekiel 33:11 NLT)

Jesus is begging every single person to knock off whatever it is we're doing that will prevent us from entering into eternal life. On several occasions recorded in the New Testament, He predicted that people who willingly reject His message of repentance and obedience would be worse off than ... (wait for it) ... the people of Sodom and Gomorrah! The homosexuals! Here's just one:

> "And you people of Capernaum, will you be honored in heaven? No, you will go down to the place of the dead. For if the miracles I did for you had been done in wicked Sodom, it would still be here today. I tell you, even Sodom will be better off on judgment day than you."
>
> (Matthew 11:23-24 NLT)

You're reading that correctly. The ancient city of Sodom would never have been firebombed out of existence if its citizens had experienced the miracles of Jesus. Why? Because those wicked sinners would have repented. This is more proof that homosexuals can stop engaging in gay sex. More importantly, Jesus went on to say that the pride-filled, parading homosexuals of Sodom will actually be better off at His return, compared to anyone (heterosexuals included) who knowingly rejects His message, as the people of Capernaum had done in this instance. The gay people of Sodom, along with all others who never had the true message of God presented to them, will still get the chance to get it right on Judgment Day! (Read the chapter on "The resurrection no one talks about.")

Ladies and gentlemen, the Bible is a book about how to reach our intended destiny, giving explicit instructions on how to gain eternal, divine life. Its mind-blowing, inclusive message is that everyone, irrespective of race, culture, national origin, sexual inclination or deviant sin, can receive this magnificent reward if they stop their satanically-inspired rebellion against their Creator and get with the program of obedience. It results in life everlasting as a divine child of God! For all those who knowingly refuse this spectacular gift from God Almighty, all I can say is: That's so gay.

Chapter Thirteen:
The world's most famous prostitute (who never actually hooked)

H ere's a quick question. Who is the most famous prostitute in history?

No, it's not Julia Roberts in "Pretty Woman" or Jodie Foster in "Taxi Driver." And while it's tempting to answer the question with American politicians who regularly whore themselves out for large sums of money, the name that comes to mind for many people is a woman from the Bible, a lady whose name has become virtually synonymous with selling her body for sex. The woman with the tarnished reputation is Mary Magdalene.

There's one major problem with that response, however. Mary Magdalene was never a prostitute. That's correct. There's neither a shred of evidence nor even a hint from Scripture that this well-known name ever engaged in what has jokingly become known as the world's oldest profession.

I know it's difficult for many to accept this fact due to the powerful brainwashing that has gone on for centuries regarding this highly slandered servant of God. Even in our time, we have seen highly inspiring movies such as Mel Gibson's masterpiece, "The Passion of the Christ," in which actress Monica Bellucci portrays Mary Magdalene, and is shown as a woman caught in the act of adultery who is subsequently forgiven by Jesus. In 2016, the popular movie "Risen" again repeated the same erroneous depiction. But as we take a look into what the Bible actually says about Mary, we won't find a single mention of sex, prostitution, whoring or harlotry, though the Bible is filled with those notions elsewhere, as we shall see.

Mary Magdalene appears at least fourteen times in verses of the New Testament. She receives more mentions than do most of Jesus' apostles. While people living in that era generally did not have last names as they do today, it's believed by many scholars that the name "Magdalene" is a reference to her being a native of Magdala, a small town on the western shore of the sea of Galilee. Just as Jesus was called "a Nazarene" in Matthew 2:23 because He lived in Nazareth, so Mary was called Magdalene because her hometown was Magdala. The gospel of Luke specifically refers to "Mary called Magdalene." (Luke 8:2 KJV)

The word "Magdala," which is of Aramaic origin, simply means "tower." There are some passages in the non-biblical Jewish Talmud that refer to "Miriam (the Hebrew name for Mary), the plaiter of women's hair" or "curling women's hair," which some have suggested might mean she was a hairdresser, or even an adulteress. But that is speculation.

What we know for certain about Mary Magdalene from Holy Scripture paints a very different picture than the image of a loose woman or an adulteress. She's actually quite a triumphant figure. Here's what the Bible does say.

Mary Magdalene had been possessed by seven demons, but those evil, fallen angels were kicked out of her by the divine power of Jesus:

> ... Mary Magdalene, out of whom he had driven seven demons. (Mark 16:9 NIV)

> ... Mary Magdalene, from whom he had cast out seven demons (Luke 8:2 NLT)

These are the only two verses in the Bible which connect Mary Magdalene to any sort of evil, but please note that prostitution is never mentioned in either verse, nor is it suggested. She was a woman who was actually victimized by seven demons taking up residence inside her, so she was likely tormented with relentless ferocity, leaving her without any peace of mind. Other instances of demonic possession in the Bible sometimes show people engaged in violent acts against themselves, even with burning or drowning. One man who asked Jesus to heal his son who was possessed by a demon noted: "The spirit often throws him into the fire or into water, trying to kill him." (Mark 9:22 NLT)

But concerning Mary, we're not given any other information as to how the seven demons affected her. We're merely told that Jesus had cast more than half a dozen demons out of her.

Mary Magdalene was also one of several women who provided some financial sustenance to the ministry of Jesus. Luke informs us:

> and also some women who had been cured of evil spirits and diseases: Mary (called Magdalene) from whom seven demons had come out; Joanna the wife of Chuza, the manager of Herod's household; Susanna; and many others. These women were helping to support them out of their own means. (Luke 8:2-3 NIV)

The place from whence Mary's financial resources came is never specified.

Mary Magdalene also is seen as one of the female witnesses to the final moments of Jesus' life as a human being, watching Him slowly die during His crucifixion:

> Many women were there, watching from a distance. They had followed Jesus from Galilee to care for his needs. Among them were Mary Magdalene, Mary the mother of James and Joseph, and the mother of Zebedee's sons. (Matthew 27:55-56 NIV)

> Now there stood by the cross of Jesus his mother, and his mother's sister, Mary the wife of Cleophas, and Mary Magdalene. (John 19:25 KJV)

Even after Jesus was laid in His tomb, we're told she couldn't tear herself away from the Master:

> Both Mary Magdalene and the other Mary were sitting across from the tomb and watching. (Matthew 27:61 NLT)

As I demonstrated in the first "Shocked by the Bible," the Bible indicates Jesus was, in actuality, executed on a Wednesday afternoon and put in the grave Wednesday evening, before the annual high-day Sabbath of the Feast of Unleavened Bread was to begin on Thursday of that week.

Then, while Jesus was in the grave for seventy-two hours, Mary Magdalene is shown purchasing spices on Friday, the day after the annual Sabbath, so she could anoint the Savior's body:

> And when the sabbath was past, Mary Magdalene, and Mary the mother of James, and Salome, had bought sweet spices, that they might come and anoint him. (Mark 16:1 KJV)

With Saturday night being the completion of the "three days and three nights" Jesus predicted He would be in the grave (Matthew 12:40), Mary Magdalene then hustled to Jesus' tomb after the weekly Sabbath of Saturday was over, before the sun had arisen early on the first day of the week, Sunday.

> Early on the first day of the week, while it was still dark, Mary Magdalene went to the tomb and saw that the stone had been removed from the entrance. (John 20:1 NIV)

Upon seeing the stone no longer there, she darted back to find some of Jesus' other disciples:

> So she came running to Simon Peter and the other disciple, the one Jesus loved, and said, "They have taken the Lord out of the tomb, and we don't know where they have put him!" (John 20:2 NIV)

Once Peter and John arrived and inspected the empty tomb, they found only strips of linen and a cloth that had been wrapped around Jesus' head for burial. The men then went home. But at least one person remained there for a while at the tomb of Jesus. Yes, it was our famous non-prostitute, Mary Magdalene. This fervent believer proceeded to converse with angels on the scene. And finally, perhaps most significantly, she was the very first person – not just the first woman – to see Jesus after He had been raised from the dead. Additionally, she was also the first person to speak with Him at that glorious moment! Here are the details in the New Testament:

Now when Jesus was risen early the first day of the week, he appeared first to Mary Magdalene (Mark 16:9 KJV)

Now Mary stood outside the tomb crying. As she wept, she bent over to look into the tomb and saw two angels in white, seated where Jesus' body had been, one at the head and the other at the foot. They asked her, "Woman, why are you crying?"

"They have taken my Lord away," she said, "and I don't know where they have put him." At this, she turned around and saw Jesus standing there, but she did not realize that it was Jesus.

He asked her, "Woman, why are you crying? Who is it you are looking for?" Thinking he was the gardener, she said, "Sir, if you have carried him away, tell me where you have put him, and I will get him." Jesus said to her, "Mary." She turned toward him and cried out in Aramaic, "Rabboni!" (which means "Teacher").

Jesus said, "Do not hold on to me, for I have not yet ascended to the Father. Go instead to my brothers and tell them, 'I am ascending to my Father and your Father, to my God and your God.'"

Mary Magdalene went to the disciples with the news: "I have seen the Lord!" And she told them that he had said these things to her.
(John 20:11-18 NIV)

What an inspiring report! Here we have a person who formerly had been plagued by seven demonic spirits, who had followed and served Jesus, not just with devotion and obedience, but with tangible financial support, who was there with Him to see his execution and burial, who purchased spices to anoint His body, who was the first human being to see and converse with the risen Christ, and who was the first person (and a female at that) to be told to spread the good news that the Creator of the universe was restored to life! Yes, this woman was the first Christian witness!

Why on Earth would anyone want to soil her reputation with this nonsense about prostitution?

The bad reputation

There are numerous factors which have contributed to this giant misconception over the years. It possibly began with Magdala, that town on the shore of the Sea of Galilee, from which Mary Magdalene's name is likely derived. According to the Jewish Talmud, the town of Magdala had a seedy reputation, and because prostitution was rampant there, it was destroyed. I like to remind people that many regions today, including Greater Las Vegas, Nevada, are known for prostitution, but that obviously doesn't mean someone who hails from there is automatically a hooker. At least I hope that's not the case.

Another reason may be the fact that Luke's mention of Mary Magdalene in his eighth chapter appears directly after an account of Jesus being anointed by a sinful woman in the seventh chapter of his gospel. Here's the story:

> One of the Pharisees asked Jesus to have dinner with him, so Jesus went to his home and sat down to eat. When a certain immoral woman from that city heard he was eating there, she brought a beautiful alabaster jar filled with expensive perfume. Then she knelt behind him at his feet, weeping. Her tears fell on his feet, and she wiped them off with her hair. Then she kept kissing his feet and putting perfume on them.
>
> When the Pharisee who had invited him saw this, he said to himself, "If this man were a prophet, he would know what kind of woman is touching him. She's a sinner!"

Then Jesus answered his thoughts. "Simon," he said to the Pharisee, "I have something to say to you."

"Go ahead, Teacher," Simon replied.

Then Jesus told him this story: "A man loaned money to two people – 500 pieces of silver to one and 50 pieces to the other. But neither of them could repay him, so he kindly forgave them both, canceling their debts. Who do you suppose loved him more after that?"

Simon answered, "I suppose the one for whom he canceled the larger debt."

"That's right," Jesus said. Then he turned to the woman and said to Simon, "Look at this woman kneeling here. When I entered your home, you didn't offer me water to wash the dust from my feet, but she has washed them with her tears and wiped them with her hair. You didn't greet me with a kiss, but from the time I first came in, she has not stopped kissing my feet. You neglected the courtesy of olive oil to anoint my head, but she has anointed my feet with rare perfume.

"I tell you, her sins – and they are many – have been forgiven, so she has shown me much love. But a person who is forgiven little shows only little love." Then Jesus said to the woman, "Your sins are forgiven."

The men at the table said among themselves, "Who is this man, that he goes around forgiving sins?"

And Jesus said to the woman, "Your faith has saved you; go in peace." (Luke 7:36-50 NLT)

Here we have an immoral and sinful woman who was blessed in having her transgressions of the law forgiven by Jesus. But her name is never provided. While this story about the unnamed woman finishes out chapter seven of Luke, the name Mary Magdalene suddenly pops up in the second verse of the very next chapter:

> Soon afterward Jesus began a tour of the nearby towns and villages, preaching and announcing the Good News about the Kingdom of God. He took his twelve disciples with him, along with some women who had been cured of evil spirits and diseases. Among them were Mary Magdalene, from whom he had cast out seven demons (Luke 8:1-2 NLT)

So, it's quite possible the textual proximity of Mary Magdalene to the unnamed sinful woman could have sparked the idea Mary was the sinful woman. In fact, in the year 591, Pope Gregory the Great, in one of his sermons, actually made that specific connection, writing originally in Latin: "We believe that this woman [Mary Magdalene] is Luke's female sinner, the woman John calls Mary, and that Mary from whom Mark says seven demons were cast out." Pope Gregory also claimed the ointment used to anoint the feet of Jesus had been used previously by Mary Magdalene "to perfume her flesh in forbidden acts." Thus, the power of the pontiff appears to have given long-lasting legs to the prostitution idea.

In similar fashion, the gospel of John recounts how another woman was caught in the act of adultery, and Jesus forgave her:

> As he was speaking, the teachers of religious law and the Pharisees brought a woman who had been caught in the act of adultery. They put her in front of the crowd.

> "Teacher," they said to Jesus, "this woman was caught in the act of adultery. The law of Moses says to stone her. What do you say?"

> They were trying to trap him into saying something they could use against him, but Jesus stooped down and wrote in the dust with his finger. They kept demanding an answer, so he stood up again and said, "All right, but let the

one who has never sinned throw the first stone!"
Then he stooped down again and wrote in the
dust.

When the accusers heard this, they slipped away
one by one, beginning with the oldest, until only
Jesus was left in the middle of the crowd with
the woman. Then Jesus stood up again and said
to the woman, "Where are your accusers? Didn't
even one of them condemn you?"

"No, Lord," she said.

And Jesus said, "Neither do I. Go and sin no
more." (John 8:3-11 NLT)

This is the scene I mentioned earlier that was immortalized in the
2004 motion picture, "The Passion of the Christ." Unfortunately, the film
perpetuates the prostitute myth, for director Mel Gibson identifies the
adulterous woman on the big screen as Mary Magdalene. The movie was
a box-office smash, earning more than $600 million during its theatrical
release and becoming the highest-grossing religious film in history.
Overall, "The Passion" stayed very faithful to the script in the New
Testament, but all those millions of people who flocked to the cinema for
this fantastic Biblical epic were once again brainwashed with the notion
that Mary Magdalene was the woman caught in adultery, when the Bible
makes no such connection.

Dirty laundry

Perhaps one of the biggest factors in cementing the idea that Mary
Magdalene was a reformed prostitute may have been the creation of
something called Magdalene asylums, also known as Magdalene laundries,
in North America, Europe and Australia.

These were institutions designed to house "fallen women," whether
they had been prostitutes, unwed mothers, women who had sex outside of
marriage, victims of abuse or merely destitute ladies. The facilities were
run by a variety of religious groups including Catholics and Presbyterians,
and the name "Magdalene" was selected because many people held on

to the mistaken notion that the Bible's Mary Magdalene was indeed a hooker. The buildings were called laundries because the ladies there were actually washing laundry seven days a week, without pay. Many of the women who lived and worked there allegedly became victims themselves of mental, physical and even sexual abuse.

The first Magdalene asylum was founded in 1758 in Whitechapel, England, followed by a location in Ireland in 1767. Philadelphia, Pennsylvania, was the first city in the United States to join the club, while New York, Boston, Chicago and Toronto, Canada, soon jumped on the bandwagon, and the Magdalene asylums blossomed in hundreds of locations worldwide. The last one closed in 1996.

A massive scandal erupted in 1993 at one of the Magdalene laundries in Dublin, Ireland, as the dead bodies of 155 women who worked in harsh conditions at the facility were found in unmarked graves. That gruesome discovery helped inspire the 2002 motion picture, "The Magdalene Sisters," which was based on true events, and was named Best Picture at the Venice Film Festival. Thus, due to the proliferation of the Magdalene asylums, the name Magdalene even in our day echoes some sort of connection to prostitution.

Married to Jesus?

There also has been plenty of talk in the media in recent years about the possibility that Jesus Christ was married during His human ministry, and the name of His alleged wife most often associated with the speculation is none other than Mary Magdalene.

This theory went viral in 2003 with the publication of author Dan Brown's best-selling book, "The Da Vinci Code." In 2006, Brown's story was brought to the silver screen in a movie of the same title starring Tom Hanks. But people need to remember that "The Da Vinci Code" is a work of fiction. It is not actual history, and it is certainly not Biblical. Yes, Jesus did exist, and so did Mary Magdalene, but the Bible never even hints the two were married, though it does give intimate details regarding the lives of many other figures within its pages.

Next thing you know, someone will take a real-life historical character such as American President Abraham Lincoln and suggest he discovered a plot by vampires to take over the United States, and then embark on a mission to eliminate them. Oh wait. That ridiculous fictional premise did make it into movie theaters in 2012's "Abraham Lincoln: Vampire Hunter." The point is, anyone can take a real figure from history and make up an elaborate fantasy about that person, irrespective of any basis in fact.

Meanwhile, there has also been a buzz about a papyrus fragment called "The Gospel of Jesus' Wife." The fragment was introduced to the public in September 2012 at the International Coptic Congress in Rome by Karen L. King, a professor of Divinity at Harvard University in Massachusetts.

The text on this small piece of papyrus contains a line that, when translated into English, reads: "Jesus said to them, 'My wife ...'"

Professor King claimed the papyrus featured a fourth-century Coptic translation of "a gospel probably written in Greek in the second half of the second century," but she also noted it "should not be taken as proof that Jesus, the historical person, was actually married."

The papyrus was slammed by a host of experts as a modern-day forgery, and in June 2016, King admitted it was likely a fake.

One other note concerning the fragment: There's no mention of Mary Magdalene. In fact, the so-called "wife" of Jesus is never named, so for all those who might have thought this was some sort of proof Jesus was married to Mary Magdalene, keep dreaming.

The Magdalene lesson

There is an important point I'd like to make about the story of Mary Magdalene. It's this fact that, after she was instructed to tell her fellow disciples of Jesus that their Master was indeed alive again, that He had been miraculously brought back to life, those very disciples and friends of Jesus did **not** believe her. Here's the account:

> Now when Jesus was risen early the first day of the week, he appeared first to Mary Magdalene, out of whom he had cast seven devils. And she went and told them that had been with him, as they mourned and wept. And they, when they had heard that he was alive, and had been seen of her, **believed not**. (Mark 16:9-11 KJV)

I think it's safe to say that if Mary Magdalene were giving the good news of Jesus' resurrection to people who had not been following the Savior, they would likely think she was insane, or at least a few french fries short of a Happy Meal. But the folks she informed were not the ordinary citizens of the day. They were Jesus' chosen and beloved apostles who spent more than three years with Him, the Messiah. They had eaten with Him, traveled with Him, listened to Him and witnessed countless eye-popping signs and wonders, including blind people given sight and other dead human beings – including a young girl as well as His own personal friend Lazarus – raised from the dead by the miraculous power of God.

They had been instructed on numerous occasions by Jesus Himself that He would suffer, die and then be raised from death. Here's just one mention:

> After they gathered again in Galilee, Jesus told them, "The Son of Man is going to be betrayed into the hands of his enemies. He will be killed, but on the third day he will be raised from the dead." And the disciples were filled with grief. (Matthew 17:22-23 NLT)

These are the men who believed Jesus throughout His ministry, even giving up their daily occupations to become His full-time students. So why on Earth would they not believe the amazing news provided by their colleague Mary Magdalene that He was indeed back, just as Jesus had predicted in detail again and again?

These people were the first Christians, the ones who were dispatched to travel across the planet to spread the good news of the coming kingdom of God, the future takeover of the governments of this world by the Creator of all things. And yet they thought Mary Magdalene was telling stories out of school, that she was actually lying to them when she asserted she had seen and spoken with the risen Yeshua.

Apparently, they made the simple and common mistake of not believing every word spoken by their God. Their hearts were hardened to the message Jesus had repeated to them about His death and resurrection. Jesus meant exactly what He said when it came to the timetable of being "three days and three nights in the heart of the earth" (Matthew 12:40 KJV).

He meant exactly what He said about being raised from death. He was raised from **the dead**, not the living. He wasn't being brought back from someplace where He was alive, such as heaven, since He didn't even ascend to heaven until after He appeared to Mary Magdalene. Even after the apostles had seen Jesus raise Lazarus, who spent four days getting ripe in his grave, they somehow could not wrap their minds around the fact that their Messiah, whom they had seen slain, was fully alive again, walking and talking.

The question I now put to you is what kind of Christian are you? Are you like the apostles who claimed with their lips to worship Jesus, but did not believe every word of the Savior, even when one of their own pleaded that Jesus' prediction of resurrection from the dead had come true?

Or are you like Mary Magdalene, the magnificent Biblical heroine whose troubled life was freed from the control of demonic forces, who set herself apart from her previous demonically influenced life of darkness to serve and even financially support the work of God, who was found worthy enough to be the first person with whom the risen God spoke, and who was the point person in sharing the good news with others? Any stain in Mary Magdalene's life was removed by her Maker thousands of years ago. We should all strive to emulate her faith and devotion, and put to an end, once and for all, to this unbiblical notion she was a prostitute.

Book of hookers

It may be surprising to some, but the Bible has no problem talking about prostitution. Scripture is actually filled with the practice from Genesis to Revelation. So, if God wanted it known that Mary Magdalene had been a prostitute at any time, there's little doubt it would have been specified.

One of the first instances of paying for sex features the story of Tamar, the daughter-in-law of Israel's son Judah. She pretended to be a hooker to entice Judah to have sex with her, because she sought to get pregnant to continue the line of her husband who was slain by God. Here it is:

> Judah noticed her and thought she was a prostitute, since she had covered her face.

> So he stopped and propositioned her. "Let me
> have sex with you," he said, not realizing that
> she was his own daughter-in-law. "How much
> will you pay to have sex with me?" Tamar asked.
>
> "I'll send you a young goat from my flock,"
> Judah promised. "But what will you give me to
> guarantee that you will send the goat?" she asked.
>
> "What kind of guarantee do you want?"
> he replied. She answered, "Leave me your
> identification seal and its cord and the walking
> stick you are carrying." So Judah gave them to
> her. Then he had intercourse with her, and she
> became pregnant. (Genesis 38:15-18 NLT)

Tamar gave birth to twins from this union, and her son named Perez is actually a direct ancestor to Jesus. Her name is even mentioned in the third verse of the New Testament in the genealogy of Jesus:

> Judah was the father of Perez and Zerah (whose
> mother was Tamar). (Matthew 1:3 NLT)

One promiscuous woman whom the Bible singles out as a champion of God's purpose is a whore named Rahab, a pagan woman living in the city of Jericho at the time the Israelites were about to begin their conquest of the Promised Land:

> Then Joshua secretly sent out two spies from the
> Israelite camp at Acacia Grove. He instructed
> them, "Scout out the land on the other side of
> the Jordan River, especially around Jericho." So
> the two men set out and came to the house of
> a prostitute named Rahab and stayed there that
> night. (Joshua 2:1 NLT)

Rahab actually helped the spies by hiding them on her own roof after she admitted:

> "I know the LORD has given you this land," she
> told them. "We are all afraid of you. Everyone in
> the land is living in terror. (Joshua 2:9 NLT)

And while the Israelites were instructed to lay waste to everyone and everything in Jericho, Joshua himself made an exception for the prostitute's household:

> Jericho and everything in it must be completely destroyed as an offering to the LORD. Only Rahab the prostitute and the others in her house will be spared, for she protected our spies. (Joshua 6:17 NLT)

There are dozens of other mentions of prostitutes. Here are a few for your viewing pleasure:

> "Do not defile your daughter by making her a prostitute, or the land will be filled with prostitution and wickedness.
> (Leviticus 19:29 NLT)

> "If a priest's daughter defiles herself by becoming a prostitute, she also defiles her father's holiness, and she must be burned to death.
> (Leviticus 21:9 NLT)

> One day Samson went to the Philistine town of Gaza and spent the night with a prostitute.
> (Judges 16:1 NLT)

Yes, folks, something you don't hear too often in church is the fact that the famous Bible hero Samson, who slew many pagan Philistines in his lifetime, actually paid for sex with a hooker! Here are some more references to prostitutes:

> Jesus said to them, "Truly I tell you, the tax collectors and the prostitutes are entering the kingdom of God ahead of you. For John the Baptist came and showed you the right way to live, but you didn't believe him, while tax collectors and prostitutes did.
> (Matthew 21:31-32 NIV)

> Don't you realize that your bodies are actually parts of Christ? Should a man take his body,

which is part of Christ, and join it to a prostitute? Never! And don't you realize that if a man joins himself to a prostitute, he becomes one body with her? For the Scriptures say, "The two are united into one." (1 Corinthians 6:15-16 NLT)

When the LORD first began speaking to Israel through Hosea, he said to him, "Go and marry a prostitute, so that some of her children will be conceived in prostitution. This will illustrate how Israel has acted like a prostitute by turning against the LORD and worshiping other gods." (Hosea 1:2 NLT)

As stunning as it sounds to some, God indeed instructed His prophet Hosea to marry a whore. This was certainly far out of the norm, but God used it as a way to demonstrate to His people how they were prostituting themselves by following the wicked ways of other non-existent gods.

Numerous times in Scripture, God has used this device of labeling His own people prostitutes, whores or harlots, depending on your Bible translation. This is important because, as you're likely aware, the Bible is a timeless book, and bad behavior that made God angry thousands of years ago, such as engaging in paganism, still makes Him furious today.

One of the clearest (and often most overlooked) examples of God indicting people who claim to follow Him is found in the sixteenth chapter of Ezekiel. I'm going to provide a fairly large chunk of the chapter here so you can see that the breaking of God's laws, not just selling your body for sex, is considered adultery and prostitution to God. In this brutally honest portion of text, Jesus, speaking through Ezekiel, addressed the people of Jerusalem who, despite God's own personal care, transformed herself symbolically from a gorgeously groomed, virtuous woman into a disgusting, rebellious skank, all due to her continued disobedience to God's eternal law:

You grew up and became a beautiful jewel. Your breasts became full, and your body hair grew, but you were still naked. And when I passed by again, I saw that you were old enough for love.

So I wrapped my cloak around you to cover your nakedness and declared my marriage vows. I made a covenant with you, says the Sovereign LORD, and you became mine.

"Then I bathed you and washed off your blood, and I rubbed fragrant oils into your skin. I gave you expensive clothing of fine linen and silk, beautifully embroidered, and sandals made of fine goatskin leather. I gave you lovely jewelry, bracelets, beautiful necklaces, a ring for your nose, earrings for your ears, and a lovely crown for your head.

And so you were adorned with gold and silver. Your clothes were made of fine linen and were beautifully embroidered. You ate the finest foods – choice flour, honey, and olive oil – and became more beautiful than ever. You looked like a queen, and so you were!

Your fame soon spread throughout the world because of your beauty. I dressed you in my splendor and perfected your beauty, says the Sovereign LORD. "But you thought your fame and beauty were your own. So <u>you gave yourself as a prostitute</u> to every man who came along. Your beauty was theirs for the asking.

You used the lovely things I gave you to make shrines for idols, where you played the prostitute. Unbelievable! How could such a thing ever happen? You took the very jewels and gold and silver ornaments I had given you and made statues of men and worshiped them. <u>This is adultery against me!</u>

You used the beautifully embroidered clothes I gave you to dress your idols. Then you used my special oil and my incense to worship them.

Imagine it! You set before them as a sacrifice the choice flour, olive oil, and honey I had given you, says the Sovereign LORD.

"Then you took your sons and daughters – the children you had borne to me – and sacrificed them to your gods. Was your prostitution not enough? Must you also slaughter my children by sacrificing them to idols?

In all your years of adultery and detestable sin, you have not once remembered the days long ago when you lay naked in a field, kicking about in your own blood.

"What sorrow awaits you, says the Sovereign LORD. In addition to all your other wickedness, you built a pagan shrine and put altars to idols in every town square. On every street corner you defiled your beauty, offering your body to every passerby in an endless stream of prostitution. Then you added lustful Egypt to your lovers, provoking my anger with your increasing promiscuity.

That is why I struck you with my fist and reduced your boundaries. I handed you over to your enemies, the Philistines, and even they were shocked by your lewd conduct. You have prostituted yourself with the Assyrians, too. It seems you can never find enough new lovers! And after your prostitution there, you still were not satisfied. You added to your lovers by embracing Babylonia, the land of merchants, but you still weren't satisfied.

"What a sick heart you have, says the Sovereign LORD, to do such things as these, acting like a shameless prostitute.

You build your pagan shrines on every street corner and your altars to idols in every square. In fact, <u>you have been worse than a prostitute,</u> so eager for sin that you have not even demanded payment. Yes, <u>you are an adulterous wife who takes in strangers instead of her own husband. Prostitutes charge for their services – but not you! You give gifts to your lovers, bribing them to come and have sex with you. So you are the opposite of other prostitutes. You pay your lovers instead of their paying you!</u>

"Therefore, you prostitute, listen to this message from the LORD!

This is what the Sovereign LORD says: Because you have poured out your lust and exposed yourself in prostitution to all your lovers, and because you have worshiped detestable idols, and because you have slaughtered your children as sacrifices to your gods, this is what I am going to do. I will gather together all your allies – the lovers with whom you have sinned, both those you loved and those you hated – and I will strip you naked in front of them so they can stare at you.

I will punish you for your murder and adultery. I will cover you with blood in my jealous fury. Then I will give you to these many nations who are your lovers, and they will destroy you. They will knock down your pagan shrines and the altars to your idols. They will strip you and take your beautiful jewels, leaving you stark naked. They will band together in a mob to stone you and cut you up with swords. They will burn your homes and punish you in front of many women. I will stop your prostitution and end your payments to your many lovers.

"Then at last my fury against you will be spent, and my jealous anger will subside. I will be calm and will not be angry with you anymore. But first, because you have not remembered your youth but have angered me by doing all these evil things, I will fully repay you for all of your sins, says the Sovereign LORD. For you have added lewd acts to all your detestable sins.

Everyone who makes up proverbs will say of you, 'Like mother, like daughter.' For your mother loathed her husband and her children, and so do you. And you are exactly like your sisters, for they despised their husbands and their children. Truly your mother was a Hittite and your father an Amorite.

"Your older sister was Samaria, who lived with her daughters in the north. Your younger sister was Sodom, who lived with her daughters in the south. But you have not merely sinned as they did. You quickly surpassed them in corruption.

As surely as I live, says the Sovereign LORD, <u>Sodom and her daughters were never as wicked as you and your daughters</u>. Sodom's sins were pride, gluttony, and laziness, while the poor and needy suffered outside her door. She was proud and committed detestable sins, so I wiped her out, as you have seen.

"Even Samaria did not commit half your sins. You have done far more detestable things than your sisters ever did. They seem righteous compared to you. Shame on you! Your sins are so terrible that you make your sisters seem righteous, even virtuous.

"But someday I will restore the fortunes of Sodom and Samaria, and I will restore you, too.

Then you will be truly ashamed of everything you have done, for your sins make them feel good in comparison.
(Ezekiel 16:7-54 NLT)

As is abundantly evident in the above passage, Jesus has a serious problem with the people for whom He personally has shown love and concern. By their intentional disregard for His laws, they metaphorically became prostitutes, and even worse than prostitutes because they actually paid others instead of getting paid for their services. Even today, people still open their wallets and pay lots of money to spiritually prostitute themselves against God by engaging in worthless pagan customs each December.

If we take an honest look at our world, even in many Christian circles, countless people continue a willful disobedience to God's laws, and, thus, we have become part of this condemnation. We all need to carefully examine everything we do in life, not taking any action or belief for granted, and ask ourselves: Are we truly being faithful to the divine instructions of our Creator, or are we merely whoring ourselves out with our own desires?

Be honest with the answer. Eternity hangs in the balance.

Chapter Fourteen:
Movies with secret Bible themes

Everyone loves the movies, don't they? Well, maybe not everyone because Hollywood has certainly produced a large crop of rancid waste in recent years, helping to rot our culture with a steady stream of films packed with images and themes promoting sinful behavior and a general anti-God bias. Nevertheless, I'd venture to say the vast majority of people still enjoy seeing a good motion picture on the silver screen or at home. Yet when folks spend time watching a major production, many don't realize they are often being treated to a story with hidden plot lines that come directly from the Bible.

I am not talking about films that intentionally re-enact events in Scripture such as Cecil B. DeMille's "The Ten Commandments" starring Charlton Heston, or Mel Gibson's "The Passion of the Christ." Sometimes these Bible films get the story right, as did 1995's "Joseph" with Ben Kingsley. Sometimes they get the story wrong, as did 2006's "The Nativity Story." The big problem with this otherwise accurate film was the perpetuation of the myth that three wise men showed up to see Jesus the night He was born in Bethlehem. The truth of the matter is that no wise men were there the night of His birth, but that eventually some wise men (Scripture never says three of them) presented their gifts to Him when He was a young child in a house, not a babe in a manger.

Then there are those films which pretend to tell a story from the Bible, but deviate far from Scripture and end up becoming embarrassments to the truth. Two recent examples of such abominations are 2014's "Noah" with Russell Crowe in the title role and "Exodus: Gods and Kings" starring Christian Bale as Moses.

And once in a while, movies will casually mention an event in Scripture, and get the story atrociously wrong. A vivid example is the 1981 blockbuster "Raiders of the Lost Ark." Harrison Ford as Indiana Jones correctly recalled how Moses smashed the Ten Commandments. However, he immediately went off the rails when he mistakenly stated, "The Hebrews took the broken pieces and put them in the ark." The truth is that the Israelites did not collect the shattered pieces to place them inside the ark. Moses climbed back up the mountain to receive a second set of the tablets, freshly inscribed by the finger of God.

Having said all that, this chapter is not about movies that attempt to showcase the Bible. It's about films with plots ostensibly very different from the events of Scripture, but which feature strong messages from the Bible secretly embedded into them. I use the word secretly because I surmise some of the directors may not even be aware how connected their works are to the Word of God. None of the films on my list blatantly say anything such as, "Get Jesus in your life and be saved." And if they did project such a message, they undoubtedly would not have become so popular. But they do include themes that are astonishingly similar to those in Scripture.

We all should realize that both God and Satan, "the prince of the power of the air" (Ephesians 2:2 NKJV), are powerful voices, and both have been broadcasting their messages of good and evil to human beings through a variety of media for ages. In ancient times, prophets (true and false ones) were employed to communicate ideas from the unseen realm to the masses living in the physical world. With today's technology, we have radio, television, books, motion pictures and the Internet to infuse ideas into the minds of millions in a short amount of time. Both then and now, some voices in all these media have been transmitting truth, while others have been blaring error and confusion.

During His earthly ministry, Jesus Himself would teach by using parables, which are cinematic stories conveying secret messages about the kingdom of God to specific men and women He was calling. Interestingly, the plots would intentionally hide the meaning from those were not being drawn to Him at that time. Here's what he told His disciples about those stories:

"You are permitted to understand the secrets
of the Kingdom of God. But I use parables to
teach the others so that the Scriptures might be
fulfilled: 'When they look, they won't really see.
When they hear, they won't understand.'
(Luke 8:10 NLT)

What I'm suggesting is that Jesus could be using a somewhat similar teaching method today, still airing His messages to His elect through some of today's pop entertainment, while hiding them from the vast majority. His ideas can be clearly understood by those who have ears to hear and eyes to see, whose minds are open to the truth of God, paying close attention to everything in our world. If Jesus told us to consider the lilies of the field and the birds of the air to understand the things of God, then why shouldn't we consider the messages that are broadcast through the air and on the screen and see how they line up with Scripture?

And, yes, the Almighty is certainly able to use the God-hating, pagan cesspool of Hollywood to produce movies with His communication hidden inside. After all, He employed the pagan king Cyrus whom He called His "anointed" to free His people from captivity in Babylon (Isaiah 45:1). And if God was able to orchestrate global events through heathen leaders in the days of Esther to secretly embed the message of the Bible (see the chapter "I AM hidden"), then He can certainly infuse His ideas in today's motion pictures, even if the writers and producers may be completely oblivious to it.

Again, as you read my list, I am making no definitive statement on whether the filmmakers themselves are aware of the Biblical connections I see. Maybe they are, and maybe they aren't. I do not claim that these Bible analogies are always exact, that the messages have all been directly inspired by God, or that they stand as absolute as Scripture. My point is that God is in control of everything, and He can present Himself and His ideas to people in a host of unexpected ways, including through the story lines in many of today's most popular films. Sometimes, almost the entirety of a movie can reflect what's in the Word of God, and at other times, it's just a profound line or two of dialogue that echoes prophecy.

Please keep in mind that I haven't seen every movie ever made, so what I'm providing here is by no means comprehensive. It's merely a list of famous films that I personally think have exceedingly strong Bible themes. You may disagree with my analysis, and that's perfectly fine. I usually don't read professional movie reviews, so forgive me if anyone else has brought up any of this before. But since most film critics may not be well-versed in Scripture, I'm quite certain that much of what you'll read here is totally new. If you haven't seen any of these films, please be aware that I'm giving away much of the stories, so there's your spoiler alert.

By this point in the book, a plethora of Holy Scriptures has been presented to you, so I'll do my best not to repeat them. If you happen to be a reader who likes to check out the end of the book first, you may not understand my full analysis without having read the previous chapters. So please do all of us a favor and stop being such a sloth. I kindly ask that you go back and read this book in its proper order so you can get the maximum impact and understanding. Now that we have that straight, it's time to sit back, grab yourself some popcorn or candy, and snack on these motion-picture gems which, I hope, you'll see in a brand-new light, the light of Bible truth.

The Matrix (1999)

Starring: Keanu Reeves, Laurence Fishburne, Hugo Weaving

"The Matrix" is considered by many to be one of the greatest science-fiction thrillers of all-time, with groundbreaking special effects that set the standard for action films moving into the 21st century. The film has two sequels, "The Matrix Reloaded" and "The Matrix Revolutions," both of which were released in 2003. For simplicity's sake, I'll discuss all three movies together in this section, since they're all highly Biblical.

The movie's plot centers on a society where people are living in a computer-generated dream world, unaware that there's a real world in another dimension outside of their perceived existence. Human beings are kept in captivity in this dream world by evil forces, specifically machines that are using human beings as a source of power. A heroic figure named Thomas Anderson, also called Neo, played by Keanu Reeves, is awakened out of his slumber to become "the One," the savior of the world. He represents Jesus.

There are countless Biblical analogies in this series of films, and I suppose there could be courses in college one day that will study them. But for now, you've got yours truly as the instructor and my humble opinions to start you thinking.

One point that may surprise you is that the word "matrix" itself is a term found in the Bible. That's right, sci-fi fans. It's not some fresh and cool term invented by high-tech gurus. "Matrix" appears five times in the King James Version, and it literally means "womb" or "mothering place," derived from the Latin word "mater," meaning "mother." The actual Hebrew word rendered as "matrix" in the Bible is "rechem," and it's also translated twenty-one times as "womb."

The reason I stress this is because the world in which we live is a giant womb of sorts. It's a mothering place, a place of gestation where we are being prepared for birth into the spirit world as literal children of God. Remember, the whole reason we exist is that God is preparing and perfecting His own offspring to be born a second time, not as physical, flesh-and-blood beings, but as divine, spirit-composed, immortal beings who will rule with Him for all eternity. So, in this sense, "The Matrix" sums up our whole reason for being.

Now onto the plot. In the film, most people living on Earth are unaware that there is an unseen dimension above them. It's called "the real world" in the movie, and it controls virtually everything that takes place inside the Matrix. This corresponds to the fact that there is an unseen dimension that exists above our physical world. The Bible calls this dimension heaven, and it's the place where God and the angels dwell and exercise control over events among the human populace, even if people are unaware of its existence.

In the movie, people are described as not being awakened from the system of deception that keeps their minds locked in a state of captivity. Morpheus, played by Laurence Fishburne, explains what the Matrix really is: "It is the world that has been pulled over your eyes to blind you from the truth ... that you are a slave ... Like everyone else, you were born into bondage, born into a prison which you cannot smell or taste or touch. A prison for your mind."

After having read the previous chapters of this book, it's easy to see how the Matrix corresponds exactly to our situation in real life. We, too, have been born into a deception-filled prison for our minds, a world of illusion controlled by powerful forces above us, some of which (the dark forces) have put us in bondage to sin and the fear of death. It closely resembles what the New Testament says about one of the reasons Jesus came to Earth:

> that through death He might destroy him who had the power of death, that is, the devil, and release those who through fear of death were all their lifetime subject to bondage.
> (Hebrews 2:14-15 NKJV)

Morpheus went on to explain: "The Matrix is a system, Neo. That system is our enemy. But when you're inside, you look around. What do you see? Businessmen, teachers, lawyers, carpenters. The very minds of the people we are trying to save. But until we do, these people are still a part of that system, and that makes them our enemy. You have to understand, most of these people are not ready to be unplugged. And many of them are so inert, so hopelessly dependent on the system, that they will fight to protect it."

This corresponds exactly to real life and the world in which we all live. It has people of all professions and beliefs, including millions of self-professing Christians, not awake to God's glorious truth about who and what we really are and our ultimate destiny as divine children of God. Their minds are in the prison operated by the devil. They march to his twisted teaching that we don't need to follow the instructions of our Creator for a variety of reasons. These people remain dependent on the powers that be in society, whether it's the government or the major religions that have been invented by mankind, both of which are strongly influenced or controlled by Satan.

Even though the Bible says Jesus came to free the prisoners, not everyone is being awakened and liberated at the same time, and most folks have not taken the steps necessary to leave the jail cell inside their head. Thus, unless they're called and have their minds truly unlocked by God, they're often hostile to the truth and will fight against it however they can, even to the point of persecuting true believers.

But, as we now know, there is a time when the masses will have their minds unlocked and unplugged from the devil's control. This will take place in the Second Resurrection, the resurrection no one talks about, when Jesus and all His quickened believers will be explaining the truth to them after the devil has been destroyed in the lake of fire. It is then that they'll be judged (examined, coached and evaluated) according to their works, what they do once they have been given the truth free from all deception.

While characters such as Neo and Morpheus represent good in the film series, there are also evil entities known as "agents." They are led by a chief agent, known only as Agent Smith, played by Australian actor Hugo Weaving. Throughout the trilogy, these powerful villains are shown to be constantly monitoring the people who dwell in the Matrix, as well as possessing their minds and bodies whenever they wish.

Sound familiar? It should. Smith and his fellow agents represent Satan the devil and his fellow fallen angels, known today as demons, who watch everything we do here on Earth. Not only do the agents jump from person to person in their instant possessions, they are also shown to be in a constant state of war with Neo's gang, a classic good-versus-evil struggle whenever they meet. This is also how demons operate in real life. The Bible shows them possessing the minds of numerous people, including Jesus' own apostle Judas, and they're in a state of conflict with the forces of good, namely Jesus and His followers who are able to cast out the demons.

At the end of the first film, Neo is killed by the dark forces, just as the evil powers in real life put Jesus to death. And in the movie as well as real life, Neo and Jesus get resurrected, attaining a variety of supernatural abilities, including flying in the sky, healing people and altering matter in the physical realm.

At one point in the movie, during an interrogation of Morpheus, Agent Smith (Satan the devil) opens up about why he sought the mass murder of all human beings, explaining, "I'd like to share a revelation that I've had during my time here. ... Human beings are a disease, a cancer of this planet. You are a plague, and we are the cure. ... I'm going to be honest with you. I hate this place, this zoo, this prison, this reality, whatever you want to call it. I can't stand it any longer." This is exactly how we would expect the devil himself to think about his status here in this zoo-like prison called Earth.

In the second film, Agent Smith waxed even more spiritual about the meaning and purpose of life during a discussion with Neo, as he explained:

> But as you well know, appearances can be deceiving, which brings me back to the reason why we're here. We're not here because we're free, we're here because we're not free. There's no escaping reason, no denying purpose. Because as we both know, without purpose, we would not exist. It is purpose that created us. Purpose that connects us. Purpose that pulls us, that guides us, that drives us. It is purpose that defines, purpose that binds us. We're here because of you, Mister Anderson. We're here to take from you what you tried to take from us: purpose.

Here, the devil is not only admitting that deception is part of life, but he focuses on the reason for his existence. And that is ... purpose. The devil is a created being, a former angel whose original purpose was to guard the very throne of God Almighty, and whose purpose now is to act as the agent of opposition for those being perfected by God. He's "here" because Jesus put him here. In other words, Jesus created him for a purpose, which agrees perfectly with Colossians 1:16 which states that everything, even rulers in the unseen world, were created by Him and for Him.

Smith's remark that he and his minions are here to take from Jesus what He tried to take from them refers to Satan's own desire to kill his Creator and take over as the Most High God. That has been the perverted purpose inside the mind of the devil for eons. He's at war with God because the Creator will not allow him and other angels to become divine members of God's family, and the Maker will kill them for their rebellion.

Once the devil is destroyed and millions of people become quickened into God's very own family, his evil purpose will be fulfilled in a very good way, for God will have saved "much people alive," as Joseph so eloquently stated in Genesis 50:20. Interestingly, immediately after this discussion about purpose in the film, Agent Smith gets into another battle with Neo (Jesus), who tears a rod of iron in the form of a tether-ball pole from a schoolyard playground to smack Smith around. In Psalms and Revelation, Jesus is shown to be ruling the nations with a corrective rod of iron, sometimes even dashing rebellious people to pieces with the rod of discipline.

The enigmatic Agent Smith almost seems to be the focus of the second and third parts of the trilogy, and he is shown replicating himself countless times by taking over the bodies of human beings who dwell inside the Matrix. This corresponds to what the devil is doing here in real life right now. He is not only possessing individuals who are void of the Spirit of God, he is also influencing billions of people on this planet with his wicked line of thinking. Satan does not actually have to be dwelling inside someone for that person to be following his footsteps. He creates cloned versions of himself by getting people to buy into his clever lies about all subjects over thousands of years.

Thus, when "highly educated" people believe that the universe came about without any designer, or that people evolved from lower life forms over millions of years, they are spiritually marching to the devil's drumbeat. It's the same on matters of religion. Hundreds of millions of people on this planet either believe God doesn't exist, or they follow some deity that is not the God of the Bible. Thus, through incessant deception, they have become a clone of sorts of the chief demon. Even across Christendom, if those who claim to worship Jesus say we're not supposed to be keeping God's commandments, they are actually pushing the same agenda as the devil, the original lawbreaker. The Bible calls such people "children of the devil." (1 John 3:10 KJV)

Perhaps the most interesting aspect to me concerning Agent Smith is that he eventually is turned into a physical human being, just as Satan the devil will become a physical man before He is executed. As we have seen, God told Satan what would become of him in the future:

> "Will you still say before him who slays you,
> 'I am a god'?
> But you shall be a man, and not a god,
> In the hand of him who slays you. (Ezekiel 28:9 NKJV)

In the film series, Smith is transformed into the physical body of a man named Bane, and then goes on to admit to Neo that he himself is indeed "the enemy," which is what "Satan" literally means. He explains that he'd prefer his existence as a spirit-being compared to someone dwelling inside a flesh-and-blood human body, saying: "I admit it is difficult to even think, encased in this rotting piece of meat. The stink of it filling every breath, suffocating cloud you can't escape. Disgusting. Look at how pathetically fragile it is. Nothing this weak is meant to survive. ... Look past the flesh, look through the soft gelatin of these dull, cow eyes, and see your enemy."

Despite having been physically blinded, Neo confronts Bane/Smith/Satan, and is able to spiritually peer through the physical body of his enemy to see the fiery spirit-entity of the diabolical Agent Smith. And what does Neo do? As you might guess, he swings another rod of iron to whack the head off of Smith, whose decapitated body then shatters like glass and becomes dust and ashes. This sequence of events is remarkably similar to prophecies we've already read in the Bible. Remember, in Genesis 3:14-15, it was predicted that Jesus would eventually crush the head of the devil, and Ezekiel 28:18 says Satan will be reduced to ashes.

In the final confrontation between Neo and Smith at the end of the third film, Neo is able to destroy Smith and all his innumerable clones watching the pair fight. He does this by causing all the evildoers to explode with the fiery presence of his own personal light tearing them apart from within. Again, the Biblical end of Satan is amazingly similar:

> therefore will I bring forth **a fire from the midst of thee, it shall devour thee**, and **I will bring thee to ashes upon the earth** in the sight of all them that behold thee.
>
> All they that know thee among the people shall be astonished at thee: thou shalt be a terror, and **never shalt thou be any more**.
> (Ezekiel 28:18-19 KJV)

With the war against evil finally over in the Matrix, a voice from a deus ex machina (a god from the machines) declares, "It is done." This perfectly matches the final words of Jesus during His execution in John 19:30 when He conquered evil and rescued His own offspring from eternal death: "It is finished."

The Truman Show (1998)

Starring: Jim Carrey, Ed Harris, Laura Linney, Natascha McElhone

"The Truman Show" is a comedic drama focusing on the life of one man, Truman Burbank (Jim Carrey), whose entire life is the subject of a globally popular television show, unbeknownst to him. Every aspect of his daily life is monitored by thousands of cameras, ultimately controlled by the show's creator named Christof (Ed Harris). The town in which he lives is actually a giant set constructed under a massive dome in the Los Angeles area. Truman, who is about to turn thirty, is the only one who does not know his true identity. Everyone else, including Truman's family and closest friends, are all actors.

This film is one of the best analogies for much of what is broadcast in the Bible, yet is never talked about in church. It focuses on the world of deception, the false reality in which we all live every single day. It is a world of lies that are presented as truth, with virtually everyone lying to us about everything, including matters of faith, and people accepting the lies as truth.

Truman (the true man) represents humanity, virtually all human beings who have ever lived, unaware they're being closely monitored by others in another dimension. The millions of people watching the "The Truman Show" with such a keen interest represent the large numbers of beings in the unseen realm of heaven – God and the angels (both good angels and bad ones) – who watch our every step and know our every thought to see if we're on the path toward life or death. They are examining and judging us, to assess our preparedness for the gift of divine life and rulership in the coming kingdom of God.

Throughout the film, Truman begins to question his life, awakening to the fact that something is not quite right with the world. At one point, the show's creator is asked why he thought Truman has never come close to discovering the true nature of his world until that time. His response is completely accurate for people who live in our own real world of deception: "We accept the reality of the world with which we're presented. It's as simple as that." That brief statement is quite profound, because it's true for everyone. From the moment we're born, we're taught by our parents, teachers and religious leaders, and we accept that what they tell us is true, with little questioning. While some information may be true, it is mixed with lies, making it difficult for most people to come to know the complete truth.

Christof, the person running Truman's world, does not represent Jesus Christ. In fact, he represents the one who desperately seeks to be like Jesus, and would replace Him if he could. He is Satan the devil who wants total control. His very name of Christof indicates he's an off-Christ, a knock-off of the true God. The world he has developed for Truman looks like the real world in many respects, but is actually artificial, with paid liars interacting with Truman, even among his best friends and wife. These actors follow a predetermined script, and at times in the movie, they are fed Christof's words via microphones and earpieces.

This is precisely how the world operates today. The vast majority of people on this planet are following the script, the instructions, of the deceiver instead of the laws of God. Many never even question their way of life. And there are times when the devil actually speaks through human beings, either by influencing their brain to say something or even personally possessing their mind.

The world that Christof has created for Truman is an island prison, holding Truman in captivity, just as we humans are held in captivity without knowledge of the truth. Christof actually keeps Truman's mind in prison by the same means the devil keeps us in captivity: the fear of death. Truman has been inundated with messages about how deadly it can be to travel off his island, plus he witnessed his own father supposedly die in a contrived boating accident. In like fashion, the New Testament states people "lived their lives as slaves to the fear of dying." (Hebrews 2:15 NLT)

One of the most meaningful parts of the film comes during a phone call between a love interest of Truman named Sylvia (Natascha McElhone) and the fiendish Christof:

> **Sylvia**: Hi, Christof, I'd just like to say one thing: You're a liar and a manipulator and what you've done to Truman is sick!
>
> **Christof**:   ... Sylvia, as you announced so melodramatically to the world, do you think

because you batted your eyes at Truman once, flirted with him, stole a few minutes of airtime with him to thrust yourself and your politics into the limelight, that you know him? That you know what's right for him? You really think you're in a position to judge him?

Sylvia: What right do you have to take a baby and turn his life into some kind of mockery? Don't you ever feel guilty?

Christof: I have given Truman the chance to lead a normal life. The world, the place you live in, is the sick place. Seahaven is the way the world should be.

Sylvia: He's not a performer, he's a prisoner. Look at him. Look at what you've done to him!

Christof: He could leave at any time. If his was more than just a vague ambition, if he was absolutely determined to discover the truth, there's no way we could prevent him. I think what distresses you, really, caller, is that ultimately Truman prefers his cell, as you call it.

Sylvia: Well, that's where you're wrong. You're so wrong! And he'll prove you wrong!

Here we have tremendous insight into the battle that's raging between the forces of good and evil in the unseen dimension of heaven which are all focused on what human beings think and do.

Sylvia, who can be viewed as an angel or even Jesus calling to help humans discover their true identity as the offspring of God with a glorious future, correctly nails the character of the devil as "a liar and a manipulator" who is "so wrong." This servant of God, **the "caller"** as she's referred to by the devil, recognizes that the grand deception is preventing people from hearing their divine call and attaining their intended destiny, instead taking babies and twisting them into a gross distortion of their original design. She even cites Truman's captivity, saying, "He's not a performer, he's a prisoner."

The devil responds by claiming people actually prefer the jail cell of their mind over the real world, which is the freedom of eternal life in the spirit dimension awaiting them if they'd only walk out of their incarceration. And one statement from Christof's devil character is completely true: "He could leave at any time. If his was more than just a vague ambition, if he was absolutely determined to discover the truth, there's no way we could prevent him."

The One who freed the prisoners, Jesus Christ of Nazareth, declared, "I am the way, the truth, and the life" (John 14:6 KJV). When people are absolutely determined to discover the truth about who and what they really are and why they're here, they will learn that it's all connected to the real Creator, Jesus. It is then that the devil no longer will have a hold on our minds, and we can simply walk out of the prison.

It does take some effort on our part, though. Just as we're commanded to keep God's commandments to enter into life, the film shows Truman taking steps – some intimidating at times – to reach his salvation. In one scene, despite his overwhelming fear of drowning in water, Truman is shown driving a car across a bridge in an attempt to get off the island. Yet the authorities (the devil's minions) do their best to keep him from escaping and learning the truth.

The climax of the film features a personal battle at sea between Truman and Christof (man versus the devil), where Truman is relentless in resisting the unseen demon's persecution. During a fierce, conjured-up storm by which Christof tries to capsize Truman's boat, the hero shouts, "You're gonna have to kill me!" Frustrated by Truman's resolve, Christof gives up on the persecution. This matches the Bible's instruction to "Resist the devil, and he will flee from you." (James 4:7 KJV)

In the final moments, as Truman is about to discover the truth about his phony world, he climbs a stairway into what appears to be the sky, a "stairway to heaven" of sorts. Even at that moment, Christof the devil tries to coax him one final time to remain in captivity. He uses his standard playbook and says: "You're afraid. That's why you can't leave."

The godly Sylvia is shown praying for Truman's strength to complete his journey, as she whispers, "Please, God. You can do it." Truman overcomes any residual fear within him and steps through an exit door into a dimension he has never experienced before, the real world, where there is real life and his true love awaiting him, sparking instant jubilation among the multitude of watchers. This reflects the boundless joy shared by God and his holy angels once people overcome all the tricks of the wicked one, finally exiting their state of death and coming to life as they personally meet and marry their God.

In sum, "The Truman Show" demonstrates that the world in which we all live is a complete sham built on thousands of years of lies orchestrated by the god of this world, Satan the devil. Although we're held in captivity through deception and the fear of death, we can, if we really desire, discover the truth. Once we know the Truth, the real Creator, Jesus Christ, we can walk out of the devil's prison, experiencing true love as we enter life everlasting with our Maker, the glorious destiny awaiting us in the real world.

Groundhog Day (1993)

Starring: Bill Murray, Andie MacDowell

Both a fantasy comedy and a serious look at the meaning of life, "Groundhog Day" is one of the most spiritually positive movies ever made. The plot follows a mean-spirited weatherman who, through a miraculous circumstance, repeats the same day over and over in Punxsutawney, Pennsylvania, where he's assigned to cover the annual Groundhog Day festivities. He is trapped in a time loop for countless days, and only through a transformation in his character from being an arrogant, self-centered jackass to a kind, altruistic friend of his fellow man can he escape his captivity and receive his desired reward, true love.

Personally, I think this film is one of Hollywood's most brilliant, fun-filled productions when it comes to broadcasting Bible messages. Bill Murray plays conceited TV meteorologist Phil Connors, who initially treats everyone, including his own producer, Rita (Andie MacDowell), like dirt. He is content neither with himself nor his job, confiding that he is actively looking to leave his station.

It is then that forces stronger than himself intervene in his life. A blizzard traps him in the one place he doesn't want to be, stuck with local residents for whom he has the greatest disdain. He cannot understand why he's a prisoner in the time warp, mysteriously restarting the same day at sunrise, 6 a.m., on February 2nd. The only way Phil is able to escape his prison of suffering is to improve his personal character and learn how, day after day after day, to become a better person, treating others with genuine kindness and helping them whenever possible. He ultimately receives his reward according to his works.

In this film, the Bible connections jump off the screen and smack us in the face. First of all, we all need to realize there are forces in the unseen spirit world, whether they're from God or angels, that are bigger than us and can impact both us and the circumstances surrounding us. The miraculous time loop is obviously the work of unseen powers. In the same way, everything we see around us in our natural surroundings is the handiwork of unseen powers, who placed us in a created world we personally may or may not enjoy. Note also that each day starts at sunrise, just like in the Bible.

The film gets philosophical numerous times, and at one point, Phil asks Ralph, his drinking buddy: "What would you do if you were stuck in one place, and every day was exactly the same, and nothing that you did mattered?"

"Now that sums it up for me," is Ralph's response. That is the exact thinking of countless people across the world right this second. Millions believe that nothing they do really matters, when, in fact, **everything** they do matters, since they will be judged according to what they do in life.

Now that we're all here dwelling in this place – this neighborhood, town, state, nation or world in which we exist – we have been given a certain number of days in our physical lifetime. These days may seem very similar or even repetitive, but it is during these days that we're allowed to make mistakes and learn from them, perfecting our character to become the righteous children of God we're commanded to be. Many forget that we're actually commanded by Jesus to be perfect: "Be perfect, therefore, as your heavenly Father is perfect" (Matthew 5:48 HCSB). Even though we may screw up at times and sin, God says that upon repentance, He will forgive our iniquity and forget our sin.

Throughout the course of the film, the once ornery weatherman realizes that truly caring for others is far more rewarding than being cold toward his fellow man, so he goes on a mission to help people in need, including changing flat tires for stranded ladies, counseling a troubled young couple, feeding a homeless man and saving the lives of a man choking and a boy who falls from a tree. His actions evincing his care and concern finally pay off, as he wins the love of Rita and is freed from his captivity. This echoes the declaration from Jesus about our coming reward: "He shall reward every man according to his works." (Matthew 16:27 KJV)

Before coming to that conclusion, however, Phil's captivity allows him to explore the limits of his debauchery. He initially becomes enthralled with testing the bounds of rebellion, enjoying, for example, the seduction of local women. This relates to how we, as human beings living in our captivity of the devil, actually can find pleasure in whatever sin floats our boat. Scripture notes that "they all may be judged who did not believe the truth, but took pleasure in wickedness." (2 Thessalonians 2:12 NASB)

While driving on railroad tracks and playing chicken with a train, Phil contemplates the fact there are no consequences to his aberrant behavior, and he boldly declares, "I'm not gonna live by their rules anymore." This, as we've seen countless times in this book, is the attitude of the devil himself. It is how many people live their lives today, making the conscious decision to disobey the divine instructions, doing whatever they wish. Unfortunately, not living by the rules keeps us trapped in our personal captivity and leads to death.

What is the final action that brings Phil out of his supernatural prison? It is not any of his good works, though they certainly are precursors that help lead up to the key moment. The ultimate event that ensures his freedom is the single act of love by Rita his producer when she spends every last dollar and cent in her bank account to "purchase" Phil at auction at the film's climax. "I bought you. I own you," Rita informs Phil. He himself also remarks, "You paid top dollar for me." In this sense, Rita represents Phil's redeemer. Her name even sounds a bit like "redeemer." She is the figure of righteousness and purity throughout the story whom Phil seeks to be like. She eventually spends everything she possibly can to "buy" the person she loves, helping him escape his captivity.

This is a perfect analogy for Jesus. He is the pure, sinless figure of the ages, who is not only the Producer of us (just like Rita is Phil's producer), He is also our Redeemer, buying us back from the power of the devil at the highest cost possible, the blood of the Creator being shed. That purchase releases us from our prison of death so that we can enter into life as immortal children of God.

Regarding our divine destiny, the film touches on the fact that we "are gods," just as Jesus twice said to human beings, "You are gods" (Psalm 82:6, John 10:34). During a meal with Rita, Phil matter-of-factly announces, "I'm a god." The incredulous Rita responds, "You're God?" Phil answers her by explaining, "No, I'm **a** god. I'm not **the** God."

This exchange puts the icing on the cake, folks, because this is the core message of the Bible, pinpointing why we're all here. God Almighty is having children. He is reproducing Himself, making additional divine beings who are meant to rule with Him, sitting on His own throne, judging (coaching and evaluating) other human beings so that they, too, can join God's family. We are not **the** God, as in God the Father or Jesus Christ. But we have been created with the potential, if we repent of our sins and follow Jesus the Messiah, to be born again into spirit-composed, immortal god bodies, receiving the crown of glory, dwelling with and reigning alongside our own Producer for all time.

One of the final comments from Phil as he enters paradise with his producer solidifies this reward of eternal life in glory as he triumphantly proclaims: "Let's **live** here!"

The Shawshank Redemption (1994)
Starring: Tim Robbins, Morgan Freeman, Bob Gunton

Considered by some critics to be among the best films ever made, the story centers on banker Andy Dufresne (Tim Robbins), who is given a life sentence in a harsh prison for a crime he did not commit. Despite severe persecution during his incarceration, Andy is able to befriend, inspire and edify his fellow inmates, eventually escaping his captivity to enjoy real life in a tropical paradise.

The marketing tagline for this film has Bible written all over it: "Fear can hold you prisoner. Hope can set you free." While the movie has a variety of ostensible Biblical references, including a few scattered

Scriptures spoken, they are not what I wish to focus on. The secret Bible theme embedded into this film is one we've already seen in others: that people in this world are being held prisoner by an evil power doing his best to keep them in captivity, forcing them to live in fear.

Tim Robbins' character, Andy Dufresne (note his initials are A.D., as in anno domini, meaning "in the year of our Lord"), can be seen either as Jesus, since he had committed no crime, or as any faithful follower of Christ, one who is being redeemed from the prison that is this world. In either case, Dufresne is treated horribly during his time in prison, even being gang-raped by sodomite convicts. The Bible reveals tremendous suffering not only on the part of Jesus, but many of His followers as well.

Despite his poor treatment, Andy, who polishes rocks as a hobby, keeps his calm and educates (polishes) his fellow inmates by teaching them to read, building a state-of-the-art library and broadcasting inspiring opera music through loudspeakers in the prison yard. He also offers hope to his friends, telling Red (Morgan Freeman): "Remember, Red, hope is a good thing, maybe the best of things, and no good thing ever dies." That word "hope" is plastered all over the Bible, more than one hundred times, and it inspires countless numbers of people in verses including "the hope of glory" (Colossians 1:27 KJV), "the hope of salvation" (1 Thessalonians 5:8 KJV), and "the hope of eternal life" (Titus 3:7 KJV). One of its best connections to "Shawshank" is this comment from Paul:

> And our hope for you is firm, because we know
> that as you share in the sufferings, so you will
> share in the comfort. (2 Corinthians 1:7 HCSB)

Andy's statement that "no good thing ever dies" can be seen either as a reference to our eternal life once we're raised from the dead, or the fact that Jesus Himself said there is only one individual who is good, God the Father, and He never has died in any manner: "There is none good but one, that is, God." (Matthew 19:17 KJV)

Satan the devil is manifested in "Shawshank" in the person of Samuel Norton (Bob Gunton), the heartless warden of the prison. When we're first introduced to Norton early in the film, he has a form of godliness, as he states: "I believe in two things: discipline and the Bible. Here you'll receive both. Put your trust in the Lord." But the very next sentence out of his mouth lets us know we're really dealing with a foul-mouthed controller, as he adds, "Your ass belongs to me." Remember, the wicked one is the deceiver who wants to be like Jesus and, at times, appears as an angel of light, so he can have moments when he seems godly, at least on the surface. But make no mistake: The wretched devil is the one running this giant prison known as Planet Earth, at least until the return of Jesus.

Throughout the film, the depth of the warden's vile character is revealed through a money-laundering operation and his torment of Andy when the former banker refuses to continue aiding in the illicit scheme. The worst affliction comes when a witness comes forward who can help prove Andy's innocence. But, just as the devil does anything he possibly can to keep people in his spiritual prison and prevent their salvation, so the warden does his best to keep Andy behind bars, going so far as to have his demonic prison guard shoot the exonerating witness dead.

Nevertheless, by enduring his sufferings and a patient hope, Andy eventually tunnels his way to freedom through the womb of a woman (actually a poster of a pin-up girl in his cell) followed by a sewage pipe to become born again, finally free from his chains to enter into a life of riches and paradise. As Red put it so eloquently, "Andy Dufresne, who crawled through a river of [poop] and came out clean on the other side." This statement at the end of the movie should prompt all readers of Scripture to instantly think of what's written at the end of the Bible, because it summarizes what happens to believers, when they're quickened into spirit bodies and are wearing spotless garments:

> After this I looked, and there before me was a great multitude that no one could count, from every nation, tribe, people and language, standing before the throne and before the Lamb. They were wearing white robes ... "These are they who have come out of the great tribulation; they have washed their robes and made them white in the blood of the Lamb. (Revelation 7:9-14 NIV)

Just as Andy endured great tribulation and crawled through a river of unspeakable filth to reach his paradise destination, becoming clean on the other side, so we, too, as believers in Christ must persevere through our own trials and tribulation, crawling through our own river of foul sewage, overcoming whatever obstacle is thrown in our way, staying on the path of righteousness to overcome the wages of sin, which is death, and enter into our own everlasting paradise of eternal life. The most memorable line of "The Shawshank Redemption" affirms the sum total of Scripture: "Get busy living, or get busy dying." God has presented us the ways of life and the ways of death. And He has commanded us to choose life. So let's get busy living.

The Island (2005)

Starring: Scarlett Johansson, Ewan McGregor, Steve Buscemi, Sean Bean

One of director Michael Bay's most-intriguing action films, "The Island" is yet another movie with the now familiar Biblical theme of people unaware of their identity, being held captive by a dark force doing his best to prevent them from discovering the truth about what they are.

The story begins by showing people inundated with messages from a God-like voice telling them an island paradise is their ultimate destiny: "You're special. You have a very special purpose in life. You've been chosen. The Island awaits you," the voice declares. The island is said to be the only place left in the world to actually live a healthy life, since most of Earth has purportedly suffered some sort of toxic disaster. The fear of being contaminated keeps people cemented in their supposedly safe dwelling place, until they win the lottery to be sent to the island.

The only problem for the people in this society is … there is no island. It's all an ingenious deception, masterminded by a brilliant scientist, Dr. Bernard Merrick (Sean Bean), who has created a society of clones who dwell in his own institute. In reality, he is replicating wealthy people who have paid exorbitant sums of money to have extra body parts at the ready, courtesy of their duplicated "children," should they ever need a transplant. (It has long been mankind's goal to cheat death and live forever, especially by bypassing the intended method of joining ourselves to our Creator.)

The clones, who are fully developed human beings, are kept in a state of child-like obliviousness, unaware of what they are and their true reason for being, thus being precluded from realizing their full potential. They're merely fed the lie over and over that they could win the lottery one day, and get sent to the island of paradise. What they're not told is that whoever does win the lottery is actually taken to a medical center where he or she is slain to acquire their bodily organs.

The business plan goes awry when one of the replicants, Lincoln Six Echo (Ewan McGregor), begins questioning his existence and eventually learns of the organ harvesting. He realizes that the paradise they've all been promised for years is a sham, and is a road that leads to certain death. He escapes his captivity with his best friend, the beautiful Jordan Two Delta (Scarlett Johansson). Once they make it to the outside "real" world, Lincoln asks a man (Steve Buscemi) with whom he conversed at the institute: "Why did they lie to us? Tell me." The response: "To keep you from knowing what you are."

This line is the most important of the film, and is actually the tagline to not only the movie, but also our perceived existence in what we all think is real life: **"They don't want you to know what you are."**

Satan, who is the lying god of this world just as Dr. Merrick is the film's deceptive chief executive, is preventing people from knowing **what** we are, that we "are gods," as Jesus twice stated. The devil has created an elaborate deception that includes the man-made religions of this world, including most of traditional Christianity, to prevent people from learning the truth, to stop us from taking the necessary steps to realize our full potential as divine rulers in the coming kingdom of God.

People have been brainwashed for thousands of years by the unseen ruler of this world who broadcasts a mixture of truth and lies. The truthful part is that we are special and chosen by God for a tremendous purpose in a future paradise. But we're not given the whole story. We're not told what that purpose truly is. We're not told what Jesus said, that we are gods, even though that's broadcast throughout the Bible. And we're not told that we actually have to take concrete steps, such as stopping our rebellion and starting to keep God's commandments, in order to develop and perfect our character so we're prepared to rule with our Creator once He returns.

Remember, we're the children of God, the actual offspring of the most powerful Being in the universe who is creating masterpieces to sit down with Him on His throne. But if we're kept in the dark as to our intended destination, as the devil has cleverly done through thousands of years of misinformation and disinformation, then we'll never get there. We won't develop and mature spiritually, and we will never bear the fruit that God has intended for us.

We were not designed to float around all day on a cloud in heaven, doing nothing but singing worship songs for trillions of years. That is part of the elaborate lie the devil has concocted. It is part of the all-encompassing hoax that most Christians today actually buy into. Just like the clones in "The Island" believed they did not have to do anything but wait around to enter their paradise, most Christian believers today also think they don't have to do a single thing except believe that Jesus is God to reach their idea of paradise. Taking only that one step, while not repenting of their sins, is still the path toward death, just as those in the film were killed when they won the lottery.

The main protagonist in the movie, Lincoln Six Echo, can be viewed as a type of Jesus who saves his fellow humans. Lincoln struggles against Dr. Merrick, the representation of the devil who wants to be like God and who falsely claims that he is the one who gives life. The name of Lincoln Echo signals that this character is an echo of President Abraham Lincoln, whose most famous act was to free the slaves. Again, this shouts the message of the Bible. We human beings are all slaves to the power of the devil: slaves to sin, death and the fear of death. But Jesus Christ is the one who has freed the slaves on this prison planet. He has liberated us from our captivity so we can take the needed steps to be perfected into our intended roles as the divine co-rulers of the future.

The last moments of this thought-provoking film represent the conclusion of the Bible story in remarkably accurate fashion. Lincoln kills Dr. Merrick, just as Jesus will crush the head of Satan, killing off evil once and for all. The holographic walls, which once kept the people in the endless captivity of deception, are done away with. The light from the outside real world gloriously beams inside the institute, just as the light of truth brightens the path for new believers and will ultimately illuminate the kingdom of God. The people, once ignorant of their true identities as members of God's own family, follow the light in breathless jubilance while they escape their prison and enter salvation, the new and true world.

The final scene shows Lincoln and his love, Jordan, sailing into paradise on a boat that he and his real-world "father" had designed. The vessel is called Renovatio, which is Latin for renewal, restoration, or, as the film indicates, rebirth. The Scriptural metaphor is complete. Jesus said at the conclusion of the Bible: "Behold, I make all things new" (Revelation 21:5 KJV). So, the Designer who created the entire plan of rebirth gets to be with His beloved bride, who has been reborn into a newly restored paradise to finally live real life, all according to the plan designed by Himself and His own real-world Father.

The Rock (1996)

Starring: Sean Connery, Nicolas Cage, Ed Harris

With a title like "The Rock," this movie gives us a big clue that the story will have some sort of connection to the God of the Bible. After all, Scripture actually calls God "the Rock" in numerous places, including:

> He is the Rock, his works are perfect, and all his ways are just. A faithful God who does no wrong, upright and just is he. (Deuteronomy 32:4 NIV)

> Come, let us sing to the LORD! Let us shout joyfully to the Rock of our salvation. (Psalm 95:1 NLT)

> … the rock was Christ. (1 Corinthians 10:4 NASB)

The plot of this action film from director Michael Bay centers on a former good guy turned bad who holds hostages on an island prison while threatening the lives of countless others if a large ransom isn't paid. It is up to a man named Goodspeed, with help from a father figure, to save the hostages from certain death.

The antagonist is General Francis X. Hummel (Ed Harris), a former guardian of the U.S. republic, who warns at the film's outset that most of the world isn't going to like what he's about to do. The devil himself, a former guardian angel of God's dwelling place, acted in similar fashion, doing something that human beings continue to suffer for. Hummel leads a crew of former Marines (a band of fallen angels) on a mission to take hostages on the island of Alcatraz, known as "the Rock." He threatens to launch VX nerve gas on the citizens of San Francisco unless a massive financial payment is made. In like fashion, the devil is holding the citizens of the world as his hostages. The staggering ransom was ultimately paid in the Bible through the self-sacrifice of Jesus.

There are two heroes of the film, FBI agent Stanley Goodspeed (Nicolas Cage) and former British SAS Captain John Patrick Mason (Sean Connery). Goodspeed can be viewed as a Jesus figure, while the older Mason is portrayed as both God the Father and Jesus at different moments. Remember that Jesus said, "Anyone who has seen me has seen the Father" (John 14:9 NIV). Using their advanced knowledge and special abilities (which can be seen spiritually as divine powers), this dynamic duo work together to free the hostages from their island prison.

The names of the characters in this film are highly symbolic of Scripture. The film takes note of the origin of Goodspeed, coming from the phrase "God speed": "If there come any unto you, and bring not this doctrine, receive him not into your house, neither bid him God speed: For he that biddeth him God speed is partaker of his evil deeds." (2 John 1:10-11 KJV)

A mason, of course, is a skilled craftsman who builds or works with rock, as God the Father is a skilled Craftsman who is building and shaping a family kingdom with the Rock Jesus. In the film, Mason has a daughter (Claire Forlani) whose name is Jade, which is also a type of rock, a beautiful gemstone to be specific. This reflects a few interesting points.

First, we are the same type of being as our Parent. Just as jade is a kind of rock, we are a type of god, created after God's own kind.

God Himself says: "Look to the rock from which you were cut, and to the quarry from which you were dug." (Isaiah 51:1 HCSB)

Secondly, we as children of God are beautiful gems in God's eyes. Finally, as gemstones, we need to be shaped and polished by the Craftsman in heaven who is perfecting our character. We must never forget that we are God's "workmanship" and "masterpiece" as stated in Ephesians 2:10.

An emotionally moving scene in the film has Mason trying to connect with his daughter with whom he has never had a relationship.

He starts off by saying something Jesus might have said during His human ministry: "I don't have a great deal of time here. But I'll be coming back." The conversation gets even more Biblical as it continues:

> "Jade, you know, you're almost the only evidence that I exist," says Mason.
> "But I don't know you," is the daughter's response.
> "That's what I want to change," notes her father.
> "Jade, I'm not an evil man. If you can believe that, then it's a start."

This exchange is fascinating when you see it with your spiritual eyes open. God is telling his child, who represents us, that we humans are the evidence that He exists. Not only are we created by Him, but we are the only part of creation made in His specific image and likeness. We look just like God with our physical attributes, and we are meant to be like God in all respects, eventually becoming quickened into our divine bodies. Yet despite our being the very offspring of God, many of us don't even recognize our own Parent, as Jade expressed by saying, "But I don't know you."

And her father's response sums up a main message of the Bible. God wants to change the fact that people don't know Him. He wants the close relationship with every single one of His children. He goes on to say that he is not an evil man. In other words, "I'm not the devil." If we can believe that God is not looking to harm or trick us, then it's a start toward building a solid relationship.

Meanwhile, before the rescue mission begins, the film reveals how there is considerable bad blood between Mason and the men running the U.S. government. It is up to one man, Goodspeed, who acts as the mediator in resolving their differences. This is analogous to the man Jesus being the lone mediator between God the Father and all of humanity: "For there is one God and one mediator between God and mankind, the man Christ Jesus." (1 Timothy 2:5 NIV)

At the film's climax, there is significant Biblical imagery, with Goodspeed lying on the ground with his arms spread out as if he were being crucified. A giant needle has been stuck into his chest, just as Jesus had a spear thrust into him during His execution. Goodspeed is then blown into the sea, where he appears dead in the water, but is raised back to life when his father figure grabs him from above and restores him to life. The final scene of the film shows that Goodspeed has married his bride, just as the final moments of the Bible reveal the Good Man Jesus marrying His bride, the faithful believers who followed His instructions.

Willy Wonka & the Chocolate Factory (1971)
Starring: Gene Wilder, Jack Albertson, Peter Ostrum

A timeless classic among children of all ages, "Willy Wonka & the Chocolate Factory" is the story of a kind-hearted, young boy whose invitation to learn the secrets of a delicious kingdom turns into a phenomenal reward once his moral character is tested by the maker of all the goodies.

This popular musical is one of the clearest, most succinct analogies for how the Creator of all things is actually testing His children's character to determine who can receive "the most fabulous prize one could wish for," as a newscaster broadcasts at the start of the film.

Actor Gene Wilder portrays the Candyman named Willy Wonka, the reclusive creator of a large variety of sweet treats that children greatly desire. He lives and works in a place that is off-limits to the rest of the populace.

Spiritually speaking, Wonka represents Jesus, the Creator of all things good, who lives in the unseen dimension of heaven that is currently off-limits to His children. Wonka holds a contest where people from all over the world have a chance to get an up-close-and-personal look at the master's secrets, just as believers are given the secrets to the kingdom of God. While millions search for the elusive golden ticket that will gain them access to the kingdom, only five invitations exist, reminding us that "many are called, but few are chosen" (Matthew 22:14 KJV).

In the film, five boys and girls from countries all over the world are then allowed to sample most of the candy maker's creations, just as we, the children of God, are allowed to view and sample most of God's creations on Earth. But during this process, Willy Wonka pays close attention to the character of each individual, to discern if the children are filled with good traits or evil. This is exactly how Jesus operates, examining the hearts and minds of His own children and studying their actions to determine who is worthy of the astonishing reward of eternal life as members of God's very own family.

Unfortunately, most of the children are filled with the character traits of the wicked one, Satan the devil, and all are shown to violate the explicit instructions of the gracious boss.

Augustus Gloop from Germany is a greedy, obese, gluttonous boy whose fleshly appetite ends up polluting the paradise that Wonka (Jesus) has created, when he drinks from a chocolate river.

Violet Beauregarde is a gum-chewing addict who directly disobeys instructions not to sample one of Wonka's creations, a gum that tastes like a three-course meal. Just as Eve was tempted to eat the forbidden fruit and failed the food test, so Violet gives in to her own lust and fails her test of obedience. She turns into a giant blueberry, thus living up to her full name, which can loosely be translated as "looks good in violet."

Mike Teevee, as his name suggests, is a TV addict obsessed with his favorite shows, just as the lives of many people today are programmed by the nothingness that is broadcast on the air. His personal pride becomes his downfall when he seeks to be the first human to be transported through TV airwaves, but ends up getting physically shrunk to just a few inches tall. As the Bible notes, "Pride comes before destruction, and an arrogant spirit before a fall." (Proverbs 16:18 HCSB)

The biggest brat of the bunch is Veruca Salt, a wealthy, rude, manipulative girl who is perhaps the closest thing to a witch with a capital B that you'll ever see on screen. Her incessant demands of "I want it now" remind everyone she is just like Satan, lusting for things she can't have. When it's determined she's a bad egg instead of a good egg, she plunges toward the furnace, which, as we all know by now, is the destination of the devil.

And then there's Charlie Bucket (Peter Ostrum), the only child who has any redeeming qualities, selflessly sharing what he has with others. But despite his meekness and humility, he, too, violates the instructions of the covenant he signed with Wonka. He and his grandfather both steal

Fizzy Lifting Drinks to be elevated into the air, just as men and women today think they can still be "raised" by God even if they break His rules. But in the end, Charlie repents of his wrongdoing, and is forgiven of his sin when he demonstrates determination not to follow the path of greed and vice by performing "a good deed in a weary world."

At that moment, Wonka exclaims, "You won! You did it! ... I had to test you, Charlie, and you passed the test."

Wonka informs Charlie that he's won "the grand and glorious jackpot," giving everything he owns to the boy because he had to "find a very honest, loving child." At the film's conclusion, Charlie soars through the heavens with his master as inheritor of all things.

This is the whole Bible in a candy-coated nutshell, folks. God is offering all of us "the grand and glorious jackpot," "the most fabulous prize one could wish for," eternal life and rulership as divine members of God's own family. But He has to thoroughly test and examine us to see if we're worthy of the reward, to know for sure if we're honest and loving enough to handle such enormous power and responsibility.

A couple of side notes on this scrumdiddlyumptious film:

The soundtrack of the movie is very similar to the songs and proverbs in the Bible. For instance, in one tune sung by the Oompa Loompas, there are verses such as:

Oompa Loompas: "If you are wise you'll listen to me"

Scripture has: Listen to instruction and be wise (Proverbs 8:33 HCSB)

Oompa Loompas: "If you're not greedy, you will go far"

Scripture: A greedy person provokes conflict, but whoever trusts in the LORD will prosper. (Proverbs 28:25 HCSB)

Oompa Loompas: "You will live in happiness too"

Scripture: How happy are those whose way is blameless, who live according to the LORD's instruction! (Psalm 119:1 HCSB)

And finally, near the climax of the movie, Charlie asks what will happen to the rest of the children who don't make it to the end of the tour. Wonka responds, "They'll be completely restored to their normal, terrible, old selves, but maybe they'll be a little bit wiser for the wear. Anyway, don't worry about them."

Biblically speaking, this is precisely what will happen to everyone in the Second Resurrection who is not raised to glory in the First Resurrection. They will be restored by God to their normal, terrible, old selves, but hopefully will wise up to their transgressions and repent. In that future time, the rule-breakers will be instructed by all of the decent "Charlies," the now divine children of God, on how they, too, can learn to do good and win the prize of immortal life with God. We shouldn't be overly concerned about their salvation in this existence, for in the Second Resurrection, they'll get the full chance to make the grade without the devil around to spoil them.

Blast from the Past (1999)

Starring: Brendan Fraser, Alicia Silverstone, Christopher Walken

This cute romantic comedy focuses on a young man named Adam who ends up with a wife named Eve through extraordinary circumstances. It begins with the 1962 Cuban Missile Crisis, as Adam, played by Brendan Fraser, is born in an underground fallout shelter that his brilliant father (Christopher Walken) has constructed in the family's back yard.

Adam gets raised inside the shelter into his thirties, being instructed solely by his parents how to live an altruistic and moral life. He then enters the regular world in the late 1990s to join his fellow citizens. And that's where the comedy begins. The people of the more modern era are far more tainted, jaded and morally corrupt than those raised with the pristine values of the 1950s and early 1960s. It has become "normal" for those living near the new millennium to have sex with anyone they wish, take illegal drugs, and buy and sell pornography. The clean-minded Adam provides a living example to the modern degenerates concerning personal conduct.

But the controlling authorities of the state, specifically a psychiatrist, seek to take him out of society and have him committed to an asylum. By the end of the film, the once promiscuous Eve (Alicia Silverstone), falls deeply in love with Adam, having been converted by the sheer decency of his clean, polite character.

In similar fashion, Jesus was instructed by His Father on what to say and do before He was sent into the physical world, where He burst onto the public scene in His thirties as well. His fellow citizens, the very children He created, had become horribly disobedient and morally corrupt, violating the letter and the spirit of virtually every instruction provided generations earlier.

Jesus was the ultimate example for human beings on how they should live, because Scripture commands us to "be imitators of God" (Ephesians 5:1 NASB). The fact that He did not fit in with the authorities of His day also prompted the state to remove Him from society at large. In the Bible, the end of the story features Jesus marrying the bride He loves, and the bride of Christ is actually more than one person. It's anyone and everyone who realizes the character of Jesus is the very character we should have in our minds, and then reverses their sinful ways to become like their Husband. So just as Adam in the film eventually gets to marry Eve, who has finally given up her sluttish, sinful ways, so Jesus will formally marry His repentant, clean-living bride once He returns to Earth.

The most poignant line of dialogue in "Blast from the Past" comes from Adam, who notes as he is getting drenched by a rain shower, "My father, who is a scientist, says that everything is a miracle. Everything. Until recently I wasn't sure what he meant by that."

We all need to realize that our Heavenly Father is indeed a scientist. He created all the scientific, physical laws which govern our universe, and the spiritual laws by which "we live and move and have our being" (Acts 17:28 KJV). And yet everything is a miracle. In other words, all things in nature happen because God has made them happen.

Whether it's the sun emitting its golden rays on our planet, the rain or snow falling from the sky, the flowers and crops growing from the soil, the birth and development of every living creature worldwide, it all happens because our Father, the most brilliant Scientist, has put it all into existence and motion. "Everything is a miracle. Everything." The sooner we all realize we're not the product of nothingness, the sooner we can take action to get on the track to life. So God is not only our blast from the past, He's also the blast in our present, as well as our glorious future to come.

Kate & Leopold (2001)

Starring: Meg Ryan, Hugh Jackman

Like "Blast from the Past," this romantic comedy adventure involves a "handsome, honest, courteous" man named Leopold (Hugh Jackman) who, as he's turning thirty, comes from another dimension, specifically 1876, to arrive in modern-day New York City. His decent morals clash with contemporary society, but he ends up being with the woman he loves, Kate (Meg Ryan), who chooses to leave her corrupted world and travel into that purer dimension to marry her love.

While some of this movie is not Bible-related, there is a key portion or two that hits the bull's-eye when it comes to the message of Scripture. One involves a scene where Leopold is filming a commercial for diet margarine, which is supposed to resemble "fresh, creamery butter," but, in reality, "tastes like saddle soap." That's when he gives a speech about acting righteously, eviscerating the world of deception and extolling the importance of not taking part in the trickery, or any sin for that matter:

"I find myself peddling pond scum to an unsuspecting public," Leopold laments. "When one finds oneself participating in an endeavor entirely without merit, one withdraws."

Kate responds: "No, because sometimes, you have to do things that you don't like. Sometimes, you have to suck it up and finish what you started. It's part of life."

Leopold's answer to her sums up the state of Opposite World, where lies are cleverly crafted and polished to make people think they are truth: "Is this what you do at work, Kate? Research methods to deceive people? Refine lies until they resemble truth? It's no wonder you dread your workweek. What has happened to the world? You have every convenience, every comfort, yet no time for integrity."

The other Biblical point in the film is that Leopold happens to be the designer of the modern elevator. The movie shows elevators unable to lift people when Leopold is out of his proper place, since he is unable to complete his work. But once he is sent back to his other dimension, everyone is able to be lifted properly. The Bible metaphor is obvious. Once Jesus (the Designer of raising people) was brought back to His original dimension of heaven, He became able to raise everyone from the dead during the respective resurrections in the future. Just as those in the film could not be lifted to their destination without Leopold's finished work, so we could not be raised to life without the work of Jesus being completed.

Knowing (2009)

Starring: Nicolas Cage, Chandler Canterbury, Rose Byrne

This science-fiction drama, replete with dazzling special effects, centers on astrophysicist John Koestler (Nicolas Cage), who, despite being the son of a pastor, is a man who has been rejecting God and the love for other people ever since his wife died in a fire.

He teaches his college students at M.I.T. about determinism versus randomness in the universe, or, put another way, purpose versus no purpose. At the movie's outset, John explains: "The theory of randomness, which says it's all simply coincidence. The very fact we exist is nothing but the result of a complex, yet inevitable string of chemical accidents and biological mutations. There is no grand meaning. There's no purpose." When pressed by one of his students on his personal belief, he graphically answers, "I think [poop] just happens."

In this sense, the professor represents the "highly educated" people of today's modern world who don't believe in the God of the Bible, and think we're the results of some freak accident of cosmic flatulence. They believe that everything came from nothingness, with no designer and no sustainer, and that there's no real purpose or meaning to our existence.

Things begin to change, though, when John's son Caleb (Chandler Canterbury) is given a list of seemingly random numbers that were placed in a time capsule fifty years earlier in 1959. It turns out that the numbers were not random at all, but rather a prophetic itemization of the precise dates, locations and body counts of every major disaster over the course of five decades, including the 9/11 terror attacks; the downed Pan Am flight over Lockerbie, Scotland; the Oklahoma City bombing and Hurricane Katrina.

The professor eventually figures out that the events in our lives are actually determined by forces bigger than ourselves, because his disaster list predicts the imminent end of the world when all life is wiped off the planet. While he is powerless to stop the end from happening, his son Caleb and a girl are spared death because they were listening to the guiding voices of mysterious spirit beings, representing angels. Caleb actually refers to the humans who are saved as "those who heard the call." In the scene's final moments, as Earth is being destroyed by solar flares scorching the planet, the people who are saved are placed safely on a lush new planet with a glowing tree, reminiscent of both the Garden of Eden and the new Earth mentioned in Scripture.

In my view, there are two key Biblical themes central to this movie. The first is the importance and accuracy of prophecy. Scripture is here for our benefit, to help us understand who we really are, why we're here, and where we're going. Even though John's scientific friend at M.I.T. ridicules him for bothering to probe any association between the list of numbers and modern disasters, the professor nonetheless continues to dig, and eventually discovers the truth.

In our own lives, we as believers need to truly understand that what's written in the Bible is completely true, even in the face of opposition, whether it's based on our own personal presumptions, public ridicule, or the twisted messages taught by many pastors. The Word of God is correct, whether we wish to believe it or not, and the more we dig into it, the more it becomes obvious.

The second point has to do with the transformation of Nicolas Cage's character. He starts out as a typical, secular person of the world, thinking we're all here by accident and that there's little, if any, purpose to life. But through his meticulous study of every number scribbled on the prophetic piece of paper – you can read that as the meticulous study of every word that's printed on the page of your Bible – he is awakened to the truth.

By the end of the movie, he has completely changed his way of thinking and realizes that there is indeed a grand purpose, life after death, and that everyone will be reunited in the future. He tells his son, "We're all gonna be together. And mom's gonna be with us, too. I know it. I know that now. I know it." Hence, the educated-yet-ignorant secular man has made the journey from rejecting the truth, to studying and learning the truth, and finally to "knowing" the truth, as the film's title "Knowing" declares. This is the path that leads to eternal life.

The Walking Dead (2010 – 2017)

Starring: Andrew Lincoln, Chandler Riggs

Yes, I know that this is a television series, but it plays like a movie and is produced better than most films. Its plot centers on survivors of a mysterious medical disaster that causes people who have died to become reanimated as flesh-eating zombies. Ironically, the title of the show, "The Walking Dead," does not refer to the zombies. It refers to people who are still alive, and still walking around, although they're all infected with a condition that will eventually turn them into roving corpses.

The very title of this program is another metaphor for the Bible. When we read the entire message of Scripture, it's very easy to see how all of us – everyone currently alive on this planet – are the walking dead. We are physically alive and walking around, yet we are spiritually dead, and will be dead forever unless and until we come to God and repent of our sins. You might understand the analogy better by recalling the moment when a man looking to follow Jesus asked for permission to first bury his deceased father:

> Jesus said to him, "Let the dead bury their own dead, but you go and proclaim the kingdom of God." (Luke 9:60 NIV)

When Jesus said, "Let the dead bury their own dead," He is explaining that people who are physically alive, yet at the same time still spiritually dead (existing without God's presence), should be the ones to bury the folks who have physically died. In other words, breathing people who don't have God in their lives are actually dead in God's eyes – they themselves are the walking dead – until they repent of their sins and come to true spiritual life. The TV series often features Biblical imagery, including people held in captivity, and one episode in which some zombies meet their final demise by walking into a massive lake of fire, providing them their "second death" mentioned in Revelation.

Blade Runner (1982)

Starring: Harrison Ford, Rutger Hauer, Sean Young, Daryl Hannah

Director Ridley Scott's dark vision of the future is actually a commentary on existential questions we all have, including who and what we are, the desire for longer life, and the fear of death. The story focuses on human replicants with a four-year life span who, despite being outlawed from Earth, return home to confront their creator, seeking more time to live.

There are several key moments in this film that echo Biblical themes. One scene near the beginning has lawman Rick Deckard (Harrison Ford) wondering how a gorgeous replicant (Sean Young) is unaware that it's a replicant. "How can it not know what it is?" he asks the creator. Again, as we've seen demonstrated in previous films in this list, most people in real life have no idea what we actually are. We are gods, as Jesus said, designed by our Creator so that "we will be like Him" (1 John 3:2 NASB).

Another famous scene has renegade replicant Roy Batty (Rutger Hauer) personally visiting his designer, Dr. Eldon Tyrell (Joe Turkel). Batty nervously admits, "It's not an easy thing to meet your maker," before explaining the reason for his visit: "I want more life, Father!" This, of course, reflects the desire of all humanity, to do away with our mortality, and live forever. It also reflects the desire of Satan himself, who knows he's going to be destroyed and will do anything possible to keep on living.

When Batty learns there is no escaping his mortality, he lives up to his last name and goes bonkers, manually crushing the head of his creator. This is a twist on the Bible prophecy where the Creator God Jesus is forecast to crush the head of the devil. With this in mind, it is very possible, if not likely, that what we're shown on screen is the true desire of Satan, to kill his own Maker, to murder God Himself. Remember that Jesus called Satan "a murderer from the beginning," and that Satan has been in conflict with God since iniquity (lawlessness) was found in him. Moments before crushing the creator's head, Batty, who is called "the Prodigal Son" by his designer, confesses to his designer that he's done "questionable things," an admission by Satan that he has rebelled against the divine commandments.

There are two moments of dialogue in "Blade Runner," both of them uttered by replicants, which reflect a recurring message in the Bible. The first statement is: "Painful to live in fear, isn't it?" The second, spoken by Batty (the devil), is similar: "Quite an experience to live in fear, isn't it? That's what it is to be a slave." Once again, we are given the very Biblical notion that we as sinful human beings are all slaves, living in the captivity of fear. We're slaves to death and the fear of death, even though God has intended us to overcome that fear, saying countless times in the Bible to "fear not."

In the final moments of the film, Deckard, who is assigned to kill the lawbreakers and thus could be viewed as a type of Jesus, is shown hammering Batty with a large iron rod, the famous rod of iron the Bible talks about. It's the same weapon with which the Jesus figure in "The Matrix" also batters the devil. During the pummeling, the demonic Batty eggs on Deckard, yelling, "That's the Spirit!" The comment is noteworthy because Jesus Himself is the Spirit.

Meanwhile, as Batty is trying to prolong his soon-to-expire existence, the evil one intentionally drives a nail through his own hand, and even saves Deckard from certain death. This reminds us of Jesus having nails driven through His hands during His crucifixion and saving humanity from death. However – and this is a big however – because it is the demon Batty nailing himself in the movie, it is another twist to what we see in the Bible. What we're witnessing on film is Satan's desire "to be like the Most High" in every way possible way, posing as Jesus when he's actually the personification of evil. Interestingly, when time finally runs out for Batty and he expires, Deckard utters the exact same last word that Jesus did before He died: "Finished." The analogy is very clear. Deckard, like Jesus, accomplished his mission to defeat the wicked one.

Star Wars (1977 – 2015)

Starring: Mark Hamill, Harrison Ford, Carrie Fisher

"Star Wars" is an epic good-versus-evil saga telling the story of a small number of outsiders, known as Jedi Knights, fighting the forces of evil a long time ago in a galaxy far, far away. The original film and its sequels comprise one of the most successful franchises in Hollywood history, venturing far beyond the silver screen and into the universe of television, books and magazines, and even toys and other products bearing its insignia, and generating vast amounts of wealth. As of this writing, there have been seven major films released, the most recent of which is "Episode VII: The Force Awakens," and there are more on the way.

The Biblical allusions in "Star Wars" are almost endless, and there have been numerous books written on the subject, none of which I have read. What I'll provide for you here is my own personal take from all the episodes in a single, condensed form so you don't get overwhelmed with galactic minutiae.

Let's start with the title. As we have seen, the Bible at times refers to angels as stars, so when we hear the phrase "Star Wars," we should instantly think of the ongoing war between good angels and bad angels in Scripture. The devil and a third of the angels are in rebellion against God and the two-thirds of the angels who remain faithful to their Creator. Thus, there is ongoing war among the angelic stars, or what we can call the star wars.

The movie takes a direct schematic outline from the Bible, assigning everything that is good to the light, and all that is evil to darkness, or "the dark side":

> And God saw the light, that it was good: and God
> divided the light from the darkness.
> (Genesis 1:4 KJV)

> The way of the wicked is like darkness
> (Proverbs 4:19 NASB)

Some of the main characters, including Luke Skywalker (Mark Hamill), Anakin Skywalker (Jake Lloyd, Hayden Christensen) and Rey (Daisy Ridley) all have humble beginnings on a very dusty planet. This reflects our own down-to-earth origin, that we are indeed composed of dust. And though we return to dust at death, we will be raised to a glorified spirit body if we follow the path of the light, that which is in harmony with God's instructions.

Each episode in the saga mentions an unseen power known as "the Force," which is analogous to God Himself in Spirit form. It is the presence and power of the Almighty Creator.

As Ben Obi-Wan Kenobi (Alec Guinness) describes it, "The Force is what gives a Jedi his power. ... It surrounds us and penetrates us. It binds the galaxy together." In other words, the Force is everywhere, just as God's presence is everywhere in the universe:

> Where can I go from your Spirit? Where can I
> flee from your presence? If I go up to the heavens,
> you are there; if I make my bed in the depths, you
> are there. (Psalm 139:7-8 NIV)

And a common saying throughout the film is, "May the Force be with you," just as the Bible has "may God be with you." (Exodus 18:19 NIV)

In the most recent episode, we're shown how the Force is actually calling people to serve its power, as Rey is told, "The Force, it's calling to you. Just let it in." Throughout Scripture, we're shown that "many are called" (Matthew 22:14 KJV) and that Jesus Himself is urging people to let Him in when He calls on them:

> Listen! I stand at the door and knock. If anyone
> hears My voice and opens the door, I will come
> in to him and have dinner with him, and he with
> Me. (Revelation 3:20 HCSB)

The Force is shown to be very active in certain characters in the film, including Obi-Wan, who is obviously a type of Jesus. He helps teach Luke the ways of the Force (the ways of God), and allows himself to be slain by the dark forces of this world for the benefit of others. After his death, Obi-Wan is raised as a spirit being, whose voice is heard guiding Luke in the war to defeat the darkness. Of course in the Bible, Jesus allows Himself to be slain by the dark forces of this world for the benefit of others. And once raised as a Spirit being, He continues to guide the light-seekers in the physical realm, endowing them with His very own Force, His divine Presence.

Every true believer is given a measure of the Spirit of God, helping to resist the devil and overcome its deceptive path toward death. Interestingly, in "The Force Awakens," those fighting against evil are actually called the Resistance, reminiscent of the instruction to "Resist the devil, and he will flee from you." (James 4:7 KJV)

Now, simply because we believers in God have a small amount of

God's Holy Spirit given to us, it does not mean we are automatically granted salvation. We need to be properly trained in the ways of God, learning to control our fears and confidently fight against the dark, unseen forces in control of this world:

> For our struggle is not against flesh and blood,
> but against the rulers, against the powers, against
> the world forces of this darkness, against the
> spiritual forces of wickedness in the heavenly
> places. (Ephesians 6:12 NASB)

The training is not easy, and it comes with some difficulties and suffering. In the film, when Luke has to be trained and tested properly, he travels to a remote planet filled with nothing but wilderness where he can focus on the Force without distractions. This corresponds to the wilderness regions where God trained and tested both ancient Israel after the nation's departure from slavery in Egypt, as well as Jesus Himself for forty days when He confronted the devil. This entire pagan world in which we live can also be considered the wilderness, and we're being trained and tested here to properly use the gifts of God's Spirit so we can perform good deeds:

> For we are His workmanship, created in Christ
> Jesus for good works, which God prepared
> beforehand so that we would walk in them.
> (Ephesians 2:10 NASB)

In the film, an "elegant weapon" is provided for those fighting for the light. It is called a light saber, and is a sword that emits powerful energy that slices through virtually anything. A similar device is mentioned in Scripture, and was the weapon of choice for angels stationed in the Garden of Eden to prevent anyone from gaining access to the tree of life once Adam and Eve got the boot:

> After sending them out, the LORD God stationed
> mighty cherubim to the east of the Garden of
> Eden. And he placed a flaming sword that flashed
> back and forth to guard the way to the tree of life.
> (Genesis 3:24 NLT)

On a spiritual level, the light saber represents "the sword of the Spirit, which is the word of God" (Ephesians 6:17 KJV). "For the word of God is alive and powerful. It is sharper than the sharpest two-edged sword, cutting between soul and spirit, between joint and marrow. It exposes our innermost thoughts and desires." (Hebrews 4:12 NLT)

The enemy, who is Satan, is represented through numerous villains in the series. He is the duplicitous Senator Palpatine, whose alter ego Darth Sidious is the evil emperor of the Galactic Empire. He is Supreme Leader Snoke, sitting on a throne like the god of this world, imploring his evil agents to act on his behalf. He is also seen through Darth Vader, a former good guy who was once a Jedi Knight, a guardian of the Republic, but became engrossed with evil and turned to the dark side. As we've read, Satan himself was a former guardian angel of God's own throne until lawlessness was found in him and he was cast out of heaven.

"Star Wars" repeats many of the same themes we've seen in other movies in my list, especially those of people held in captivity by evil forces, but are finally set free. Some of the characters in bondage are:

  • Princess Leia (Carrie Fisher) held prisoner by Darth Vader and later by Jabba the Hut

  • The Millennium Falcon ship and its passengers held captive by a tractor beam compactor intended to kill them

  • Han Solo frozen as a prisoner in carbonite

  • Lando Calrissian (Billy Dee Williams), Leia and Chewbacca held by the Empire in Cloud City

  • Young Anakin Skywalker, who is a slave originally, but gets liberated from captivity by those fighting for the light

  • Poe Dameron (Oscar Isaac) held by a tether cord while trying to escape in a TIE fighter

  • Rey held prisoner and interrogated by Kylo Ren (Adam Driver)

In the Bible, the devil is the dark force holding human beings in captivity, preventing them from knowing who they really are and from reaching their divine destiny. But the ultimate Light, Jesus Christ, has set the prisoners free from bondage, so they can overcome sin and reach their intended destiny, their divine thrones in the kingdom of God.

Another familiar theme in this film series is that of deception employed to keep people captive in darkness. In one instance, after Anakin Skywalker has a prophetic vision of his wife (Natalie Portman) dying in childbirth, Palpatine (Ian McDiarmid) deceives Anakin by claiming that the dark side of the Force holds the power to save his wife's life. Anakin, thinking he is doing something good, submits to the false teachings and becomes the evil-minded Darth Vader. This brings up two points we've seen so far in the Bible.

One is the fear of death mentioned in Hebrews 2:15, the fear that keeps us in slavery. Since the beginning of time, people have been gripped by the fear of death, and they want to believe any idea that can prevent mortality. Thus, the false notion that we "shall not die" was easily believed by Eve in the Garden of Eden, and millions of people across many religions glom on to that same erroneous view today, all because they are still slaves to the fear of dying.

The second point has to do with the religious powers of this world, who appear to be acting with good intentions, when, in fact, they are actually doing the deceptive work of the devil:

> These people are false apostles. They are
> deceitful workers who disguise themselves as
> apostles of Christ. But I am not surprised! Even
> Satan disguises himself as an angel of light.
> (2 Corinthians 11:13-14 NLT)

We all need to keep in mind that there really is only one truth, and that truth is displayed in the pages of the Bible. When preachers of any faith or denomination deviate from what's in Scripture, they are tricking you, though perhaps unknowingly. No matter how good they look or sound, and no matter how many good works they may do, such as feeding the hungry, they are leading people to death instead of life if, for instance, they teach that the commandments of God are not meant to be followed.

The "Star Wars" saga reveals that there is very good news still to come. Evil in all its forms is destroyed, usually by fire, and there is a resurrection from the dead and a rebirth into a glorious, spirit-composed body for those deemed worthy. This is perhaps best demonstrated in the ending scene of "Episode VI: The Return of the Jedi."

Once the second Death Star is exploded (representing an end to the second death), a massive celebration begins with not only the chosen people, but also Ewoks (who could represent non-believing Gentiles who join themselves to the light) taking part. In fact, Ewoks are the ones blowing animal horns (Biblical shofars) as trumpets to start the party, reminiscent of the Feast of Trumpets. There is singing and dancing as friends who resisted and overcame the evil are reunited, bringing to mind the Feast of Tabernacles and resurrection.

Additionally, Luke is given a vision of his fellow servants (Anakin, Yoda and Obi-Wan) who appear in their shining, glorified, spirit bodies. The Bible recounts an almost duplicate incident in Scripture, when Jesus transfigured Himself in the seventeenth chapter of Matthew:

> "His face shone like the sun, and His garments
> became as white as light. And behold, Moses
> and Elijah appeared to them, talking with Him."
> (Matthew 17:2-3 NASB)

We must remember that Jesus stressed in verse nine of this chapter that the transfiguration was only a vision, a supernatural preview of who would be in the kingdom of God in the future. At the time of the transfiguration, Moses and Elijah were actually dead and in their graves, since Jesus said in John 3:13 that no one has gone to heaven except Himself. But it is astonishing how this Bible scene that shows a supernatural glimpse into the glory-filled future still ahead of us has been embedded into one of the most popular motion-picture series of all time.

One final point about "Star Wars" and the Bible: The most recent installment as of this writing, "The Force Awakens," highlights the fact that everything in Scripture is an accurate declaration of the truth. Because, sadly, we live in an age where the stories of the Bible are regarded by many to be myth, recounting events that never took place. The so-called educated people of today are "always learning and never able to come to a knowledge of the truth" (2 Timothy 3:7). But as Han Solo notes on this matter, "I used to wonder about that myself. Thought it was a bunch of mumbo-jumbo. A magical power holding together good and evil, the dark side and the light. Crazy thing is, it's true. The Force. The Jedi. All of it. It's all true." So is Scripture.

The Big Short (2015)

Starring: Christian Bale, Ryan Gosling, Steve Carrell, Brad Pitt

Based on the true story of the 2007-2008 financial collapse, this comedic drama tells the story of a handful of outsiders able to see disaster coming years in advance, and are ridiculed for their belief, but in the end, receive a staggering reward for their efforts. It also reveals how the entire world system in which most of us put our trust is completely fraudulent.

This movie, perhaps more than any other in my movie list, sums up the message of the Bible for our time, right now, as you read the words on this page. While it's not a film that blatantly evangelizes in any way, it uses humor and graphic language to wake people up to rampant deception and warn them of coming catastrophe if they don't change their harmful behavior. "The Big Short" was nominated for five Academy Awards, including Best Picture, Best Director, Best Supporting Actor for Christian Bale, Best Film Editing, and winning Best Adapted Screenplay. The main characters are Dr. Michael Burry (Christian Bale), Mike Baum (Steve Carrell), Jared Vennett (Ryan Gosling), and Ben Rickert (Brad Pitt).

Burry is a California hedge-fund millionaire who discovers in 2005 that the entire financial system is rotting severely from the inside. He makes this find by doing an extraordinary thing. He actually reads the details of the top-selling mortgage bonds to learn the disturbing truth about their underlying defaulted-upon mortgages. His boss is stunned at this method, asking: "How do you know the bonds are worthless? Aren't they filled with [bleeping] thousands of pages of mortgages?" Burry answers: "I read them." His boss incredulously responds: "You read them? No one reads them."

Despite fierce opposition from his colleagues, Burry asserts that based on the truth of what's in the pages, the housing market is an unseen bubble about to burst and plunge America into a dark abyss, irrespective of bright forecasts offered by the powers that be in government and on Wall Street. "Everyone's wrong," he maintains. "It's possible that we are in a completely fraudulent system!" Burry is proved right in the end.

Burry's discovery of the deceit cracks open a window to the light of truth, and others, including Wall Street hedge-fund manager Mark Baum, also see the light. They eventually join Burry in betting millions of dollars that a massive economic collapse will happen, all the while being laughed off by top bankers. Baum laments the sordid state of the financial sector, telling his wife (Marisa Tomei): "It is a [poopstorm] out here, sweetie. You have no idea the kind of crap people are pulling, and everyone's walking around like they're in a [damn] Enya video. They're all getting screwed you know. You know what they care about? They care about the ball game, or they care about what actress just went into rehab."

When Baum starts to learn how deep the deception goes, he proclaims: "We live in an era of fraud in America. Not just in banking, but in government, education, religion, food, even baseball." He tells his partner Vinnie Daniel (Jeremy Strong): "It's time to call bull----." Vinnie asks: "Bull---- on what?" Baum declares: "Every [bleeping] thing."

Even when some of the outsiders go to the news media to warn the public of the impending economic doom, the powers in the press refuse to sound the alarm. Once the crash does take place, the final text of the movie notes that five trillion dollars from pension funds, real-estate values, 401ks, savings accounts, and bonds had disappeared. Eight million people lost their jobs, six million lost their homes, and that was only in the United States. But the few number of outsiders who bet against the system profited immensely from their labors, receiving an astounding reward.

The Biblical themes in "The Big Short" jump off the screen from start to finish. We're shown how a few, ordinary, honest people living in today's high-tech world can discover a startling, life-changing truth that no one else is able to see due to worthless and endless distractions such as sports and celebrities. And how do they learn the truth? By simply reading the words on the page and believing them! Just as Burry's boss was stunned that Burry read all the pages detailing the mortgages, so too are many people astonished that a few outsiders in today's society learn truth by reading, studying and believing all of Scripture.

In the film, the probers study the words in the mortgage documents, and follow up with deeper research that leads them to the inescapable conclusion that the entire world system – the economy, government, education, and yes, **even religion** – is one giant fraud, a house of cards ready to collapse. Those who read the Bible – all of it, delving into every nook and cranny of it – will also learn the truth, and it may be truth that those in charge of the major religions have missed before.

The truth may even seem quite disturbing at first, as the conclusion about the global sham becomes obvious. The outsiders in the movie were paying attention to everything that is real and important, and that was the key to their success. The Bible in many places urges us to **pay attention** and consider everything: "Pay attention, you stupid people! Fools, when will you be wise?" (Psalm 94:8 HCSB)

Those seeking truth will discover that virtually everyone running the world is wrong, and what has been written down in Scripture is correct. Now, it's hardly a news flash that government officials lie to their citizens, but it is a surprise to many that leaders in the education and religious sectors are falsifiers as well. When high schools and universities teach there is no divine Creator and that we're all an accident of space flatulence, they are lying to us.

When religious leaders, especially many in ostensible Christendom, teach that it's perfectly fine to ignore the commandments of God or that celebrating winter and spring holidays that originated with the worship of satanic gods is a holy and healthy practice, they are deceiving us. In order to verify the truth, all that people need to do is read the details already written down in Scripture. As the Bible commands us: "Prove all things" (1 Thessalonians 5:21 KJV).

Another major theme of the film is how deep the fraud and deception go. It's not just one person being dishonest. It's almost everyone, especially top executives and those meant to police them. They're all lying and getting rich off their dishonesty. As we've seen, the Bible has pegged the devil as a liar from the beginning and as the father of lies, so his society and the standard business practices he has developed here on Earth are, as Mark Baum put it so eloquently in the film, truly "dog [poop] wrapped in cat [poop]." God has noted in the Bible how Satan himself has become extremely wealthy through his dishonest trade: "By your great skill in trading you have increased your wealth, but your heart has become proud because of your wealth" (Ezekiel 28:5 HCSB). We all need to remember that honesty in business dealings is of prime concern to God:

> The LORD detests dishonest scales, but accurate weights find favor with him. (Proverbs 11:1 NIV)

> Lying lips are abomination to the LORD: but they that deal truly are his delight.
> (Proverbs 12:22 KJV)

As Baum complained in the film: "What bothers me isn't that fraud is not nice. Or that fraud is mean. ... Fraud and short-sighted thinking have never, ever worked. Not once. Eventually you get caught. Things go south. When the hell did we forget all that? I thought we were better than this. I really did."

The people who discover the truth in "The Big Short" clearly represent people who suddenly, and sometimes unexpectedly, learn the truth about God in real life. They have faith that what they have perceived is, in fact, real in the face of staunch opposition and ridicule. They subsequently make the decision to stake all they have against the entire evil system, working against the nefarious masterpiece of Satan the devil whose toxic tentacles extend into every sector. These few people, whether prophets who warn others or just ordinary believers who resist the devil, are the "few" who Jesus said will receive the ultimate reward:

> "Enter through the narrow gate; for the gate is wide and the way is broad that leads to destruction, and there are many who enter through it. For the gate is small and the way is narrow that leads to life, and there are few who find it.
> (Matthew 7:13-14 NASB)

The film shows how both the deceivers in power and those they deceived were destroyed in the financial meltdown. They represent the many who try to enter at the broad gate, which people have been tricked into thinking is the easy and correct way. But in the end, it led to their destruction – millions of jobs lost and stored wealth vanishing into nothingness. As the Bible states: "Wealth is worthless in the day of wrath, but righteousness delivers from death." (Proverbs 11:4 NIV)

Yet those very few who knew the truth, who stuck to it despite heavy persecution, were given an astonishing reward according to their works. The reward for believers in God's truth, the real truth which stands in opposition to the phony teachings and governments of this world, is everlasting life, reigning with the Creator of all things.

"The Big Short" is more than just typical entertainment. It is actually a real-life parable – a warning being broadcast to everyone today. It smacks us in the face to show us how corrupt our society has become, how far from the laws of God we have strayed, and that there is certain destruction ahead of us if a massive turnaround does not take place. This message has been sitting in the Bible for thousands of years, voiced by prophets, apostles and even God Himself. Yet very few seem interested, as they continue to love the darkness more than the light, being more fascinated by social media, sports scores, the sex lives of others and every possible non-God-centered activity to ignore the path to life.

Few are aware that God has destroyed many kingdoms of this world in the past because of disobedience to His instructions, including the kingdoms of His own people in Israel and Judah. He has sometimes sent small-scale disasters as attention-getters and wake-up calls for repentance before unleashing a major cataclysm that wipes everything out. It is possible, or even likely, that the financial apocalypse of 2008 was a wake-up call for all people to stop their rebellion against God's laws and deal honestly in every facet of their lives, because severe punishment in the form of destruction and death is the only other alternative.

There may be something far worse coming in our future if people continue in their selfish, rebellious ways, not having learned their lesson. The film's conclusion suggests that people have not learned their lesson, stating, "In 2015, several large banks began selling billions in something called a 'bespoke tranche opportunity.'" This, according to Bloomberg News, is merely another name for the monetary sleight-of-hand that led to the 2008 catastrophe.

One final note on this movie: The film states that after the destruction took place and Mark Baum had received his huge reward, his wife commented that he "actually became gracious after the collapse and never said 'I told you so' to anyone." This is an important message expressed many different ways in Scripture. Even when believers are correct and victorious, we are not to be filled with pride and arrogant boasting. We are to be humble servants of God who are always mindful of others' feelings, treating them the way we wish to be treated. We are to be gracious to others, because God has extended His divine grace to us, actually saving us by His grace.

People who are in the wrong at this time, especially because they have been deceived, will still have a chance to repent in the Second Resurrection, since God gets no pleasure from the death of the wicked, and wants as many as possible to come to life and fulfill their divine destiny.

Now that you have seen the Bible messages embedded in all these popular films, maybe your eyes are now open to more of God's glorious truth. It should be easy to see how themes from Scripture are constantly mentioned and sometimes repeated in different motion pictures. Here are some of the main ideas we can glean:

- There is a Designer who made all things and placed us here.

- Human beings are the personal evidence that God exists.

- Most of us do not know what type of being we are, not even recognizing our Parent when He presents Himself.

- We were designed by our Creator to become gods, spirit beings just like Him.

- There is a desire among human beings to have longer life, even eternal life.

- There is a global deception taking place designed to keep us from learning the truth.

- Countless distractions and diversions have been created to capture our attention and inhibit us from learning the truth.

- We are all slaves living in captivity by an evil force until we are called out.

- There is a good-versus-evil battle going on.

- Light represents all that is good and godly, while darkness represents all that is evil and of the devil.

- There is another dimension all around us that is invisible to our eyes, from which other beings are monitoring us.

- There are beings in the other dimension calling to us.

- The world as we know it is evil, and we're meant to abandon the ways of the world.

- People are instructed to stop selfish, sinful behavior and return to the laws of the Creator.

- What is written in Scripture is the truth, and needs to be studied and put into practice.

- If we "pay attention" and "prove all things," we can understand the truth in spite of massive deception.

- People have to be properly trained in the ways of God and experience suffering to resist and overcome evil, perfecting their character.

- The devil is a real individual, tricking virtually everyone on the planet into following his deceitful Opposite World ways.

- Some preachers are actually deceitful workers who disguise themselves as angels of light and apostles of Christ.

- People can overcome the deception of Satan and leave captivity by following the instructions in Scripture.

- There is an unseen force – the power and presence of God – looking to help us.

- We are spiritually dead in God's eyes until we change our behavior.

- Our character is being tested by God at virtually every moment, in good times and bad, so He can determine if we're worthy of receiving the phenomenal reward of becoming divine members of His family.

- It is a small number of outsiders who fight against deception and evil but eventually receive a tremendous reward according to their works.

- God uses evil actions and destruction at times to accomplish His purpose.

- There is an end to the devil, whose head will be shattered by Jesus.

- There is a paradise coming for those of us who hear and respond to God's call.

- And the Good Guy marries His bride at the end of the story, and they live happily ever after.

As is obvious from the above list, when we actually focus our minds on the instructions of God and pay attention to everything in our modern world, we can plainly see that God's messages are still being broadcast to the masses. Those messages may not be in every single movie, but they're evident in many of them, and my list is just a beginning point. I could have gone on and on, but my point has been made, and now it's time for you to get in the picture. It's good exercise for your spiritual growth to pay attention and discern which messages of God are in any film. You can start with your own favorites to discover what hidden treasure has been secretly embedded. It is up to you to incline your ears to hear it, learn it and live it, so you can become part of the divine life that is happily ever after.

Conclusion:
We live in Opposite World

And now, ladies and gentleman, before I close out this latest venture into the Word of God, I would like to ask you a question or two. Do you ever get the feeling that something is not right with the world in which we live? Do you sense that what we're often told is the exact opposite of how things should be? I ask because we're constantly bombarded with mantras that are contrary to reality. For instance, we're often told to believe:

- Illegal immigration is fine, even preferable to legal immigration

- There's no such thing as radical Islamic terrorism

- Man-made global warming is threatening the extinction of life on Earth

- The news presented to us is always an unbiased, accurate depiction of what has taken place

- Government is the answer to our problems

- If you like your doctor, you can keep your doctor

But everyone with his or her head on straight knows instinctively that the truth is the opposite of what is being broadcast by the powers that be. There's a reason for that. It's because we are living in what I call Opposite World. It is a world where seemingly everything that is right is portrayed as wrong, and everything that is wrong is portrayed as right. God Himself commented about this strange reversal thousands of years ago, since it's actually not a new phenomenon:

> Woe unto **them that call evil good, and good evil**; that put **darkness for light, and light for darkness**; that put bitter for sweet, and sweet for bitter! (Isaiah 5:20 KJV)

Other terms accurately depicting the place in which we exist could be Deception World, Prison World, Distraction World, Dumbed-down World and Satanic World. But I think Opposite World best sums it up in an easy way for everyone to understand what's taking place here.

Opposite World is our society where the devil has snookered people through thousands of years of lies, so that millions think that what is wrong is what is right. We must never forget that Satan is a real individual, a powerful spirit being who holds a strong grip on the minds of the vast majority. He is keeping people captive in a state of ignorance, making sure they don't even know who or what they really are and why they're here, preventing them from reaching their intended destiny.

He has developed this marvelous habitat so that most people believe the opposite of the truth, or conduct themselves in a way that blatantly violates the instructions handed down by our Designer. Our society has been held hostage for thousands of years by this very clever demon who is intentionally trying to turn God's ways upside down, twisting the truth just enough so that people actually believe the exact opposite of what was meant.

This explains why we have so many problems today, and they rarely, if ever, get solved. At any given moment, there is plenty of murder, war, theft, disease, hunger, lying, economic turmoil, religious strife, lusting, adultery, fornication, unwanted pregnancy, abortion and people having a lack of care and concern for their fellow man. It's all because human beings are living in direct opposition to the teachings of their own divine Parent. This is even true for millions of Christians, who have been instructed by their pastors that there is little reason to obey the specific instructions of their Creator, whose name they like to praise, while at the same time blatantly disobeying His laws:

> The Lord says: "These people come near to me with their mouth and honor me with their lips, but their hearts are far from me. Their worship of me is based on merely human rules they have been taught." (Isaiah 29:13 NIV)

> "So why do you keep calling me 'Lord, Lord!' when you don't do what I say? (Luke 6:46 NLT)

It's high time that people of faith, and even those of no faith, finally come to grips with the fact that humanity as a whole is living in rebellion against what is intended and beneficial for us. We're simply doing it wrong, as can be seen by so many examples in Opposite World. Here are some of the obvious ones:

> Many of the most educated people on Earth say that there is no Creator God, and there is no real purpose for human life. The truth is that there is a Creator God who does indeed have a Master Plan for human beings.

> Many schools teach that the universe and life itself are the result of an accident, some sort of cosmic flatulence, and that life evolved over many millions of years to its current state. The truth is that the universe is not an accident; it was created by a family of Divine Beings who designed and created all life, including human beings. Evolution is non-scientific nonsense. A complete lie.

> The prevailing belief is that life forms that eventually became human beings originated in the sea. The truth is the opposite, as we came from the ground, the dirt, the dust of the earth.

> People of many religious persuasions are taught by their leaders that they don't really die when their physical lives expire, that they go on living in some other place or form. The truth is they do completely die and return to the dust from whence they originated.

> Most Christians are under the impression their dead loved ones are alive in heaven right now, watching their every step. The truth is those deceased people are dead in all respects, completely unaware of anything, but will be raised from the dead in one of two resurrections in the future, the resurrection of life when Jesus returns, or the resurrection of judgment a thousand years later.

> We're told to obey the laws of our country, but at the same time we're instructed by many religious leaders to disregard God's laws. Millions are taught that God's laws

are done away with or simply not meant to be followed any longer. But Jesus Himself said not the slightest part of any of God's laws is done away with, and anyone who teaches that will be called least in His kingdom. He also said if we wish to enter into life, "Keep the commandments."

Millions of Christians think that just believing that Jesus is God or their Savior is all they need to do for salvation, while ignoring the mandates to repent of sin and become perfected. Jesus says He will reject many so-called "believers" because they practice lawlessness.

Many think that God always enjoys hearing the prayers of people, but they don't realize "God detests the prayers of a person who ignores the law." (Proverbs 28:9 NLT)

Countless pastors claim to be teaching God's truth, when they are in reality teaching disobedience, leading people astray with beautiful-sounding sermons. God says He is an enemy of those shepherds, calling them false apostles and deceitful workers.

When it comes to food, people generally think they're free to eat any animal they wish. But God has said otherwise and has provided specific lists of non-edible animals in Leviticus 11 and Deuteronomy 14.

There is a very popular notion that God never causes evil or harm, and that the devil is solely responsible for all that goes wrong. The truth is that God says He Himself is responsible for natural catastrophes, and sometimes creates mayhem in our personal lives.

Annual holidays such as Christmas and Easter are viewed as perfectly proper and holy ways to worship God. The truth is that God has condemned the customs associated with such holidays in the most ardent terms, based upon their evil, pagan origins, including the horrific murder of young children on behalf of Satan the devil.

Millions of people cut down and decorate green trees every December with silver and gold ornaments, when God has specifically instructed not to do that very thing, calling it a worthless fraud.

Countless Christians are under the impression that God's holy days such as Passover and the Feast of Tabernacles should no longer be celebrated, when God Himself says they are to be observed "forever." (Exodus 12, Leviticus 23)

Many people have little problem lying to others. Thus, we have lawmakers in all political parties who say one thing to get elected, and then do the exact opposite once they're in office, governing against the will of the people. We have men and women who cheat on their spouses. We have parents eagerly lying to their own children about a guy with magical reindeer who flies through the sky to place gifts near trees and fireplaces. The truth is that lying lips are an abomination to God.

Millions of people think Mary Magdalene was a prostitute before becoming a follower of Jesus. The truth is that the Bible never mentions prostitution or any sexual sin in connection with this woman, who was actually the very first witness to the risen Christ.

Many people refer to their religious leaders as "Father" or "Rabbi," when Jesus said not to use those specific terms. (Matthew 23:8-9)

Countless Christians believe that God promotes only loving and not hating. We're also taught in society, "Don't be a hater." The truth is that God hates many things and some people. The Bible even commands us to hate, and specifically to despise evil.

The vast majority of Christians are taught that the wages of sin is not death, but eternal life in a fiery place of never-ending torture. The Bible says the opposite, that the wages of sin is death, involving a fire that will completely consume and annihilate the enemies of God.

Many believe Satan's destiny is to be alive forever in the lake of fire. The truth is that the devil, like all wicked individuals, will die in the lake of fire, with no further existence of any kind.

When most hear the term "Judgment Day," they assume it's a bad thing, a time when everyone who didn't follow God is thrown into a fire. The truth is that Judgment Day is actually a very good thing for most people. It's a time when they will be given a final chance to repent and get with the divine program, being examined, coached and evaluated by others who have become part of God's family.

It is legal in America and elsewhere for women to have their unborn babies slain in most circumstances, sometimes even after they have been born alive outside the womb. God has made it clear that murder, especially of an innocent baby, is disgusting to Him.

It is thought by many to be perfectly normal and right for unmarried men and women to have sex with each other, and have a variety of sexual partners in life. The truth is that God warns against fornication.

Many people see no problem with decorating their own flesh with tattoo ink, but God has instructed us not to do that very thing. (Leviticus 19:28)

Young people often think it's cool to rebel against the rules of morality, and that acting in godly fashion is uncool, and only intended for geeks and nerds. The rebels don't realize that they're actually killing themselves with this line of thinking.

The powers of this world start days in the middle of the night, while many Jews and some Christians commence their days with the darkness of evening. The truth is that each day begins and ends with the light, just as the pattern was established in Genesis, and later confirmed by Jesus, who calls Himself the light of the world as well as the bright

Morning Star, personally being the beginning and the end.

People presume their daily problems are the result of conflicts with other flesh-and-blood human beings. The Bible says the battle is not against flesh and blood, but against evil spirit beings in the unseen dimension.

As should be obvious by now, the world as most people know it marches in direct opposition to the ways of God. It is a fraud, a giant hoax based on the deception of the devil. It continues to operate in darkness because, as one might expect in Opposite World, most people actually prefer the darkness of the devil over the light of God. Those are not just my words. They are the words of Jesus:

> "This is the judgment, that the Light has come into the world, and men loved the darkness rather than the Light, for their deeds were evil. For everyone who does evil hates the Light, and does not come to the Light for fear that his deeds will be exposed. But he who practices the truth comes to the Light, so that his deeds may be manifested as having been wrought in God."

(John 3:19-21 NASB)

We all need to keep focused on why we're here. We need to remember that this place in which we live is a testing ground for our character and we need to practice the truth. God is looking for people to come out of Opposite World, this Babylon of confusion, and live obediently according to His ways, not the ways of rebellion. He wants to grant us eternal life in His coming kingdom, to join the divine, spirit family running the government of God, according to the laws He has set in place.

But we have to take major steps to reach our destination of glory. We cannot be lazy believers. We can't sit back and think to ourselves that mere belief in Jesus will save us. We actually have to do His will, following His instructions. It takes time and focused effort to put into practice the directions we have been given. We need to develop our character to become like God, so He will welcome us into His family. We don't want to get shocked by the Savior when He rejects us upon His return. None of us knows how much time we personally have left to be living and breathing here on Earth, so time is of the essence when it comes to repentance.

Your intellect is not going to grant you eternal life. Neither is the government. Neither is your money, your pastor, your church or the smiling evangelist on TV. Only God has the ability to raise your dead self from the grave, and give you a glorious life of joy and peace that will never end. So you may want to listen to Him for a change, instead of the illusions offered in our world of deception. I urge everyone to read the Bible as much as possible and believe what it says, even if it goes against what religious forces claim. Because the Bible is God in written form. It is the truth. It is the way. It is the life.

Now that you have read this book, the choice is up to each and every one of you regarding which path to choose:

> "Today I have given you the choice between life and death, between blessings and curses. Now I call on heaven and earth to witness the choice you make. Oh, that you would choose life, so that you and your descendants might live!
> (Deuteronomy 30:19 NLT)

About the Author

Joe Kovacs is a Bible-believing Christian, unaffiliated with any church or denomination, and author of the #1 best-seller, *Shocked by the Bible: The Most Astonishing Facts You've Never Been Told*, which is the prequel to this book, and *The Divine Secret*, which also hit #1 on Amazon.com.

He's an award-winning journalist and broadcaster who has run newsrooms in television, radio, and online for more than 30 years, both in the United States and overseas.

A frequent media guest, Kovacs has appeared on *The O'Reilly Factor* on the Fox News Channel as well as on countless radio programs across America and the world, including *Coast to Coast AM* and Michael Savage's *The Savage Nation*.

Follow Joe on Twitter @JoeKovacsNews.